FIT LIKE, NEW YORK ?

AN IRREVERENT HISTORY OF ROCK MUSIC IN ABERDEEN AND NORTH EAST SCOTLAND

PETER INNES

With research assistance from Bob Spence

First published by
Aberdeen Journals Ltd., Lang Stracht,
Mastrick, Aberdeen AB15 6DF

ISBN Number 1 901300 02 1

An Evening Express Publication

Printed by BPC-AUP, Aberdeen

FIT LIKE, NEW YORK ?

AN IRREVERENT HISTORY OF ROCK MUSIC IN ABERDEEN AND NORTH EAST SCOTLAND

CONTENTS

INTRODUCTION

Two Gordon Highlander squaddies were captured by the Germans during World War II. Despite most brutal Gestapo interrogation, military information was unforthcoming from the NE loons. When all else failed, their inquisitors perpetrated the most horrendous torture conceivable: they nailed the Gordons' feet to the floor and then played a Jimmy Shand record.

The North East of Scotland, and music. . . Jimmy Shand never played Be Bop A Lu La, but ye ken fit I mean. I had always thought that our rock 'n' roll experience was worth the telling. I have no personal musical talent (during my childhood, our house was flooded. My dad floated out the front door on the table and I accompanied him on the piano). I do, however, have great memories of nights at different Aberdeen music venues, some of which I was too young to frequent legally. Some of our first wave rockers have already gone to the big ballroom in the sky so the challenge was to pull together memories and photographs, all rapidly fading. Exiled from Aberdeen for a few years now, my original appeal for input appeared in the letters page of the Press and Journal in September of 1994.

Responding to that first item, Bob Spence, a self-confessed, incurable vinyl junkie and Scottish beat freak, came on board. His efforts in spreading our collective net and hauling in some prize catches (as well as some red herrings) have been invaluable to the project, to the extent that I promised Bob in the very early days that he would share the credit for this book. Without having him on the other end of the phone to listen to my illogical and sometimes depressed ramblings, it wouldn't have happened. We've had horrendous telephone bills over the last three years.

The original concept was to pick the story starting with the early Sixties beat boom which marked the beginning of my own musical excitement, fuelled by seeing "The Tsars" chalked on Aberdeen walls. The logical point at which to switch off my memory and the word processor appeared to be when punk detonated. This identified a manageable music and style oriented package of about 14 years. However, two things soon became apparent. Firstly, so many others shared my experiences and affection for the music, they also wandered the streets, pubs, dance halls and clubs in search of that rock 'n' roll buzz and its attendant good times. What did come as a surprise was the willingness and enthusiasm shown by others to share their recollections of the Aberdeen and North East scene, from Fifties youth club skifflers through to guys with chart number ones to their credit. Secondly, once I opened the lid on this thing it was only going to stop when it was good and ready. It took a life of its own and wouldn't let me quit until I told the whole story. Then I found that writing a book is ultimately like sex: no matter how much time you have, you always finish in a helluva hurry.

This is for anyone who ever tried to look cool after getting cuffed at the dancing, for every punter who ever stood at a bus stop with that month's 'in' album under his arm, for all those musicians who burned the wee small hours of their lives in battered Transit vans. If nobody acknowledged you fellas at the time, this is my way of showing appreciation of your efforts.

Inspired by the first rocker I knew, my uncle Charlie: thanks for playing Chuck Berry on Pye International, The Shads, the Big O and The Beatles on deleted orange Polydor. Dedicated with love to my wife: Yvonne, thank you for tolerating all those Midnight Hours. Thanks also to my ma for all the fish soup.

Young man made it to the city
searching through the wet streets
looking for a rock roll band
caught the rip off train to freedom
a line of agents holding out their hand

Work your arses off forever
midnight highways really bring you down
but you're there and you're working
so don't complain so many miss the train

(From Rip Off Train - words and music by Phil May (© Lupus Music)

Chapter 1

"We hadna' seen a hot tattie in ages'

Despite its prominence as a major port, the Aberdeen of the early 1960s was somewhat insular, in comparison with its modern cosmopolitan situation. Foreigners were few and far between. These - comprised an infrequent English person, bicycle-riding French ingin Johnnies or seamen from Polish ishing vessels (equipped with more cold-war radar systems than Jodrell Bank) which docked in the - harbour. In return for what they supposed to be hard British currency, these sailors traded Polish cigarettes, vodka and checked cotton work shirts with canny Aberdonian dockers and fish workers. However, attempts by this first wave of Iron Curtain trawler men to spend what they understood to be Scottish bank notes proved problematic: imagine their disgust when the Anchorage and other harbour pubs refused to accept the proffered Embassy cigarette coupons.

American accents, so familiar to Aberdonians from the mid-1970s onwards, were then heard exclusively in John Wayne movies at the Grand Central or the 'Torryers'. The only people who worked in oil were students at Grays School of Art, or mechanics in the engine rooms of Europe's biggest trawler fleet. The heart of the city lay in fishing, ship building, granite, paper and, less importantly, textiles. Such industries funded recreational activities for Aberdeen's youth and it was from these that city juveniles gleefully escaped into the weekend music scene. It was only in the Fifties that the the term 'teenager' came into existence, hence acknowledging that middle ground between childhood and adulthood. Whilst in the previous decade youngsters had been barely and indifferently acknowledged, in the Sixties their amplitude in society increased. They also enjoyed more recreational time and spare cash than ever before. Impatience, and the concept of choice as a pubescent prerogative replaced naive acquiescence. Such choice inexorably converged on music and fashion. The latter spelled the end of barkit white jimmies with black laces, plastic sandals and economically sound brogues. (Easiphit were soon to experience a run on their cheap leather-effect winkle pickers, toes curled up after one soaking leaving the wearer resembling an extra from a Sinbad movie). During bleak North East winters, mothers had dressed these kids oblivious of aesthetics. Hence itchy balaclava helmets (knitted by well-intentioned, domineering grannies) ruled the roost, in the company of mitts with string attached, and long wrap-over scarves, safety-pinned at the victim's back. At every trumpet-announced opportunity, it was out to the rag mannie to barter these woollen instruments of torture in exchange for essential water pistols, goldfish and balloons. A lucky tattie or a candy epple at the Timmer Market had been a big deal, scant compensation for repetitive tales from their elders of how empty jam jars secured entry to the pictures in byegone years. And who was that Johnny Norrie they raved on about? Just why did he insist in going through those doors in auld Torry? Peeing in the kypee was an enjoyable, if futile, cri de coeur. In 1960 Aberdeen the cinematic horrors of Alfred Hitchcock's latest movie Psycho paled in comparison with the sickly smell of smoking caney (cinnamon sticks) with which under-age picture-goers clouded the Majestic's atmosphere.

This was when Bucksburn, for example, was in the countryside. . . television sets were scarce in working class homes, children were expert in memorising numbers that related to the then financially important Co-op divi, rather than telephones. Dear reader, if you fall into this age bracket then pound to a penny you know what your ma's coapy number was?

Even before Butlins at Ayr (replete with dreaded, plastic palm-treed Beachcomber Bar) provided an affordable trade fortnight destination for working class families, Arbroath's Red Lion caravan site typified Aberdonian vacations.

Gordon Hardie's 1950's Castle Jazz Club in the Hardgate provided a parent-free refuge for youngsters who were now on the threshold of finding their own stylistic and cultural feet. . . as these kids grew in age and buying power, new teenage-targetted music came through a fog of pops and crackles from Radio Luxembourg on cheap Hong Kong transistor sets, smuggled under the kids' bedcovers each night. Beach Ballroom, Palace and Palais apart (we shall return later to these nirvanas of dance), early Sixties Granite City pop heaven secreted itself in housing estate and town-centre youth clubs. Bruce Miller, Telemech, and Mac's in Marischal Street were primary sources of chart singles, whilst Woolies had their own Embassy budget label, with four or six anonymous cover versions on one release. These were spun on multi-stacking Dansette record players in gyms, church halls and scout huts. Not much, but the best the kids had to let out their generation gap frustrations. We were still a decade away from the concept of the DJ and his mobile disco, with flashing coloured light bulbs and his inane accent from the USA (Union Street, Aberdeen). In good old Scottish grannie's heilan' hame style, 1956 saw the release (escape?) of a chunky four track EP, recorded live at the Tivoli theatre. . . a young Sydney Devine gave it laldie as he assaulted Blue Suede Shoes replete with teddy-boy drape jacket, Brylcreemed DA, and tartan trews.

For several years the 62 Club was home to the city's rocker and biker fraternities graduating there from Northfield's Beehive Club. The latter was perhaps the busiest live music location. It was also a dangerous gig as far as musicians were concerned. One bass player recalls an incident when a hallyrackit punter exploded from the crowd onto the stage, knocking over everything and everyone in his way. When our bassist halted his playing, the thug shouted "Dinnae you stop - it's your drummer I'm efter.' On occasions, group members achieved a safe exit by swinging their guitars around them, cutting a path through the Beehive's rioting clientele. On the site of today's Lemon Tree venue, the St Katherine's Club (known affectionately as St K's) enjoyed regular capacity attendances under the watchful eye of Father McClachlan: the almost forgotten Belmont Street church hall-based Philemon Club was another avidly attended teen forum.

Musos and wide boys congregated at Allan's Bar in George Street, a Winchester Club frequented by Arfur Daleys with Aiberdeen accents: Shark Gray was one such habitué. The Castlegate and East End areas encompassed many venues for live music, numbering within their constituencies the Hop Inn (where Lennie Benzies and Sonny Pearce played in pre-beat piano, drums and vocals acts), the Cras' Nest and the East Neuk. The latter King Street venue witnessed the inception of Aberdeen's primeval rock 'n' rollers, Eddie Watson's Alligators. They were exponents of a hybrid swing-jazz, before the fusion of R & B and country music in the USA brought rock 'n' roll to teenagers world-wide. Colin Fraser was a 17-year-old trombonist and recalls "Along with sax player Jimmy Gray, I appeared every Sunday night at the Swing Club on the top floor above Burtons. One evening, this drummer Eddie Watson approached us and asked if we fancied joining a rock 'n' roll band he was forming. We thought we would give it a go and began rehearsals in the community room at Castlehill Barracks. It was a dump.' They adopted See You Later Alligator as their signature tune: it also provided the band's name. "We made our own equipment' says Gray "We bought electrical bits and pieces from Alexanders in Holburn Street and got a joiner to knock up some speaker boxes.' Soon Eddie's reptilian tail-lashing swamp dwellers had their fearsome teeth locked into the new sound from the US South. By 1956 and Rockin' Through The Rye, Eddie's snappers were well entrenched into the style of The Bill Haley Comets.

With dual guitarists Jackie Fearless and Jock Stewart, Sandy Bright vocalised the latest stuff from Elvis and Little Richard. Alex Evans on fiddle bass completed their founding line-up, with pianist Alan Payton joining later. Their East Neuk and Music Hall shows led to peripheral rave-ups from Montrose to Tain, sporadically sparking juvenile mayhem (similar to, and probably in imitation of, the riots improbably induced by the Haley-scored movies The Blackboard Jungle and Rock Around The Clock). Such Alligator frenzy saw them "pretty well paid, but we always set a sum of money aside so we could improve our PA and instruments.' They would have done well to listen to Peter Pan's cautionary words Never Smile At A Crocodile. "We went up to Eddie's hoose one day and he had done a bunk for Canada wi' the cash. He has never been heard of since.' Later the boys were to fe-fund themselves and re-form as The Hihats.

By 1960, you had to dig it dad, but dig it good. Like make with the cool sounds daddy-o, straight out of the fridge, man. Get over and out in back street cellars where drink's for squares, man, kids' stuff. Who laid the square discs on us? Oh man, send for the body snatchers. Well, in London maybe, but in Aiberdeen such fey arty jive talk would have been an open invitation to a Torry handshake. The Sixties ushered in a boisterous music scene, which included amongst its most vociferous The Royal Teens, The Facells, The Playboys and The Strollers. This voyage through our beat heritage sets sail with the latter combo in 1961 onboard a P&O passenger liner Orion, plying to and from Australia. At sea Frank Milne became friendly with fellow Aberdonian shipmate George Barker: both were guitarists, with Frank doing vocals, as they entertained crew and passengers. Their first gig ashore together occurred at Melbourne's Flying Angel Hall, where Frank remembers that "George managed to get his lead knotted up inside his semi-acoustic guitar, leaving him with only about 16 inches of guitar lead to plug into the amp. So he played on his knees and introduced feedback to Australia.'

Five months after that Orion trip they parted company, going off on different ships but agreeing to keep in touch with the intention of forming a group when they got ashore. They met again at the Silver City Cafe in George Street the following March. George had assembled a few of his mates and had been trying to track down Frankie. The first Strollers line-up, led by George on rhythm guitar with Frank on vocals, had Bill Gauld on drums, Denny Greig on lead guitar and Hammy Harwood on bass. The singer resided in Stockethill where he organised their first gig at his local church youth club. Fine for him, but the others lived in Garthdee and had to cart drums, guitars and their sole Selmer amp on the bus. Appropriately for these aspiring pop stars, their fee was one bottle of soft drink each.

Contemporary music was on the cusp of the skiffle boom and derivative Brit rock 'n' roll, microscopically studied and Xeroxed from the genuine American material. Aberdeen was no different from the rest of the country in being awash with Brylcreem and hair lacquer. Frank again "Cliff Richard and The Shadows were big although personally I preferred the authentic US stuff like Jerry Lee, Elvis, Little Richard and Fats Domino. The first number we ever played was Eddie Cochran's Twenty Flight Rock with all our instruments coming through our one amp.' Nonetheless, they went down really well and moved rapidly into the big time, negotiating their terms up to two bottles of juice each.

In view of his forthcoming marriage, George went back to sea that October to get some money together. The group struggled on for a while in his absence but eventually collapsed without his dominating presence. Thanks to Syd Weaver (his own group was Sheriff Syd Weaver and The Deputies) Frank pulled a spot with The Midnighters, one of the city's top combos. Their previous vocalist was the mysterious Johnny Dark (such stage aliases were commonplace) but deflatingly and less exotically, his real name was Ronnie Robertson. These nocturnals were Ian Taylor on lead guitar, Billy Speirs on bass, Jim 'Swannie' Swanson on rhythm guitar, with Ricky Whitelaw on drums. Andy Anderson took Ricky's place when he later moved on. The Mids circulated on the Aberdeenshire country dance circuit and supported chart acts coming through the North East on the national tour rota. Packed gigs at St K's had Frank taking short-cuts in learning top-20 lyrics. "These were screaming days when the girls would howl like banshees, especially during the rocky numbers. I soon wised up to getting them screaming during the verse, so I only had to learn the chorus. They couldn't hear the rubbish I mumbled for the racket they made themselves.' Mandatory hit parade material apart, the group were dipping into the blues of Lightnin' Hopkins, Muddy Waters and Big Bill Broonzy.

Wise to teen-pop razzamatazz, the band caused a mini riot at St. K's, appearing in new bright red suits, with quiffed and Cliffed vocalist Frank dressed in blue. Ian sported a sparkling new scarlet Fender Stratocaster. . . the Strat was virtually unobtainable, with other local guitarists using equipment like the Hofner V3. (Brian Youngson owned probably the only other Strat in Aberdeen at the time). This flash hardware was damaged when the band's dormobile rolled over on the Alford road in September of 1962. Undeterred by injuries to Bill and Swannie, they carried on with the show the following evening, looking like local heroes back from a war.

Meanwhile Barker, ashore from the merchant navy, had galvanised his Strollers back into action. Frank casts his mind through 30 years to pick up the story again. "George tried to get me to back but I was really busy already. On my recommendation Roger Benzie got the job as Strollers' co-vocalist along with George's sister Julie.' One night she turned up at a Midnighters' gig with Denny Greig's fiancee. When the set ended Julie introduced herself, proclaiming "The Mids are rubbish, you should go back with The Strollers.' Frankie says "She may have had bad manners but she did have good taste.'

Frank left Aberdeen and The Mids for Liverpool, performing at The Iron Door club's folk and blues night. . . at other times, Johnny Wood and June Cowie were also featured Midnighters' vocalists. June had visited her uncle Jim 'Rusty' Russell at New Year and joined in a sing-song next door at Johnny's mother's. It was suggested that June try out with the band and rehearsals took place in Johnny's bedroom, where they learned a couple of new chart numbers each week. After a much-travelled sojourn with the band, June moved on to club and pub work with bassist Jim Forsyth.

Back in Aberdeen after a few weeks at Merseyside's Iron Door, Frank found that The Strollers were already flying high. Bill Speirs had replaced Hammy, enticed on board on the strength of his having access to the group's white Fender bass. Unhappy with Benzie's vocals, George tried to talk his former shipmate around again. Frankie really preferred to play guitar and in any case was under the impression that Roger had settled in. Firey Dod's answer was "He's leaving but he disnae know yet'. . . Frank's recollection is that "It wasn't very nice, and I later felt that Benzie was hard done by. The Strollers had a regular job at The Beehive and it was a really popular spot. Dod wanted to make sure they kept the gig. So I ended up re-joining'.

By the end of 1962 they were also working regularly at St K's and the Beach Ballroom, by now second in Aberdeen's group heirarchy only to Tommy Dene and The Tremors who held down a prestigious Palace Ballroom residency. On the back of The Strollers' upsurge George had the old van sprayed bright yellow, overlaid with blue stars containing the lads' names. In big lettering was the legend "Frankie and The Strollers with Julie.' This vehicle carried group and equipment to rural dates at Inverurie Town Hall, Mintlaw Station and Pitmedden. A fleet of buses departed from Aberdeen's Mealmarket Street, transporting the city's screamage fans to these country dances.

Saturday afternoons saw the top end of George Street littered with vans belonging to various groups, as they congregated in the Silver City Cafe and at J T Forbes guitar shop. In this music emporium George Barker earned his nickname 'Firey Dod', a reference to neither his red hair nor his temperament, but rather to his customary position perched on top of the shop's heater. The fish market cafe was a post-gig late night assembly point for night-owl musicians, harmonising I'll Take You Home Again Caffeine when they met for post-gig bacon softies, egg baps and other unidentified frying objects. "We wouldn't talk much about the 'name' acts we had supported, but we often enviously discussed the fancy equipment they had'.

Early in 1964 The Strollers successfully negotiated a Glasgow audition for a contract in Germany. Newly-weds Frank and Julie deciding against travelling, Bill Wood came in to share vocals with Dod. The lads set off for Germany in May, leaving Frank behind in Aberdeen playing guitar with Brian Still's group. The band did well abroad and had a good time, but found it difficult to extract money from clubs, agents and promoters. They returned home disappointed but maybe a bit wiser. Despite these difficulties, the ever-optimistic George reckoned they could still make a success of it in Germany, given another chance.

Julie was pregnant as Frank re-joined what was now a pretty hot band. Before leaving for Europe again they played a farewell gig at the Beach Ballroom. Frank Milne on lead vocals, guitar and blues harp, Denny Greig on lead guitar, George Barker on bass and vocals, Alex Craigen on drums, and Freddie Ellis on keyboards and vocals, played a predominantly R 'n' B set to a raving Beach crowd.

On the strength of that goodbye show, Alex Craigen was offered a permanent spot with Johnny Scott's resident Beach Ballroom band. His acceptance of the job forced another shuffle, with Freddie moving from keyboards to drums: nae bother for Fred, he was to become known as 'the Godfather of Aberdonian drummers.' The journey began inauspiciously, with all of the travelling money spent before Newcastle. This set the standard, proving to be invaluable training for their forthcoming campaign. Being skint was a way of life for British beat groups in Germany.

They regularly played the Savoy Club in Hanover, promoted by Wolfgang Heillemann through his Studio 7 organisation. A bit of a star in the Jerry Lee Lewis mould on the German Fifties rock 'n' roll scene, Wolfie had operated under the stage name Bubi Haynes The Piano Wrecker.

German audiences were mental for Merseybeat and were also digging R 'n' B and blues, right up The Strollers' strasse. The boys' experiences display parallels with The Beatles' early struggling days in Hamburg. "We could never get paid and right from the start it was a battle to survive. We were performing club sets of eight hours at a stretch. The problem was we couldnae get any sleep after being so high during the night's frenzy, the slightest little noise woke us when we were trying to get our heads down. It took forever to wear off. We were starving half of the time and would go banging on the promoter's door, shouting 'Come on Wolfie - give us some money!' We were pretty rough buggers ourselves, not to be messed about with. But basically he just ripped us off.'

However, laughs were plentiful at venues varying from top class night clubs to downright weird dives, throughout the Hanover and Dortmund areas. During all-night sessions Freddie was a real driving force: audiences, with their mach schau (make a show) demands, orgasmed over his power drumming. Notwithstanding his value, internal band ructions resulted in Fred being replaced temporarily by a local drummer Hans Dieter, but this all settled down eventually. Freddie was at his chaotic best during this

German campaign, causing all sorts of mayhem "We would be in the middle of a packed city street when he would suddenly shout things like 'Long live Audie Murphy!' (Murphy was World War II's most decorated American GI who personally killed many German troops). But Fred was definitely the loudest, wildest, beatiest drummer the clubs had ever seen.'

As with dozens of other expat British bands, Dod's boys found themselves billed aus Liverpool (regardless of their actual origination), as promoters capitalised on The Beatles. Other UK acts (notably Tony Sheridan and Scousers King Size Taylor with his group The Dominoes) were enormous in Germany, but remained virtually unknown back in Blighty.

The Strollers' van was an attraction in itself. "One time on tour we came off the autobahn and went down an ausgang instead of an einfart. The politzei pulled us up but when they saw our van they asked us for autographs and pictures, before telling us to always remember to go in an einfart. This proved to be important advice that we immediately forgot.' Driving through the countryside to a gig, the vehicle broke down (all those ausgangs and einfarts had done for it). Denny and Freddie travelled on with a local group, The Shouters (so named because they couldn't afford microphones), while George and Frank stayed put, in vehicle mechanic mode. En route to the venue the van stopped again, this time terminally, the big ends had gone.

Wandering about in the middle of nowhere they happened upon a wee village where assistance might be gained. The place to source vehicle repairs was obviously the local pub, their entry into which brought reactions from the pils drinking natives akin to that of an invasion from Mars. These mangy rockers, attired in battered winkle pickers, weird clothes and greasy long hair, were something new. "They eyed us up and down, looking for our collecting tins' says Frank "We tried to explain to them that we were just poor lost Scottish heart throbs with a kaput van.' With their hybrid Aberdonian-pidgin German failing to gain a flicker of comprehension, the desperate duo dropped speilen guittaren and 'Rolling Stones' into the conversation to get the message across.

"Suddenly they lashed us up with food and loads of drink, VIP treatment. It took us a while to twig that they actually were under the misapprehension that we were the Rolling Stones. We were in no hurry to put them straight. . . it was only when they drove us to our gig and asked for autographs that they realised that we were Dod and Frunkie fae Aiberdeen. This naturally pissed them off, so they dumped us there and buggered off.'

Following the death of the vehicle and the Stones impersonations, they had to hire a van to transport themselves and their equipment. This burned further holes in their already aerated pockets - it had been difficult enough to send Deutchsmarks home to wives and families. A German group, The Trotters, had a regular gig at Emden's premier club Moulin Rouge. . . a few blocks away The Strollers were packing them in at their venue (which, had it been cleaner, might have been a slum). The Scots, watching the local boys do their stuff, were asked by the cordial, clean-cut, nice-guy Trots to do a couple of guest numbers on stage. This impromptu performance proved fruitful as the favourable audience response saw them being offered steady employment there in their own right, at The Trots expense. Which was how they came to steal the Moulin Rouge residency from the affable German band and breach their contract with the fearsome Wolfie. The Strollers had a basic motivation for accepting the gig. "The thing was, there was no way we could turn down the offer. The wifie who owned the place gave us a decent meal and we hidna seen a hot tattie in ages.'

Hassle from the piano wrecker, combined with the desire to get home for Christmas led to the lads strolling back across the North Sea. Now re-instated at the Moulin Rouge, The Trotters recruited Freddie on drums but the remaining poverty-stricken Strollers were forced to sell one of their prized Fender Strats to raise the necessary cash to get back to Aberdeen. Mid-December 1964, they rattled out from Emden rail station, waving auf wiedersehen to their old kamerad Fred.

Back in Aberdeen they were big news. The P & J's banner headlines included "Strollers return from triumphant tour of Germany', "Didn't have to sell a Strat to get home', "Musicians' wives not dying of malnutrition', and "Germans capture fearless Freddie.'

When the bratwurst had finally worked its way out of their systems, Bob Milne came in to replace Freddie, as Dod negotiated a residency at the Looking Glass, the Market Street lounge. The Palais on

Diamond Street, attempting to attract a younger clientele, inaugurated what they called 'group spots'. So after finishing their gig at the Looking Glass, The Strollers went up to the Palais to strut their stuff for a second time each night. When the Double Two lounge in Torry opened for business, they relocated over the river. "George's singing had improved out of all recognition and we were doing some really nice harmony stuff. We thought that our set was quite versatile, different to what other groups were doing. . . Ray Charles influenced blues-rock, with a jazzy bias. Unfortunately we unwillingly acquired the wrong sort of reputation because of the audience we attracted. This crowd was pretty rough and followed us about causing trouble.'

George then proposed that the band go over to Australia to try their luck (a drastic, but not unknown move for Scots in the Sixties). With Svengali-like timing, the Firey one took the £10 Assisted Passage Scheme plunge mid-1966, hence avoiding the whole football World Cup multiple orgasm that discharged out of England that summer (it still spasms on to this very day, given the remotest excuse). He wrote letters home praising the Australian lifestyle and its unlimited potential, having already found steady work with an Aussie group. Inspired by these rave reports, Frank and Julie also emigrated, with Denny Greig and his family following soon afterwards. The final configuration of The Strollers to play in Aberdeen saw Bill Speirs on bass, Morgan Adams on drums, with Frankie on vox, lead guitar and blues harp.

. . . .

Brian Kennedy asks if he may consult his wee black notebook as he gives evidence on the Aberdeen beat scene, this time centred on the adventures of The Strangers. During his Grammar School sixth year, he combined with fellow aspiring guitarist Derek Freeland, and biscuit-tin basher Tony Blanchard: crumbs!

Brian used his cousin's clubbie book acoustic guitar for sessions at the YMCA in Skene Terrace, and passed his lunch times ogling Hofner and Burns electric models displayed in JT Forbes' shop window. The first electric guitar he played was Derek's £13 self-assembled model, at a Grammar school end-of-term dance. However he soon acquired a Guyatone solid body guitar. Brian's neighbours, the brothers Johnson, each brought one of these back from a merchant navy trip to the Far East. . . (Johnny Johnson had won talent competitions in Singapore). When Johnny's brother gave up on his guitar Brian bought it and promptly set himself up with a Watkins Dominator amp on tick. Johnny practised with the embryonic Strangers, using his Guyatone six string as a bass, before building his own copy Fender Precision. The arrival of drummer Raymond Riley and singer Dave Laing (stage name, Barry Wayne) turned them into a 'real' group, for whom the Inverurie based impresario Bert Ewen arranged a first paid gig at the Rescue Hall, Peterhead. On the eve of this inaugural performance, Dave broke his leg and Norman Shearer jumped in at the deep end as replacement vocalist. "Somehow my name was suggested. I had never even sung in public before, let alone with a band - but they came looking for me. Derek told me much later that when they first saw me, their instinct was to drive on past - my drainpipes and drape jacket put them off. Anyway, they did pick me up, so I fronted a group without rehearsals and no idea what we were going to play. Somehow our enthusiasm pulled us through, and The Strangers were on their way.'

This young Aberdeen group worshipped at the tapping feet of their gurus, The Shadows. Not only was their musical repertoire so sourced, they named themselves after the B side of a 1960 top-five hit by Hank Marvin and his boys. The Shads showed that even the most basic player could soon be a Fender bender. Their move out of the Two Is skiffle bar, with their dinky smart-stepping stage movements, opened inumerable doors for young players across the UK, including The Strangers. Brian soon mastered Hank's cultured tremeloed sound - that echoed single note lead, consolidated by Derek's strummed innocuous rhythm. Once they had the taste of paid rock 'n' roll, The Strollers were back up to see Harry Lord in George Street, buying a Hofner guitar (Strats were still on the unaffordable shopping lust-list) and two Vox AC30 amps.

Brian is most complimentary when he remembers Harry Lord. "When he took over the JT Forbes business, he frequently loaned out equipment. He deserves a lot of credit for helping many aspiring young musicians to fulfil their dreams. Harry's home was a Hogmanay magnet for most of the groups, some great jam sessions. . . or maybe the alcohol made it all seem better than it actually was.'

Reinforced by the experienced drummer, Syd Green (former member of George Lawrie's Palais band and resident for some time at Dundee's JM Ballroom), they went full tilt for duplicating The Shadows' sound. A Watkins Copycat Echo unit became their next acquisition, along with now-affordable matching salmon pink Fenders - a Strat and a Jazz bass. Cash for the HP repayments on the new equipment came from a regular round of engagements at Mintlaw, Udny Station, Pitmedden, Peterhead and the Dalrymple Hall, Fraserburgh.

At the latter venue they supported Jet Harris, their lean, brooding hero who had recently come out of The Shadows. The Aberdeen boys impressed Harris's manager such that he immediately offered them a six month initial tour in Europe as Jet's backing band. . . all having full time day jobs, the lads declined. ("Fit d'ye mean jobs?' shouts the youthful Norman Shearer "I was still at school')

Derek was injured in a road accident. Norman suggested that his cousin might be the ideal man to temporarily fill the rhythm guitarist's pointy-toed shoes. The stand-in easily passed the audition, making his inaugural public appearance at the Mill Inn Maryculter. He was the 15 year old Billy Bremner who turned out to be something of a find, going on to be one of the best respected guitarists in British and American rock music.

Brian Kennedy is the ideal person to comment on the Aberdeen beat - he joined the city police force. Let's see: It was 30 years ago today, Sgt Kennedy taught the band to play. . . hmm . . . nae bad, it just needs a wee bit of work.

. . . .

Time changes everything. . . from the early Sixties onwards, the fortunes of the Dons fluctuated dramatically. They were a disgrace, annihilated regularly by the Glasgow teams, and escaping relegation by the slimmest of margins. Tommy Pearson scuttled off amid loud celebrations and Eddie Turnbull arrived to put out most of the playing staff along with the rest of the rubbish: boy, were the scaffies confused that morning. Then came 'cup tie' McKay, Zoltan Varga, Joe Harper, captain Willie Miller, the sunshine of Easter Road and Hampden, the rain of Ullevi, manager Willie Miller. . . and it was, briefly, almost back to square one. The team that Willie managed looked good on paper but unfortunately they were crap on grass.

Popular music experienced equally quantum changes and travelled an unfathomable course through a million fads and trends to the present.

Only two things have remained constantly with us each and every week, regardless of what else happens in the universe: Wee Alickie. . . and The Facells.

As The Strangers became strangers, Derek Freeland and Norman Shearer, weary of sophisticated MOR tremolo-arm-governed Shadows' Brit quasi-rock (with its accompanying black dinner suits and cummerbunds) did a flit away from the conventional neighbourhood of lead, rhythm, bass and drums. Norman sets the scene "That period invokes thoughts of Cliff and The Shadows clones: Shane Fenton and The Fentones, and Malcolm Clark and The Cresters. With music in the doldrums, Derek and I had to do something different so the break-up of The Strangers was inevitable.' Derek echoes these Shadows of boredom and ennui "Brian Kennedy was an excellent guitarist but was also such a bloody perfectionist - the more difficult the number was, the happier he was. The concept of having a blast at rudimentary rock 'n' roll was beyond him. On the other hand, we thought it should simply be fun without working so hard at note-perfect performances. The Facells was our reaction to all that.'

A self-confessed sax maniac, Norman recruited George Smith, a clarinetist on Aberdeen's jazz scene (his cousin Atholl Smith also played clarinet with the boss man of Granite City jazz Sandy West). George converted into a rock 'n' roll saxophonist as they commenced Sunday rehearsals at the Torry Community Centre, "deafening the neighbourhood and the seagulls' as Norman remembers.

Those antediluvian run-throughs resulted in The Facells gigging initially with George Rose on drums and Sandy West's brother Brian on keyboards. However, the team selection soon settled down to Norman on vocals, Derek on rhythm, Ricky Whitelaw on drums, Ian Philip on lead guitar, with George 'Sporty Dod' Smith on sax. Bass player was the south-paw Bill 'Hovis' Richardson: not many left-dukers on the scene then (although McCartney wasn't doing badly, and a young James Marshall Hendrix was learning his incomparable tricks and licks on the US chitlin' circuit). For The Facells, matching black polo-necked jumpers were the order of the day.

During this period, it was trendy for groups to have names that ended in -ells and -ettes. A contemporary French car was the Facell Vega. . . let's hear it for Gary Vega and The Facells! Problems with pronunciation of the new group's name around the North East saw a Muggarthaugh loon tell his pals that The Fackells or The Facels were coming to town.

It was curtains for the band right from the outset. An inaugural gig in the Highlands finished unfeasibly late and there was no conceivable way back to Aberdeen that night. With nowhere to rest their rockin' young heads, the promoter took down the stage curtains to provide make-shift bedding for the boys to sleep on. The following morning they pulled themselves together and phoned in with lame excuses. . . Norman skived off school.

Gary Vega very soon died of embarrassment, but The Facells remained to become regulars at the 62 Club, the Beehive, St. K's and the enormously successful Philemon Club. Initially simply another covers group, their individual talents created a fundamentally unique sound. Norman describes Ian's inimatable guitar style as "one of the hallmarks of the early Facells - he was the only local guy into string-bending effects, which he did with some sophistication. He garnered the technique from Joe Brown, himself a much under-rated guitarist.' A veteran of The Midnighters and Syd Weaver's Deputies, Ricky was a fine drummer who was destined to lead The Facells for many years. Hovis Richardson had earned a crust with The Commancheros.

1964 found The Facells touring the ubiquitous weekend country dance circuit, with Thursday nights in the city devoted to the Palace Ballroom, alternating their residency weekly with co-equals Tommy Dene and The Tremors. Hosted by Rank Organisation MC and vocalist Clive Ahmed, the Palace engagement involved supporting visiting, principally Merseybeat, groups. Norman's rueful "how unfair it all was' recollection: "The Hollies did 45 minutes and we worked all night, but they got all the money.' Maybe those Hollies' million-sellers had something to do with it.

Live sets kicked off with Ray Charles' What'd I Say, which became their signature tune, guaranteed to get their crowd going. The group played this number ever louder and faster as Norman theatrically descended the Palace stairs, with bouncers restraining pumped-up, screaming fans. He occasionally miscalculated his tormenting of hysterical teeny-boppers and was pulled feet-first into the heaving crowd. Ricky says "The Palace was really jumping in those days.' Derek remembers that material such as the Wolf's Smokestack Lightning and Rufus Thomas' Walkin' The Dog, picked up from the early Rolling Stones, as being "a breath of fresh air compared to impotent British pop.'

Facellmania found expression in badges bearing the motto "The Fabulous Facells Fan Club', worn by female acolytes, congregating around the Palace stage and chasing the band down Union Street. One anonymous report describes how three groupies just happened to be on board the van, hurtling through the Aberdeenshire countryside one night. The unaccredited driver brought the vehicle to a halt alongside a field before jumping out. He then opened the back door of the Facellmobile and hoisted a bale of hay inside, shouting "Feeding time!'

With The Beatles annihilating hitherto staid, sanitised British popular music and breaking the mould for ever, university cliques transferred their elitist affection from trad-jazz to the new beat groups. . . The Facells became darlings of the student set, playing the Pre-Torcher and the Arts Ball for a number of years. Derek remembers the era as one of "terrific excitement, even when we were not gigging we watched other groups to check out the opposition.' He also name-drops a couple of the acts encountered during travels throughout Scotland: Russ Saintly and The Newnotes sound grim enough, and what about Johnny Carr and The Cadilaccs?

After four years in the band Norman called it a day. . . for him, the thrill had gone. A potential work posting away from Aberdeen precluded his accepting the offer of a spot with Johnny Scott's band at the Beach Ballroom. Now a touch crusty, Hovis also went stale. Ian Philip followed The Strollers and emigrated to Australia . . . and the first phase of The Facells came to an end. As witnessed by that fleet of yellow artic wagons carrying drill pipe and diving gas to and from East coast harbours, Derek Freeland just keeps on trucking. . . whilst Norman does his duty with HM Customs and Excise, making sure that we pay ours.

Maintaining the band's continuity, Ricky recruited Johnny Barclay on guitar, whilst one of Aberdeen's favourite faces Sonny Pearce, filled the vacant vocalist's spot. Sonny had been an early starter. "My mother always encouraged me to sing and when I was a bairn I was doing a couple of songs in social clubs, as a kind of a novelty thing.'. . . Several years on, he became known as a pub singer specialising in Nat King Cole and other classic crooners' stuff. . . before the beat group eruption, pubs attracted customers on the strength of the vocal, piano and drums music on offer.

Sonny attended a Saturday afternoon Palace Ballroom session, spectating at a talent competition run by The Press and Journal. Unaware that one of his chinas had entered him as a contestant, he was eventually chivvied into going on stage when his name was called. The Diamonds provided the backing for the various entrants - Syd Weaver was the winner with his rendition of Cut Across Shorty, Sonny came second with Choo Choo Train. A couple of days later The Diamonds' drummer Freddie Ellis came knocking on Sonny's door, asking him to join them and 30 years later he remains a legend on the city's group scene.

Apart from Fred and Sonny, that Diamonds line-up had Davie Whyte on guitar and Brian Nicholson on bass. . . (previous members had included vocalist Sandra Ewen and lead guitarist John Cummings). According to Sonny, these were rough Diamonds. "We had a few dates for Albert Bonici, starting in Elgin. Then we were off to Oban where we had to meet up with this bloke who had just had a hit record. . . he must have been really good, so good that I canna mind his name. We were going to be backing him for a couple of shows. Bonici told us to pick him up, appropriately enough (he was a real smoothie), outside Burtons in Oban. We came roaring roon the corner in our Bedford van, smoke spewing out everywhere. There he was, carrying three mohair suits on hangers. We never treated any of these so-called stars any different from anybody else. . . anyway we went to the hall, a right dilapidated wreck of a place, and did a 20 minute rehearsal to run through three or four numbers. He wanted a big build up, his sticking his head through the fire-door at the side of the stage was my cue to give it lots of "Here he is. . . blah blah' and he would run to the middle of the stage. All that sort of stuff.'

"That night we had done a couple of numbers ourselves before the door opened and it was time for Mr Big to make his entrance. . . Ladies and gentlemen, here he is etc etc. . . He made a big jump into the middle of the stage . . . it gave way and collapsed, he disappeared right through it. The crowd were still sort of half way through their first cheer. . . their applause died as he dropped through the floor. We were in stitches but kept playing, we couldnae think what else to do. He clambered back out of the hole onto the stage, covered in cobwebs and shite, and tried to pick up the song. It was just a bloody scream.'

For Sonny, The Diamonds were not a bad band as far as they went, but "our lack of professionalism let us down. We would just stick on a record and listen out for our own parts. Then it was just a case of go for it and do your best.' When The Diamonds stopped sparkling, he then had a short spell with Andy Lawson, Brian Nicholson, Eddie Lawson, and Bob the mystery drummer, in the Steve Cameron-managed Classix.

The Diamonds' 'just go for it' philosophy diametrically opposed the very professional approach of The Facells, whom Sonny joined after the Vega had driven away. "We rehearsed a helluva lot and were as polished as we could be. Ricky of course was the boss of the band, I'm not sure if he knows it, but we used to call him God - what he said was gospel. On the other hand, they called me the Bully. . . people used to approach me about fixing up gigs for the group, but I didn't then have the temperament for dealing with business. . . I had a short fuse. So I told them "If you want to sort things out, contact Richard. If it was left up to me, we would never have got any work.' Sonny's talent moved The Facells into a close harmony style, concentrating on Hollies, Four Seasons and Beach Boys material - he says "I brought Ricky's singing out of him as well, he had never really thought himself good enough before, but it fitted well into our new harmony format.' Success continued unabated but November 1965 brought fireworks in the shape of a fine from Charlie Styles, local secretary of the Musicians' Union. Ricky allegedly failed to give adequate notice of boys' unavailability for a Beach Ballroom commitment - the ensuing fracas saw his being threatened with expulsion from the MU. Sonny's quote at the time was "Without Ricky we will have to fold the band'. Resolution came when the group settled with the union to the tune of £50, a not inconsequential sum 30 years ago.

After Charlie was placated, local promoter Gordon Hardie arranged a Facells' visit to Albert Bonici's Two Red Shoes in Elgin where they taped two tracks for Bonici. In betweens Johnny and The Copycats' I'm a Hog for you Baby on Albert's Norco label and this effort from The Facells, came The

Trawler Song by Grampian TV regular Dave McIntosh, the Singing Coalman. Let's put that one on the back of the fire. Thus the sole vinyl testament to The Facells was recorded live at 'The Boots' on a pair of reel-to-reel tape recorders. The A side was Bonici's choice and a conservative one at that. If You Love Me I Won't Care, the much covered standard, sounds to these CD coddled ears as if it suffers from distortion or tape flutter. In contrast the B side So Fine, a Johnny Otis number culled from Ike and Tina Turner's repertoire, presents a rocking George Smith sax-driven charge from a cooking, live Facells: Wooly Bully on heat, and a fine snapshot of this hot Aberdeen band in 1966. Sonny confirms they "put heart and soul into it' but reveals that the primitive recording set-up (blankets over the drums, mufflers, and a solitary set of cans for the vocalist) limited what they could produce. Hopes were understandably high, but Ricky must have been out buying the NME to check on the single's progress, when Ready Steady Go called him to come on the show. And the postie must have pinched the massive Norco royalty cheque.

After The Beatles arrived on the scene, Sonny felt that audiences became encouragingly more educated about the music. "Earlier, people would hear really an overall group sound, and mainly focus on the singing. The majority of times the music could have been shite (within limits, of course) but the crowds were pretty naive about what they were getting. Later though, fans were more discerning. . . they developed quickly, in some cases faster than some of the bands could. So even through a really grim performance a punter was able, for instance, to pick up on the fact that the bass lines had been terrific. I felt much happier with that quality of appreciation and criticism, rather than the way it had previously been. I didnae take kindly to being slagged by somebody who didnae know his arse from his elbow.'

Personnel changes were commonplace amongst Aberdeen groups. "Fans must have got confused and annoyed at times, seeing the same faces but with different acts week by week. A lot of the music was 12 bar, easy for any player worth his salt to drop into any specific group's routine. That was one of the appealing things about The Facells for me. Apart from lead guitarists, who did tend to fluctuate, we kept a steady team together for a very long time.'

Aberdeen bands were not renowned for pandering to prima donnas. At a Bert Ewen-promoted Inverurie Town Hall gig, The Facells turned up early (standard practice, indicative of dedication to the job in hand). They set the gear up, checked the sound balance and hung the immaculate stage suits on a rail. Then it was across to the Butchers Arms for a half of shandy or a nip, before returning to the venue to change for the show.

Dismay and consternation, as the suits now lay in a wrinkled heap in a corner of the dressing room. A pissed-off Sonny challenged "Who the f—k threw them down like that?' The culprit was one Peter Noone (Herman of Hermits fame, perpetrator of I'm Into Something Good and dozens of other similar crimes to be taken into account) who, on the TV screen appeared to be the dentally-endowed, clean-cut cuddly type who would get a piece at anybody's door. In reality he was somewhat bigger. . . (he had to be bigger, the telly screen isn't very high) and was extremely full of himself. . . as we say in Aiberdeen, a right bam.

"It was me' he said "And I'm Herman, top of the bill.' Which impressed Sonny not in the slightest. . . "I dinna care who the f—k you are. Pick them up, or. . . ' And when one of Herman's heavies loomed into view, he also had his fortune told, free of charge. "And you'll be first. . . '

Sonny then ran into marital problems and had to decide between his music or his marriage. So he left the band and set off to London with his wife to start afresh. For The Facells, his departure forced a fundamental change of direction into contemporary rock of a Deep Purple persuasion. The combo's reduced vocal resources determined the choice of material with Ricky was now singing lead as well as drumming. "Heavy rock was the only stuff I could get away with on my own.' During the following years personnel fluctuated frequently: passing through the ranks were bassist Brian Nicholson, and a succession of guitarists in 17-year-old deposed Tsar Billy Spratt, Jim Witter, Johnny Wood and Alex Wallace. Five years earlier Wallace had played in Ellon group The Daltons along with bassist Peter Whimster and drummer John Thompson. John spent 24 weeks in the UK hit parade in 1972, including a prestigious five weeks at the top of the charts. We shall reveal his 840 minutes of fame at the end of this chapter: the reader might endeavour to identify this massive hit record in the interim - no cheating.

Another new recruit was vocalist Sandy Davidson, who had previously played in city lounge bars with Lennie Albiston (who had experienced difficulties with his stools, a most unsavoury event in Aberdeen's rich rock tapestry. . . catch up with this exclusive revelation later). When Sandy joined The Facells, they were holding down a residency at the Broadsword public house in Tillydrone. The band was soon to head down to the harbour area when Dougie Argo approached them to provide the live music at his new venue, the Argo Lounge. This was an all-seated venue, where The Facells were to play a mix of current chart material and standards for the next seven years. Sandy remembers that they "specialised in close-contact stuff, involving the audience in the show.' Their popularity at the Argo prompted Alex Johnstone to invite the band to take up residency at his newly-converted Palais Ballroom. . . they stayed at Ruffles for almost five years. At this revamped Diamond Street night-spot, The Facells supported and backed visiting acts as diverse as The Drifters, Labi Siffre and Del Shannon.

Backing these turns without the luxury of proper rehearsals was hit or miss situation, as Sandy recounts "It was just a case of showing up an hour earlier than usual and having a quick run through. Then, show time and away we go.' A year into their Ruffles residency, the band lost their leader when Ricky hung up his drumsticks, work commitments saw him beat it offshore. His replacement was Sandy's relative Gerry McRobb.

Lulu appeared at Ruffles using expensive and complicated PA equipment set up for her by Grampian Television. "She had just started her first number when the fancy sound system packed up. I was crawling about on my hands and knees at the back of the stage, trying to be as inconspicuous as possible with wire and plugs everywhere. Of course everybody saw me, and the whole place was in hysterics as I tried to connect her into our amps.' Sandy doesn't say whether Lulu was appreciative of his efforts, but he does remember with good reason the reaction of Tony Christie. "I messed up my introduction for him but he came on and did his act. However when he had finished, we came back on stage to continue the show. Instead of handing me the mic he dropped it on the floor and walked straight past me.' Is This The Way To Amarillo? Maybe not, but it came bloody close to being the way to Woolmanhill casualty department. . . By now, The Facells had become a more-rounded entertainment act with humorous take-offs of Elvis, The Stones, and. . . Shirley Temple? In particular, a Gary Glitter spoof with Davidson cast as Sandy Sparkle went down like Linda Lovelace.

A move to Jimmy Wilson's original premises in Exchange Street saw The Facells packing out the upstairs lounge for four years, with a line up of Gerry, Sandy, Brian and Johnny Barclay, who was later replaced by Graeme Smith. A short stay at the Park Hotel marked the return of George Rose, a participant in the band's initial rehearsals all those years before at the Torry Community Centre. Across at the Sunnybank Club former Midnighter Andy Anderson appeared on drums during a four-year engagement as Gerry temporarily defected to the Metro Hotel. Andy Lawson brought with him his impressive guitar pedigree stretching back to The Freddie Ellis Combo, The Royal Teens and The Classix.

John Lafferty enticed the band and its loyal following to Caesar's Palace. Whether or not The Facells were able to laff-a-lot, they played dance hall material at Johnny's empirical chateau to Aberdonian jigging and libation enthusiasts. A warm spell followed at John Dawson's Hot Box: the venue had begun its live music days during the Sixties as the Elite Lounge. Sandy describes how the scene had come full circle. "Women who came to see The Facells on their own hen-shines years before were now bringing their daughters along for the same reason. We were obviously playing different material but we were using the same close-contact audience rapport, with equal success.'

Wanting a complete change of scene, Sandy bid adieu to the band 1991 and has played as a duo with Graeme Smith at hotels and clubs since then. He agreed with Gerry McRobb that the name and identity of The Facells should be kept alive. "Why not, it's a shame to let the name die after all these years and if you can make some money. . . '

A million years ago, we began by making a comparison between The Facells and The Dons. Management and players inevitably change with the passing years, but faithful fans are smitten for life. The Wee Red Devils are still causing heartache and happiness down Merkland Road way, and The Facells' party night continues every weekend doon the shore. Who would be rash enough to predict when these legacies might end?

. . . .

Brian Kennedy of The Strangers has already provided a glowing testimonial for Harry Lord, who assisted many Aberdonian musicians during the pioneering beat era. Harry is an ex-WW II code-breaker Yorkshireman who started work at the JT Forbes music shop in Aberdeen's George Street in 1961. Along with two sleeping partners he took over the business which then primarily dealt with accordions, and began tailoring his stock to satisfy the demands of local rockers.

It is noteworthy that Harry, a well-respected figure amongst his clientele, did not actually play an instrument himself. He believes however that his method of dealing with his customers adequately compensated for this. "When a lad came in looking for a guitar, I would ask what his price range was - little point in selling something that the customer couldn't really afford. I would get what I thought was an appropriate instrument down off the shelf, and let the customer handle it and play it. The transaction was, to me, a special type of sale. After all, each player had his own style and preference, and every guitar is different.' One musician with a photographic memory tells us that Harry's 1961 price for a Fender Strat was £166 16/6: an ex-loan Precision bass was 105 guineas.

As for lending out guitars: " I suppose I would have been in trouble earlier on if JT Forbes had found out about it, but my idea was to let the lads get the feel of the guitar by playing it at home or at a show. Mostly this paid dividends because if I didn't sell that specific instrument, I would eventually get a sale. Again, there was no future in saddling the player with something he ultimately wouldn't be happy with.' Whilst Harry's main rivals Bruce Miller guaranteed their instruments were shiny and free of finger marks, Harry gave his customers the best deal available, even if there was the odd scratch here or there. East Coast Flames and Mr Fantasy guitarist Allan Park recalls "It was not unknown for Harry to be disturbed at home at ten o'clock in the evening by a panicked musician seeking his help because, for example, an amp had blown. Maybe at times he was too nice for his own good.'

As a spokesman for Aberdeen's drummers, Graham Spry doesn't beat about the bush. "Harry was supremely obliging as far as looking after the punters was concerned, but he was also progressive with his merchandise. Most people think that the Ludwig rock 'n' roll kit became commonplace only after The Beatles and Ringo Starr made the big time, but Harry had one in stock way before then.' Predictably, Harry's good nature was sometimes taken advantage of: one drummer had a kit out on 'appro' for three years. When Harry eventually nailed the individual down, the response he received was "Na, it's nae for me, I'll bring it back in on Monday.' Bad patter, simple as that.

"My shop was mobbed from before nine in the morning until half past six. They were nattering to each other - finding out who had gigs at what venue, and who was short of a bass player or a drummer. If I had been able to sell cups of tea and sandwiches I would have made more money than I did from my instruments.' The close-by Silver City Cafe was in the fortunate position of picking up such passing trade from Harry's predominantly male disciples, who developed their own language and catch phrases, using the shop as a musicians' job centre.

The business ended due to the financial recalcitrance of his sleeping partners "I felt that we were carrying too much obsolete stock, and that we needed some re-investment to update our merchandise. The problem was that my partners (I wish they had slept more than they did, they kept interfering), wouldn't sink further money into the shop.' Harry's acquired Aberdonianism predominated when he decided that, in the absence of goodwill from his partners, he wouldn't fund the show on his own. The next morning, he instructed his lawyer to instigate voluntary liquidation. . .

There was an awkward pause from Harry when I told him that a Yorkshireman is an Aberdonian with a generosity by-pass, but his sense of humour returned when informed about the success enjoyed by some of his former customers. . . Billy Bremner, Speedy King et al. The former proprietor of the George Street guitar shop commented, somewhat tongue-in-cheek "So they are big stars now; maybe I did some good after all. But they have forgotten all about poor old Harry.'

. . . .

Of Harry's percussive customers, one alone is singled out by his peers as being the big beat man. . . Freddie Ellis. He possessed a precocious talent that saw him playing drums, and bringing the house down, at the Tivoli theatre when he was only 13-years old. A multi-skilled musician, when the need arose he turned his hand to practically any instrument. "Freddie was into Buddy Rich techniques when everybody else was banging on biscuit tins', according to Andy Lawson, one of our most enduring guitarists, "He was years ahead of his time and must have been one the best drummers in Britain, let alone Aberdeen. He was the guy who educated and brought on virtually hundreds of local musicians. . . so many guys have Fred to thank for showing them the ropes.' Praise indeed from Andy who normally refers to drummers generically as being "not so much musicians, more musicians' pals.'

. . . .

The last we heard of the post-Freddie Strollers, Denny, Firey Dod and Frankie had emigrated to Australia in 1966. Based in the North Queensland holiday resort Townsville, George established himself as lead vocalist with The Rhythmaires, playing at a top venue the Allen Hotel. When his Aberdonian reinforcements arrived, he wasted no time in creating space in the band for Denny and Frank, with sister Julie doing occasional cabaret spots. They changed their name to The Clansmen, clichÈd perhaps but in fact half of the group were Scots.

Townsville contrasted fundamentally from Torry, a far cry from the Double Two, the Rats' Cellar and the Nineteenth Hole. "The quality of the live music surprised me, but we had to change our approach to blend in because it was all short hair, tidy appearance, white suits and bow ties. All of this, combined with having two trumpets in our line-up, was so different to our Strollers' rocking days. We got into the cabaret circuit, playing a plush hilltop location called the Panorama House and appeared on many radio shows. We were very much big fish in a small bowl and I always had the impression that the local musos actually believed that the Townsville show-biz hoopla was for real. They thought they were bona-fide stars.'

"Across the tracks in South Townsville, the cowboys were living legends of their own imagination. So the choice was an Englebert cabaret scene in North TV or Australian C&W on the other side of town, and neither was very stimulating musically. By 1970 Dod had developed a bit of a Tom Jones fixation. He played for the crowd and became very good at it - maybe tolerable for a short time but I found it soul destroying month after month, which developed into year after year. I kept saying "Can't we get away from this stuff?' but nothing changed.'

This frustration ultimately resulted in the Milnes quitting and relocating down to Perth, in Western Australia. 'Firey Dod' moved North to Darwin, followed later by the Greigs.

Frank did a guitar and vocal spot on local television, bringing him a few offers. . . he joined a band called Equity, playing hotels and night clubs. "The music in Perth was a big improvement to Townsville - in the big city clubs, Clapton was God and that suited me fine. There were all types of bands but one of the most popular was The Prankstars. A big-name comedy band in mid-Sixties, they developed into a six-piece all-round act. One of their guitarist-vocalists had to leave through illness (they got sick of him) so I joined the queue and got the job. A mix of Australians, New Zealanders and Brits, they were fronted by a guy called Roy Lawrence and were undoubtedly the best band I have ever played with. Amazingly professional, with a great variety of material.'

Playing Perth's top venues and sell-out tours of Western Australia, they recorded The Pom Song in 1974 (you don't need to hear it, the title tells all). In the WA chart they were at number nine and climbing when the disc was banned. Apparently the authorities regarded it as being a xenophobic insult to the Queen (now you know where The Sex Pistols got the idea from). Despite being purged from the shops, the band continued punting the single at live gigs. Sales actually improved but were not reflected in the official charts. By this time Julie and Frank had divorced: she went up to Darwin to join brother George and his band.

Among the many visiting acts which The Prankstars supported, Frank remembers blowing The Searchers off the stage at The Booragoon club. "They must have had an off night as I've heard them sound better - when we came back on again, we took the house down. The crowd was right behind us, being the local band.' The house physically came down during Christmas of 1974 when Cyclone Tracey flattened Darwin. The Aberdonian expats were among the hundreds evacuated to Perth. Strollers' memorabilia: photographs, tapes and posters - all gone with the wind. Frank, Denny and George had 'a good old get-together' in Perth, where Dod did a few gigs with The Prankstars, including a top of the bill spot on a Darwin disaster fund-raising concert: "a terrific night.'

Frank stayed in Australia until 1977 when he decided to return to Scotland for a year to show the old country to Jane, his new wife. That first year drifted into two. . . and they have remained in the North East ever since. "In Aberdeen, I didn't want to get back into a band situation but I did look up some of the guys I knew. Bill Speirs was working offshore and freelanced when he was at home. Freddie Ellis was playing keyboards for Stevie Cameron at the Four Mile in Kingswells along with Morgan Adams, the young drummer I took on at the end of The Strollers.'

The main thing that hit Frank when he came back from Oz was how little the musical style of the Sixties bands had progressed "Sure, different material, but played in the same way as before I had emigrated - most were either on a nostalgia kick or playing country and western.' Notwithstanding this disappointment, some of the newer bands impressed him. "For me, Superklute were the best in town.'

"When his work routine allowed I had Bill Speirs playing with me on bass. I did some harmony stuff with my old friend Tucker Donald at the Covenanter pub in Kincorth, and worked with Davie Whyte at the Imperial Hotel. Now I'm 50, too old to do new wave material - and too young and tasteful to do Sydney Devine and Daniel O'Donnell rubbish. I could easily have got myself more lucrative bookings by compromising but I thought "is that really what I want? You have to have some pride in what you do. I resisted going into the Sixties revival scene, but have been real busy locally using the stage name Frank Breck. I found a gap in the market playing R 'n' B, blues, rock and old jazz standards - throwing in some Gordon Lightfoot and country, depending on where I was playing. I already had a good name with the blues harp and guitar, but if you want to eat, versatility wins the day.'

Frank's Aberdonian sense of value versus cost is exemplified by his decision to take on a wee Japanese drummer who "lives in a box and I don't have to pay him.' A trio of Bill Speirs, Frank and the wee Nipponese silicon-chip-off-the-old-block unintentionally upset British political and economic affairs in 1980. "We made a cassette, it was really pathetic but I managed to get rid of all 500 copies down in the Fife miners' clubs. The week after I sold the last one the national pit strike started - I hope it was just a coincidence.'

Earlier, we briefly mentioned Frank's 1962 stint at Liverpool's Iron Door Club. Amongst the bands he encountered were The Dennisons who at one point numbered Clive Hornby, Emmerdale's Jack Sugden, amongst their members. Despite not making Brian Epstein's stable they shared joint third place in Mersey Beat magazine's popularity poll for 1963. Frank "did a few bluesey Sonny Terry and Brownie McGee-type numbers. A backing guitarist was amazed that anyone from Aberdeen played the blues, he thought it was all sheep and cows up here. Dressed in my blue Midnighters' suit, I told him there were some terrific bands in Scotland, but he gave it the usual Scouse tirade about how good the Merseybeat scene was. I told him to calm down but we kept arguing about how the Liverpool groups compared to those in Aberdeen. Then he asked me if I had heard The Beatles. To be honest, I had never even heard of them, but I told him straight away that The Beatles "are nae as good as Tommy and The Tremors.' Never mind Frank, you can't be right all the time.

. . . .

You will recall how vocalist Sonny Pearce left for London after many years with The Facells. When he came home to Aberdeen a few years later, he thought it was time to recover his equipment from the band, or to receive financial recompense for it. Instead he was talked into returning to the fold. "Somehow it didn't work the second time round, and by the time I was discharged from hospital after suffering a collapsed lung, The Facells and myself were history.'

After working briefly with organist George Munro as a duo, they went to the Waterton Hotel to put together a band at the request of co-owner John Low. Inspired by the singer's lung problem, this combo was dubbed Sonny Pearce and The Second Breath, in which Aberdeen thoroughbreds Alex Craigen and Jim Peacock also featured during two years at the Bucksburn venue. A subsequent move to the Carlton (Sonny returning to the Hop Inn after many years absence) brought a three-year guitar orientated sound . . . before he packed a pair of Redwings in his kit-bag and went to work offshore.

His equal-time routine allowed him to do fill-in spots during his fortnight ashore and, in unfortunate circumstances, he helped fulfil the ailing Tucker Donald's engagements. Some time later Sonny's own health failed when he contracted cancer (which he has thankfully conquered). When the bombshell of his illness hit, his offshore employment came to a close. . . struggling to survive financially on sickness benefit, he cast his thoughts around for an alternative source of income. Strangely it was not until his wife suggested that he get back into singing that he gave it any serious consideration. He was not, however, interested in getting involved in a band situation again - it came to his notice that his peers Tommy Dene and George Duncan were packing them in at their respective lounge bar locations. Both used professional backing tapes, and Sonny admits to being hurt when a friend unfeelingly stated "Jist think, you could've done something like this, but you're too late now.'

Sonny's recalls "It wouldna have bothered me if I had given it a go and fallen flat on my arse, but I was a touch annoyed that I was written off before I even tried.' Despite his initial misgivings that his moment of popularity may have passed, Sonny's career took a new lease of life when George Mitchell at the Metro Hotel approached him.

Mitch sent Sonny up to Bruce Millers with an open cheque to get whatever hardware he needed, and soon recouped his outlay as Sonny developed an instant and enthusiastic, if unexpected, following. "I admit that I was astounded by the attention and popularity for what was not really an intentional comeback, especially at 54 years of age.' He has subsequently performed at several Aberdeen venues, being selective about the frequency of his appearances. His weekend gigs continue to attract the punters in droves. "As far as my music goes, I have two priorities. Firstly I have to make decent money. Secondly, I love singing. . . well, that's not really true. I love to hear myself singing. That's being honest, but if you think about it, if I don't like the sound of my own voice then there's not much chance of an audience enjoying my singing. I am totally enthused with what I am doing now.'

Sonny strays into Edith Piaf Je Ne Regrette Rien territory, although admittedly more Torry spurdie than Parissiene sparrow. "You look back on it after many years and sometimes you get to thinking about missed opportunities. Like the time The Facells were playing at a rock band competition at the Beach Ballroom in the Sixties.' (Actually August of 1967: The Beathovens were the winners, the vote apparently being gazumped due to the hundreds of young Mormon converts who supported them). "The compere was Alan Freeman, who suggested that he could easily use his contacts to fix management and recording deals. I naturally assumed that he was referring to the entire band. It soon became obvious that the group as a whole was of no interest to him, but I turned down the solo chance there and then. Maybe loyalty to the group got in the way of personal advancement but that's the way it was.' If truth be told, he still harbours a secret desire to get that Facells line-up back together. "OK, so the high harmonies would be a problem but I am certain we could still put together an incredible act. And, without being big-headed about it, we would sell-out any stage in Aberdeen, no problem.' In the meantime, until a soon-to-be-rich Aberdeen promoter takes Sonny up on his dead-cert idea, most weekends we can catch this maestro at his best. . . go on, spoil yourselves.

. . . .

Several years back in our saga, we briefly mentioned former Ellon beat musician John Thompson's five weeks at the top of the hit parade of 1972. Having allowed the reader to stew for few pages, it can now be revealed that he played drums on Amazing Grace during his time with The Pipes and Drums of The Royal Scots Dragoon Guards. . . and just for the record, my ma's coapy number was 19304 and my grannie Jean's was 56729.

THE STRANGERS
L-R Brian , Derek, Syd, Gary Vega,
Johnny Johnson

THE FIRST FABULOUS FACELLS

THE CLANSMEN
Australia
Bottom 3 steps, going up the way
Firey Dod, Frank, Denny

EDDIE WATSON'S ALLIGATORS
New Deer 1956
Jock Stewart Guitar
Alex Evans Tea Chest Bass
Colin Fraser (on floor) Trombone
Jimmy Gray's Feet

THE STROLLERS
1962
L-R Bill Gauld, Bill Speirs, Frankie Milne, Firey Dod,
Denny Greig

Chapter 2

The Beatles Do A Midnight Flit. . . and the case of the disappearing reporter

The conditions under which The Beatles undertook their inaugural visit to the North East of Scotland were gey rough: comparative light years away from the luxurious jet-setting to which they were to become accustomed.

The most powerful and influential entrepreneur in the British music business in the early Sixties was Larry Parnes. He ran a stable of artists and groups and had a policy of re-christening his stars with stage names calculated to (hopefully) provide a blatant sexual allure, offsetting their generic musical sterility. An exception was Billy Fury, a moody, good-lookin' son-of-a-gun. Hence Parnes' employees included such as Duffy Power and Vince Eager. The Silver Beetles failed the audition as Fury's backing group, but drew a consolation prize in playing behind Johnny Gentle for a Scottish tour. Gentle was in reality John Askew, a 20-year-old apprentice joiner and former merchant seaman, well down the pecking order in Parnes' galaxy.

With a line-up of Lennon, McCartney, Harrison, and Edinburgh born Stuart Sutcliffe on bass, their lack of expertise and talent precluded The Silver Beetles from attracting a regular drummer. Manager Alan Williams resolved this quandary by hiring Johnny Moore, a bottle factory forklift driver. At 36, Moore's attitude and style differed fundamentally from those of his teenage co-musicians.

The eight day Scottish tour was thus far the biggest event in their rudimentary careers: McCartney, coming up to exam time at the Liverpool Institute, told his father he had some term-leave. Sutcliffe and Lennon skived off art college, the latter's future wife Cynthia submitted her work under his name on a lettering exam. Harrison managed to swing time off his work as an apprentice electrician. Williams persuaded Moore to abandon his full-time forklift job, on the strength of great things to come. George became Carl Harrison in homage to his idol Carl Perkins. Sutcliffe became Stuart de Stael after a Russian artist and McCartney adopted the latino stage-name Paul Ramon.

Duncan Mackinnon of Scottish Border Dances (and of pig-farming fame) booked these Scottish dates which ran from May 20th to 28th, 1960. The Silver Beetles and their instruments set off on the trail of rock 'n' roll fame. . . in an Austin van. Private jets and Lennon's psychedelic art nouveau Rolls Royce were an unimaginable universe away. The trail was to take them to such high-profile venues as Alloa Town Hall, Inverness, Fraserburgh's Dalrymple Hall, Keith, Forres Town Hall, Nairn, and Peterhead. It cost five bob to see Gentle and his backing band that May in Forres, where the support act was Rikki Barnes and his All Stars. . . next time we meet Rikki will be in Hamburg's Top Ten Club.

As Gentle was a minor-hit minor attraction in the first place, his tour was never going to set the heather on fire. At one venue they were relegated to playing a small upstairs room, whilst the main attraction downstairs was an old time Scottish country band. Each musician earned £18 for the entire tour. We don't know if they received their wages as they went, but they definitely ran out of money way before the end, with subograms being sent ineffectually to Parnes. Reduced to surviving on a daily bowl of soup, living in digs without running hot water, they booked into the Royal Hotel in Forres, but did a moonlight flit without paying the bill.

Gentle says "They were about the roughest looking bunch I had ever seen in my life. The promoter Duncan Mackinnon thought they were no good and wanted to sack them. I remember that we all sat down together in a bar in Inverness and went over each number for hours until they had got the sound right. They were terribly depressed, I felt sorry for them and persuaded Mackinnon to let them finish the second week. One night after we'd finished a show, a girl came up and asked for their autographs. John was so thrilled he couldn't stop talking about it. He even asked me whether I thought they should chuck everything up and go full time'

To add injury to insult, their van was in a collision at a Banff crossroads when Gentle crashed into a parked car occupied by two old ladies. The others were merely shaken up but a flying guitar case smacked Moore in the mouth, smashing his front teeth. When the group showed up at Fraserburgh's

Dalrymple Hall without him, the Broch promoter refused to pay for a drummerless act. . . he and Lennon unsympathetically hauled Moore out of his hospital bed to play the gig.

Gentle again "We said goodbye to each other at Dundee station, and as my train pulled out they were still saying - ask Larry Parnes if he wants us again. . . ' When they returned to Liverpool, Parnes had already received reports of their performances. He did not offer them further employment. Instead, they dropped back into Merseyside's low-level youth club and coffee-bar circuit.

. . . .

In November of 1962 The Beatles were booked to return to North East Scotland. Much had happened in the 30 months since their disastrous low budget tour with Gentle and Moore. Seemingly futile and dispiriting rounds of small venues in and around Liverpool had eventually paid dividends. Alan Williams had taken them to the St. Pauli district of Hamburg, initially playing the sleazy Indra Club. Forced to play all-night sessions to audiences of drunken sailors, dockers and whores, their act became a manic, nothing-to-lose rock 'n' roll show. Subsequently they climbed Hamburg's league table to the lofty heights of the Star Club via the Kaiserkeller and Top Ten venues.

Their first professional recordings were made during their Hamburg apprenticeship, backing Tony Sheridan's Polydor tracks. Originally issued only in Germany, a single credited The Beat Brothers (Polydor's generic name for Sheridan's group, regardless of the personnel involved). The later UK release of My Bonnie, however, carried the legend Tony Sheridan and The Beatles.

There are various versions of how they and Brian Epstein came together: the latter's account was that a request for My Bonnie at his NEMS Liverpool record shop brought them to his attention. Concurrent with riotous Hamburg scallywagging, phenomenal local success in Liverpool progressed into domination of the scene soon to be tagged 'Merseybeat'. Epstein allegedly visited the Cavern to find out what all the fuss was about. . . Since the debacle of May 1960, Stuart Sutcliffe had left the band to concentrate on art studies but died of a brain haemorrhage four months later. McCartney had moved to bass and popular drummer Pete Best had come and gone, being replaced by Ringo Starr.

For their first bona fide UK single Love Me Do, Ringo's loose-swinging style wasn't recognised by EMI as the innovative talent it really was. They called for a second recording, at which Starr was relegated to shaking the tambourine. Session drummer Andy White replaced him, although the Ringo version hit the shops on a later re-pressing when initial stocks of the White-drummed cut had sold out. Ringo's cut also made it on the Please Please Me LP. Andy White will resurface later in our travels, crossing drumsticks with Tommy Dene and The Tremors. A month after Love Me Do hit the UK top-20, Epstein exchanged contracts with Albert Bonici for The Beatles to appear at five Scottish venues during January of 1963.

Guiseppe Bonici had come to Inverness in 1892 from Burgo di Taro in Northern Italy and began work in a newspaper shop. Years later his Scottish-born son Albert studied and worked in engineering before gravitating back to the family business. By 1952 this was centred on Elgin's Park Cafe and Albert had become Scotland's principal promoter of popular music, establishing his reputation through big band and trad jazz dates. He developed a promotional network throughout the country and consolidated his pre-eminence by opening his own night spot The Two Red Shoes, behind the Park Cafe. This became a mandatory venue for acts visiting Scotland, and also for his own indigenous combos including Johnny and The Copycats, and The Jacobeats.

The shrewd Bonici incorporated a fruitful clause into The Beatles' contract. . . amateur in many ways, Epstein missed it (although he was not alone in making this mistake when dealing with Bonici). Clause ten said "The Management - in this case Bonici - to have the first option to present this attraction in Scotland following this booking'. In the normal course of events such a clause was totally acceptable, but importantly, it generally limited the right of first refusal to a specific city or town, not a whole country: a telling example of English perception of Scotland being a village. Effectively The Beatles (and many others who fell into the same trap) could not legally perform North of the border without Bonici's prior agreement. It was quite some time before London-based agents wised up.

The five date tour in the first days of 1963 was to include Longmore Hall, Keith (January 1), Two Red Shoes, Elgin (January 2), Dingwall Town Hall (January 3), Bridge of Allan Museum Hall (January 4) and finally Aberdeen Beach Ballroom (January 5). Having played in Hamburg on Hogmanay night 1962 the group managed to fly only as far as London on New Year's day, but onwards travel to Scotland was hampered by a merciless winter storm. The Keith date was correspondingly cancelled.

Bonici's associate Gordon Hardie handled promotions in Aberdeen. "I went to see The Beatles at The Bridge of Allan along with the Dundee promoter Andy Lothian. He had been enthusing about them, saying that they were going to be very big. That night I just couldn't see it at all. I remember thinking that they could all do with a good haircut, and that they were far too loud'. The quality of The Beatles' performance (and the crowd's reaction) the following night at the Beach Ballroom have been codified via popular Aberdeen myths and hearsay. Were the mop-tops actually flop-tops at that Sunday night three-bob show? Were they indeed mediocre, booed off the stage? Supposed attendees swear blind that the fab four were appalling: conflicting accounts abound surrounding the Granite City's biggest mystery.

But pray hear the verdict of Norman Shearer, founder member of The Facells. "I had already heard Love Me Do on Radio Luxembourg, and thought that it was something special - but I knew nothing about the group so I didn't know what to expect. They were bloody terrific, my over-riding memory is of John Lennon holding his guitar high and square to his body, belting out Chuck Berry's Sweet Little Sixteen and Roll Over Beethoven.' Gordon Hardie's evidence is "One definite fact was a crowd of autograph-hunting girls waiting for The Beatles after the show. However, it's fair to say that these same girls would hang around every act that appeared there, regardless of whether they were any good or not.' Nevertheless, there is one vital, previously overlooked clue as to the quality of The Beatles' live performance that night.

The final Hamburg engagement had ended at the Star Club on Hogmanay Day , with the boys earning 750 DM each per week. Cliff Bennett and The Rebel Rousers arrived in Hamburg that same night. Their guitarist Dave Wendels recalls "We drove straight to the club with suitcase and guitar in hand and we walk in. People are throwing wine around, girls draping themselves all over. The curtains open to four guys in leather jackets playing Roll Over Beethoven. It was The Beatles of course. They weren't very good though! I remember thinking how bad they were as a band, but in between the cheesey, rotton covers, they'd do one of their own songs and you could tell they had something special. They stood out, you knew they were gonna happen big time.' Ted Taylor of fellow Merseybeaters, King Size Taylor and The Dominoes (with whom Aberdeen group The Strollers co-starred in Hanover) taped the show. In the packed, chaotic club, Taylor's Grundig reel-to-reel tape recorder and hand-held microphone captured several hours of The Beatles playing live over a backdrop of drunken German New Year's Eve celebrations. Taylor later offered to sell the rudimentary tapes to Epstein, but turned down the derisory £20 offered. After lying unattended for 15 years, they were finally edited and cleaned up: the resultant double album The Beatles Live! at the Star Club in Hamburg, Germany 1962 was released in 1977. This material has been re-issued under various titles and is widely available on cheapo CD.

The listener will obviously have to make allowances for the circumstances under which the recording was made. Nevertheless, it must definitely be representative of what happened in Aberdeen only six days later. It includes the first recorded version of I Saw Her Standing There, along with their current club repertoire: Twist And Shout, Hippy Hippy Shake, A Taste of Honey, Your Feet's Too Big, Little Queenie, and the like. McCartney even does a version of Marlene Dietrich's Falling in Love Again. It is not suggested that this evidence is conclusive: it's there, if you want to investigate or refresh your memory.

Gordon Hardie "bought The Beatles for £42 for that date and sold them on to the Beach Ballroom for £45.' Lennon, McCartney, Harrison and Starr (more than anything or anyone else), slapped the Fifties on the bum and dragged it into the new decade. The band stayed on in Scotland for another two days, performing their new song Please Please Me on a Scottish TV kiddie show Round Up. Within a fortnight of that Beach engagement they were at number two in the hit parade, on the way to changing the face of popular music for ever. For Scottish dates subsequent to that January tour, The Beatles commanded £300 in October and £1,000 a year later. Also on the bill at these latter concerts were Tommy Dene and The Tremors (Dundee Caird Hall), and The Copycats (Glasgow Green's Playhouse and Edinburgh Odeon). Under the terms of clause number ten, Bonici participated in sharing in the profits from these sell-out performances: that's why his Copycats snuck on to the bill. Their vocalist Johnny Stewart, who watched the Scousers from the wings, is adamant that they were fabulous.

In collaboration with Bonici, Gordon Hardie materialised the concept of the pop package tour for the North East. He remembers a specific show at the Capitol: "One bill which I promoted in May of 1964 featured eight acts, all in that week's top-ten. The Rolling Stones were in their ascendancy, rising stars yet to hit the heights, and closed the first half of the show, a spot normally filled by the lesser lights. Herman's Hermits (looking over their shoulders for Sonny Pearce) headlined the package as bill-toppers - it shows you how fast things changed in the pop business.' As the direction and scale of youth music tangented, this type of pop package venture would soon become impossible to finance, co-ordinate or manage.

The Stones' bassist Bill Wyman recalls their subsequent gig at the Capitol in June of 1965 (by which time they had notched up four top-five smashes, including three successive chart toppers). "After two mad shows at the Usher Hall in Edinburgh, we set off by road for Aberdeen. . . when we stopped off for a fry-up at a country pub in Laurencekirk, a 75-year-old character named Tom Cairney sang Scots folk songs to us. In a broad accent he told us "You look awfully like lassies, but I like ye!' The Stones' 1965 dates brought riots, havoc and destruction to Scotland together with considerable overtime for the police forces of Glasgow, Edinburgh, Aberdeen and Dundee.

Mick Jagger was reported as suffering from exhaustion the night after the Capitol appearance, resting at the Gleneagles Hotel rather than flying back to London as scheduled. Jagger defended the group's followers in an NME interview. "The fans don't mean to break the seats, they just stand on them to see better and in some of the older theatres the seats cannot take it. Sure, you get a couple of fellows who come along to throw tomatoes but nobody turns up with the idea of wrecking the joint.' Hang about, are we talking about Aberdonians here? Tomatoes don't come cheap.

Gordon Hardie was "struck by the naivety of some of the lads who played then. They often had no conception of where they were. About 40 minutes before they were due to start their Beach Ballroom act, one group realised they were missing a vital piece of equipment. I can't recall exactly what, perhaps an amp. They had left this item behind at the previous night's Glasgow gig. One of them located the ball-room manager Sam Gill and asked if he could borrow Sam's car keys. This chap seriously thought he could nip down to Glasgow to retrieve the missing kit, and get back in time to start their act.' Gordon continues "Ignorance of Scotland's geography didn't end with musicians. I was personally more into the jazz and cabaret scene, regularly engaging that type of act from a South Shields agency. The directions they gave their musicians were, basically "Take the A1 North to Edinburgh and cross the bridge, then you'll find Aberdeen.' Music business people south of Stonehaven treated the North of Scotland with disregard and indifference. When trying to attract London media attention for his Oily Records label more than 20 years later, Jim Allardice discovered this attitude still prevaled.

Back to Gordon Hardie "Timing was always crucial in putting a successful promotion together. Andy Lothian and I thought that Georgie Fame was worth supporting, and guessed that he would do well. We put him on for two nights and lost money on both. But only three weeks later he had a number one record and was selling out everywhere.'

One of the many groups that toured the area for the Bonici-Hardie axis were The Pretty Things. Their line-up which hit the charts and made The Stones, by comparison, seem like refined gentlemen was Phil May (vocals, state-of-the-art sneer and the longest hair in the business), Dick Taylor (himself the original guitarist with the embryonic Stones), John Stax (bass), Brian 'Yeti' Pendleton (rhythm guitar) and the maniac Viv Prince (drums, arson, main mover in the Pretties' deportation from New Zealand). They brought their frenzied Anglophile R 'n' B to the Capitol in 1964 (their hits that year were the primally snarling Rosalyn and Don't Bring Me Down).

Dick Taylor remembers that appearance with mixed emotions. "We had no problems at the gig itself where we went down really well to an appreciative crowd. Afterwards we stood in the hotel reception area and decided to go out for a few drinks. We were just on the point of stepping out of the door on to Union Street when an almighty fight started. There were bodies flying everywhere. It didn't take us long to agree that such quaint northern Scottish customs wouldn't mix very well with five long-haired beatniks with very English accents. So most unusually for us, we stayed indoors and had a quiet night in the hotel bar.'

The Evening Express carried a story in 1965 about The Pretties' non-appearance at the Two Red Shoes in Elgin. Dick again: "We were travelling over the Devil's Elbow or one of those country roads, through the snow in the middle of winter. For some reason that I forget, Phil and I were in a big American car. Brian and Lofty, our roadie, were in the van with all our gear - Viv and John were in another car. Before we set off, an old fella at the local garage warned us "You winnae get through this road the nicht.' (Dick Taylor's attempt at a Scottish accent is endearingly awful.) ''Phil and I left after the others and half an hour later we came upon the van slewed right across the road. Brian was giving Lofty directions, as he backed the van to the roadside to try to get going again. Unfortunately, what he thought was snow-covered road was actually a snow-filled ditch. The van ended up with its rear wheels in the hole, well and truly stuck.'

No van meant no equipment, and no equipment meant no gig. The following day, with their transport back in one piece, a local reporter visited them. The idea was to do an article about the wild men of English rock being tamed by the wilder Scottish weather.

"He lined us up in front of the van to photograph us for his story, The Pretty Things and their van. Because he was having trouble getting us all into the picture he took a few paces backwards and was last seen disappearing, with a loud Scottish scream, through the snow bridge he had stepped on to. All we could see was the top of his head. As you can imagine, we cracked up and were rolling about in tears. I remember that very clearly.'

Chapter 3

Tremors In My Kneebone

Ask Tommy Dene about the explosion of skiffle and rock 'n' roll music in the late Fifties, and he will tell you it was an unplanned, uncoordinated and fortuitous. Its detonation effectively liberated a repressed, excitement-starved youth population. Tommy was 12 or 13 when the sounds of Elvis Presley and Glaswegian-Cockney Lonnie Donegan fired the imaginations and ears of British adolescents. The message came across from Luxembourg and AFN broadcasts, the BBC's home service being strictly rooted in such musical productions as The Billy Cotton Band Show. It was many years before the Beeb's dinner-jacketed, old school tie mandarins acknowledged the existence of rock 'n' roll. Before Six Five Special and Oh Boy!, British TV seldom broadcast youth orientated, teen-appeal entertainment: in any case, few families in Aberdeen possessed a television.

Certainly the city had no guitar shop, but the brother of one of Tom's friends, Mike McDonald, brought back a guitar from a foreign merchant navy trip. Another mate also acquired one by mail order from a News of the World advertisement, driving Tommy to persuade his none-too prosperous folks to purchase one for him. Practising at their various homes with washboard and tea-chest bass accompaniment, a kazoo or comb-and-paper solo provided variety: the first number they played with any accomplishment was It Takes a Worried Man. These efforts led to a spot at the Smithfield youth club on Provost Rust Drive. Tommy is of the opinion that this rudimentary musical effort was perhaps the very first performance by a 'group' as such in Aberdeen, 'group' in this context being fundamentally different from the old 'band' format. There was nothing previous by way of live music for juveniles in the city. His enduring career as a vocalist was founded in that embryonic concert: when the curtains opened on the group, the rest of the lads froze. Tom was the sole member to begin singing. . . and is still doing so 30-odd years later.

He combined with his lead-guitarist Brechin-based cousin Byron Grant together with bassist Mike Reoch and rhythm guitarist John Roft, also from Angus. Aberdonian Eddie McKenzie (Ed The Ted) took part in pre-electric acoustic sessions, but the final member of the original Tremors was Dennis Morrison, an drummer from Aberdeen. The families of the Brechin guys were "fairly well-off', funding decent instruments and sharp suits. As Tommy says, appearances counted for much, even hinting that "looking the part' contributed substantially to the combo's promotion from St K's to the Palace Ballroom. There, The Trems played support to visiting hit parade groups on Thursday nights (back-to-back weekly with The Facells) and headlined Saturday afternoon sessions in their own right. The queue for the latter dance stretched right down Bridge Street, although the self-effacing Tommy reconciles such popularity with the dearth of alternative attractions in Aberdeen. "Other than youth clubs, there was precious little else for young people to do.'

The soon-to-be-married John Roft left the group in July of 1963 just as the rest of the lads turned professional. The 21-year-old Tommy poached Donald Stewart from Aberdeen band Midnighters Incorporated as a replacement. Successes at the Palace Ballroom notwithstanding, the influence of Dundee-based promoter and agent Andy Lothian saw Tommy and The Tremors far and away the most popular group in the Jute City, to the extent that many laboured under the misconception that they were native Dundonians. For a period they played just about everywhere in Scotland apart from Aberdeen. Their Tayside fame level mirrored that of the Beatles in Liverpool: Dundee Top Ten Club appearances saw the group being mobbed by fans, (slavishly reported by the Dundee Courier centre-page spreads). . . Tom and Don Stewart travelled The Road and the Miles To Dundee countless times.

Such was their Tayside status, they shared top billing with touring chart acts rather than filling the less prestigious local support spot. A case in point was when they played with Brian Epstein's stable (The Beatles, Tommy Quickly and Cilla Black) at the Caird Hall. Having finished their own set The Tremors joined the audience but caused a minor riot by leaving early, being recognised by the local fans. These were doubtless members of the reported 2,000 strong fan club who voted The Trems North of Scotland rock band champions.

Lothian arranged for an audition with Joe Meek (legendary producer of late Fifties and early Sixties British rock) at his studio, above Violet Shenton's leather goods shop at 304 Holloway Road in London. Personal idiosyncrasy and paranoia dissipated the fame and respect which Meek's phenomenal output deserved. His impressive track record included many major hits for The Flee-Rekkers, John Leyton, The Honeycombs, Lord Sutch, Freddie Starr and The Midnighters, Lonnie Donegan, and The Tornados. . . the latter's million-selling Telstar (composed and produced by Meek), was the first double-bubble UK and US chart topper by a British group. Meek hand-built his studio in the summer of 1960, out-fitting it with second-hand RAF radio equipment costing £3,000 - it was here The Tremors auditioned. "The set-up was unbelievable, with the studio inside the house and electronic apparatus everywhere. Cables ran from room to room, up and down the stairs. Our session finished and we went out for a pint so that Meek could have a news with Andy Lothian. When we returned to hear Meek's verdict, he said our group was no different from hundreds of others in London.' However the producer said "he could do something with the vocalist'.

Tommy turned down this solo opportunity without hesitation - it was the whole group or nothing. With the benefit of hindsight, this was probably the wisest decision. Unbeknown to The Trems at the time, in an age when homosexuality was a criminal act, Meek had been fined £15 following a seedy episode in a public toilet. Blackmail and death threats ensued when the case was publicised. In 1967 the police were interviewing known gays following the grusome murder of a 17-year-old lad who was known to Meek. When his landlady Mrs Shenton went upstairs to see him unexpectedly, Meek killed her with a shotgun that he then used on himself, committing suicide. . . "I could do something with the vocalist', indeed.

Back home, with Lothian ensuring his charges kept a high profile, for three consecutive years the readers of his monthly Scottish Beat magazine voted The Tremors Scotland's best group. On a Pete Murray-compered STV pop show they co-starred with The Barron Knights and an up-and-coming Glasgow group Lulu and The Luvvers, plugging their new single Shout. The young Lulu lifted this Isley Brothers scorcher from the live set of Glasgow's immensely popular Alex Harvey. With obvious warmth and affection Tom says "I could spend a couple of hours talking about Alex, he was something else. On tour on Arran we had terrific beach parties, drinking and playing guitars. His charisma just wisna real. He could have worked wi' anybody in the world without batting an eyelid.' If anyone gets around to writing the Alex Harvey story, Tommy is a guy to look up.

November 1963, and we catch up with Kelly, the song that henceforth was mandatory at every East coast dance for decades to come. "It was on the B side of Del Shannon's Hats Off To Larry. When I had heard it a couple of times I told the guys that I thought it could do the trick for us. We rehearsed it until we thought we had it down really well and it proved to be a terrific success. Kelly became a highlight of our repertoire, audiences simply wouldn't let us away until we played it.' The song set the standard for smootchie dances, referred to by testosterone-saturated Nimrods as 'a knicker trembler.' It was also instrumental in The Tremors returning to London to resume their recording efforts. Tommy explains "Andy got in touch with various A & R guys from different London record companies, telling them we were the biggest thing in Scotland. . . I suppose that wasn't far off the truth. According to him we would sell thousands of copies of anything we might release. To consolidate the popularity aspect he brought these sceptical A & R people up to Dundee where we were stronger in our natural habitat, rather than playing cold in some studio we had never seen before. Andy orchestrated events that night such that the Top Ten Club was full to bursting point. These London guys had to fight their way through the crowd just as we went into Kelly, the fans' favourite.'

Lothian's hype caught Decca's interest and a session took place at Olympic Studios, where The Stones cut their early singles and where Johnny and The Copycats also worked. The session was over-seen by Terry Kennedy who worked for Southern Music and laid claim to having discovered Donovan. "They wanted a couple of numbers and the obvious choice was Kelly. We also did Bobby Day's Rockin' Robin. They didn't like our drummer so they brought in their own guy, a Glaswegian named Andy White.' (White also displaced Ringo Starr on The Beatles' Love Me Do: an identical fate befell Ronnie Millings, drummer with Them on Here Comes The Night). "White was a great drummer, no danger there but the next thing was that they didn't like our own backing vocals either. In came two session singers, the wee guy who did the falsetto stuff with the Ivy League and another bloke. . . Decca eventually rejected the single, so we hawked the demo around London, but couldn't even get anyone to listen to it. As far as they were concerned down there, Scotland was all haggis and bagpipes. They didn't want to know, whether you had talent or not.' Is this sentiment already becoming familiar?

Lothian toured the band with another of his acts, the highly un-cred McKinlay Sisters. Byron Grant recalls "We didn't like it much, feeling that it got in the way of what we wanted to do.' The Trems also suspected that Tom was a tad dissatisfied with them and maybe hankered after a more heavyweight line-up from Aberdeen's more renowned musicians. "From memory,' says Byron "Tom and The McKinleys were being chauffeur-driven to and from the more distant venues, whilst we were left to drive the van and meet up with them at the other end. We felt it was unfair that, for example, they were flying down from Scotland to London, but we had to slog it out on the road. So we told Tom our side of it and we agreed to part. It was mutual, amicable and better for everyone concerned.'

The Tremors were now without a lead singer. "We had only done backing vocals before, and were a bit stymied as to the best way forward. Tony Fortunato at The Locarno in Montrose loaned us his premises to practise every afternoon, which led to a few smaller gigs. But we couldnae get close to the bigger engagements, which Tom kept a hold of. Andy Lothian suggested that our best bet was try the clubs in Germany. We knew it would be really hard graft but the idea was to improve our act in front of live audiences.'

Travelling to Germany in May of 1964, the lads were destined initially for a month's residency at Hamburg's Crazy Horse club (allegedly located in the city's West end, distant from the heady temptations of the Reeperbahn's Grosse Freiheit and Herbertstrasse. Aye OK Byron, sure thing). Just after New Year of 1965, he reported "We have to work for our money, playing 42 hours a week.' Feeling they had something to prove they pulled out all the stops, giving their all. After that original engagement a further two-month contract came, which stretched into three months. . . then a six-month deal followed with work throughout Germany (Flensburg on the Danish border, to Travemunde on the Baltic Sea, via Berlin). Contemporaneous performances were fossilised on Polydor LPs Beat City, Album Of Evergreens, 16 Beat Groups Of The Hamburg Scene and Go Go Go Teen Beat With 12 International Bands. These were cut by Polydor's German area recording manager Paul Murphy. "A crook and a con man, but a nice one.' A couple of singles also appeared on the Fontana label.

By now it was 1966 and Dennis and Don came home to Scotland - the original month had developed into two years. Mike and Byron kept at it in Germany. "We met up with John Law, vocalist with Glasgow group The MI5. They sacked him when his voice gave up due to the repetitive, nightly eight-hour sessions all the bands played. But he got over the throat problem and when we picked up a German drummer, we were back in action as John Law and The Tremors.' Other Scottish acts who have settled into the remnants of the German club scene include Dundee folkie trio The Wally Dugs, Jovial Brown (black Dundonian lead guitarist at The Star Club), Isobel Bond (formerly of The Staccato Five, at the Top Ten) and veteran Alex Young from The Easybeats and AC/DC dynasty. Of the old-time Brit rockers, Cliff Bennett and Roy Young are regulars. Tony Sheridan still makes a decent living on the back of his Sixties club days and Beatles associations, but is reputedly "a pain in the damned neck. We will never work with him again.'

During a shaggy, heavy period they recorded an eponymous 1970 album for Philips under the briefly-held name of Light of Darkness. Some 15 years ago they reverted to British roots material (The Stones and The Beatles) blended with a touch of Scottish folk rock, a pinch of Rod Stewart, and (inevitably) some country licks. Their musical melange has seen them through busy annual schedules, from off-season small pub gigs through to major summer festivals (with The Rattles, Wayne Fontana, and Status Quo). Young Angus Young recently sat in for a few numbers with The Trems, but left his shorts and school cap at home. The private function scene holds a lot of pull: the guys recently picked up DM 3,000 for playing at a dentist's wedding. . . by gum! Now into year 31 in Germany, it's been a helluva long month.

. . . .

In 1964 the original Trems left for Hamburg. Back in Aberdeen Tommy Dene surrounded himself with drummer Jim Lunan, ex-Stranger/Royal Teen Billy Bremner on lead guitar, Syd Weaver (by now he had handed in his sheriff's badge and had lost his Commancheros), played rhythm guitar and shared vocals with Tommy. Bassist was Speedy King who was Aberdeen born, but was brought up in a 'nissen hut' in Crimmond before councils began to catch up with post-war housing shortages. His dad was a stonemason who had also worked in the coalmine and steel industries in his native Tyneside area, and moved to his wife's home patch of Fraserburgh upon demob from the army. Speedy was another skiffle enticee: a female neighbour's boyfriend loaned him a guitar and he was hooked. Schoolmate Willie Donaldson "played a mean boogie-woogie piano, he was really wicked. That is, before he discovered religion and became a minister.' Radio Luxembourg hissed its way into young Pat's brain. . . he was an altar boy who harmonised Bye Bye Love with the Everlys daft Kincaid brothers ("I was more into Little Richard') as the three boys walked to church. Aunts and uncles had already exposed him to Glen Miller, The Inkspots and Johnny Ray and later bequeathed him a hand-me-down gramophone. Pat's own young nephew is now the proud possessor of an oak-panelled cabinet which today is the world's plushest doos' hut.

In 1959, Michael Robertson, Bill Summers and Ronnie Grant combined with the 14-year- old Doogie Burnett, Margaret Gauld and Speedy to form The Rockefellers. At the likes of Buckie's Fishermans Hall, they laid their dance band efforts on an audience whose birth certificates bore equally wet ink. Having safely negotiated the vast expedition to Aberdeen to enrol at Grays School of Art, Pat joined Ricky Whitelaw and Johnny Wood in The Midnighters, thereafter depping for The Strollers and working with El Cyd and The Commancheros, The Royal Teens and Tommy Dene's new Tremors line-up. They were soon to take on Germany themselves, following the example of the original lads. A successful audition in Paisley generated a residency offer from reputable John Marshall at his Frankfurt and Cologne Storeyville clubs. Contrasting with The Strollers' grim experiences, Tom had no complaints about the promoter, "a really straight, nice guy.' Tom enjoyed his first class return flights to Cologne, but Speedy's recollections are different, bringing train and ferry ordeals, lugging guitars and equipment, to mind. However it was in Germany that the boys discovered pizza (unknown back in Scotland) downstairs from the Storeyville club. A culinary revelation for these mince 'n' tatties-nurtured chiels, and one of the more printable incidents in their education on the road. Until then, anything South of Dundee had been an adventure but in Speedy and Billy "a burning desire was awakened to try for something different to the cosy Aberdeenshire system we graduated from.' Alternating monthly between the two Storeyville venues, a seven-night-week plus Saturday afternoon schedule was the exhausting norm.

Several months after returning from what had been a succesful engagement, Marshall flew in to meet with Tommy in Scotland, calling for The new Trems to resume work at his Frankfurt venue. . . where they replaced Shane Fenton's band, The Fentones. Repatriated again from that second residency, a batch of demos were recorded at Lothian Studios in Edinburgh. From the scratchy, done-to-death acetates 35 years later, you can still glean the Trems' prowess as they steamed professionally into I Can Tell, What Would I Do, When Will I Be Loved and Gee But It's Lovely. Now faced with the daunting challenge of touting themselves around an indifferent London, and aided ineffectually by an agent with trustworthy name of Richard Nixon (Tremorgate?), a road-weary Tommy returned home, resting his voice for a few years, hoping for a better deal as a Blue Chip casino croupier. Jim Lunan also soon travelled North (his replacement was Freddie Ellis, a recent escapee from those nice Trotters in Emden). Working Blackpool and Great Yarmouth holiday resorts, this English-based version of The Trems backed the likes of The Walker Brothers and Mike Berry on national tours. Softly singing God speed the day when I'm on my way to himself, Syd eventually headed for the hills leaving only Bremner and King holding out in London. Both experienced difficult times before ultimately acheiving major success in the business. . . in an ensuing chapter we shall exclusively expose Billy's penchant for kinky socks.

The song Kelly has become an albatross around Tom's neck. "I still get asked for it and to be honest, I don't even like it. As a matter of fact, I'm sick of it. One time I was playing in Kintore where this woman obviously didn't know the background - she told me I wouldnae go down well if I didnae know Kelly, every other turn they got out there played it. I won't tell you what I felt like telling her; you couldn't print it anyway.' Until Tom explained the song's history, the author could never understand why that particular song featured unerringly at every Aberdeen dance.

After his Blue Chip sabbatical, Tremors' fans Kenny Jensen and Adrian Vitesse, members of the Montrose based Blackhawks, approached Tom. He accepted their offer to join their band and worked out of Montrose with them for two years. Subsequent Friday night gigs at Bucksburn's Cloverleaf led to the owner of the premises, Bill McWilliam, talking to Tom about the Waterton Hotel, Bill's new business venture. Live music at the venue had hitherto comprised a good old accordion and drums routine, which unsurprisingly brought very few customers through the door.

Tommy accommodated McWilliam's request to put a Waterton band together, although their opening night proved to be traumatic. Tom relates "If you knew that massive room that easily held 300 people, you will understand what I'm saying. The band was myself on vocals, Jim Lunan on drums - he hadnae played in ages; and Freddie Ellis on a Wurlitzer organ without a Leslie pre-amp all going through the house PA. . . no guitar or bass. A couple of days after I had fixed Jim up I met Freddie. He had heard I was recruiting and asked if I had a gig for him. When I told him I already had a drummer his reaction, absolutely typical of him - was "nae problem, I'll play keyboards instead.'

Of course Freddie carried the deserved reputation as one of the city's most naturally-talented musicians, but a minor technical problem soon became apparent "Freddie was accustomed to playing piano (his father, himself an accomplished club pianist, had taught him) but couldnae work out the foot pedals on the Wurlitzer. He did OK wi' his hands but the feet were about as good as Ernie Winchester's. We had music scores but he couldnae read them anyway. So basically he read the chords and got away with it.'

The Waterton's clientele formed queues outside for future sessions, evidence of the band's rapid improvement as the venture triumphed resoundingly. It took the allure of a radical diversification from the pop experience to entice Tom from his Bucksburn success. Tommy Samson (he had written scores for, and conducted, big bands) found himself with a contract from the Douglas Hotel to recruit an orchestra. He opted for Tommy Dene as the man to head it up: seasoned campaigner Syd Weaver also signed up for what developed into a 12-piece band.

During this period Grampian Television heard Tom doing a couple of Sinatra-type numbers at a Dee Motel jazz club. Hence came an invitation to Queens Cross and an audition for Grampian. Tom was placed in a room with a pianist, without mic or arrangements, and un-nervingly told "let's hear you'. What Grampian heard was good enough for them to present Tom on a one-off show, he did a couple of Sixties numbers and a Tony Bennett standard.

The Douglas Hotel paid their brass players for rehearsal time, something totally new for Tommy Dene with his background in pop where payment was made by the gig, and sometimes not at all. However, the experience was an enjoyable one for him, "I learned how to count in a big band, nerve-wracking in front of 1,500 punters. The formally trained musicians were hoping I would mess it up - you know, kind of "who does this upstart pop singer think he is?' The other thing that sticks in my memory about the Douglas was all those punters packing the place out, but they couldnae get a drink.'

He is now tweaking a painful nerve, familiar to anyone who habitually frequented 'the dancing'. Six deep, trying anything to attract the attention of uncaring, amateur and undermanned bar staff, in order to buy warm and over-priced alcohol in plastic glasses. Woe betide the fool who, having spent a king's ransom on hooch bearing striking similarities to the Girdleness Lighthouse (blinking near water), was careless enough to appear a wee bit boozy.

The only female interested was likely to have a thirst like a warehouse full of blotting paper - and then enter the dreaded bouncers. Not so much as 'thank you for your custom, do come back again' as they threw the bon viveur down the stairs into the street, with a few playful kicks included at no additional cost. To think we paid entry money for the privilege of undergoing such torture - and the civilised delights of the late night taxi queue were still to come. . . However, we are now way off the track, so let's return to Tommy Dene.

After two or three years at the Douglas Tom played in four-piece bands at the Argo Lounge and the Double Two, where he confides he was "earning a pittance', deciding to spend his time more fruitfully with his children, then aged five and seven. The low wages commanded by such combos are both sad and surprising, considering the pedigrees of the musicians involved. Aberdeen's music public has always been notoriously hard to please; never mind your Baker, Bruce and Clapton. Tommy Dene, Alex Craigen, Jim Peacock and Andy Lawson deserved better.

Revival gigs at the Beach Ballroom excepted, Tom absented himself from the Aberdeen music scene for seven years. Re-activated, he now works sporadically in town when the fancy takes him. Understandably pleased that he attracts young punters as well as wrinklies, he modestly credits this to his material rather than his delivery of it. His current routine may not be causing major tremors, but he says "I am enjoying it as much now as I was 30 years ago.' Even if that albatross lands on his shoulder every so often. . .

TOMMY DENE & THE TREMORS

THE CLASSIX
L-R Brian, Bob, Eddie, Andy, Sonny

THE ROYAL TEENS
L-R Tooter Dod, Andy, Ricky (note the absence of collar and tie), Kenny, Andy Willox, Brian

THE ROYAL TEENS
L-R Andy, George Munro, Kenny, Gus, Speedy

BOBBY VINCENT COMBO
L-R Alan Taylor, Eddie Keith, Bobby Vincent Barclay,
Andy Lawson

MR FANTASY
L-R Jim McKenzie, Allan Park (B),
Mike Wilson (F), Robert Vince Vincent

Chapter 4

We will fight them at the Beach. . . . and Snuffy Ivy makes an entrance

The Beach Ballroom was the weekend destination for thousands of Aberdeen teenagers for decades. Musical styles and crazes came and went but the Beach perpetually offered excitement: music, dancing and the chance of a trap, or a fight by way of a consolation prize.

In 1918 drummer George Elrick formed a trio with Jimmy Ross on piano and Alton Locke on alto sax. Soon earning a big white fiver for private dances, they expanded to the Lucinians (latin for song-birds) quintet. With waggish fans referring to them as The Loose Onions, the boys became The Rialto Band and finally The Embassy Band. After coming second in a regional Melody Maker dance-band competition the Aberdeen boys won the Edinburgh final. This triumph spurred a move into full professionalism, and Mrs. Elrick's wee boy George assembled a new combo for the newly opened Beach Ballroom. After he moved to London, the Beach entered its ten and 12-piece orchestra days, when Blanche Coleman's all-female band ruled the jitterbugging roost, later succeeded by Leslie Thorpe. His band held down the residency throughout the Fifties. Thorpe was London-born and began his musical career in Australia. For some years he was accompanist to "the renowned coloured singer' Josephine Barker. Sam Gill worked at The Beach from 1949 until his retirement 35 years later, working his way up from maintenance man to manager. His advancement was due, apart from the obvious hard graft he put in, to his genuine interest in the venue. He witnessed Joe Loss, Ronnie Scott, Ted Heath and Ambrose appearing with their high-profile swing and jazz bands, bringing Aberdeen's punters out in force. Sam talks of "between a thousand and 1,200 turning out for mid-week shows and 1,500 customers for licensed Friday events.' Jaw-dropping attendances: a thousand customers habitually showed up on Sundays. Between 30 and 40 staff members catered for such amazing crowds. The mid-'50s inexorable charge of rock 'n' roll, with its wild rhythms and sexual undertones, inevitably changed the agenda (without diminishing the scale) of the Beach operation.

In May of 1960 Leslie Thorpe was succeeded by Johnny Scott, who secured the council's £150 per-week contract. Five years later Derek Sanderson took over with The Sanderson Sound before trying to move with the times by renaming the band The Big S. The resident band did their best with current chart material, sharing the bill with favourite NE groups and visiting 'name' acts. Because the local 'pop boys' couldn't read music they were often treated disdainfully by their elders in the Scott and Sanderson outfits. . . but no matter, as the immediacy and enthusiasm of the young guns far outweighed sometimes stilted brass-dominated big-band arrangements. How many dozens of times could Vehicle, 25 Or 6 to 4, Spinning Wheel and You've Made Me So Very Happy be credibly passed off on a pissed-off (and invariably pissed) pubescent audience? Nonetheless, never let it be said that trombonist Sandy 'Satchmo' Cuthill ever failed to be the life and soul of any party. His When The Saints Go Marchin' In needs to be seen and heard to be believed. And even then you're not sure.

Too young for the Palace Ballroom or the Douglas Hotel, the city's young trendies out-grew school-hall and scout hut youth clubs and headed en masse down the Boulevard.

A ritualistic anti-clockwise perambulation around the dance floor (supposedly eyeing up the talent, leading to 'cattle market' comparisons) made it relatively easy for Sam Gill's team to identify potential trouble-makers. "If we spotted someone walking against the flow, nine times out of ten he was looking for bother.' The famous dance floor was set on steel girders, roller-jointed to coiled springs: effectively a maple-wood trampoline. Beach Babies (the tribal name adopted in their golden youth by a generation of Aberdeen quines) would rendezvous under the clock after a dance: a no show indicated a lumber for the night.

Mrs Tucker Donald describes how her late husband, a legend in Aberdeen entertainment circles, secured his spot as vocalist with Johnny Scott and remained at the Beach for most of the Sixties. "When I met Tommy at the Bucksburn Argosy dance hall in 1955 he was a Torry trawlerman. He was always singing, often doing a couple of songs in pubs like the Cra's Nest, he also did the odd turn at the St Katherine's Club and at dances out the road. Christmas 1959 he and a friend went to the Beach Ballroom, where his pal asked on his behalf if he could get up on stage for a song or two. For a start they said no but eventually they relented and up he went. They liked what he did and offered him a job on the spot. He worked there for the next ten years.'

Whilst dance sessions throughout the weekend were crowded, Monday nights offered a special entrance deal of 'two for the price of one'. As these teen jigs were unlicensed, dancers invariably smuggled a dram inside the premises and musicians would walk a short distance to the Gaiety for a drink in between sets. Hogmanay celebrations saw traditional half bottles being involuntarily checked in with the coats on.

As a regular venue for nationally popular acts on British tours (most notably, booed-off or not, The Beatles) the Beach frequently played host to Emile Ford and The Checkmates, with their eight hit records between 1959 and 1962, including the chart topping What Do You Want To Make Those Eyes At Me For. Emile took a liking to Tucker's vocal style and invited him to come down to London to record with him. With the sessions complete, Ford hit a problem before the records were pressed. His wife started divorce proceedings, freezing his assets (a similar fate befell many mid-Winter would-be romeos round the back of the Beach Ballroom). Tucker came home to Aberdeen.

Mrs Donald again "The tapes lay gathering dust for 15 or 16 years. Lennie Benzies was a good friend of Tommy, and in 1978 Lennie's brother Robbie privately pressed up a thousand copies and sold them locally.' These three tracks were written and sung by Tucker with backing vocals from The Breakaways featuring Vikki Brown (Joe's wife and Sam's mother). When they appeared as a Clubland Records single, they were revealed as credible examples of British poppy ballads from the classic crooner school. As the big band scene declined, Beach sessions in that format finished late in 1969. Subsequently Tucker appeared at pubs and clubs throughout the city including the Rats' Cellar, the Torry Bar, the Caledon in Garthdee and a lengthy stint at the original Swan Bar in Loch Street. Tucker's Beach Ballroom decade was, in all probability, a record for the longest vocalist residency in Scotland. Such contemporaries as Robbie Benzies and Sonny Pearce gladly offer their own opinions. "When Tucker was on form he was absolutely terrific, he was an absolute master at his own Sixteen Candles style.'

. . . .

'By public demand' was a fully justified claim made with reference to the increasingly frequent appearances at the Beach by 'General' Geno Washington. An ex-GI from Indiana based in England, he toured the country perpetually in the Sixties with his Ram Jam Band, virtually monopolising the British soul scene. Geno established himself as the darling of London's 'in' set (The Stones and The Who included), through sheer hard work and exhaustive gigging at fashionable Southern venues such as the Ricky Tick and the Uppercut clubs. Appearances at London's Bag o' Nails club brought him into contact with Portsoy's My Dear Watson, whose lead vocalist John Stewart recalls how Geno "was a bundle of laughs. We got along so well that we even talked about playing with him on a steady basis but we were trying to do our own thing then.' And My Dear Watson's own thing was something magical, but more on that subject later.

Following Geno's first Aberdeen show word soon spread around the town and each successive gig was even more sardine-can-packed (fishy and greasy) than the previous one. We didn't know at the time but his act was to be the closest thing to the genuine article (with due deference to the valiant endeavours of our own Gordon Lemon) that Aberdeen would see for 25 years, until James Brown played the Exhibition Centre in 1993. Geno's singles sold disappointingly, surprisingly unable to capitalise on his dance-hall and club popularity (four releases reached only the lower reaches of the top-50). However his live-set-replicating albums acheived top-ten status. Hand Clappin' Foot Stompin Funky Butt Live peaked at number two and sat in the chart for over a year. Indeed only The Sound Of Music and Bridge Over Troubled Water outsold it that year. Ironically he recorded his two successful 'live' albums in a studio, set up to simulate a club atmosphere (stage, lighting, invited audience, show clothes). A third LP, catching his set genuinely in-situ at the exotic Bolton Casino and recorded on a mobile four-track unit, didn't sell sufficiently to make the charts. Geno's back-catalogue is out on budget-priced CD for anyone wishing to replace their scratched vinyl or to remember those sweaty sessions on that bouncing dance floor. If The Ram Jam Band fell short in musical perfection, then adequate compensation came in their spontaneous drive and funk. Fuelled by dynamic guitar and horn sections their non-stop, high octane dynamic pop/soul revue played to increasingly busy, enthusiastic houses. Aberdeen's soul fraternity were Hipsters, flipsters, finger poppin' daddies. Aberdeen's non-soul fraternity were simply gypit.

. . . .

The Fireflies (a young West of Scotland semi-pro band) got together during 1965 and with a change of name to The Chris McClure Section they launched their inaugural expedition North into the Aberdeenshire tundra. Here they established a faithful and durable teenage fan base developed through regular country circuit gigs. The Section was Jim McIsaac on keyboards, Alan Montgomery on guitar, Ian Ogram on drums, and Andy Cumming on bass.

Chris recalls rural locales with some affection. "We did places we had never heard of before we came up here, like Inverurie, Kintore, Strichen, Aberchirder and Mintlaw Station. These were more or less village halls which we normally filled. We always stayed at the Burnett Arms in Kemnay, looked after by the Elricks who made it a home-from-home for us. When we were regular fixtures in Aberdeen, we had the run of the kitchen when we got back from the gig and there was always a dram as well.'

"I remember we played in a massive marquee in a field out the road as part of the Oldmeldrum Sports I think. The enormous tent was hooching with people and our sound struggled through two, ten-inch columns on each side. We must have been nearly inaudible. . . I'm sure that most of them couldn't hear a thing.'

By the time Chris graduated to the Beach Ballroom his set developed into "an amalgamation of current chart material and stuff which, quite simply, we enjoyed playing. We went down really well doing dance music, Drifters and Ray Charles' What'd I Say come readily to mind. For some reason no-one else in the area seemed to be playing our up-tempo style.'

Concurrent with his monthly gigs at the Beach, Chris recorded two Polydor singles, I'm Just a Country Boy and The Answer to Everything, both ballads. A firm favourite with the Beach's clientele, he has returned to Aberdeen and the surrounding area frequently over the last 25 years, latterly billed under the stage name Christian, adopted in 1978. "I was looking for a change of image and it was close enough to my real name, I thought it was just a wee bit different.' He now plays the social club circuit as well as occasional nostalgic gigs back at the Beach with his current cabaret act. But Chris encourages his audience to get up and dance during the finale of his set. As he says "That's what it's all about, having fun.'

. . . .

 So. . . the resident big band at the Beach Ballroom became unfashionable to the point of obsolescense in the late Sixties: the day of the teeny-boppers' favourites was upon us. . . get into the loft to look out your old platform soled boots, lads . . . and get ready to start screaming, lassies - we are now entering The Twighlight Zone.

From the remnants of the mid-decade Shades of Blue emerged a three-strong Torry mob of Ronnie Sinclair on guitar and vocals, Andy McFadyen on bass and Ian Barrie on drums. The latter came up with the name for this new trio, Twighlight Zone. Ronnie remembers their premiere appearance in a social club at the bottom of Market Street, where his father was on the committee (early gigs more typically happened at the Tullos youth club, Powis School and the St Katherine's Club). At St K's, they purloined The Facells' gear while the big boys went off for a pint: The Zones had not yet acquired their own equipment.

In contrast with later incarnations of the band, early references were the progressive guitar blues of Jimi Hendrix and Cream (not dissimilar to stuff being played by Albert Fish, another intense, long-hair Aberdeen group). Disraeli Gears, Piper at the Gates of Dawn and 'the all powerful' Sgt Pepper's Lonely Hearts Club Band were omnipresent on the turntable chez Zones. Laudable and credible as these aspirations were, targets were re-adjusted in recognition of their own musical capabilities and the need to crystallise dreams into hard cash. Improving their professionalism, Mike McFadyen took responsibility for advertising, bookings and transport. At the time the band were far from appreciative of his hard work and the hassle he endured, only later realising the contribution he made. Achieving popularity meant that punters, rather than the band-members, had to be pleased. So rock-blues was jettisoned in favour of MOR pop, from whence came Twighlight Zone's teenybop reputation.

Fronting the realigned band was trained singer Teddy Trowbridge, Ian was elbowed in favour of John Whyte, Adam Fowler was recruited on keyboards, and Mike McFadyen got Jim Fraser in to help him out. Twighlight Zone developed a friendship with Northern progressive shaggies Spiggy Topes. The latter combo lived in a caravan on a Nigg site when they were on the Aberdeen circuit; the bands hung out there sharing guitar licks and techniques.

With their revamped line-up, a strong following developed (initially in Torry at humble youth club appearances) but the predominantly female teenage fan base soon extended throughout the city. Appearances at the Beach Ballroom increased. Ronnie estimates that regular warm-up slots for The Chris McClure Section eventually saw them overtaking Chris in popularity.

1970 arrives. The Dons win the Scottish Cup as The Twighlight Zone win a recording opportunity with RCA Victor and are offered a long-term residency at the Beach. Turning their backs on Aberdeen they opt instead for Bright lights, big city. . . In London the RCA contract de-materialised almost immediately and attempts to attract other record labels to the Zone's heavier, original material achieved results no more tangible than Tommy Dene's almost a decade before. With Spiggy Topes also having relocated to London (now working with Cliff Bennett) the boys crashed at their flat before finding a place of their own. On the back of a hot News of the World shock-scandal exposÈ (concerning the alleged hedonism of Glasgow's Marmalade), English agents proved ambivalent to Scottish bands. An audition at Decca brought the comment "Your songs aren't bad, keep writing and try to get back in to see us in a year or so.' What they were supposed to do for money during that year is anyone's guess. The Decca agent had around 1,500 bands on his books and made no concrete or vinyl promises. "Not so much little fish in a big pond, more like tadpoles in the Atlantic ocean.' However, Ronnie cites the ill-health suffered by Andy and Jim as the reason for aborting the London expedition.

Re-grouped in Aberdeen, the band re-established themselves on the local circuit where Ronnie was singularly unimpressed. "We eventually settled down in a sleazy club for a four-year residency. Adam left when he got married so we settled for MOR as a four-piece until we dissolved in 1975, never having regained the enthusiasm or momentum of the London venture.'

There was, however, a concluding close encounter of the Twighlight kind, when the band re-zoned in 1994 to raise £600 for a youth club charity. Normally open and forthcoming about the highs and lows of his band, Ronnie kept schtum on the 64,000 dollar question: whatever happened to those gargantuan loon pants, such a familiar sight a-flapping in the bracing Menzies Road breeze?

. . . .

In the beginning there was St K's but as beat surrendered to rock, the haunts of the Silver City's music cognoscente also began changing. Stickers and posters carrying the legend "I'm a Place Face' swamped Aberdeen. Located at the non-Union Street end of Chapel Street, bands played 30 or 45 minute sets in rotation from three stages in the one room. Stalls sold fashionable clothes and trinkets. . . it was a brave attempt at innovation, based on the template of Edinburgh's venue of the same name. Its failure proved that Aberdeen wasn't ready for such a groovy experience.

Located in Albyn Place and officially run as an RGIT club, The Dive was a favourite spot for local performers. A small venue, it is remembered as being atmospheric, intense and sweaty. A couple of miles away The Holburn Disc, upstairs from the Holburn Bar, was probably the first attempt at a discotheque in the city. It took some time before its clientele got wise to the incompatibility of UV lighting, dental gunge, and dandruff. One lad wore what was obviously a brand new made-to-measure jacket: the tailor's chalk marks were clearly visible yards away.

Concerns about diminishing attendances at live shows in the area during May of 1966 manifested themselves at a meeting between the Musicians' Union and local magistrates. MU secretary Charlie Styles claimed that discotheques held on licensed premises present "a moral danger to youngsters'. . . these events have "special lighting which attracts teenagers'. . . were these kids or moths? Charlie appealed to Aberdeen Trades Council for their help in the matter. The subject gathered steam when a local school teacher reported how he found a number of his pupils at "a discotheque session'. Just what a teacher was doing in such a joint was not clear. This under age drinking scare prompted Baillie Ronald Bruce to demand a police enquiry.

Charlie was in action again in September of 1967, this time demanding protection for his members and their equipment. Fifty bottle-throwing teenagers attacked The Out as they left The Beehive. Rhubarb's Brian Youngson established a petition at Harry Lord's shop. "These animals will murder some-one. More bouncers are needed. The slightest excuse is enough to set a pack of up to 300 of them off. Rhubarb, The Facells, The Quantrells, The Method and all the groups are behind me.' Marginally safer than The Beehive, the Looking Glass in Market Street was just the place to sit nursing a pint of snakebite. Just the place in fact, to listen to some band murdering a Thin Lizzy number. Snuffy Ivy made a colour-ful entrance and loudly harangued (in her own distinctive nasal style) the semi-pro endeavours of two young painted ladies of the night. This brought the house down - a helluva floor-show, certainly better entertainment than the band provided.

As the Seventies approached, the Elite Lounge and the Harriet Street Bar became essential, if compact, live venues. It took only comparatively few customers before these premises filled to over-capacity, and then some. Inability to gain access to the room where the bands played was not, in itself, a major disappointment. Almost equivalent, self-deluded cred was derived from sitting on the stairs, pint and sleekit jazz-woodbine in hand: really cool, especially in January. In Rosemount the downstairs level of the Silver Slipper was home to progressive outfits such as Whitehart and pulsated for a few months until police began weeding customers out. Who knows if grassing took place? Pressure from the Grampian constabulary eventually forced the closure of the venue due to its unusually smoky atmos-phere.

If the Grill, the Bridge Bar and the Hairy Bar were for mannies, then Aberdeen youth felt compelled to spend their time and money in places of their own desire. Regular habituÈs of the outrageously fash-ionable Blue Lampie and Shep's Moorings soon sussed a method of actually feeding the superlative, but over-subscribed juke boxes and actually getting to hear their selections before kicking-out time. A simple technique, the required music had to be sequentially upstream from the disc playing at the time - uniniti-ated customers wasted their cash. It seemed the thing to do at the time, nose to nose, cradling a pint glass close to the chest to avoid a soaking in the scrum, shouting at mates over the din. If a pub had elbow room it wasn't a place to be, or to be seen.

The power cuts of 1973 in a candle-illuminated Prince of Wales saw the winter of our discontent made glorious summer when Nick (grumpy head barman, motto Ich Dien but only when I'm good and ready), oblivious to the open trap door in the flickering half light, fell through the gap to the cellar below. Loud clattering and oaths were greeted with rapture by the pub's cold, die-hard clients. Arthur Scargill won himself many supporters that night. Neither the Prince nor Ma Cameron's would ever have won pub of the month, but they were 'in' and that was that. Co-incidentally, it was never too difficult for those of dubi-ous legal age to obtain a drink in such places.

Pub crawls inevitably lured young men 'doon the shore' to Peep Peeps (Commerce Inn or any way you like) and to such exotic destinations as the Bond and Spa bars. Those young punters with sufficient common sense and sobriety avoided the Caberfeigh and the Royal Oak, to avoid catching a flying beer mug in the face or catching something of a more infectious nature. The Palace Ballroom in Bridge Place was the starting location for Aberdeen's prototype teenybop group. When he was only ten-years-old in 1963, Robbie Benzies went round to his pals' gang hut to play the guitar - by the following year he was a member of The Tsars, 'Scotland's youngest group.' The others were comparative has-beens: Billy Spratt (later to star with The Quantrells and The Facells) was already 14. Bill's relative Robert 'Vince' Vincent was the group's bassist, with Stephen Wiseman on drums. Davie Fraser was later to sing with the group, and became DJ at The Palace.

The Rank Organisation had converted The Palace from its previous cinema incarnation, opening in 1960. "It really lived up to its name' remembers local sax player Jimmy Gray. "Facilities were first class, a terrific stage and good quality amps.' Some 20 bands auditioned for the spot as resident band, the win-ning combo being Jimmy's revitalised Alligators with vocalists Francis Main and Bobby Vincent. As The Tsars became active, trombonist Roy Pinder led the new resident Palace band, the brass section of which included ex-Alligator Colin Fraser, Wally Robinson, Frank Burnett, Sandy Stewart and Vic Canale (also on sax was Binner's dad Bill Innes Snr). Female vocalist Eileen Bremner, bassist Johnny Smith, pianist Munce Angus, drummer Bill Angus, and finally, vocalist-MC Clive Ahmed completed Roy's labour-inten-sive orchestra. Ahmed became The Tsars' manager in an era when a gimmick was all in getting groups recognised above (or in this case, below) the others: he flew his fledglings into a sky crowded by wrinkled, wizened crows in their late teens and twenties.

A vital initial step was edging into Palace Saturday afternoon sessions, playing a couple of numbers during Tommy and The Tremors' break. Robbie Benzies remembers The Tsars as being "reasonably good, nothing brilliant. . . but it was our youth that was such a novelty and got us so much work.' With a Stones, Beatles and top-40 repertoire, they crept on to the Thursday night bill. Due particularly to Robbie's tender years, care was needed over the whens, wheres and durations of Tsars' performances. Such restrictions eventually led to young Benzies being dropped in favour of the more chronologically advanced Jim Peacock.

"My older brother Lennie had been in action for quite some time. Even before groups broke through as being the new thing, he was in a piano and guitar act. Lennie played regularly at The Hop Inn in the Castlegate where I used to hang around as a kid, getting to know lots of the blokes in the different groups, all of them older than me of course.' Successive associations with Tucker Donald, Jim 'Rusty' Russell and big brother Lennie kept Robbie busy on the Aberdeen club and pub circuit.

A Roy Pinder engagement ended in the sack, but he was off to London where former Alligator Alex Evans looked after him. With Alex's co-reptile pianist Alan Payton they formed a jazz trio in Tottenham. Robbie was invited upstairs for a drink, to a bar where local band Storm were playing, and "Come and do a couple of numbers with us' developed into a semi-permanent engagement. Many years later came a phone call from Frank Kane requesting Robbie's participation in Storm's reunion London gig in 1993, from which a photo appeared on the Islington Gazette's front page.

When the first Storm subsided in 1970 Robbie was reunited in Aberdeen with his old Tsars mentor Clive Ahmed at The Harbour Bar. With drummer Stan 'Spike' Milligan they became The Clive Ahmed Trio, moving on to a residency at The Argo Lounge. Spike's day job at the Employment and Benefits office at the bottom of Market Street made him very edgy about playing lounge bars close to the 'broo'. After one especially hassle-filled day, Spike couldn't handle a gig at The Looking Glass for fear of being filled in by some of his disgruntled, boozed-up day-time customers. Such pub entertainment didn't prove too rewarding either for one of Robbie's acquaintances, a long-term Aberdonian drummer. This percussionist had played at the East Neuk right from the pub's earliest live music days in the Fifties through to 1973. Lets say he was picking up three tenners (nothing to do with Domingo and his mates) for six nights work. . . with a corresponding weekly bar bill of £50. When the gig finally ended after 20 years roughly speaking, the day of reckoning revealed that the much-battered drum kit actually belonged to the pub and not the much on-the-batter drummer. 17 years with nothing to show for it. . . goodnight and thank you.

No such problem for Robbie himself, his versatility on several instruments provides him 'fill in' work when he doesn't have a steady gig. He was also the guy who took Tucker Donald's Emile Ford tapes, pressed them up and issued them as a three-track single. They were working together at the Torry Bar when Tucker told Robbie about the London recording sessions. Robbie remembers that "Tucker always wanted to record his work, to have something in his hands. More or less to document his work. And the songs were certainly good enough so I issued a thousand copies.' Most of which were sold at live venues and outlets like New Market Tapes, a credible sales performance without local radio to push it along. Robbie's greatest satisfaction came from his friend Tucker saying "See this guy, he went out of his way and made an effort on my behalf.'

TUCKER DONALD

THE TSARS
Scotlands Youngest Group

CHRIS MCCLURE SECTION

GENERAL GENO

TWILIGHT ZONE

Chapter 5

The Jacos, Johnny and Big Jim

Outwith Aberdeen a flourishing band scene existed in the North East's outback. Most eminent of the rural rockers came out of Albert Bonici's Elgin organisation in the shape of The Jacobeats and The Copycats.

To excavate down to the foundations of The Jacobeats we travel back to Portsoy in 1953, where we find The Diamonds skiffle group, 13-year-old members of the church youth club and bible class run by the Reverend Montgomery. Supportive of youth activities, he ran hops for his juvenile parishioners and allowed the skifflers to use the church hall for their practice sessions. The boys, who had adopted their name from Lonnie Donegan's Jack Of Diamonds, were also permitted use of a room (at the top of the church hall turret) for storage of their rudimentary equipment. Awkward in terms of lugging their gear up the spiral staircase after gigs, but it was free and was welcomed by the boys at the time.

In California Leo Fender would doubtless have quaked in his blue suede shoes had he known that Dougie Maclennan and John Rennie were making their own Spanish-style acoustic guitars at home, from plans sourced from a woodworking hobby magazine. John in particular suffered for his art. "On a mid-winter night I was cutting out the sides of my guitar from very thin plywood, using a one-sided razor blade. The electricity failed, plunging the house into darkness. But undeterred and full of youthful enthusiasm, I determined to persevere and complete the job that night. I lit a candle and got on with the task. However I wasn't making much progress, and closer inspection revealed a pool of blood over the wood and the table I was working on. I had been using the blade the wrong way up and gashed my thumb to the bone several times.' When John's hand healed he finished his Portsoy Telecaster, which proved to be fit for rudimentary skiffle purposes. The group thought about a change of name to Blood Sweat and Tears or Badfinger.

The suite of Diamonds included, apart from John and Dougie, George Milne and Leslie Anderson at various times on tea-box bass, the Green family (James, Martin, Eric otherwise known as 'Plum' and Mrs Green's washboard) with Sheila McIntyre on vocals. Eventually the day came when the DIY guitars could be replaced, as John explains. "I vividly recall travelling to Aberdeen on the train on a Saturday morning to buy our new Hofner acoustics from Bruce Miller. We returned to Portsoy entertaining local fishermen all the way on the 4 o'clock service, known as the 'trawler train' because it transported local boat crews home for what remained of the weekend.'

Necessity being the mother of invention, the group moved into crude electrification of their equipment. Microphone crystal inserts, which shattered instantly if dropped, were purchased mail-order, as were speakers. Mounted into boxes they outputted between five and 10 watts. Valves from old wireless sets were built into amplifiers, with pick-up sockets fitted for instruments to plug into. Mic stands were fabricated from electrical conduit screwed into lead-filled car hub caps. As we said, crude. . . but effective.

From his corporate international entertainments management nerve centre in Inverurie, Bert Ewen finally permitted The Diamonds to appear during Saturday Macduff dance intervals. The only mode of transport available to the lads was the service bus, onto which they loaded their voluminous equipment, much to the disgust of the exasperated driver. At the Macduff knees-up they hung around digging the various groups and dance bands until Bapper gave the nod for their turn. The skifflers returned home to Portsoy on the late dance bus (if there was one) or by taxi. It was some time before they saw any rewards but eventually Bapper would hand over a few pounds.

Sheila McIntyre left and both Leslie Anderson and George Milne were obliged to concentrate on their day jobs. The musical Green brothers went to college and hence were lost to the group. John, Dougie and Bill McKenzie were joined by Joe Mowatt from Cullen and Bill Murray from Buckie. The group's personnel were now stabilising into a reasonably consistent format.

Rehearsals took place at the Rathven Hall on Sunday afternoons and occasional weekday evenings. By now retitled The Apaches (after The Shadows' hit of the same name) they became North of

Scotland Rock Band Champions, winning the title at the Aberdeen Beach Ballroom in November of 1961. Granite City favourites The Midnighters were second with The Sabres from Elgin taking third place. The Press and Journal report of the event gives a snapshot of the times. "A 17-year-old blonde receptionist Miss Josette Lawrie was chosen Miss Young Set 1961. Voted 'King and Queen of Jive' were Aberdeen couple Andrew Adams (21) and Audrey Grimmer (20) from Torry.'

Within months of their triumph in Aberdeen The Apaches, under the sponsorship of Albert Bonici, were regularly backing and supporting his visiting acts at the Craigellachie Public Hall, Cullen Town Hall, Buckie St Andrew's Hall, Huntly Stewart's Hall and the Elgin Drill Hall. Major local players included Erle Jacobsen and his Erle Blue Stars, Dean Travis and The Tempests, and The Johnny Douglas Combo. From outside the area came Bert Weedon, 'a very nice guy', Tucker Donald's recording sponsor Emile Ford, 'an absolute perfectionist', Shane Fenton (later to recreate himself as Alvin Stardust) and Johnny Duncan, who "would rehearse his set in great detail in the afternoon but then turn up at night after a few pints and sing whatever came to mind.'

John feels The Apaches experiences in backing such a diverse array of acts, and replicating the latest records, was to stand them in good stead for future adventures. A Buckie Town Hall dance above the public library was sorely overcrowded, to the extent that the organisers were seriously worried about the floor collapsing. The decision was taken to open a double-door fire exit, permitting a controlled and safe evacuation of the premises. By the time the doddery old duty gadgie actually got around to opening the doors, the pressing throng of panicked dancers stampeded. Only when the hall was empty was he was discovered, trapped behind the door, ribs broken and nose flattened.

Transferred elsewhere by his employers, Mowatt dropped out of the picture to be replaced by schoolboy vocalist John Stewart. He stayed with The Apaches during the school summer holidays, enabling the band to fulfil their existing commitments. Primitive recordings reveal this line-up rehearsing contemporary chart material by Joe Brown, Lonnie Donegan, Chubby Checker, Cliff and the Shads. Like opening a dusty, yellowing scrapbook, the tapes transcend a long 35 years. . . earnest young hopefuls endlessly reworking and polishing their repertoire in that tiny rural village hall.

When Johnny returned to school at the end of the hols, new vocalists were Kenny Lawson and Margaret Riddoch. Margaret had "an extremely strong voice, she could easily have performed jazz instead of pop.' Kenny was the group's comedian, climbing up over the stage curtains at a gig in Ellon, waving to the audience whilst hanging upside down from the rail during one of Margaret's slower, dramatic numbers. Ian Young came in on drums replacing Bill Murray. The group proudly showed-off their Gibson EBO bass with their Levan Goliath and Fender Stratocaster guitars, beaming in their collarless sky-blue Beatle suits.

Albert Bonici put his considerable weight behind the act introducing fundamental, important changes. Adios to the trendy suits in favour of full Hunting Stewart tartan Highland dress at £80 a shot. Albert thought this crucial, imparting a gimmick value indispensable if his charges were to appear different from a plethora of other beat combos throughout the country. Matching the Highland image came a name change to The Jacobeats. With its reference back to the 1745 rebellion and contemporising the early Sixties beat music craze, The Jacobeats was either excruciatingly painful or very clever. Having carefully saved their wages, they turned professional. Six months of solid rehearsals ensued at the Rathven Hall, honing routines and sets to perfection.

The first be-kilted gig was in Dunoon with the group detouring into Scott's kilt maker shop in Aberdeen to be outfitted on the road south. On-the-spot alterations to the kilts delayed their arrival in Greenock, too late to catch the last ferry. However, the local policeman found a local worthie to transport the group and equipment in his small boat. The bobby telephoned ahead to Dunoon and a black maria met them at the other side to drive The Jacos to their dance venue. Yet another panic: The Jacobeats were ignorant of the complicated procedure of dressing in traditional Highland garb. The star of that night's show was Lulu who came to the rescue and sorted them out. We don't know if the lads were true, free-swinging Scotsmen on that occasion . . . did Lulu sing " You know you make me want to shout'?

Dunoon's US submarine base became a regular haunt, as recorded in local press. "One of the loudest and most appreciative welcomes came last week when they appeared in Dunoon, wearing their gay Stewart tartan kilts before US naval personnel. Said drummer Ian Young, "cameras were clicking left, right and centre. It surpassed our wildest hopes." Tain Town Hall was less enthusiastic, as The Jacos were "jeered by several youths in the audience, the kilt being the main object of their derision.' A severely hacked-off John Rennie located a portable fire extinguisher that he placed between his legs and directed at the hecklers. Apparently the threat in itself was enough to put the rowdies' gas at a peepie, hardly surprising when combined with the gay tartan kilts factor.

In 1964 they set off on the much-used rock 'n' roll highway from Scotland to Germany, October and November being spent as resident combo at Dusseldorf's Casino night spot. One night stands at US military bases followed through to January with Alex McKay on rhythm guitar during extended merchant Navy leave, with John switching to bass. Fellow North East beat musicians Eddie Leppard and The Leopards were spotted along the ausgangs and einfarts.

The forthcoming marriage of lead vocalist Margaret Riddoch precipitated the band's return to Portsoy. Her subsequent departure saw the arrival of sisters Lorna and Deirdre Cameron (aged 18 and 16 respectively) from Jimmy Dingwall and The Electrons, a semi-pro band in their native Nairn. Bonici revealed that no less than Ed Sullivan had been desperate to get The Jacobeats on his coast-to-coast American television show. By the time the US and British Musicians' Unions had agreed on an exchange group coming over from the States, The Jacos had signed up for the German tour. Ambitious plans for Mexico and Brazil also foundered, reputedly for similar reasons . . . Ed Sullivan, networked US TV, Mexico, Brazil. . . hype? Albert Bonici? Giwa, nae Albert!

Domestic touring continued unabated. . . John recalls the hospitality proffered by the citizens of Kirkwall. "On the boat over we had such a rough crossing the girls were violently seasick. The gig involved us in first performing a concert along with a local act and then playing again for the dance, finishing at some uncivilised hour in the morning. The promoter laid on transport for us but the driver was so drunk there was no way we would get in the van with him, it was safer for us to drive. Because of their bad experience on the trip over, Deirdre and Lorna decided to fly back to the mainland rather than risk the sea crossing again. It turned out to be a hot breezy day and their plane was thrown about in bad turbulence. The girls were sick again.'

Securing weekend engagements was comparatively easy but The Jacobeats travelled as far afield as Manchester and Birmingham to fill mid-week itineraries. Nights at home in their own beds were infrequent and sporadic. This chaotic, demanding lifestyle with its hasty, irregular junk food eventually caught up with Rennie. Medical problems compelled him to abandon the road with his doctor telling him "treat your body with more respect or you're in trouble.' His enforced departure from his beloved Jacobeats was soon followed by the resignation of fellow founder Dougie MacLennan who developed into a leading local photographer.

Effectively now minus one of his major acts Bonici turned to Graham Nairn, already at the Two Red Shoes ballroom. Under Alex Sutherland's direction Graham had joined on a summer engagement after graduating from art college in Dundee. Three years later he was still at the Elgin nightspot when Albert asked him to re-activate The Jacobeats into a working unit. Coincidentally Eddie Leppard and his Leopards had also recently gone off on separate trails, allowing their bassist Rae Rogers to change his spots and enlist with The New Jacos. Extensive rehearsals at the Two Red Shoes and at the Arradoul WRI hall, with rest and recreation at the Square Cafe in Buckie, resulted in a set predominated by R 'n' B, with modern jazz leanings. These young pretenders to the Jacobeat throne thereafter trod the same ground as the original incarnation of the group, opening the door for odious comparisons. Fortunately these fears proved unfounded and the new kilts on the block were voted a success.

Working two clubs on the same night (common enough on the lower budget cabaret circuit the band now inhabited) they shared the bill with a conjurer who certainly had the better deal. The New Jacos had to set up their bulky, heavy equipment, play an alacritious full set, strike their equipment, reload their van and drive speedily to the second club to repeat the exercise. The magician, on the other hand, simply stuffed his rabbits back in his top hat, reunited his glamorous assistant's top half with her legs and conjured up a taxi. At Mr Smith's Club in Manchester they found staff and customers alike in a state of paranoia, anxiously glancing over their shoulders. Nairn thought "Christ, they must have heard really bad reports about us.' Finally the edgy barman whispered that only two weeks before, a gangland shooting had taken place on the premises. John Rennie and his fire extinguisher would have sorted them out.

Perpetual gigging resulted in a tight little band and a dedicated fan-base from Thurso to Manchester, with outposts as distant as Swindon. Notwithstanding their undoubted popularity they were heading towards their final fling: ultimately the New Jacobeats tired of uncivilised road life. The kilts were handed over to The Bambis from Buckie, mais bientÙt the sporrans were sent to Valhalla and ceremonially burned on a pyre of heather and Chuck Berry 78s.

Graham returned to the 'Boots' (the colloquial tag for the Two Red Shoes). Performing pop and rock covers, the ten-piece Jimmy Martin Band would read his arrangements on Wednesday's first run-through, and have them up and running for Friday and Saturday hops. The Boots was, according to Graham "an institution that was always packed to capacity.' Technology bulletin up-and-coming: with the house band Graham used a Burns short scale Jazz guitar through a Binson Echorel Baby into a Burns Sonic amp, adequate for the size of venue and the music played. Alan Rodgers used a Rickenbacker 'Monster' bass. To provide additional 'beef' Graham went on to the dependable AC30 amp fitted with a Selmer amp head, customised with a bank of push-button effects grafted into the amp. Powerful for the time, their PA system had a 50-watt Vox head coming through two Selmer Goliath cabinets containing four, 12-inch speakers. If the music wasn't heavy the hardware definitely was, as Graham has good cause to remember. "I carried the gear all the way up the fire escape at the Dalrymple Hall, Fraserburgh. I was close to death by the time I got them into the place. I can't recall who else was on the bill that night but my back will never forget those speakers.'

Bonici's stable of East coast beatsters also produced The Copycats (who would develop into one of Scotland's best bands): their vocalist Johnny Stewart ultimately carries the twin-edged distinction of being the country's most under-rated, and unknown songwriter.

As 11-year-olds Stewart and Iain Lyon featured in rival crude, adolescent skiffle bands, The Saints and The Sinners. Performing novelty acts in local Portnockie and Buckie group competitions, these kiddie combos combined under Iain's leadership as The Cimmarons in 1962. During his school holidays Stewart had already been war-crying and rain-dancing with The Apaches. Originally a five-piece The Cimmarons also had Billy Cameron, Robert Lawson and Alistair Ewen but the latter dropped out within a year. The name changed to The Copycats who rehearsed at the same rent-free WRI hall used by The Apaches/Jacobeats. Early repertoire hinged on easily accessible and familiar Shadows' material but the rock 'n' roll of Chuck and the Georgia Peach soon infiltrated. Unusual for the North East at that time, authentic American soul (basically unavailable in the UK other than from specialist London import shops) soon predominated.

Lawson's uncle carried exotically-labelled vinyl back from his American merchant Navy trips. These first slabs of R 'n' B were quickly reinforced by Marvin's 1964 You're A Wonderful One together with discs by Smokey and The Miracles. Stewart's mother brought the latter Tamla gems from a visit to his aunt in the USA. Those Detroit soul icons inspired and influenced the Moray Firth combo and Stewart in particular. "A lot of it was way over my head, I didn't really appreciate what some of it was all about then and it was basically no good for our home white audience. But I was amazed and knocked sideways by the music.' The seeds had been sown and before long they came under control of Albert Bonici who was responsible for personal representation, publicity, and management. Musical direction was handled by Alex Sutherland and personal management by John's brother Alex. Ken Smith was their road manager and was therefore tasked with outfitting and operating the group's "specially constructed van, containing reclining seats for sleeping, fitted wardrobes, radio, tape recorder and record player.'

Stewart says that Bonici "was always one step ahead'. The manager realised that securing The Copycats a major label recording deal meant relocating to London, overmuch of a culture shock for his young provincial protÈgÈs (average age 17). They instead featured on Scotland's first independent record label, Bonici's Norco, with I'm a Hog for You Baby/I Can Never See You in 1964. The A side was a stylish period cover of the Leiber-Stoller-composed Coasters favourite and the flipside was an original Iain Lyon number. . . admittedly a basic, parochial Mersey-washed beat sound, but it was a start. Under Albert's protective gaze a couple of London gigs at least part-funded recording costs at Olympic Studios. Thus the project was undertaken totally within Bonici's control, independent of any record label whims. The initial pressing of 1,000 were quickly snapped up and a copy of the much sought-after single recently changed hands for more than £40.

John obviously had a lot of time for Bonici. "Some people thought of Albert as being a rogue entrepreneur, but I liked him. He certainly had vision in the late Fifties when he changed his Park Cafe into a skiffle joint modelled on the Two I's in London, making it one of the first youth venues in Scotland. As far as our first single goes he took the chance on financing it and I don't think he lost money on the deal.'

Easily hurdling the regional Elgin heat of a national beat contest, The Copycats advanced to the Scottish finals in Hamilton. West coast bias predominated and the event was a shambles. Despite being scheduled to do their stuff at two in the afternoon, their grudgingly conceded nine o'clock slot was never allowed to happen. John was struck down with laryngitis so Syd Weaver, at the venue without a backing band, had agreed to deputise. This sorry episode meant that The Copycats never made it on to stage. The thing was fixed in favour of the Glasgow-based Beat Unlimited Showband with their version of Neil Sedaka's I Go Ape, dressed in gorilla suits. Syd was having none of it and appropriately went bananas with Musicians' Union representative Charlie Styles. (His wrath on unearthing unregistered group-members was a thing of beauty). Chas and Syd forced a re-staging of the event which The Copycats won legitimately in Perth in November of 1963. Second place went to Dundee's Mark Drayton and The Hounds.

The Cats flew the Scottish flag in the UK finals at the Tooting Granada chasing the first prize of a recording contract plus musical equipment valued at £500. Headlined by established acts Joe Brown and Heinz, the competition was won by the Moray marauders. The boys were too young to sign a legally-binding contract and Albert felt unable to commit them without consent from their parents. Imagine the disappointment at being relegated to second place... nonetheless the story brought terrific publicity and catalysed the abandonment of their final vestiges of caution. Turning professional surely was the way forward?

By default the winners of the event were The Excaliburs and other competitors were The Warriors featuring Jon Anderson and Tony Kaye (later of Yes) as well as Dave Foster. The latter will reappear in this musical Mein Kampf 30 years hence in the North of Scotland.

For these fishing port kids, the allure of professional rock musicianship was undeniable: in Johnny's case, his parents intended for him to enter the family butchery business. Dizzy with the music, there was no competition. Remote as it may have been in reality, they saw a possibility for inhabiting another world and lifestyle populated by The Beatles and The Stones. Making a way through life by playing a guitar had to be better and was at least worth trying. Bear in mind that, for The Copycats, Aberdeen had previously been a biggish, Saturday deal. A metaphoric Red Sea parted and they walked into the chasm.

An exhaustive schedule of gigs in Scotland and the North East of England ensued with gigs supporting The Hollies and The Beatles, thanks to Bonici's clause ten. Of the hundreds of groups he worked with, Stewart talks about Johnny Kidd and The Pirates in glowing terms. "A terrific band that was years ahead of their time. Kidd himself was a great guy who epitomised British rock 'n' roll for me, he must have spent years of his life travelling to and from gigs up and down the country. I always felt that he never did receive the credit he deserved.' Grown too big for the Boots, a Copycats' move to Germany was born of necessity to escape what had become a restrictive circuit. They felt stifled and were learning nothing new. So in Germany their first five months were spent playing American military bases in Giessen, Saarbrucken, Mannheim and Offenbach. These were segregated but being daft Scottish loons the Copycats didn't know the code. Exposed to black music in the Negro billets, ideologically their cultural and ethnic horizons broadened. As a band they began developing an idiosyncratic style of original unhackneyed material, nonetheless remaining indebted to authentic R 'n' B sources.

John takes a quiet satisfaction from an incident which united two guys, previously diametrically opposed racially, through the band's music. The story involves a civilian black soul brother with the improbable name of Robert Burns (a friend of the boys who lived in Frankfurt), and a redneck GI also with a Scottish name Dick McDonald. The latter opined that he did not like 'monkey music.' On the train journey through to a Copycats' gig these two refused to share the same compartment. There was a shortage of accommodation in town that weekend, presenting Burns and McDonald with the choice of sleeping in the street or crashing at the group's flat. Opting for the comforts of the Cats' apartment, their barriers dropped through beer and music to the extent that come Monday morning they were big buddies.

Still on the amis connection, Iain Lyon must have ruefully reflected when he sobered up on the potential consequences of his drunken antics. After a long and presumably enjoyable night on the pils he decided his best bet for breakfast was the local US military base. Hence, at the height of cold war tension, a civilian VW driven by a drunken unlicensed Moray marauder roared erratically past the GI gatehouse, unnoticed and unmolested.

An 18-year-old female vocalist, Eithne Alexander, flew in from Elgin International Airport to join the group in February of 1965 to give those GI audiences something to look at even if they didn't dig the music. We don't know if she cramped the boys' style but they certainly didn't hang on to Eithne too long. Approached by Rudi Pfeifer, a mature student who opportunistically booked a hall in Waldorf on the outskirts of Frankfurt, they agreed to play his civilian club. The guys walked into an enormous and daunting hall where Rudi had optimistically set up seating and a dance floor for 800. The gamble paid off in spades with the venue being filled to capacity on its first night. The Scots' growing reputation was further enhanced as the venture continued to prosper. Pfeifer pulled in such night club luminaries as John Marshall, owner of the Storeyville clubs in Frankfurt and Cologne; Peter Eckhorn, owner of Hamburg's infamous Top Ten Club with his club manager, Glasgow R 'n' B legend Ricky Barnes; and Peter Naumann, representing Munich's PN Hit House venue. The Cats were henceforth ensconced as regulars at Eckhorn's Hamburg establishment performing a set which John describes as 'a mix of original compositions and black bluesey/R 'n' B soul material.'

John also recorded for the Top Ten record label (Eckhorn capitalising on his club's fame). John says that the sessions were not over-sophisticated. "We simply poured the last punters out the door at five in the morning before Peter brought in his old local rock 'n' roll pals, both black and white. Ricky dusted off his saxophone, we got a couple of cases of bier and some uppers in, then switched on the tape and went for it. The results were nothing special, pretty rough actually - but I bought a new suit from the proceeds of the session.'

Further recordings were made during German tours of duty (nine months annually for four years), for the indigenous Cornet label. At the Waldorf studio where The Beatles had recorded Komm Gib Mir Deine Hand the Cats taped the Stewart-Cameron Angela (an infectious falsetto-vocaled, up-tempo poppy number) and I'll Never Regret You. A second German effort, Start Thinking About Me/Pain Of Love emerged from Munich's Bierkeller studio where a wee Austrian painter named Schicklgruber had addressed his Hitler Youth fan club when he was top of the Third Reich charts. Start Thinking About Me presents great progression in John's writing, with his vocal showing an early maturity, auguring well for the future. The flipside moved into intentionally discordant pop, not so easy on the ear and an interesting contrast to previous oeuvre.

April of 1968 saw French immigration authorities at Saarbrucken take exception to the 'I'm Backing Britain' slogans and Union Jacks adorning the group's van. Refused entry to France, committed Parisienne night-club and radio broadcasts were unfulfilled. The British record industry did not reciprocate by backing the boys. Demos and tests for Pye and Decca floundered, the latter turning up their noses at a 12-track album. . . Decca had also thought The Beatles were rubbish, so what the hell? Help arrived with the intervention of Harry Vanda and George Young of The Easybeats (The Cats worked with them in Germany). The Young family had emigrated from Glasgow to Australia in 1963 under under the Assisted Package Scheme. Friday On My Mind was an 1966 international hit for The Easybeats and brought George back to Europe. His younger brothers Malcolm and Angus Young of AC/DC became a school-uniformed, heavy metal guitar inspiration for Aberdeen's Bash Street Kids. Another siblng was Alex, stalwart of Hamburg-based The Big Six and later of Apple label hit-makers Grapefruit. Harry Vanda was a first generation Dutch emigrant to Australia.

Quasi-Aussie George helped secure a recording contract with EMI subsidiary Parlophone but the deal was not unconditional, the record company insisting on a name-change. Johnny Stewart winces "My Dear Watson was Albert's idea and we never did like it. Watson doesn't come across as a strong character in the Holmes books, a bit of a wimp really. We didn't care much either for the image that Albert put together for publicity shots, period Victorian clothes and daft bowler hats. But he was the boss'

Elusive Face/The Shame Just Drained was recorded at the two-storey De Lane Lea studio in London where Pete Dello's Honeybus occupied the other floor. Released in 1968 the A side was a Stewart composition with the flip written by Young and Vanda, who also produced the single. Arlo Guthrie was Melody Maker's guest reviewer that week and reckoned that Elusive Face, later covered by Inverurie's

Steele Combo on their Good Times album "wasn't a bad record, the singer sounds like Ritchie Havens'. Arlo, didn't you hear the warnings not to touch the brown acid at Woodstock? "Not a bad record' eh? Where John was finding the heartbreak is anyone's guess but if ever a record deserved success this was it: an enormous, emotionally draining snatch of love-sick angst.

Attempting to break the single the boys worked flat-out in London, pulling a four-month Tuesday night residency at the Bag o' Nails. A favoured hang-out of London-based stars the club was the first social port of call for incoming American artists. It was here that The Watsons encountered a blues and rock guitarist non pareil in a gadgie named James Marshall Hendrix. Jimi's bass player Noel Redding was already an acquaintance. His previous bands (The Lovin' Kind, Neil Landon and The Burnettes) had shared German stages with The Copycats during European jihads. Hendrix "basically wanted only to listen to the band and to relax without people hassling him. He sat right at the front wearing his cool hat, smoking a small cigar, having a drink. . . he would ask us to play more Impressions numbers, Curtis Mayfield being a favourite of his.'

The omnipresent Geno Washington frequently sang with the Watsons during their Bag residency and suggested that their association became more permanent. John's affectionate memory of Geno: "He wasn't the greatest singer in the world but he really knew how to have fun.' The 1968 Parlophone power-pop of Stop, Stop, I'll Be There/Make This Day Last should have blown the pop chart apart. With an extravagant arrangement busier than the late Dick Donald's sales ledger, Young and Vanda went in with all guns blazing: a belter, a diamond, a true North star.

John was married by this time and his wife initially accompanied him on the road. This proved logistically problematic and unfair on the marriage. The solution was simple, it was in fact elementary My Dear Watson ('fraid so dear reader, had to use it sometime) as John swopped beat for meat, returning to the family business back in Portsoy. The Watsons continued by drafting in Findochty's Alex Ziggy Slater, a former member of Buckie's Grey Woolly Affair, as they moved from Parlophone to the DJM label. There they recorded an album's worth of material with an unknown staff session keyboards player by the name of Reggie Dwight.

Even in their incomplete demo condition these dozen eloquent Johnny Stewart numbers leave the listener incredulous at DJM's artistic negligence in not bringing the project to fruition. This album would have proved a winner for both label and the band. A sublime coalition of fizzy country pop (It's Too Late, Things Look Good Today, Watch Out For The Hurricane, and Serious Business with its infectious poppy hand-claps) and the introverted gloom of In The Meantime and Runnin' Away From Himself. The keyboards work wasn't bad either. . . but sadly the only tracks to gain public exposure became the final single Have You Seen Your Saviour/White Line Road in 1970. These are tragically ignored classics with mature and wistful vocals, powerful and understated country influenced melodies.

DJM had promised the lads the earth but redirected their all into promoting the same session keyboardist Reggie Dwight, now re-christened Elton John. The partnership between Reggie and lyricist Bernie Taupin had initially resulted in the promising Lady Samantha and Border Song. Finally recognising the talents that had been under their noses for some time, DJM were pushing Elton towards the big time. Frustrated by such reprioritising delays The Watsons abandoned London to return to Scotland. Never again would their cultured pop talents grace Tin Pan Alley or 221b Baker Street.

Iain Lyon subsequently played guitar with John Wayne (OK Kincaid, let's get the hell out of here. . . others in the band were Glaswegians Noddy Kerr, Freddy Mail and Sandy Newman), acoustic act McCulloch-Lucas and finally The JSD Band. Bill Cameron attempted to recapture good times in Germany before ultimately settling back in Morayshire, whilst Rob Lawson went to work within Albert Bonici's Elgin agency. The original Copycats have re-assembled for sporadic local charity fund-raisers and 'why not?' gigs. . . their thirtieth anniversary was marked by a 1992 Elgin Town Hall bash.

Returning to the lost DJM album. . . given an even break, it would have been The Watsons' ticket to the big league, a cornerstone for enduring careers for all concerned. Ultimately, the label's lack of interest drove My Dear Watson to disappear without due recognition or credit, leaving behind a clutch of consummate singles and their forgotten LP: a testament to a fine band in the wrong place, at the wrong time. How ironic that Scotland's best music of the Seventies became the decade's best-kept secret. As for Dick James, the owner of DJM - has the business ever seen a more appropriate Christian name?

. . . .

A decade after My Dear Watson shared the spotlight with Geno Washington at London's Bag o' Nails, another Moray Firth marauder was beginning his steady climb to the top of the British singles and albums charts. As The Copycats were burning the midnight oil in Germany's beat clubs, back in Portsoy primary school, Jim Paterson's interest in music was beginning - this developed further through his principally classical training at Banff Academy. He remembers that his cousin watched Johnny Stewart and the boys locally whilst Jim himself enjoyed Chris McClure's gigs at "the local tattie shed'. Cupboard-inhabiting skeletons begin rattling as he bravely admits to paying money to see The Bay City Rollers and Slik at Cullen. Early preferences encompassed soul music and Alice Cooper's theatrical rock, although Jim's liking for the latter was very much image based. However, he didn't form part of any local pop groups, playing brass instead eventually with the Scottish National Brass Band.

Wishing to diversify his skills into a more modern sphere he couldn't find the right course at a Scottish college. Jim therefore moved to Leeds, where he was tutored in jazz and 'light' music. He returned to Portsoy after his studies and 1978 saw him working at the local Ewing's oatmeal mill. Three months into the job he spied an advertisement in the 'sits vac' section of Melody Maker from a band seeking a brass player. The ad was placed by Kevin Rowland, who with his partner Kevin Archer (they had met in The Killjoys, a punk band) was turning his world domination master plan into the flesh and blood of Dexy's Midnight Runners. Jim's Friday telephone call in response to the ad was followed by an audition in Birmingham, and his becoming a Midnight Runner all within a fortnight. "Dexys are close to my heart, when I moved down from Scotland to join I fell in love with the group.'

Taking their name from dexedrine the amphetamine stimulant favoured by the Northern Soul set and under the co-management of Clash guru Bernie Rhodes, Dexy's initially rehearsed in Wolverhampton, where their first gig took place at The French Duck, a pub. Rhodes was already well connected with London's rock music Mafia through his experiences in breaking Strummer, Jones et al during the cataclysmic first wave of punk. He released Dexy's debut single Dance Stance on his own Oddball Productions label - this inaugural blast of Midlands working class soul dented the chart at number 40, a respectable start for a previously unknown act. Dexy's image of donkey jackets, black toories, and building site boots, was Rowland's creation. The band was presented as a gang based on the stevedore chic of the Marlon Brando movie On The Waterfront. As part of Dexys' instant mythology, Jim was thereafter referred to exclusively as Big Jim Paterson.

On the strength of the encouraging Dance Stance, Rhodes secured Dexys a support spot on the second portion of a national tour by The Specials, Madness having played the first half. Jim remembers the exposure gained on these dates effectively universalised the band, which was then picked up by EMI. The second single, the consummate Geno, appeared on an EMI subsidiary Late Night Feelings. By the time it hit the top of the pile in 1980, Dexys were one of the country's hottest attractions. Featuring Hammond organ, two saxes and Jim's trombone they were fired by the epochally defining talents of James Brown and Aretha Franklin. . .

Rowland's homage to the artist he described as 'The King' Geno Washington, dominator of British club soul throughout the Sixties, was a horn-laden gem. Dexy's leader had been fundamentally affected by the experience of seeing The Ram Jam Band at the tender age of 14: join the club, Kev. Jim says that Rowland raved on about the man: those packed, perspiring nights at Aberdeen's Beach Ballroom had obviously been replicated in the Midlands. "Hot and sweaty down in the club as you know, Whoa Geno. . .' Dexy's brass section included Geoff Blythe who had heroically been a member of the RJB, hence amassing major street cred in Rowland's eyes. Blythe (now resident in the USA), was responsible for Dexys brass arrangements, a task later inherited by Big Jim. The B side of Geno was an energetic, forceful tribute to Breaking Down The Walls Of Heartache, Johnny Johnson and The Bandwagon's 1968 hit, a show stopper on Dexy's 1980 tour. Whatever else might be said about Rowland, there aint no denying the man's musical taste.

Favourite records invariably fix a specific time and place for the listener, on a personal level. Thus it is ingrained eternally in the author's memory how, after the Dons hammered Hibs 5-0 at Easter Road in the sunshine of that memorable May day in 1980 - Premier League champions for the first time - Geno was played in Edinburgh's clubs throughout that boozy Saturday night. This was the occasion when our four-strong posse of Beach Ballroom veterans was denied access to an off-Princes Street den where we sought a late celebratory drink (as if we hadn't had enough already). The reason given for our non-admittance was "Sorry lads, couples only.' His brain being full of whisky, Big Neil was thinking on his feet as he huddled confidentially with the more senior of the doormen and then, hey presto "Okay in you come but nae trouble or you're out.' Making our way downstairs to the bar, we asked our hero how he had done it - had he slipped the bouncer a Harold Melvin? The gob smacking reply came "No, I told him we're gay.' Happy admittedly but gay?. . . What could a boy do, other than shrug his shoulders and get on with the bevvy?

All of which was fine until two hydraulic hours later, full of Championship boisterousness and beer, our dance floor carousing was getting too much for the club's staid Edinburgh clientele. They were, after all, out for a moron-free Saturday night, half of them wanting to drown their Hibees relegation blues. Imagine our shame and mortification when the DJ shut the sounds down and announced loudly to a quizzical and soon to be even more disgusted crowd: "I'm nae putting the music back on until the poofs from Aberdeen sit doon and behave.' Rubislaw Quarry, where were you just when we needed you most? Not that we could have climbed the fence anyway.

Come July the Edinburgh hangovers had almost gone and Dexys' There There My Dear continued the white-skinned blue-eyed soul blitzkrieg, peaking in the singles chart at number seven. For their inaugural LP, Dexys were promoted to EMI's higher profile Parlophone label. The Searching For The Young Soul Rebels album (opening with Rowland's impassioned plea Big Jimmy, for God's sake burn it down! hit number six, and included the first of Jim's dozens of compositions for Dexys, I Couldn't Help It If I Tried. With EMI refusing to re-negotiate the band's six percent royalty contract, even after the label's incredible returns from Geno, drastic action was called for. So the band stole the album master tapes from Chipping Norton studios, refusing to return them until the deal was improved. In a meticulously planned operation, producer Pete Wingfield and an engineer were enticed from the control room, allowing other Runners to swipe the tapes. The group's getaway van, engine running, sat outside along with a decoy vehicle. In a vain attempt to prevent the hijack, the foolhardy Wingfield threw himself in front of the van as it hot-rodded out of EMI's car park - he escaped death by inches.

The scam worked and with a new, near-double percentage contract in the donkey jacket pockets, another single was released in March of 1981. But Plan B stiffed at number 58 much to the delight of the cock-a-hoop music press. Rowland had proved difficult to deal with as far as Fleet Street was concerned. His refusal to grant interviews was read as his being at odds with the world in general and the NME in particular - instead he issued hand-written manifestos, proclaiming the gospel on his Intense Emotions Limited letterhead. "Spiritual passion and a craftsman's care, a positive force with a touch of despair. . . ' His incandescent talent often went unacknowledged by the music press who took great pleasure in castigating Rowland. . . his aloofness did him no favours but he was fiercely committed to a puritanical safeguarding of his unique new soul vision. Dexys body-swerved NME's conventional strategy: the mag first champions the cause of a fresh act, proclaiming them as new saviours before casting stones as their adoptees are adjudged as selling out to commercial pressures. With Rowland refusing to play their game they wrote him off as an arrogant, demented poseur, although in many cases a feeling of grudging admiration hid within such journalistic voodoo doll-pinning. He talked a good fight but he played an even better one, as Jim confirms. "Sure he could be difficult at times but maybe that temperament was a bonus, contributing to our music's dynamism and enthusiasm. He had a good side as well and certainly I got on well with Kevin. I learned a hell of a lot from him.'

Rowland decided to sack his drummer, but word got out before the foul deed was consummated. Despite the majority of the Runners voting for his dismissal instead, Kevin won the day. In the putsch The Birmingham Five departed tails between their legs, to become firstly The Bureau and then General Public. Mick Talbot later became Paul Weller's partner in The Style Council. Kevin Archer also left the camp although, in his case, on good terms. This left Rowland and Paterson as the sole (soul) originals, who set to recruiting a new band and creating a new image. . . Kevin now had them dressing in hooded running gear and boxing boots. On tour they performed early morning roadwork and existed under a Spartan training-camp regime. Ian Dury would surely have shuddered at this puritan existence. . . No sex or drugs or pints of Skol, doo doo doo de doo doo. . . Despite the band's unsmiling image, Jim says "We weren't really that miserable. We used to have a lot of fun given the chance when Big Brother wasn't looking.'

That summer saw Kevin shooting again for different goals when he had the brass section learning the cello, which he says "wasn't bad but was not stunningly successful.' A recent burst of honesty from the born-again Rowland reveals how he recruited the leader of his string section Helen O'Hara. "Kevin Archer found her at music college in Birmingham and let me hear her demos. He suggested that I contact her to ask if she knew anyone who could play cello for Dexys. Then I pinched her for myself.' Nice one. Following their sell-out Old Vic Projected Passion Review, Rowland's purist, ever-questing soul fundamentalism saw him sacrifice that second version of the group. . . he headed off on yet another unpredictable tangent. . .

1982's Too Rye Ay album showed him blowing his cover in a big way. Having got his infatuation with Geno Washington off his chest it was cheery Van Morrison's turn for exorcism. Kevin enthusiastically absorbed his mentor's pained emotional excess aesthetic. The resultant annoyingly catchy Come On Eileen returned Rowland and Dexys Midnight Runners to the top. All anguish, raggedy dungarees and Irish itinerant hoe-down, it is probably their best-remembered song and was the year's top seller. The Morrison fixation was never more clearly stated than in the lovingly recreated top-five cover of Jackie Wilson Says. Another calculated, deliberate Rowland stroke of genius saw the athletic look ditched in favour of holey dungers, Irish-Celtic tinkerism now being the man's fixation. Too Rye Ay also marked Big Jim's departure from the band he loved. "To be honest, I left out of jealousy when the string section joined. I felt a bit neglected. It was on an impulse and it was wrong but I'm a stubborn bloke.'

Although credited to Dexys Midnight Runners, Because Of You (theme music to BBC television's Brush Strokes) was effectively a Kevin Rowland solo project. Its unlucky number 13 placing in November of 1986 marked the end of the glory days. . . a couple of years later his self-credited album The Wanderer sank faster than a pint of lager in Joe Harper's hand. Soon Rowland was declared bankrupt with debts in excess of £100,000 and he was on the dole. Big Jim also had to sign on. "We were both unemployed for most of the three years up to 1993. It was very hard to find the money for demos and so on but at the same time the struggle was good. We didn't take anything for granted and we shared the load.'

Dexys were back together on Jonathan Ross' Saturday Zoo on television in February of 1993. Rowland was adamant that "The Runners are back, no question about it.' Jim remembers things were looking good for them as a unit again, with about half an album in the can. Rowland certainly seemed more mellow, even deigning to speak to the previously reviled music press. Perhaps a case of him now needing them more than they needed him. . . yesterday's hero and all that?. . . With his new humble persona, he revealed that this time round he was "just one of the band', confessing that glory for the band's greatest achievements had not actually been laid on the right doorsteps. He admitted that the Too Rye Ay sound came from Kevin Archer "He was responsible for that sound but it was credited to me. He found it but I stole it.' And for the album tracks Rowland came clean that "I never gave Big Jim his due desserts, he co-wrote them with me.' Jim's laid-back reaction to this is "He's worried about stealing my thunder back in the old days but I wasn't aware of it.' According to Jim the revitalised Dexys "Seemed to fizzle out, with personal differences between the members of the band.'

As far as Jim's own musical tastes go, he is "a sucker for anything with a good melody, I like something with a good tune you can sing along with. I have a soft spot for melodic traditional Scottish folk music, ballads of Corries ilk.' He has been resident in England for 20 years but "when I'm old and decrepit I'd like to come back to a small Scottish village rather than live in the big city'. Recently Jim has been doing low-key session work and concentrating on writing. A flux of compilations and live material signalled an enduring support for Dexys and thankfully Alan McGee's Creation records, continuing their search for the perfect pop rainbow, have signed Kevin to a new contract. Rowland without Paterson is like the Eiffel Tower without steel; like the pyramids without sand; like a fish supper without fish. First off the Creation blocks was a re-issued Stand Me Down, to be followed by a Rowland solo cover-versions project (co-produced by Jimmy), in advance of a brand-spanking-new Dexys album. One dead-cert for inclusion is the co-composed My Life In England. "I'm nae thinking about buying a mansion or anything daft like that, but things are now looking pretty good really.' In the meantime, our eternal gratitude goes to the Wee Red Devils and to Jim (himself a red-hot Dons fan who suffered the 1995 relegation sword of Damacles along with the rest of us) for that unforgettable Edinburgh Saturday . . . Come on Big Jim Too Rye Ay. . .

DEXYS MIDNIGHT RUNNERS
"We weren't miserable all the time"

THE PHANTOMS
From Buckie

THE JACOBEATS

L-R Doug McKennan (Lead G), Ian Young (Drums), Margaret Riddoch (Vox), John Rennie (Rhythm G), Josh (Temporary Bass), *Front* Kenny Lawson (Vox)

MY DEAR WATSON

Chapter 6

By appointment to His Royal Highness, Prince Moulay Abdullah

As our odyssey progresses ever Northwards, the harder the music (as well as those playing it) becomes. Caithness was the seemingly improbable source of a major influence on the Scottish beat scene in the untameable shape of Johnny Sutherland, the founding father of Northern rock music. Our investigation of his invaluable contribution commences with an analysis of the historical and geographic circumstances that were to detonate a mini explosion of Caledonian rock that would echo throughout contemporary Western popular music.

On the face of it Caithness is the remotest community on the UK mainland. Until the early nineteenth century, it was a de facto island: there were no roads over the difficult Ord of Caithness until then. The reality was however somewhat different with the sea being a unifier; the Pentland Firth has been an international trade highway of importance for centuries. Many generations of Caithness seafarers acted as pilots for shipping in these difficult narrows with very strong currents. Visiting captains would not risk undertaking a local passage without the benefit of local knowledge. From the Viking invasions through to recent times there have been regular strandings of ships, the crews of which found it virtually impossible to achieve repatriation. Consequently, the local population has traditionally had a mongrel genealogy. The frequency of contact with people alien to the area no doubt broadened indigenous minds in a way impossible for those residing, for example, in remote Highland glens. Natives of lowland Caithness have spoken English since it overtook Norn (an antiquated language not dissimilar to modern Faroese) in the sixteenth century.

In the early 1800s, Caithness effectively took control of the North Sea herring fishery industry, including curing and processing, which had hitherto been the almost exclusive domain of the Dutch. A significant fleet of Caithness-owned merchant schooners plied the Baltic (hence the existence of Baltic blood in the Caithness ethnic mix), with herring and flagstones, the latter to satisfy the demands of a burgeoning North European market for railway station platform materials.

The economic success of the herring and flagstone businesses enabled Caithness to resist the worst excesses of the post-1745 Highland clearances. Indeed the area was to offer shelter and employment for dispossessed crofters (up to this point few people bearing the surname Mac. . . inhabited the region). Revulsion at the gross vindictiveness of the clearances was probably one of the early catalysts in installing a socialist ethic into Caithnessians. . . one of whom, Donald MacFarlane MP, sponsored the 1884 legislation which promoted security of tenure for crofters.

Following the decline of the herring fishery and pavement trade an interim boom up to the 1930s saw the area second only to Aberdeenshire in granite quarrying. However (rest assured dear reader we will soon get to the point) it was the construction of the Dounreay fast reactor nuclear research facility that catalysed the emergence of rock music in the area. In the face of a Suez crisis-induced oil shortage the project was a rush job, employing some 30,000 construction hands. They were billeted in the 'Boston Camp' at Dounreay and included site painters from Glasgow Dave and Bill Fehilly, the first arrivals on what was to prove more than a parochial platform.

With proto-rock 'n' roll breaking through in the mid Fifties the first local band to champion this genre was The Rhythm Four With Johnny Curran, a baker from West Lothian who had moved North to make bread from the expanding Caithness populous. Drummer Chris Duncan, a World War II naval veteran, recalls that he was "about 40 at the time but most of the others in the group were in their early Twenties.' The Fehilly brothers abandoned their Dounreay work to establish Glasgow Dance Promotions, responding to demands for modern entertainment. Their regular venue was the large wooden Boys' Brigade hall in Wick with capacity for more than 1,000 people. They engaged such acts as The Clyde Valley Stompers and Bob Wallis's Storeyville Jazzmen, as well the Shadowy first wave of rock groups from Glasgow and Aberdeen. The brothers also ambitiously promoted seminal American rocker Gene Vincent.

Thurso's Princes Cafe transformed under their direction into The Spot, the town's first juke box cafe. For two decades it was to be the teen scene and its juke box was to have a major impact on the progression of local rock music. There, young locals heard Painter Man and the Jeff Beck-Rod Stewart version of I've Been Drinking Again, both of which were incredibly popular locally. Stewart had played at the Thurso Town Hall in the early Sixties as a member of Jimmy Powell and The Dimensions.

Upon the legalisation of bingo in the UK, the Fehilly brothers moved into that field and also into gaming casinos. By this time their operation was headquartered in Dunfermline where they decamped into rock music management in a big way. Apart from persuading Alex Harvey to come out of retirement (to get together with Tear Gas as The Sensational Alex Harvey Band) the Fehillys also managed Nazareth, the Kingdom of Fife's most notable rockers until The Skids went Into The Valley with Albert Tatlock years later.

As well as construction crews, Dounreay attracted some of Britain's best scientific brains - 'the Atomics' North to live and work, creating fierce competition between their children and those of local parents, at Thurso High School and at the new Technical College. When the Dounreay Fast Reactor was commissioned, young locals had the opportunity of securing good professional employment on their own doorsteps. Some 30 apprentices drawn from the Northern counties were trained at the facility each year - some of these became active in local beat groups. Notable amongst these was Shetlander Magnus 'Sonny' Flaws, who persuaded Johnny Sutherland to take his group The Federals to tour Shetland. Twenty-five years later, Magnus was very much in the public eye when the oil tanker Braer stranded near Sumburgh Head in 1993, in his capacity as councillor for Shetland's most Southerly ward.

The impact of Dounreay on the area cannot be underestimated with the population of Thurso trebling in the late Fifties. Traditional local families were determined not to be outdone by the incoming 'Atomics' in what was a very cosmopolitan Thurso.

A converted Victorian school, the Wick Assembly Rooms became the principal local venue, with groups being supplied to local voluntary sector promoters, primarily via Albert Bonici. This venue has excellent acoustics: in this regard, Jeff Beck is quoted as saying that the Assembly Rooms was the finest he had played. Beck was with The Yardbirds on the occasion that prompted this praise, playing dual lead guitar with Jimmy Page.

Local bands such as The Federals and The Aktual Fakts provided ever improving backing and support music to visiting acts. Inasmuch as Dounreay represented the white heat of British technology, local musicians were spurred on to demonstrate that they were up with the times and did not have heather growing out of their ears. Johnny Sutherland, who fulfilled a crucial role in those early days, was not only able to play his Gibson behind his back, he was one of the few British guitarists with the ability to play with his teeth, emulating that great My Dear Watson fan from Seattle. During this trick at a Stornoway gig a confused female fan screamed . . . "Hendrix!', before fainting. Johnny's obsession for musical perfection, combined with his almost public espousal of the drugs culture and his inability to get on with other musicians, created problems in his maintaining a band on the road. He therefore had to train up some very young players and developed an excellent reputation as a tutor, attracting disciples from well outside the area. One of his notable early bands was The Jam which included schoolboys Graham Walker and Johnny Gray.

A further important factor to the musical awareness of Caithness was the clear radio reception of signals beamed from American Forces Network: AFN Europe. The station played R 'n' B material at a time when bland, Brit quasi-rock and cover versions dominated the UK charts. Much American material was picked up by Caithness groups well in advance of its appearance in this country's top 20. AFN also previewed Elvis Presley's releases before their issue here, providing added stimulus for local listeners. In common with his fellow American servicemen Elvis regularly sailed through the Pentland Firth on board big grey troop ships. Radio Free Europe was also received legibly, but was less popular due to its excessive US cold war propaganda content.

Two young Caithnessians, Donnie Sinclair and George MacBeath, represented Scotland in Radio Moscow's World Youth Folk Music Championships: the station was also much listened to, its attraction being attributable to the area's socialist leanings. On the final leg of their journey from East Berlin to Moscow they shared a train compartment with entrants from Pakistan. George, a brilliant musician with the deserved reputation of being able to get a tune out of any instrument no matter how obscure, experienced 'Paki black' for the first time. Apart from its more obvious results, George developed an intense interest in Eastern music. With the Beatles bringing Indian influences into the Western rock domain, George tutored Johnny Gray and was often critical of George Harrison's sitar playing.

Through his civilian employment at Forss, equidistant between Thurso and Dounreay, at the US navy base (in itself another factor in the area's familiarity with American music), George was posted to college in Newcastle-on-Tyne. Whilst furthering his professional training he discovered that Northumberland's main musical equipment stockist had a large inventory of imported Indian flutes. The problem facing the owner of the shop was the inability of his customers to make any headway with the instruments. One Saturday morning George intervened by picking up one of the flutes and immediately producing a tune from it. The shop keeper was so grateful that he paid George to come in on successive Saturdays until the consignment had completely sold out.

Saxophonist Donnie Sinclair (the other half of that Midnight In Moscow duo) became a teacher. Several of his Thurso High School pupils became members of his American soul specialist band Eileen and The Talismen. Their drummer was Wick's Andy Munro whose composition On The Midnight Prowl won him the North of Scotland song writing contest in December of 1966 at the age of 17. Dick Levens was also in that Talismen line-up and subsequently worked professionally with Pete Brown. The latter subsequently collaborated with Jack Bruce in writing some of Cream's cream: Tales Of Brave Ulysses, Sunshine Of Your Love, Strange Brew. . .

US soul bands frequently appeared at the US Navy NavRadSta Thurso base, a military radio station that primarily communicated with missile-bearing submarines. Local musicians often accessed these gigs. American nationals also featured in local bands: The Opium Trail, starring schoolboy musicians Graham Walker and Roger Niven, included American Ron Gershwin in its ranks. Petty Officer Third Class Bruce Bartow also brought a wealth of On The Road experience to the scene. An accomplished New England guitarist with a folk music background, he was a failed draft dodger who had hoboed his way across the USA on goods trains heading for San Francisco where he shared an apartment with Jack Casady, bassist with The Jefferson Airplane. Through this association Bruce came to know many of the contemporary bands emerging from the West Coast movement and was a regular attendee at the original Fillmore Hall and Avalon Ballroom venues. With the authorities on his trail, Bruce fled from San Francisco and made it as far as Phoenix, Arizona before he was caught. Given just 24 hours to sign up for military service, he elected for the US Navy which he erroniously considered a safe bet for avoiding combat action in Vietnam. A short-back-and-sides later, he was on river patrol in the Mekong Delta on PBRs (rapid, small, four-man patrol boats with machine guns fore and aft). Subsequently he was quite badly wounded when his tank landing craft downed its ramps on a mined Da Nang beach. After hospitalisation he requested a transfer to Scotland with the Holy Loch in mind, but finished up in Thurso instead.

Bruce brought with him his authoritative collection of West Coast albums, introducing the far North of Scotland to Moby Grape, Captain Beefheart, Spirit, and The Grateful Dead. . . as well as Jefferson Airplane. Such material being difficult to obtain in the UK at the time, local band members enthusiastically familiarised themselves with the new music. Reflecting the extent of local interest, Caithness Courier editor and rock band manager Bill Mowat persuaded Bruce to give a public seminar at Thurso Town Hall. To an audience of some 40 acolytes, Bruce played and discussed West Coast psychedelia, open in its espousal of peace and love with advocation of the drugs culture being only cosmetically disguised. The American was far from chuffed when the newspaper report on his dissertation, written by Mowat under the nom de plume Tim Hunt, deleted all references to cannabis. Living off base, Bruce later got himself in trouble for bidin' in with Sheila Whittaker from Stonehaven, an art teacher at Thurso High. Sheila was also a part-time go-go girl with Johnny Sutherland's band.

One semi-pro combo worthy of mention is The Jigsaw Puzzle, formerly known as Umeandus, who capitalised in a socialist manner on a hiatus in promoting visiting 'name' bands in the area. Primarily working in professional day jobs at Dounreay, their most influential member was the half-Malaysian Ian 'Sally' Campbell. His father was a local World War II serviceman who met his mother on the last boat to escape Singapore before it fell to the Japanese. Ian shrewdly conceived the idea of hiring the Wick Assembly Rooms on Fridays and the Thurso Town Hall on Saturdays. The band therefore employed the visiting chart acts and also put themselves into the show as support group, frequently with a greater fee than that negotiated with the bill toppers. Arrangements for bookings with the Council were entrusted to their only non-Dounreay member, insurance salesman Sandy MacLeod. The system allowed the band to maximise financial returns on these ventures and to gain valuable experience of rock music economics.

Jigsaw Puzzle's cartel came to grief when MacLeod left the band to establish Caithness Dance Promotions, through which he claimed the right to local gigs. Local musicians then found themselves effectively debarred from such work and Johnny Sutherland championed the cause in the ensuing political battle. His delegation included the young Johnny Gray, and addressed the Provost, Baillies and Councillors over the affair. All of this focused the minds of several Thurso rockers on the possibilities of turning pro on a full-time basis.

Dounreay and the community were the subject of a BBC documentary in May of 1967. On the suggestion of Bill Mowat, producer Finlay MacDonald, a native of Skye, used The Opium Trail performing Hold On I'm Coming as a central part of the programme. This band crystallised the area's cosmopolitan mix, comprising schoolboy sons of 'Atomics' (Graham Walker and Roger Niven), a 'local', and the American Ron Gershwin - as well as an excellent female vocalist, Monica Rodgers. She later appeared throughout Europe with Johnny Sutherland's The Blend. Opium Trail's drum kit logo was a creation of Peter Blake, internationally famous for his design of The Beatles' Sgt Pepper album sleeve. His Opium Trail connection was the aforementioned Sheila Whittaker, a graduate of the Royal College Of Art in London.

As beat mutated into rock and groups somehow disappeared to make way for bands, Gully Foyle emerged as pioneers of hard rock in Scotland. Their roots are found in Thurso where guitarist Stefan Kocemba and bassist Robbie Manson, together with Johnny Sutherland and Dennis Thompson, formed The Aktual Fakts (Dennis was later to form part of Grit, an Aberdeen combo). Stefan moved to Edinburgh with his family, whilst Robbie came down to Grays School of Art in Aberdeen, meeting drummer Billy Allardyce. With brothers Kenny and Brian Ross they became Phase Two. Sutherland later came down from Thurso to trio with Wee Billy and Robbie. The latter stayed on at Grays as Sutherland and Allardyce moved to Edinburgh to rendezvous with Stefan.

Manson drops momentarily out of the Gully Foyle saga - but fear not, he makes a welcome return several thousand miles and 40 countries later. He continued playing on a part-time basis in Aberdeen initially with The Haze, where his co-members included Johnny Barclay, Bill Kemp and Eddie Somebody. . . evidently a haze in more ways than one. Robbie and Johnny B's next musical amalgam Rhubarb was sweetened by respected city rockers, former Playboy Ian Dowbekin, guitarist-keyboardist Brian Youngson and the inimitable Ricky Munro on drums. Back on the trail in Edinburgh Billy, Stefan and Johnny had joined forces with Jim Scott on vocals, Peter Goldie on rhythm guitar, and bassist Sandy Wilson in a conglomeration named Just Us. Wilson departed after only two or three months, to be replaced by Wee Freddie. Sutherland departed for Switzerland to meet up with local musicians, including bassist Werner Frolich. Under the name Second Chance they did their best, but according to Johnny "we weren't getting on that great.'

On the strength of well-received Edinburgh and Glasgow club gigs, Just Us followed Sutherland to Europe with Wee Freddie. He travelled about as well as Mark Thatcher. In Zurich an exchange of bassists took place, Just Us apparently getting the best of the deal according to Sutherland. "Werner had pretty good equipment and lots of money.' Johnny returned to Caithness where with Dick Levens and Andy Munro he formed The Blend. . . blues, soul, jazz and when they could get away with it, op-art/pop-art proto-psychedelia. In short, they played anything to keep the customer satisfied.

Just Us became Switzerland's most popular club rock act. But it wasn't all tax-exile, Toblerone, holey cheese and Alpine horns (if you get my snow-drift). Becalmed in Klosters with only two gigs a week to occupy their creative energy, terminal boredom set in. The devil made work for idle hands. Having found a dead bat in the grounds of the hotel, little Billy slipped it in Stefan's cornflakes bowl the next morning. The joke continued when they nailed it to the door of the local church, just a laugh for the band, which they thought no more about.

The following day all hell broke loose. A quaint Swiss chalet situated close to the church had burned down during the night and the indigenous population and police blamed the Scottish satanists, inferring they had caused the inferno through devil worship and black magic. . . just the tasse de the of L'Express du Soir, the local rag. Its Saturday evening sports edition Le Vert Eventuel (which each week featured Petit Alexandre, a football-supporting scallywag) jumped on the band-wagon, carrying a stop-press item to the effect that the band had been arson about. A Swiss army knife-wielding lynch mob gathered, but just in time the boys high-tailed it out of town over the German border. They were to become fixtures of the German clubs, touring there a dozen times. North to Denmark, making several TV appearances and taking the clubs by storm. . . before being deported.

Leaving cold Scandinavia behind, Morocco became the next exotic work-place, a short journey across the Straits Of Gibraltar from Estepona in Southern Spain (scene of previous gigs at the Sin Favor club). Why Morocco of all places? Indigineous herbal relaxants surely tipped the scales. . . ? Their original engagement was for a fortnight's work at L'Amphitheatre, a swank tourist club in the capital, Rabat. Playing a melange of original material and Who and Creation covers to expatriate French and bemused Arabs, their stay extended to nine months. Touring with a travelling circus on the Algerian border, to a background of border skirmish gunfire they performed with magicians, belly dancers and native groups playing tribal pipes. Stefan recalls "people came from miles on horseback and camels to see us. We were the only white faces in the show and were regarded as being freaks. Berber horsemen, dressed in black robes and armed with scimitars, showed their appreciation by firing rifle shots into the night sky.'

The Casablancan studio where their first album was taped was rudimentary by European standards, its normal product being Arab folk music. The LP's sponsor was Ali Bussif, a North African Andrew Loog Oldham equivalent. The specific amount of the fee is long forgotten but Stefan recalls that it "was enough to live on for three or four months. We didn't want the album to surface in the UK because, apart from the primitive recording facilities, Billy had resorted to raiding the local slaughterhouse for goat skins and we couldn't find proper guitar strings. We were also hoping to pull a recording deal when we got back home, and didn't want to jeopardise our chances.'

The band's publicity material made much of a royal command performance at a bash organised by Prince Moulay Abdullah, the brother of King Hassan II (Moroccan head of state since 1961). The party was in celebration of the engagement of a pasha's daughter: if you are sitting comfortably (on the edge of your seat?), we'll begin. . . The boys were friendly with Zladco, a Yugoslav who had deserted from the French Foreign Legion by walking across the Sahara from Algeria. Of all the gin joints in all the world, Just Us were by now playing a Casablanca club owned by Rachid, a local hood. They wanted out and Zladco hired a moped to set off with Stefan over 200 miles of mountainous terrain for Kenitra, where they secured a month's work.

Stefan telephoned back, telling the guys to pack their bags, load up the van and travel over to the new venue. Leaving their digs, they were intercepted scarily by a squad of plain-clothes police. Billy explains. "First off, we thought they were Rachid's heavies, we had already told him we were finished with his club so we thought we were in big trouble. When they explained who they were it was a big relief for us.' His elation was short lived, as the suits ordered the band to appear at Prince Moulay Abdullah's party the following evening, resolutely unreceptive to Billy's tales about departing Casablanca immediately for the new gig. Dragged off to the local jail, they were shown some poor wretches, locked up in the dungeon downstairs. It was then gently explained to them that "this is what happens to people who do not obey the King's instructions.' Billy thought to himself "Ah well, if only you'd said that in the first place. . . '

More compliant now, the band nervously related how Stef and his Gibson semi-acoustic were 200 miles away and how they couldn't perform for the royals without him. The authorities instructed their counterparts in Kenitra to bring Stefan in; achievable in a couple of hours, they thought. However it took a full day before they apprehended the Thurso guitarist and drove him, Zlad and the moped back to Casablanca in their Moroccan black maria, arriving barely in time for the reunited band to play for the Prince. The problem in locating him in Kenitra still puzzles Stefan "We were the only white people in town, and I had hair down to my feet.' The party itself was a real hooley. At the 100-room desert palace, they co-starred with French heart-throb Johnny Halliday. A supporting cast included 40 belly dancers, a dozen snake charmers, and a wall-of-death motorcyclist. . . just a touch different from your typical Saturday night at Ma Cameron's. Soon after, the Prince was the target of an unusual assassination attempt when the royal jet was unsuccessfully attacked by fighter planes, flown by disenchanted Moroccan air force pilots. Perhaps they hadn't been invited to the party.

. . . .

Meanwhile, Johnny Sutherland had taken The Blend to Germany, doing the rounds of the same US military bases where The Copycats earned their spurs. He established useful American contacts and secured a job with a New Jersey-based group. Thus in 1968 he became the first Scottish rocker to play in the USA as part of an American group. Suitably impressed with Johnny's performance when performing together in the States, Rod Stewart reputedly offered to organise a recording and management deal for him. . . the small matter of Sutherland's deportation to Canada prevented the offer being accepted. During his Canadian sojourn he jammed on stage with Arlo Guthrie, author of Melody Maker's off-hand review of My Dear Watson's Elusive Face. With the intention of forming 'the ultimate band' Johnny came home to Scotland at the end of 1969. Turning to Dick Levens from The Blend and original Spiggy Topes drummer Graham Walker, Johnny christened his dream-team Gollum The Underdog. . . the name coming from a character in the then indispensable Lord Of The Rings, written by John Ronald Reuel Tolkien. Johnny recalls "We were really active on the Aberdeen scene with an exotic mix of Blood Sweat and Tears, Manfred Mann and blues. . . but a drug influence was creeping in by then, along with my experiences in the States. Although the term hadn't yet been used, I suppose we were playing acid rock.'

When Stefan and Billy returned from souking up to Prince Moulay Abdullah, Just Us became Gully Foyle (science fiction devotees will recognise this reference to the novel Tiger Tiger). In Thurso, Robbie Manson re-enters the picture. . . the royal command performers knocked on his door, to be answered by Robbie's father. "My dad came in and told me that there were two long-haired gentlemen to see me. They wanted me to come back on bass because Werner couldn't get a British work permit. I abandoned my gig with Rhubarb to work with Gully Foyle, semi-pro initially. . . I still had six months to go on my course at Gray's so they decided to hang around Aberdeen until I could go full time with them.'

Hebridean gigs resulted from a disgruntled Oban Times letter complaining of the islands' status as a pop music desert. . . one wonders if the young Runrig MacDonald brothers witnessed those Gully Foyle performances, in all likelihood the first rock shows on North and South Uist. Billy recalls an episode on Skye when they bumped into fellow Caledonian rockers Spiggy Topes. "We had arrived as they were ready to leave, but they stayed to have a drink with us. Some time later we were sat outside the quayside pub on Portree harbour, pretty boozy. This baby in a pram started geein' it laldie, making a helluva racket. Spiggy Topes roadie Mick Kluczynski blearily asked the bairn's mother "Can it do that under water?' Ever the businessman, manager Bill Mowat piped up "Be quiet Mick, that's a potential future punter.' A gig at the Kyle of Lochalsh saw the boys setting up at the hall, the only source of electricity coming via a coin-operated meter. One sound check and a couple of quid later, the disapproving caretaker confirmed triumphantly that they would also have to feed the meter again to get juice for the gig itself. Billy says "We thought, bugger this for a game of soldiers. After we finished playing that night, we waited until he wisnae looking and screwed the meter on the way out.'

Publicity hand-outs deaclared "We used to be a freak out group with long and complicated guitar solos, a raging light show and an act that culminated in our speaker cabinets and cymbals being set on fire. We realised fully a year ago that we had just jumped on a bandwagon - and one that wouldn't last, at that. We re-arranged our whole act. It's not blues influenced and it's far from soul - but it's not trivial pop either. All our numbers have a heavy beat, and all are danceable. Many are our own compositions, and many are by writers we've met on our travels.'

Own compositions or not, neither the Morayshire police nor Baillie Douglas Simpson were impressed. The constabulary was called to Elgin's Bishopmill Hall at 9.30 one evening to investigate complaints about noise, and were assured by the venue's manager that he would get things quietened down. However the officers felt compelled to return when the promised hush was not forthcoming. The manager explained that Gully Foyle had ignored his pleas; he must have been Gullyble to think Stef would dampen his guitar flash in the first place. The resultant breach of the peace case was heard at Elgin police court. Burgh prosecutor Allan Horne described how the quartet were "impudent and abusive to the police when warned about the noise they were making. So loud that the officers found it impossible to carry out a conversation, even when they shouted at the top of their voices.' Well, wasn't that a surprise at a late Sixties progressive rock concert. Mr Horne also explained to the court how the band "struck up The Grand Old Duke of York as the police walked out of the hall.' For this heinous crime against humanity the lads were each fined two pounds. As if they cared - whilst the prosecutor, police, baillie and the P & J were making such a song and dance (When they were up they were up) the culprits were yet again back on the German autobahns. Robbie does recall however, that with promoters shying away, the band lost a lot of local work after this farce. Such is the power of the Press! . . . and Journal.

December of 1969 found Gully Foyle in London's Central Sound Studios laying down tracks for recording engineer Terry Kennedy (he had been involved with the recording aspirations of Tommy Dene and The Tremors earlier in the decade). At this time, Ian 'Clash' McLeod had been playing drums but when he was taken ill, Billy came to the rescue. Optimistic noises emerged from the camp to the effect that a single Purse Of Red Leather might be picked up by CBS. However these, and similar hopes that Kama Sutra-Buddha would release the album, all came to naught. Jim Scott having left the band, the vocalist for a successive European campaign was Jim Diamond, a Glaswegian who had been singing in clubs since he was 14. Jim had already been with Jade and Black Cat Bones. The latter blues outfit folded in London so Jim returned home, showing little interest in music for the next few months. It was actually his father who noticed a Glasgow Evening Times advert, from a band seeking a singer to travel Europe with them.

Jim tells of his introduction to Gully Foyle. "When my dad showed me the paper, I thought 'that'll do for me'. I went over to Edinburgh where I met Robbie and Stefan at Stef's mother's house in Portobello. We ran through a couple of numbers and I was in. The problem was that I didn't have the cash for my train back to Glasgow so I bummed the money off Robbie.'

Despite doubts from the Thurso duo that Jim would ever be seen again, the following Tuesday he returned to meet with them for the mid-winter journey to Aberdeen, where rehearsals were planned. Robbie travelled in the comparative luxury of the British Rail rattler, leaving Stefan and the new hand to hitchhike. Despite the snow outside, Jim had shown up without a coat - which was how, thanks to Stefan's mum, Jim Diamond took his first steps to glory on the North East beat dressed in an Edinburgh bus clippie's jacket, complete with badges. . . Jim defensively claims that he thought he looked 'quite hip' so attired, as they thumbed their way up the road. He had plenty time to think during this cold expedition. "When they said in the advert we would be travelling to Europe, I didnae realise they planned to do it the hard way.' He should have known better. . . ?

No regrets, though, about undertaking the trek as his first impression of Aberdeen has stayed with him. "We eventually got a lift in a petrol tanker. The seats were really high up, and I distinctly remember when we came over the top of the Stonehaven road, and clearly saw Aberdeen ahead. It was covered in snow and looked absolutely beautiful.'

If Jim's Arctic odyssey was a harsh introduction to rock 'n' roll domination à la Gully Foyle, the first band job he undertook in Aberdeen didn't help matters. Not rehearsing, writing or sourcing venues - but coating an old van with black paint. Paint It Black indeed and a wasted effort according to Robbie. "We had bought a real piece of scrap that simply wouldn't move, no matter what we tried. . . for all I know, it might still be lying there in Aberdeen.' Initially Jim stayed with Billy and his girlfriend before he and Robbie shared a flat. The band played warm-up gigs in readiness for the much anticipated continental tour.

Roughly concurrent with Gully Foyle readying themselves for Europe, Johnny Sutherland was fundamentally affected by tragic events in London. "The life went out of rock music when it went out of Jimi Hendrix. The rock community universally felt a great sense of loss. Gollum had a gig at the Station Hotel in Stonehaven the night after it happened. We played all the Hendrix stuff we knew and then played it again. An immensely sad occasion.' That sombre September Johnny packed away his Gibson and AC30. For the next three years he was an (un)civil servant, a tramp, a minstrel, a busker. . .

But for his prodigies Gully Foyle, Bandol in the South of France was an idyllic port of call at l'Enclume (The Anvil) club, owned by the proprietor of the local shoe shop. Jim: "He was a really nice guy who looked after us well but he simply didn't have a clue about the music business. We had a great time - three meals a day in any restaurant we chose, living in a beautiful place where we mostly lay on the beach. The club was packed on the opening night but it soon fell away to being busy only at the weekends. As he was paying wages to three bands (ourselves, Magnet, and Killing Floor) something had to give. We were the best so the others got the sack.'

However they were soon farmed out to other venues, mitigating losses at l'Enclume. Half way to a Marseilles gig they were told that they had been billed as Deep Purple. "We didnae know any of their material' says Jim, "but somehow we faked the gig, and got away with it. We were also seconded to a discotheque in St. Tropez, all great at the time but the Bandol dream ended when the owner went bankrupt. Then we hit reality in a big way.' This big reality came in the shape of Munich's Big Apple and Frankfurt's K52 clubs, playing to local German and GI audiences. "Long hours for little or no money, absolute slave labour' comments Jim. When they ran out of engagements even as unfulfilling as these, Gully Foyle were driven to deal with a gig-fixer by the name of Paul Vonk who called a meeting in Denmark to discuss a deal. Arriving in Copenhagen they found things not so wonderful, wonderful - Vonk wasn't there. Stranded in KBH without petrol for their van or the price of an Elephant beer between them. Jim remembers Stef shouting "Keep going, don't stop!' at roadie Mike Gordon as they approached European border posts. Robbie says "We were supposed to have these carnets - customs documents - to allow us to import and export our equipment in and out of different countries. Of course, we either hadn't bothered with, or couldn't afford, the paperwork. We had shot through one border post without them seeing us, but the officials on the gate house of the adjoining country were on the ball, and wouldn't let us in. They sent us back over to the other side - but as they hadn't seen us leave in the first place and didnae know what we were yabbing on about, they wouldn't let us in either. We were stuck in no man's land for hours. Eventually, they escorted us into the nearest town, where we forcibly abducted the first English speaker we could find. The idea was that he would translate, so we could get ourselves out of the mess. He was the local dentist and we hauled him off, still in his white coat, leaving some poor punter in the chair half-way though a wisdom tooth extraction. Later, an old and spicy episode saw Jim bribing a frontier guard with a bottle of after-shave (a Christmas present from Jim's mum). Jack Kerouac, eat your heart out!

Notwithstanding the hardships of this period, Jim reveals that these "were the best days of my life'. Yes, even the moonlight flit from Frankfurt. "We didnae have the money to pay for our digs so in the middle of the night, we were lowering our stuff out the windae on bits of rope. We had some daft idea that if we could clear the German border by morning, they couldnae touch us.' Eventually limping back into Aberdeen they found the P & J carrying reports not dissimilar to those which heralded the Strollers' Stratless return from Germany ten years before. "Gully Foyle back from European triumphs', "Belgian border guards were not offered Old Spice', and "Midnight flit was not required.'

Jim refers to Stefan, Robbie and Billy as being "brothers - it simply wasn't the same when Billy wasn't with us. The other drummers we had (and I emphasise, no disrespect to the blokes, they were smashing guys themselves and did their utmost with us), simply were not part of our family.' The Dunkirk spirit having seen them through their evacuation from Europe, they performed in Aberdeen as Pleasance, a drummerless acoustic trio playing the Treetops, the ABC Bowl and the Inverdon in the Shiprow. Jim says "We fair thought we were the thing with our close harmony vocals.' Robbie suggests that they were trying to bring 'quality acoustic rock' into the pub environment, rather than the then prevalent MOR material.

In this format they returned to London, having made an influential music business contact in the shape of Bob Halfin of Campbell Connelly Music. He had travelled to see the band play at the Caledonian Hotel in Inverness, and liking what he heard, brought them down to try out in the studio. Bob already had the right credentials, having co-composed the Max Bygraves heavy rock classic You're A Pink Toothbrush. No comment from your correspondent. It's a fact.

This second London sojourn saw the boys gigging at the Marquee and playing BBC radio sessions on Stevi Merik's show, performing a handful of band originals which formed the core of an album recorded at DJM in Denmark Street, with Billy back on board. Small fry, though. . . Having carted all their equipment inside the building, into the lift, down to the basement, out of the lift again and along a lengthy corridor. . . they were told to get it all off the premises, the studio was busy. Naturally hacked off at the situation, the band found out that the sitting tenant was the short podgy guy dressed in a black fedora hiding his already-receding hair, a long scarf, and Coca Cola-bottle glasses. Jim alone recognised the mystery man as an emerging singer-songwriter who was in the process of saving DJM's bacon, with his single Lady Samantha. Elton Hercules John, rising like a Rocket Man, leaving session work for My Dear Watson in his wake.

Despite being neglected by DJM the guys persevered with the album but found the label disinterested. Only months before, the Watsons' LP had met the same fate. Robbie says: "I played the acetate again recently - what strikes me now after all this time, is how Scottish it sounds, which is something we were not aware of at the time. Our inexperience in the studio really shows. They should have put a seasoned producer on the project to bring out the performance of our material, which I think wasn't bad. If you can imagine the rock thrust of the Who combined with complicated arrangements towards the Yes end of things - that's kind of where that album was. The engineer and producer DJM put on the job were both rookies, without the know-how to pull the project through.' Jim is more blunt in his appraisal "At the time, we were chuffed, we had recorded an album and we were going to be stars, all that stuff. When I listened to it some time afterwards, I thought "Mother of God that's a load of crap. Obviously too many heavy drugs going down.' You can take Jim Diamond out of Glasgow, but you can't take Glasgow out of Jim Diamond.

Unwarranted self-criticism? Perhaps the guys are too close to the work, even after a quarter of a century. The demos tell a different story to fresh ears. Shadows is a darkly brooding number, written by Stefan and Billy in Morocco. A dramatic rocker, its staccato instrumental opening leads into Jim's immediately identifiable vocal. Shadows creeping closer to me. . . the drum kit flailed maniacally by Billy who suggests that Roger was perhaps "a subliminal reference to Jim and his clippie's coat. Roger was a bus conductor on the early morning run'. Frantically paced with falsetto backing vocals, the middle eight is probably one of Robbie's 'Scottishness' references, a Caledonian hoe-down when Big Country were just twinkles in their daddies' sporrans. A blatant, tongue-in-cheek attempt at commercial pop, From Now On has a catchy sing-along chorus over a twice-removed Townsend-Moon-Entwhistle backing. If you can get an aural picture of The Rocking Berries transfused with heavy but melodic Thunderclap Newmanesque guitar then you've got If I Was A Rich Man. These tracks were way too good for the big acetate pile in the sky and even today they certainly stand on their own merits.

Back to an acoustic trio in London, circumstances contrived to bring their fraternal coalition to an end. "The pub rock scene in London was vastly different to Scotland's, with big venues and very little below that level' says Robbie, "We were living in different parts of the city and it seemed to get more difficult to get together to play.' Jim's memory is that "Stef was helping his dad out in a wee shop he had bought and I started doing solo stuff. But it wasn't a leaving situation as such, for any of us. The fire flickered on but eventually went out. In retrospect I feel that the band really died when Billy left (for short spells Denny Alexander and the onomatopoeic ex-Dixion Angel Ian 'Clash' McLeod, played drums. Carl Douglas was also bassist at times) but this was a really special time for me.' In 1975, there was talk of Stefan and Billy, along with Neal Smith and former Hedgehog Pie-man Dave Hepburn becoming Jim's London-based band. Treja-vu? Would the boys really be up to trying for a third time? Stef says "We were basically settled and working in Aberdeen and we didn't really fancy uprooting ourselves again.' Jim therefore formed Bandit with Jimmy Litherland, Cliff Williams and Graham Broad - this led him to work with the Godfather of British blues, Alexis Korner. . . subsequent super-group gigs with Carmine Appice and Earl Slick went un-recorded before he released an eponymous album on the Arista label. PhD, Jim's association with Tony Hymas and their album Is It Safe produced the first of many smashes I Won't Let You Down Again, a classic haunting piece of Euro-tinged pop. When asked about his experiences in the big time, he immediately differentiates between artistic acheivement and selling records. "When I started working with Alexis I felt that simply mixing in such circles gave me credibility, an accolade of a special kind in itself. I'm known to be a bit of a recluse. Even when I've been at number one in the charts, I won't go through the expected music bizz hoopla. I am proud of, and want to be judged only on my work, not on any image thing.' Even so, it is probably just as well that the Edinburgh clippie's uniform has stayed in the back of the wardrobe.

When Gully Foyle's fire eventually died, Robbie stayed in London where he auditioned for such 'name' bands as Roxy Music and Chicken Shack. . . with little success, as the years he had spent with GF had left him with a particular style of bass playing. He therefore made a conscious decision to "change from being a professional musician into one who made a living.' This new realism led to a Mecca ballroom residency and into a band called Cold Water Morning with whom he appeared on television's Opportunity Knocks. If you find the concept of Gully Foyle's bassist enduring the Opps Nox clapometer in a band named after a Neil Diamond song incongruous - read on, you aint seen nothin' yet. Having escaped from Zavaroni hell, Robbie put together Sunday Gage, a more conventional rock outfit began moving up the league. With Ricky Munro on drums, they were getting themselves noticed - a showcase gig was organised for them at the Roundhouse. Former Roulettes and Argent guitarist Russ Ballard, then an influential figure in production and A & R, was impressed with their demos. He showed up to evaluate the band's potential - but the London curse struck yet again. According to Robbie, Ricky went on a bender and couldn't play. The whole thing was a shambles. . . SNAFU. What would be the next logical step in Robbie's career: this former student of Gray's School of Art had, after all, laid his psychedelic bass patterns on freak-out rock heads from Caithness to Cologne. Just when the author began thinking "Now I've heard it all. . . ' In this long and curious journey through the annals of Northern rock history, yet another bolt from the blue. Or rather, from the bluebeat - is it not predicable that Robbie then played in Desmond Dekker's band? My ears are alight!

In 1973 Johnny Sutherland returned to the scene, picking up on a new generation of musicians whom he formed into Snark (Hunting Of The. . .) These were Pete Keddie, formerly with Prairie Wolf and Roadworks, Tommy Robertson, Stan Wolarz and Bob Leslie. For a period John McGlynn played drums before engaging in an acting career. In John Byrne's majestic TV series Tutti Frutti, McGlynn played Lachie, the Radio Buckie 229 metres MW disc jockey who shambolically interviewed the terminally hungover Danny McGlone and Bomba MacAteer at six short minutes after the big hour of six in the morning. Snark were Edinburgh-based new disciples (on average ten years younger than Sutherland himself) who made waves, albeit on a small, localised scale. However, Johnny's itchy feet again got the better of him. Slinging his acoustic over his shoulder he wandered throughout Morocco and Afghanistan. "Not so much the school of life more a higher university. I saw many, many things they don't tell you about in classrooms.'

The many influences (some of them musical) absorbed during these meanderings came back with Johnny in 1977, by which time he concentrated on his own music rather than worrying about performing to, and pleasing, an audience. In Wigan, his new band The Brothers had Ricky Munro on drums. One year on found Johnny in the mists of space thanks to the debatable delights of magic mushrooms, leading indirectly to his mutated strain of C & W music, incorporating his many and varied musical and psychological experiences. . . curiouser and curiouser. He then recruited yet another generation of musicians when he brought his nephews into The Wild Geese (the title clashed with another group of the same name, and had to be dropped). During the synthesised Eighties Sutherland recorded as The Auld Yin and Tartan Special. . . an old fella playing traditional whistle in front of Johnny's rock band. Yet another innovation: handed-down Scottish music, contemporised into the rock genre, several years before such an amalgam became fashionable.

In Aberdeen, Stefan, Billy and Neal Smith formed Drambo, an occasional acoustic trio Drambo at the ABC Bowl and at the Albany in Shiprow, owned at the time by George Leiper (himself an accomplished guitarist). Jim Diamond deputised at least once when Neal was ill and played a benefit with the guys in aid of a local youth detention centre. At the latter appearance, Jim met the New Zealand lady who was to become his wife. All things considered, he is pretty pleased with Aberdeen. "It has given me my best friends, my best times - and my wife.' Based in the South of England, he has fought through ill-advised contract-induced bad times and continues to produce quality top-20 albums, appearing sporadically in the singles charts with his unique distinctively crafted songs, neatly encapsulated by 1993's Jim Diamond Polydor CD. Given his affection for his Gully Foyle days, it is perhaps unsurprising that, during the latter part of 1994 he travelled North from Edinburgh and his Radio Forth show to sit in with Billy and Stefan's band at the Blue Lampie. During 1995 The Lemon Tree hosted his first gig in Aberdeen for twenty-odd years. You are welcome back anytime, Jim.

These days Robbie Manson edits videos in Norfolk, but also plays traditional R 'n' R with Mel Stevens and The Strollers. In Aberdeen, Stefan and Billy are The Barrelhouse Blues Band, a stonking slide-guitar electric blues combo, with George Leiper, Charlie Walker and Tam Murray. The intuition developed throughout Bill and Stef's many years together is glaringly obvious on their 1996 CD In Town, featuring 13 tracks performed with guts, emotion and the boys' self-evident enjoyment of Delta and Chicago blues. Mastered at Gush in California, and with glass-mastering and CD production at Data Pulse in Singapore, it puts the so-called big boys of British blues in the shade. And not an Armani suit in sight.

In Caithness a rock tradition, unarguably attributable to Sutherland, is typified by pub juke boxes stocked with Grateful Dead, Moby Grape and Neil Young. Successive waves of bands pick up this music and play it themselves. Johnny's own family have not escaped this indoctrination: for a period, he and his boy gigged and recorded as Sutherland And Son. Their 1990 album, recorded on 12- track analogue, unfortunately stalled financially before it got as far as record companies. Whilst he freely admits to his ensconcement in the drugs culture, its influence is far outweighed by the music. Currently this is 95% improvised and brings early Sixties jazz leanings (Eric Dolphy and Charlie Mingus) into a place where Hendrix might have been today had he still been with us. . . (something developmental from The Man's 1970 legacy, as distinct from most other covers of, let's say Purple Haze, which are predominantly copied note-for-note from Jimi's recorded gospel).

Johnny states that his music "is in the public domain. . . I make it available for anyone to hear, they can do what they want with it.' He runs a small recording studio in the lighthouse cottages at Dunnet Head, the most Northerly outpost of civilisation on the British mainland. If his plans come to fruition, his unambiguous single Smoke Up The Ganja / Free The Weed should be rolling up soon. . .

GULLY FOYLE

L-R Robbie, Stefan, Jim Scott, Billy

SERVICE COPY

Under the Summary Jurisdiction (Scotland) Act, 1954

In the POLICE COURT of the BURGH of ELGIN

The COMPLAINT of ALLAN MAXWELL HORNE, Burgh Prosecutor

WILLIAM ALLARDYCE, professional bandsman, 32 Huntington Road, Aberdeen.
STEFEN KACENBA, professional bandsman, 6/1 Coilladene House, Coilladene Drive, Edinburgh.
JAMES SCOTT, professional bandsman, 11 Elmbank Road, Aberdeen.
ROBERT MANSON, professional bandsman, 15 Princess Street, Thurso.

You are charged at the instance of the Complainer that on 2nd August, 1969, within the Bishopmill Hall, Grove Place, Bishopmill, in the Burgh of Elgin and County of Moray, YOU the said William Allardyce, Stefen Kacenba, James Scott and Robert Manson all members of the group known as 'Gully Foyle', DID play musical instruments and amplify the sound of said instruments in such a manner as to creat excessive noise and on being requested to abate said noise did refuse to do so and thus did cause annoyance and disturbance to the leiges and commit a Breach of the Peace.

.....(Sgd.) A.M. Horne................*Burgh Prosecutor.*

WARRANT TO CITE.

ELGIN,   5th September,   19 69

The Court assigns 29th September,   19 69 at 9.45 a.m.   within the

Burgh Police Court, Room 19, County Buildings, Elgin, as a diet in this case.

Chapter 7

The 25 year fade

In parallel with Gully Foyle's European and African conquests, a second Northern Scottish progressive rock outfit were setting the heather alight on the domestic Highlands and Islands circuit.

We have already discussed earlier Northern bands The Jam and Opium Trail. Other period combos in the Caithness area included The Web, Gale Force Eight and the delightfully titled, in a round-about, deathly sort of way, Zebidee's Morgue. Taking their name from the John Lennon-inspired leader of The Turds (Peter Cook's fictional running-gag rock group in Private Eye magazine), Spiggy Topes emerged in 1968 as a distillation of existing local combos. Formed by Thurso teenagers Johnny Gray on bass and Graham Walker on drums, the line up was completed by Roger Niven on lead guitar, and vocalist Dennis Thompson. Soon the latter was replaced by Marek Kluczynski, 'a multi-talented musician', according to the band's manager Bill Mowat. "He played harp well, was reasonable on sax, and his flute work was impressive.' Whilst Ian Anderson and Thijs Van Leer clearly popularised the flute within a rock music setting, Marek's style was unusual in that he played in harmony with the guitar.

The Caithness Courier's Tim Hunt column reported on the fortunes of Northern pop and rock groups, periodically receiving bulletins from Stefan Kocemba, full of Boys Own yarns of Just Us/Gully Foyle on their European and African adventures. Apart from being good copy the resultant newspaper articles provided parables for young up-and-coming musicians: effectively a Rough Guide through the pit-falls of life on the Rip Off Train. Bill also was also a stringer for such Sixties and Seventies Scottish pop publications as Shout and Transplant, wherein his Hunting About The North articles appeared. His early Spiggy Topes publicity made use of the place of birth of each member, a ruse to disguise their unfash-ionable Thurso residential status.

Parental pressure soon forced Roger and Graham to temporarily abandon their rock 'n' roll aspirations in favour of attending college. In came Glaswegian Arthur Farrel and Derek 'Corky' Weir from Airdrie, on lead guitar and drums respectively. Corky had been based in London but wanted out of the big city - hence his keenness to travel North to work with Spiggy Topes. Arthur had previously been with Glasgow groups The Argonauts and The Tardy Host.

Marek's brother Mick was the band's roadie: the story of how the Kluczynski clan became Invernessians is worth a book in itself. Kluczynski is the Polish word for locksmith, the trade by which the brothers' grandfather earned his living in Krakow. After the Russian revolution, he was deported to a Siberian labour camp where their father was born. Having attended school in Manchuria, he and his colleague Bruno travelled from Blagoveschensk into China upon the outbreak of World War II. They jour-neyed through dangerous territory, scene of heavy fighting of the tripartite Russian-Sino-Chinese war. British embassy authorities in Harbin, having accepted the young Poles' offer to enlist in the Allied army, directed them to Peking to muster with British forces there: a 700-mile trek undertaken mainly on foot.

Their odyssey next brought them to Hong Kong from whence they sailed just prior to its fall to the Japanese. Basic army training took place in North Africa, where the Second Polish Corps (later to cap-ture Monte Casino), was commanded by General Wladyslaw Anders. Due to the impressive educational standards amongst Polish servicemen, the ratio of officers to enlisted soldiers was incredibly high. This seeming absurdity, combined with their favourable experiences during the voyage from Hong Kong (the impressionable lads had never seen the sea before), changed their plans.

Volunteering instead to sign on for the Free Polish Navy (such as it was), their course was altered for the North East of Scotland and service on the Murmansk convoy. This eventually explained how the Kluczynski dynasty arrived in Aberdeen.

When the war ended Anders became leader of the 140,000 strong Free Polish community in Britain, including several thousands of Polish servicemen demobbed in the North East of Scotland. Those unwilling to return to their homeland (which had been magnanimously traded to Stalin under the Yalta and

Potsdam carve-ups), remained in Britain. Having met and married an Aberdeen lassie, Kluczynski Senior stayed in the city, as did his great friend Bruno. Both became adopted Torry trawlermen.

Bruno lost his life in the 1959 George Robb trawler tragedy, two miles from John O'Groats at the Stacks of Duncansby. Later Mr Kuczynski suffered a bad injury and was hospitalised in Klaksvig on the Faroe Islands. (Faroe would, in a strange turn of the cards, feature in the future career of his son, Marek). Funded by his injury compensation money, Mr K set up business in a corner-shop but was over-generous in allowing credit to customers. Well, we all know whatTorry's like for tick. Subsequently he worked in the dairy farming industry and the family migrated ever Northwards to Inverness, described by the young Ks as "the first place where we felt settled'.

Mick had messed about with radio from an early age, handled the gear for most Inverness bands, and roadied for the aromatically-named Sweet Soc. When approached to work with Spiggy Topes permanently, Mick abandoned his career in psychiatric nursing. Apart from carrying responsibility for the band's sound he also carried the band's equipment, took the gate money, occasionally fixed gigs and was general dogs-body. All for a fiver a week.

Mowat recalls Mick's determination that, from the outset, unplanned and unwelcome on-stage feedback would be prevented. This was symptomatic of his innate talent for electronic sound - one of his first recommendations to the band was not to purchase any new PA hardware. Instead he advised the acquisition of second-hand ex-MOD speaker equipment. His rationale was that military specifications were in excess of those in the commercial civilian market - thus Spiggy Topes appeared with equipment painted in military grey, an unfashionable contrast to the then prevalent groovy psychedelic spectrum of rainbow colours adorning other bands' hardware.

Mick's version: "I don't know about keeping feedback under control, we didn't have enough power to cause any. All we had were four, twelve-inch Selmer columns with 100 watts of power. It was all pretty rudimentary, basic stuff. The military equipment was Vortexian radio kit designed for two-way radio comms, with 35 watts per channel. I rescued it from a garage which caught fire, it was a helluva mess but I re-built it. Good, dependable stuff, it's quite possibly still lying in Inverness somewhere in working order.' Electrical spares were unknown, fabled items: "When our gear packed in, I cannibalised bits off the other bands' equipment' One appearance at Glasgow's Maryland Club with Beggars Opera saw them obliged to use the house sound system, banks of brand new, immaculate state-of-the-art white Marshall science. Repeated criticisms to the effect that Spiggy's sound didn't meet its usual high standard eventually brought Mick's exasperated response "What do you expect when we're playing through that f———g shite?' This sparked him to contemplate how the gear could be improved: he later sold some of his patented inventions to Marshall.

An inaugural gig had been arranged for the Wick Assembly Rooms, supporting teenybop sensations Love Affair. The latter's hit record Everlasting Love was recorded by session musicians: their live performances gained them a terrible reputation. When the Wick promoter discovered that Spiggy Topes intended bringing their own PA system with them, the implications of Love Affair being outclassed in volume as well as performance became a serious concern. So he cancelled what was to have been their first engagement which instead was re-arranged for the Halkirk near Thurso. With female pop music fans out in force screaming at Stevie Ellis in Nairn, a predominantly male audience turned out for Spiggy Topes' debut. Twenty minutes into the set the punters out-violenced Culloden Moor 1746, oak benches were tossed caber-fashion. Nevertheless, as Mick remembers "At the end of the night we had made 20 quid. That focused our attention on the money-making potential of what we were getting into.'

Innovatively self-managed Highlands and Islands gigs proved lucrative in previously unconsidered surroundings: they were probably the only rock band to play Fort William's Kilmallie Hall, use of the premises being granted by Mrs Allison, wife of the local doctor. Mick summarises the cash flow for these events "We could hire village halls from Orkney to Oban for ten bob including cups of tea and sandwiches, and charge 200 punters five bob each. Later I took some of my big mates with me as bouncers and there was still enough money to go round. . . when you consider 12 gigs in as many nights with the Watsons from Albert Bonici's agency, we were making good money for the time.' Despite being possibly the highest earning band in Scotland, they hedged their bets over recruiting a keyboards player. The sound would have benefitted (and Arthur Farrel had the ideal man waiting in the wings for six months) but the prospect of another slice coming out of the cake deterred them from making the commitment.

The first gig extraneous to the Highlands went down in Thorshavn, capital of the Faroe Islands. The band shared an Icelandair charter with footballers from Shetland, travelling to play Faroe in the North Atlantic Cup. . . Faroe were some years off competing in the larger European championships arena. As man walked on the moon for the first time in July of 1969, Faroe was still without a television service. Three years after its British release, the 1966 World Cup movie Goal ! (yes, bloody Geoff Hurst again) was showing at the Havnar Bio cinema. Spiggy Topes therefore provided a week's much-needed entertainment, being paid DDK 2.00 per ticket sold, with a minimum guaranteed 475 tickets each show. At the prevailing exchange rate of 20 Danish crowns to the pound, a night's work generated a respectable £47 10/-. "All the group's living expenses. . . including necessary meals' were paid by the promoter Mr Torgard, who also ran the local Loschen temperance lodge. He was singularly unimpressed with the boys' gift from Scotland, a bottle of duty-free malt whisky. Nonetheless, he brought the act back for another visit, when the Faroese pop public voted Spiggy Topes the World's Best Group, following in the illustrious footsteps of previous poll winners Steppenwolf and Taste.

Firmly committed to progressive rock, Spiggy Topes railed at their manager's suggestion of recording Painter Man, brought back to Scotland in Gully Foyle's repertoire from a Swiss tour with Creation, who made it a minor hit in 1966. The band dismissed the song as being too 'poppy' (Boney M carried it to the top-ten in 1979). Spiggy's music was "relatively straightforward and devoid of outrageous gimmicks - jazzy inclinations with a similar vibe to Spirit (Randy California's US West Coast combo) although they fast developed their own specific style.' The Faroe experience, however, introduced a different vein to their music. The local kids screamed all night long, and the adults danced the waltz, the only steps they knew. Thereafter, the band incorporated waltz rhythm in their rock setting, exemplified by Sailor Till The Day. And at all times, the music was presented clearly and powerfully: "What I remember is how loud they were' says contemporary Aberdeen drummer Graham Spry.

Spiggy Topes may have been the inventors of Celtic (with a K) rock, as in White Ghost written about the Brahn Seer. A Moment Fine typified Johnny Gray's developing composing capabilities, its inspiration being his then-sweetheart Janis Kelly. Lead soprano with the English National Opera, she has in recent years recorded a series of albums based upon music featured in the Inspector Morse television series, the first British operatic diva to sell in excess of a million albums. She is now married to a crab fisherman she met in Anchorage, Alaska. How shellfish of her. . .

Gray's resources seem to have been allocated equally to music and romance. Typical twisted trysts involved Curved Air vocalist Sonja Kristina and Josephine Barker. Jo's father was then Chancellor Of The Exchequer Anthony Perrinott Lysburg Barber, later to become life peer Baron Wentbridge. If Johnny engaged in nocturnal activities at 11 Downing Street, he may well have physically bumped into the furtive figure of fellow Northern rocking bassist Jimmy Bain, plucking the strings of Barber's other daughter, Louise. The level of daddy's annoyance may be guaged by an esoteric taxation introduced in one of his budgets. Income tax at 315%, applicable only to long-haired bass players with Scottish accents.

Drummer Corky Weir was married to American Nicole, daughter of French writer Charles Tacet. Nicole was a backing vocalist with Joe Cocker, Neil Young and former Spencer Davis, Traffic and Blind Faith vocalist Steve Winwood. . . whom she married after her divorce from Corky.

Live engagements from Shetland to Gretna via Orkney included the inaugural Aviemore winter festival, sharing the bill with Gully Foyle. The latter and My Dear Watson travelled many Northern rock 'n' roll miles with the Topes. Mick's recollection is that "We had as much work as we could handle, in winter our problem lay in getting to the gigs through the snow.'

In and around Aberdeen (where the band lived on the Nigg caravan site, associating with Torry hopefuls Twighlight Zone), engagements were undertaken through Gordon Hardie's Stag Entertainments Agency. A typical appearance at Maud Village Hall, for the amateur football team's dance, saw Gordon collect his standard 15% of the band's £30 fee. The show was praised in broad Doric by the venue's caretaker: "Ye maun nae be a bad group kis there wis nae fechtin the nicht.'

In the Morayshire, Inverurie and Carlisle areas, promotions were arranged by Albert Bonici, Bert Ewen and Richard Jefferson respectively. Edinburgh and Dundee were economic no-go areas. "We didn't bother because the money was rubbish. Bay City Roller clones were playing for sweeties.' Glasgow work came through John McGlone and Brian Adams' Intercity Entertainments, including a support appearance to Scottish debutantes Deep Purple at Sauchiehall Street's Electric Garden. A typical Glasgow Saturday demanded a lunch time set at the Burn's Howff, followed by an evening students' do, before a final late night blast at the Picasso Club. Billed on high-visibility, fluorescent day-glo posters as providing 'original quality progressive rock', the band agreed to play an Easterhouse benefit gig in aid of Frankie Vaughan's crusade against gang warfare in Glasgow. The kick-stepping crooner had organised a weapons amnesty and improved youth club facilities in the sprawling housing estate.

Just before show time, Marek discovered why they, in particular, had been approached in the first place. Local bands were too scared to play. He cracked mid-way through an Elton John song and stopped singing, not knowing with which foot the audience might kick him if they reacted to Elton's lyric My Rosary Is Broken.

Nairn's Ballerina Ballroom was the venue for a support spot to Status Quo who were then charting with Down The Dustpipe. On stage the number's harp solo was played, not very well, by a roadie. The Spiggys ensured that they started their own set with Marek blowing his usual excellent harp performance, totally outclassing Quo: stick that down your dustpipe!

DJ David Christian had met the band met in Faroe and began featuring them on his Radio Luxembourg programme. Ben Lyons, the Scottish controller of Radio One, also gave the band coverage. The station broadcast a handful of live Spiggy Topes performances, some from Aberdeen's Beach Ballroom with My Dear Watson. Songs from the Aberdeen shows included Johnny's First Time Loser and the aforementioned White Ghost. During its monopolist phase between the outlawing of the offshore pirates and the advent of commercial stations, Radio One regularly attracted an audience of between 20 and 25 million listeners.

These shows were therefore important in respect of raising the band's profile - although the opportunity to participate almost slipped away, as Bill relates. "I had a late night call from the BBC, desperate for the band to fill in at the last minute. Vanity Fare, in the charts with that daft pop song Hitchin' A Ride, pulled out with little notice, leaving a gap in the programme. However, our lads were already travelling to do some work in Orkney. I phoned the police and asked them to intercept them as they went to board the ferry, with instructions to contact me straight away.' ("Oh no, what do the tarry hats' want' from the band, followed by enormous sighs of relief). A different situation admittedly, but similarities exist with Gully Foyle being pulled in by the Moroccan CID on behalf of Prince Moulay Abdullah. By way of an apology to Orcadians for having cancelled the visit in favour of the radio show, the band played a number "specially for Liz Groat at the Albert Hotel, Kirkwall' This live, nation-wide radio dedication was a talking point in itself on Orkney. The band ensured that they got over to the islands for the following night. The gig proved so popular after the radio plug that people were turned away at the door.

A subsequent 24-hour voyage in a force nine gale from Orkney to Shetland resulted in the band of off-colour Highlanders gingerly crawling off the boat in Lerwick. Rocking out for their anticipatory Shetland audience was damned difficult: not only were the band's hearts not in it, the contents of their stomachs were still feeding fish off the Fair Isle.

December 1969 and the band are in London, performing at the Marquee and demo-ing tracks for Concord records, an offshoot of Campbell Connelly Music publishers. A single was scheduled for release the following February. The introductions for this venture were made by Bob Halfin, the song plugger who also brought Gully Foyle to London. Bob was a Jew who fought in the International Brigade against Franco's fascist forces during the Spanish civil war and then served in the Royal Navy in World War II. His Navy service took him up to the Hebrides and his writing Lovely Stornoway (a hit of sorts for Calum Kennedy. . . you may recall that other popular ditty I can sing like Calum Kennedy, wish to Christ I knew the remedy). Bob's other song writing triumph You're A Pink Toothbrush may not have won any trophies, but he didn't get the plaque. His son Ross is now a major-league rock photographer in the USA. During these Concord sessions, Jimmy Johnstone - owner of Grampian Records in Wick, also travelled to London, taking with him rudimentary Spiggy Topes demos recorded at his premises. Later, his meeting with Campbell Connelly's managing director Roy Berry led ultimately to Wick Records becoming a major manufacturer of pre-recorded cassettes, primarily for the European market: their workforce recently exceeded 100 persons.

The A side of the proposed single was 'a haunting instrumental' Love In The Wind, written by Dave Humphries, a London recording engineer. The B side was Mr Sullivan, an Arthur Farrel number. The project was produced, and was supposedly to be sold on to a major label, by a former member of Joe Brown's Bruvvers named Johnny 'Bev' Beveridge. The latter, co-composer of Brown's hit A Picture Of You, was apparently well-connected with the Philips record company. His connections worked themselves loose and Love In The Wind blew itself out. For later London sessions (produced by Amen Corner sax-ophonist Mike Smith) a bottle of malt whisky was the negotiated fee. . . was it the same one the Faroese tee-totaller turned down? These tracks were bent and shaped only as far as demo stage and were there-after lost, never to be issued on vinyl. . . or were they? We shall return to the subject later. . . a quarter of a century later, give or take a few months.

The band had pre-arranged to play Midlands' gigs en route to London to finance the journey. A few nights earlier they shared the billing at a Dingwall date with Slade. Noddy and the lads invited the Spiggy tribe to a party in Wolverhampton two nights hence. However, having arrived at the Bedford Hotel in Wolverhampton the Scots' entrance into the bar was greeted by an acquaintance from Inverness, a gas fitter piping up the Midlands to North Sea gas. "Kluczynski and Mowat! What the f—k are you doing here?' A couple of celebratory re-union pints developed into a helluva session and they never made it to Slade's party.

During another English sabbatical a substantial £100 was slapped on the table for a Barnsley Christmas Eve bash. However, already committed to Albert Bonici to appear at Elgin Town Hall (with My Dear Watson and Writing On The Wall), they simply wouldn't miss the Moray bash for all the tea in Yorkshire. Indeed, Bonici reputedly expressed a desire to manage Spiggys, but was already financially committed to the Watsons.

In London, rock manager Clifford Davies was having trouble with his principal money-makers Fleetwood Mac. Their hedonistic lifestyle, combined with Peter Green's tragic schizophrenia (exacerbat-ed by LSD shrapnel) foretold of a potential collapse of Davies' star attractions. He looked around for an act to fill any future void, focussing on a vocalist already on his books. From the British blues/soul holler school, but with his Rebel Rouser chart days behind him, Cliff Bennett's current band was Toe Fat. Not the outfit to solve Davies' perceived problems, so Bennett was recommended to source a new line-up. At Mother's Club in Beauly Bennett decided he would start by replacing his drummer, Lee Kerslake. Attempts to recruit Spiggy Topes' Corky Weir were rebuffed. "No way. You take us as a package, all or nothing.'

Soon Spiggy Topes were transformed into Rebellion, with Bennett as lead vocalist and Marek as second singer. This meant a move to London, which didn't suit Arthur. . . he quit and returned to Glasgow where he bought a taxi. His spot was filled by Robert ''Smiggy'' Smith, formerly lead guitarist with The Embers, Three's A Crowd and Writing On The Wall. Not that any of this worried Toe Fat's ex- guitarist Ken Hensley or the sacked Kerslake: both finished up with the mega-selling Uriah Heep. Spiggy Topes-Rebellion were now able to bring in a long desired keyboards player, in the person of Lou Martin from Belfast.

Mick Kluczynski vividly recalls how the band sat down with Davies to "sign away their souls for a hundred quid each', a down-payment on their CBS Rebellion LP and a single, Jerry Reed's Amos Moses. Bennett said "The album was recorded on a budget of three grand, and therefore wasn't very good.' Lack of money and recording haste saw Rebellion selling only between 8,000 and 9,000 copies, the majority being shifted in all probability to fans in Scotland. The Clifford Davies deal would have worked if the boys had played the club and cabaret game, behaved themselves and picked up decent wages for their trou-ble. Events did not, however, follow the script.

Whilst the Scots were comparatively cheap for Davies to recruit and run, the arrival of Curved Air in his stable (with no demands for a signing-on fee and an existing track record of sorts) spelled the end for the boys. . . Rebellion's promotional budget was diverted to Curved Air. Arriving in London in March of 1970, it took only six months to record the LP and play some promotional gigs before becoming totally disolussioned with the whole set-up. The Rebellion was quelled by the year end. Despite frequent visits to London, Bill Mowat still didn't know who he could and couldn't trust.

The Davies' episode spelled the end for Spiggy Topes as a working unit but conversely opened very big doors for Mick Kluczynski. He was to stay with Davies for seven years. . . early in the piece, Mick met Chris Adamson who was involved with Peter Green's Fleetwood Mac. Once he identified Mick's background, Adamson felt it would be possible to get him a job on Pink Floyd's road crew for a forthcoming tour. Adamson went off on the road with The Byrds, followed by a Grapefruit - Herd pop package, leaving Mick to fill in his time and pockets by doing landscape gardening work, not even thinking about Chris' employment idea. The latter's return brought with it confirmation that Mick would indeed be hitting the road (and Arnold Layne) after Christmas of 1970. At the time Mick was unappreciative of what the Floyd experience was to bring:'Obviously I had heard of them, but really only the early pop singles like See Emily Play. When I joined up, they were touring on the back of the Atom Heart Mother album - the one with the cow on the cover. Initially, all I did was to hump gear in and out of places, but gradually I was able to progress into a more technological thing.'

Whilst PA manufacturers such as WEM and Marshall serviced and stored equipment belonging to the major bands of the day, (Floyd, The Rolling Stones, ELP and Led Zeppelin) they were not over keen on doing so. Their warehouses were full of band gear, with little space left for their own hardware, which they either sold or rented into the rock market place.

Access to the equipment during storage periods between tours was therefore problematic for band's technicians and roadies - upgrading and development was difficult. Mick was able to ascend electronically because Floyd held their PA systems in their own warehouse: he increasingly came up with improvements and inventions. He eventually fullfilled the demanding role of Pink Floyd's production manager, with total responsibility for equipment, road personnel, travel arrangements, contracts and settlements. All of this was undertaken for a weekly wage, with little time off. Whilst the Floyd themselves toured only six or seven months every couple of years, guitarist Dave Gilmour would frequently lend out their gear to other bands. The equipment was of no value to the lendee without someone who understood it and could operate it - so Mick was also lent out as part of Gilmour's generosity, Queen at Hyde Park being one such third-party gig. He managed only two holidays in nine years.

In 1976 Kluczynski branched out into freelancing on a tour-by-tour regime, soon realising he was able to increase his earnings on this sporadic routine. In short, more money for less work. Early self-employment included Montreal's Olympics stadium production, an eight-week US tour of with Texan albino blues guitarist Johnny Winter. . . and on it went. Mick remained in the States throughout the late-Seventies and missed out on the plukey British punk blast. Returning to Blighty in 1981, he encountered a band equipped with the talent and the make-up to survive punk's ephemeral safety-pin stage. Hence he produced gigs and major festival appearances by those gurus of gloom The Cure. Mick's boast-list soon included Sting, Darryl Hall and John Oates, The Fabulous Thunderbirds and Peter Tosh. By this time his clients were to be found in rock's Who's Who as distinct from his hard Highlands and Islands days. Back then it was simply. . . Who?

Whilst his business remained centred in UK and Scandinavian-based rock music, Mick diversified into presentations for the Classical Spectaculars company and for the London Chamber Orchestra. A chance meeting with a guy involved in conferences and trade fairs prompted further diffusion into boxing matches, and the World Student Games in Sheffield. Mick also produced the public celebrations of the Duke Of Edinburgh's seventieth birthday, the LCO in Geneva and a Light The Darkness fund-raising event for the Red Cross. He next secured the prestigious and demanding presentation of a spectacular from Red Square to a live audience of between 80,000 and 100,000 people: a logistical nightmare beyond compare, he hauled 42 truck loads of equipment from the UK and Western Europe into Moscow, for three nights of classical and operatic music. Mick now runs his own London-based company, working internationally. A further feather in his already well-decorated war-bonnet came with his producing the 1995 and 1996 Brit Awards, laying the ghosts of fiascos past (Fox and Fleetwood spring to mind). The 1995 VE Day fiftieth anniversary bash in Hyde Park was also an MJK stage production.

Brother Marek's retreat from the Rebellion saw him also remain in London, where he encountered Andy Roberts and Bill Hatje (a Fort Augustustian former member of Gollum The Underdog). Each composed music, and an audition brought in a bass player, also writing his own material. Different styles and tastes, producing an ecclectic and talented musical mix. Bill and Andy already had a publishing contract. Under the name Summer, the band's demos brought Marek's songs to their company's attention.

Approaching Clifford Davies, attempting to buy out Kluczynski's contract. . . problems. The secretaries at the two companies fell out. End of negotiations, because the typists didn't get on and Marek finished hand-cuffed to a dead contract. Thus Summer endured exactly that long: come the Autumn, Marek took on a 'real' job (meaning a job with regular money, sleeping in his own bed, and without endless all-night, every-night dangerous travel in dodgy vans).

"When you don't have anything, you don't need it. But when a steady supply of cash comes into your life, you get used to that as well.' Marek Kluczynski hasn't played since: but has he finally scratched that rock 'n' roll itch which drove him crazy in the first place? No chance. "Every time I hear a great guitar line or catch something new and special on the radio, it drives me just as daft as it ever did. The difference now is that I am just an avid listener, with catholic tastes. . . I'm just as likely to dig music from Africa or South America as mainstream rock.' Marek displays the same healthy disregard for current pop music he showed when poo-pooing Bill's Painter Man suggestion 26 years ago. "I'm still a snob.' He is also quick to shine the Spiggy Topes spotlight in a previously unlit corner. "Bill Mowat was the man without whom we would never have got past a few wee rehearsals.'

What of those original members Roger Niven and Graham Walker, both of whom bailed out to further their educations? Lost to music, d'you think?

Roger (co-founder of Northern rock-traditionalist fusionists Wolfstone, with Dave Foster) is an accomplished classical guitarist: he established the Scottish International Guitar Festival (an annual residential teaching course for classical guitar). As well as his lute playing with Coronach - a Highland based group specialising in renaissance music - he has formed a traditional but beaty Scottish duo, The Rant. Roger's partner is Andy Munro, now a well-known day time TV kiddie's entertainer, Mr Boom. Late in 1994, The Rant released a CD entitled Mixing It on the Celtic Music label, recorded at Rowan Studios in Ardross. The album's title is so apt - good time guitar led Caledonian rock with a solid bass line, high energy reels and jigs, 17th Century Scottish lute music, traditional American airs, and a buoyant take on Joe South's The Games People Play. In short, Hogmanay music for the whole year and you don't have to be half-canned to enjoy it. Cover art on the CD is the work of Dick Levens, former member of The Talismen and The Blend, running his own Orcadian graphics design company.

Mixing It's producer is Dave Foster (Wolfstone co-founder), during the Sixties a member of The Warriors from Liverpool, along with Jon Anderson and Tony Kaye. This group (finalists in the British beat competition of 1964 along with The Copycats), worked the German circuit extensively. When The Warriors demobbed Foster, Kaye and Anderson went to London individually looking for new engagements. The latter two initially formed Mabel Greer's Toyshop (which we shall visit later) before founding Yes and recording Dave's compositions, notably Time And A Word, Sweet Dreams and Yours Is No Disgrace. Kaye subsequently worked as Badger with Foster, King Crimson's Ian Wallace and Roy Dyke (he of Ashton, Gardner and. . .) After touring Europe and the USA and recording the cult album One Live Badger, Dave met his wife who is from Ardross where he relocated to and established his recording studio. Dave had the elevating experience of being stuck in a lift with Jimi Hendrix, where the guitarist from Seattle and outer space introduced Dave to LSD for the first time. . . going up?

Club and chart dance updates of Appalachian hillbilly and Celtic hootenany music from Red Nex and The Grid got The Rant to thinking "We can do this stuff better and more authentically'. . . which resulted in their white label single Rantin'. After trying unsuccessfully to look inconspicuous in a night club (armed with a stop-watch, checking out the BPM) of popular dance cuts, they went off and unearthed an old Shetland tune Spooda Skerry which they reworked almost beyond recognition as Rantin' : it kicks arse good 'n proper. A Europe-wide deal for the single was under negotiation. However, one wonders how kindly the Beeb will take to seagulls dropping deposits on the Top Of The Pops stage. They probably know they've got enough shite on the show already.

Graham Walker re-appeared on the early Seventies Aberdeen progressive rock scene, with Johnny Sutherland in Gollum The Underdog. . . Everybody's Tolkein At Me? A full-time professional since completing college in Aberdeen, he recently gigged with former Jethro Tull and Blodwyn Pig guitarist Mick Abrahams and in 1993 he played drums for short-lived Inverness teenage band Jumpin' The Gunn. Forming part of Gary Moore's Midnight Blues Band for the After Hours and Still Got The Blues albums (the latter selling over four million copies) and 1995's Peter Green tribute LP Blues For Greenie, Walker has also fulfilled ambitions nurtured since his early teens. Graham performed with the not-inconsiderably talented B.B.King on an MTV special. . . hobnobbing in the higher echelons of contemporary blues. . . Woke up this morning baby, had them Dounreay decommissioning blues. . . continued with Albert King, Buddy Guy and Albert Collins. At a Musicians' Union benefit at London's Hammersmith Odeon, he appeared with The Rolling Stones. And somehow he finds time for television-radio music and jingles.

Guitarist Arthur Farrel now runs a driving school in Glasgow where his two sons are following in dad's musical footsteps. One of the Farrel boys was the local young musician of the year, the other is on an HND course in sound engineering at Stowe College. Lou Martin, the late Rebellion recruit, subsequently joined Rory Gallacher's band. Most recently he has been part of Blues 'n' Trouble, one of the country's hardest working live bands, led by Fraserburgh's John Bruce.

Johnny Gray has worked steadily during the post-Spiggy Topes years. He was involved with sometime Thin Lizzy guitarist Brian Robertson in a band called Heidi, and also played with Curtis Knight, the New York guitarist who made a life time career out of his association with Jimi Hendrix in the Sixties (prior to the Electric Gypsy's move to England and world fame).

Knight came to the UK, signed a lucrative publishing deal with Essex Music and put a band together to perform live dates. In the company of Scottish guitarist Ian Sorbie, Johnny Gray remembers that "We spent a long time rehearsing and writing together but we always had to chase him hard to get our money. Ian and I wrote one of the two singles with virtually no input from Knight. When it was released, the composing credit mentioned neither of us, only him. . . and that was just about enough for me. Nobody warned us about Knight's stage routine. . . we had worked hard at putting a decent sound together. We treated our music pretty seriously. Curtis came from that New York street-sharp background, and he also had something in his brain about actually being a Red Indian. That first gig was in Nottingham where we started up on stage without Knight. It was something like Gimme Some Lovin' and I looked over my shoulder to see him come on, dressed in war paint, an Indian head-dress, the whole bit. Then he went into a war dance. I thought "Na, this isnae for me.' So I quit after that first show. I heard later that he took another set of guys to Europe then bailed out back to The States leaving them stranded and skint.'

One of Johnny's other groups, AWOL, included Lossiemouth-based Glaswegian Jerry Eadie (later a roadie for Led Zeppelin), former Agatha's Moment Andy Roberts and Zimbabwean Ivor Rubenstein. Eadie and Gray were both signed to publishing deals by New Acme Music and recorded an album on Ronnie Laine's mobile studio at Atlanta Rehearsal rooms in North London. The LP was primarily produced by Bob Potter, fresh from his work on Marianne Faithfull's Broken English album, although the musicians also produced some material themselves. Paper Music (owned by Lulu's brother Billy Lawrie and Laurence Ronson, younger brother of insider-dealer Gerald) were desperate to push AWOL in the USA, body-swerving the post-punk UK scene. However, to quote Booker T. Jones and William Bell If it wasn't for bad luck, I wouldn't have no luck at all: Paper Music were mid-litigation with New Acme. . . when their disagreement couldn't be resolved, AWOL were dropped faster than the hot tattie Frankie Milne hadnae seen in ages in Germany. Johnny says "this virtually tore the heart out of the band. . . we folded shortly thereafter.'

Today, Johnny forms half of Crooked Jack, probably the country's busiest Scottish folky-ceilidh duo. Their participation in Aberdeen's Union Street bicentenary celebrations was followed in 1994 by their single Dancing In The Streets Of Raith which marked the wee Rovers' League Cup triumph over Celtic. Indeed, Johnny has tackled football songs with relish, witness his previous Raith epic Blues Run The Game and for those of a jammy persuasion, We Are The Hearts.

We now return to the Scottish North in 1970 where Johnny and the guys were filling in time before Cliff Bennett's arrival for Rebellion gigs. In Inverness they hung out at the flat of their hitherto manager Bill Mowat. With the weekend fast approaching Bill planned on going away for a few days. Knowing full-well how this crowd (or rather, didn't) behave, he told them to find another flop-house. Bill's neighbour was Carole Currie, a Scottish-born Eurasian lady who had moved to the Highlands from Port Glasgow. He asked her to keep an eye on his home. Fine, until Saturday night when a boozy Johnny Gray invited a pub load of reprobates back to the missing Mowat's abode for a party (Johnny had a spare key tucked in the pocket of his Levis). In full and noisy swing the party was interrupted by a whirlwindesque Carole who switched the sounds off and told the revellers "Tidy the place up NOW and then leave.' An argument culminated in her calling the police, who arrested those obstinate die-hards, Johnny included, who refused to depart peaceably. The bad lads spent the rest of the night in police cells before being released next morning, suitably ticked-off and hungover, cursing the over-zealous Miss Currie.

Twenty-five years down the line in January of 1995, with a song in their hearts, haggis-flavoured condoms in their kit bags and an Alexander Fleming-inspired prescription in their pockets, Crooked Jack jetted off from Kirkcaldy (where linoleum is made because they've got a flair for it) to the appropriately named Bangkok. There they performed storming Burns night gigs at the Royal Orchid Sheraton Hotel for the Unocal petroleum company. How well the chieftain o' the puddin' race travelled to South-East Asia is a matter of conjecture. However their post-gig residents' bar question to a female audience member "Which part of Asia do you come from ?' brought the reply "Greenock, but I've been over here for years now.' It should be borne in mind that the official population of Bangkok is 7.5 million, but unofficial esti- mates are nearer to 10 million people. This magatrolpolis appears in The Guinness Book Of Records as suffering the world's longest and slowest traffic jams. Lots of people to bump into, not far off twice the population of Scotland.

Some time and several drinks elapsed before Bill Mowat's name ghosted eerily into the conver- sation. Thinking at first that the Sheraton's five-star air conditioning couldn't cope with the tropical Thai humidity, a sticky, disbelieving sweat of recognition gradually formed on Johnny's forehead. This was the very same Carol Currie (now Carol Aswar) who had him nicked in Inverness all that time ago. After she threatened to call the police if Crooked Jack didn't keep the noise down, they had a laugh about the sit- uation: Carol ensured they were well looked-after for the rest of their stay.

You might remember that we previously touched on the Spiggy Topes numbers recorded at dif- ferent London sessions in the late Sxties, seemingly destined for that great demo tape box in the sky, in the company of Tommy Dene's Kelly and My Dear Watson's lost album. Imagine the author's incredulity on discovering a bootleg album issued in the summer of 1993 in Pennsylvania USA entitled A Bucket Full Of Rubbish. This LP, a limited run of 1,000 copies on the Grants label, brought daylight to obscure previ- ously-unreleased tracks from various Sixties and Seventies progressive bands, including Tomorrow, The Four Leafed Clovers and the post-Warriors pre-Yes Mabel Greer's Toyshop. The tapes were purchased from a London market stall for 50 pence each, being saved from the garbage skip literally by hours. Hence the album's title.

Joy of joys to unearth four long-forgotten Spiggy Topes tracks, the origins of which lie in Wick's Grampian Studios and in the London sessions. A review of this material by Mike Stax in his San Diego based freak-beat fanzine Ugly Things suggests "My instincts tell me it was cooked up by bearded, welling- ton boot-wearing ex-students in an English farmhouse around 1969.' Close Mike, but no cigar. First up is The Weavers' (Come Away) Melinda, a minor UK hit for Barry St. John in December of 1965 but better remembered for Tim Rose's cover. Timed at over five minutes this take has a 'work in progress' feel, indicative of its early Wick origins. Paced somewhat disjointedly, the ideas are obviously there but the muddy mix do them no favours, with Arthur's wah-wah guitar over-controlled. Perhaps too much of every- thing, lacking specific focus: better production could have given it the direction it screams out for. My Only Chance Is You is a relaxed, pastoral, jazzy piece. The instrumental Love In The Wind starts slowly and builds rapidly to impressive guitar and flute interplay. This could oh-so easily have been pumped up into something special. Finally, Arthur Farrel's Mr Sullivan is a rocky pop number with an infectious sing-along chorus. With more catchy hooks than a fishing tackle shop, it grooves on into the fade. . . which lasted 25 years.

After the Bucket Full tracks were resuscitated from their long coma, an English record label com- mitted itself to a complete album of vintage Northern groovyness. The LP will be on shiny black, heavy vinyl (none of your lightweight silvered rainbow laser technology here, thank you very much). Thus, the original quality progressive rock sleuths are a-sifting through dusty tapes, in a Bermuda-ish triangle between Caithness, Thorshavn and London. Keeping to the spirit of A Bucket Full Of Rubbish, the work- ing title for the new long-player is Scuba Diving On A Sewage Farm: Going Through The Motions With Spiggy Topes and The Turds.

SPIGGY TOPES
L-R Marek, Johnny, Corky, Arthur

SHORT LIVED REBELLION
L-R Cliff Bennett, Smiggy, Marek, Corky, Johnny

Chapter 8

Freshly caught - Lemon Soul and Albert Fish

Gully Foyle tramped along Europe's autobahns and Morocco's wadis, engaging in satanic rites and eating sheeps' eyes at desert palaces. . . Spiggy Topes freaked out from Forfar to the Faroes. . . In Aberdeen, polarised heavy rock heads and Stax-Atlantic soul men faced each other across narrow divides, at gigs by two much loved city combos. The tie-dyed, great-coated unwashed were championed by Albert Fish, whilst devotees of the Wicked Pickett and Otis Redding were catered for by Lemon Soul. Despite their common musical Mississippi Delta and Chicago South Side blues origins, any symbiosis had gone, as these popular styles fractionalised into the disparate rival factions of progressive guitar-based rock, and horn-driven soul.

Trevor Hart screamed I am the god of. . . as he brought us The Fire, before Albert Fish appeared in 1967, taking their name from a Victorian mass murderer. Both The Fire and Albert Fish had Keith Milne on guitar, Graham Ogston on drums, Sandy Smart on bass, Doug Smith on guitar, with Trevor on vocals and keyboards. Playing material at the progressive end of the blues 'n' rock scale (Cream and Jimi Hendrix), inspired by a Pink Floyd TV appearance, they introduced psychedelic slide light shows to Aberdeen. Groovy, amoebaic images were projected on to pub walls by Mal's brother Duncan 'Dutch' Strachan.

Albert Fish regularly packed out the Beach Ballroom, the University Union, the Gaiety on the Beach Prom, and all known civilisation between Inverurie and Keith. Featuring welly boots and strobe lights in their stage act, the band's status was officially recognised when Aberdeen City Council booked them for a Summer Union Terrace Gardens gig. Quite an achievement in itself, as Scottish country dance teuchter bands had previously entertained at these al fresco hoolies. An interminable heat wave (through the haze of days past, this seemed normal in the halcyon days of youth: as Neil Young would have it, when time was just a joke. . . a massive audience turned out. However a council jobsworth, not a progressive blues aficionado, judged that they were "affa loud, fit a racket', pulling the plug on the band, mid-number. From thunderous, amp-melting power-blues to deafening silence. What the f-k was going on? To set this incident in a global context, remember that, extraneous to the cosy confines of Aberdeen, college campuses throughout the world were on fire: Molotov cocktails were the drink du jour. Student-worker revolutionaries took to the barricades, rioting in the streets of the Western world. The censorious, fascist act of de-powering the proletariat's heroes Albert Fish spurred a cataclysmic uproar from the teeming Union Terrace weekend hippies: they sent letters of complaint to the Press and Journal.

When the Fish went off, Trevor's follow-up band, starring John Proctor, Mal Strachan (brother of the light show technician), Harry McFarlane, Robert Wilson, and Bill 'Binner' Innes, secured a residency at the Treetops Hotel. A young female fan occasionally turned up at rehearsals to hang out and play flute. Her name was Annie Lennox, never heard of since. A word of explanation of how Bill Innes acquired the moniker 'Binner'. . . As a pupil of the Aberdeen Academy in Belmont Street, he regularly helped the school dinner wifies carry the bins outside, thus ensuring that he received preferential treatment when seconds and thirds were up for grabs. By the early Seventies this band developed into Whitehart, shaking Rosemount to its sturdy granite foundations from the Silver Slipper, and scaring the occupants of the Pets' Pantry from the Harriet Street Bar. Aberdeen's supergroup of the time, its members emanated from other famous city combos. With Trevor were Bobby White on lead guitar and vocals, ex-Cat Squirrel Richard Grant on lead vocals, Malcolm Bruce on bass and vocals, and ex-Cousin Mary drummer Martin Pottinger. Related to Whitehart were Bruce-Hart, an occasional band that featured adventurous horn arrangements. In a courageous and innovative move they had neither drums nor lead guitar in their armoury, previously unheard-of in those guitar-dominated days. Familiar names like Innes, Stark, Hyland, Fleming, Bruce and Hart got together in this loose jamming sextet.

Trevor's next aggregation of note was The Red Brighte Signals, a brass-heavy, fluid 11-piece at the Treetops Hotel and Grays School of Art. By the time he affiliated himself with the already-established Once Upon A Band, there remained only Dave Flett on guitar and the late Dick Osborne on tenor sax and flute, from their original personnel. Other musicians in what effectively was twice Upon A Band included a bassist and drummer with the showbizzy names of Marvin West and Jeff Strong. These guys uncannily resembled Martin Johnstone and Graham Ogston. Don't over-tax your brain working out why such pseudonyms were adopted: what did any of this have to with Centre 1 anyway? This left-field version of the combo lurched instrumentally into The Mothers' Peaches En Regalia. Pretty wild for Aberdeen at that time. Or at any time, come to think of it.

Following an appearance on Grampian Television's Sounds 73, a restructured clique speculatively headed for London with common targets of jobs, money, making music and having a wild time. The band Jock seems then to have been conceived, the name designed to attract expat Scots in London, enduring through later incarnations back in Aberdeen. With Keith Milne on drums, things were looking bright by the year end. A useful acquaintance was Gavin McDonald, an Aberdonian with a recording contract, resident in London. Despite recruiting another vocalist it all came to a dramatic finale with a massive on-stage punch up. Sporting keekers and bruises, the band folded and returned across Hadrian's Wall to lick their wounds.

Embarking upon a social work training course in Edinburgh, Trevor continued playing with Osborne and Flett. The latter subsequently himself moved to London where, as we will later discover, he found fame with Manfred Mann's Earthband. But, as Flettie packed his bags prior to departing from Aberdeen, that doyen of the drum-kit Graham Spry cautioned him "Don't do it Dave, you'll regret it.'

Social work took Trev to Glasgow, where his semi-pro musical efforts concentrated on The Glasgow Works Band, with Al Fleming and Sandy Smart (the latter had been Annie Lennox's paramour for some time in Aberdeen). Both Al and Sandy are still on the Glasgow circuit with The Red Green Blues Band.

In 1977 Trevor returned to London and renewed his friendship with his old mate Dave Flett, at that time filling between MMEB and Thin Lizzy contracts by playing pub gigs. The third member of this Hart-Flett combo was Matt Irving, bassist at different times with Longdancer, Alison Moyet and Paul Young. Still intent on pursuing his rock 'n' roll dream, Trevor quit his day job in favour of recording with Flett and Irving. In time-honoured fashion, his advert in Melody Maker for like-minded musicians attracted 275 replies. Amongst the applicants was Rod Coombes, fresh from drumming for The Strawbs and Stealers Wheel. He became a member of Hart's new outfit The Lasers.

Securing a recording contract was top priority as The Lasers spent most of 1979 rehearsing and demo-ing their material, concurrent with an extensive gigging campaign at London locations such as Dingwalls and The Venue. Signing with Yes' management company, Trev thought "We were a pretty good band, but there were many high-quality acts on the scene, competition was fierce'. Ultimately they fell out over money and since his final retreat to Scotland, his contact with any of these gadgies has been limited to one solitary encounter.

Back in Glasgow he engaged in management and PA hire during the mid-eighties, and dabbled in the semi-pro pub scene with a swing-blues outfit. His social work career again to the fore, in 1989 he came home to Aberdeen where he sold out Caesar's Palace with an Albert Fish re-union gig a year later. His musical activities were thereafter limited to sporadic one-off appearances, until a synchronistic development in 1994 was to close a 30-year musical loop. But for the time being, let's leave Trev with the accolade of being a key player in Aberdeen's rock heritage.

. . . .

Having now covered the progressive blues of Albert Fish and its descendants, we change from our greasy Levis and manky trainers into our sharp soul suits. . . let's sniff out The Lemon Soul.

The righteous soul light shone on Aberdeen in 1966 - on the road not to Damascus but to Glasgow - where Kevin Henderson, Graham Spry and Quantrell Raymond Ross witnessed a Stax-Atlantic package show. The performances of Otis Redding and Carla Thomas that night proved pivotal in the founding of an Aberdeen musical dynasty - the guys returned home inspired to embark upon a mission from God, to bring the Muscle Shoals message to the people.

The origins of The Lemon Soul, our definitive exponents of the genre go back to the pre-history of Sixties beat groups The Triads, The Delinquents and The Cult. The first of these featured Ian 'Snowy'

Thompson on vocals, Tim 'Tipu' Pullman on bass, Ronnie Lumsden on vocals and harp, (replacing the original guitarist) Gordon 'Rossi' Ross on lead, Kevin Henderson on rhythm guitar and Bill Riddoch on drums. Riddoch's penchant for the dramatic was evidenced by his showing off, wearing hairy Joke Factory monster hands whilst knocking out The Triads' backbeat, engaging in stunts copied from his idol Screaming Lord Sutch.

Wild horses couldn't keep Riddoch from seeing Sutch when the latter appeared at Inverurie Town Hall. Bill and Graham Spry drove off in the middle of a blizzard across snow-covered back roads from Banchory. A vehicular breakdown enforced a stop at a desolate cross-roads garage: when the car was again operational, they boldly resumed their journey. Some 40 minutes later in hostile white-out conditions, they realised that they had taken the wrong turning and were back in Banchory.

Lesser mortals would have given it up as a bad job to curl up in front of a cosy fire with the Broons annual, but not Riddoch Of The North. Yoking Spry up in Eskimo-husky dog-team fashion, with a cry of 'mush' and a crack of the whip, he yet again pushed on, heedless of danger and discomfort (especially to Graham). He who dared won: eventually a way was forced into the bright metropolitan lights of the capital of the Garioch, two minutes before his role model Sutch started his show. Bill burst into the venue, casting in his wake pools of melted snow bigger than the Loch of Skene. He left the faithful Spry in the corner, knawing a Caribou leg, a reward for his valiant pack-doggish exertions.

Sutch's band came on stage without his Lordship, to play rock 'n' roll very badly. . . 'Crivvens' thought the munching Graham, casting his thoughts to the comforts of home, "So this is what all the furore was about. Hmm, I wonder what japes the bairn, Hen, grandpa and the rest of the mirth-making Glebe Street family are getting up to?'

Eventually arrived the moment which the North East of Scotland . . . well, Billy Riddoch at least, had been waiting for. An announcement: "Ladies and gentlemen, Lord Sutch is about to begin his performance and his act is extremely dangerous. For your own safety, please move away from the stage area.' Which was greeted with a typically spontaneous chorus of "F—k off' as the crowd charged to the front. Sutch's act that night revolved around his acting Jack The Ripper in prostitute-dismembering mode. The prophesised danger lay in Sutch's axe, an enormous, authentic implement that he employed recklessly in what was, frankly, a very dodgy stunt. There was no denying the Raving Monster Loony's physical strength: during a recent festive season (goodwill to all men, etc. . .) gig in Sweden, he had lifted a 30-foot Christmas tree and launched it into the terrified Scandinavian audience. Young Tsars-Born 5 guitarist Billy Spratt was far too close to the Inverurie action, perched atop an on-stage piano. Sutch's swing of the axe whistled millimetres past Spratt's napper, almost decapitating him in the process. Riddoch, however, did lose his head - this was all right up his macabre, theatrical street. . . his addiction to such pre-Alice Cooper gore was soon to cause knock-on shock and dismay in Aberdeen.

After the stage was cleared of blood and guts, Bill refused to let Sutch off the hook until he stood him a celebratory four-course meal. Thus Riddoch's claim to fame is that he shared fish, chips, salt and vinegar with the adulated one, in an Arctic snow storm in Inverurie's George Square, outside Davidson's chipper. . . Never mind Hendrix at Monterey, the Angels at Altamont, or The Beatles at Shea Stadium: this was rock history in the making. Well, as far as Riddoch was concerned.

Hendo and Rossi moved on to the John Davidson-managed Delinquents, who also had Tommy Forsyth, Stewart Kemp and Johnny Douglas in their line-up, with Jim Smith briefly on drums. Second division leaders, they coveted a first division place alongside The Facells, The Royal Teens, The Tremors and The Strollers. In July of 1965, The Delinquents loaded up their van and drove to Edinburgh to pay homage at The Place, Scotland's innovative rock happening venue. As Rossi relates "We turned up at the door and told them we just wanted to play. No money involved, we simply wanted to be able to say we had performed there.' Spread over five floors, live bands and discs played incessantly to Auld Reekie's hipsters, The Place inspired the Aberdeen venue of the same name that bravely, if abortively, attempted to replicate the original's ambience and popularity. Lugging their back-breaking gear up all those Edinburgh stairs was fully justified, judging by the boys' braggado when they got home.

Far away from such dizzy heights were The Cult, for whom Riddoch also drummed. It is strongly emphasised that we are now addressing the original incarnation of that group. The ensuing catalogue of calamity is attributable solely to this being a first band for all the inexperienced personnel involved.

Subsequent versions of The Cult were (by all accounts), much more organised, to the extent that the guitars had all their strings.

Bill called off from one of their regular gigs at The Hop Inn (the nearest pub to the Castlegate Barracks) and asked Spry to dep for him. "Screaming Lord Riddoch set me up' says Graham, "The place was packed, soldiers at one side of the room and prostitutes on the other. The music was just an excuse, as if they needed one, for them to get closer to each other.' The Cult's authentically scruffy, long-haired Stones-ish image differed totally from the well-scrubbed, shiny appearance of other local contemporary groups. The rhythm guitarist wasn't plugged in half the time and the guitars had Esso tiger tails hanging off them. The leopard-skin covered bass amp was enormous but contained only a solitary 12-inch speaker. By all accounts they were awful, which explains the wages, a fiver between six guys for four or five hours work.

Transport for band, instruments and amps was constantly problematic. In his cosy house, a law-abiding, dormobile-owning citizen read in his EE of the Dons' 2-1 away win at Cathkin Park (goals from Bobby Hume and Charlie Cooke). Miss Lesley in the Romper Room flickered unheeded in the corner. This idyllic reverie was disturbed by a loud banging on his door. He responded to this summons, to be confronted by a triad of hirsute, unkempt R 'n' B types, delicately explaining in a step-by-step, idiot-proof manner: "Heymin, we're in a band, right? We hinna got a van, see? See yer van ootside, we're takkin it ti tak oor stuff ti a gig the night, right? So gee's the keys now.' Faced with such a logical and polite request, the dismayed vehicle owner acquiesced after bravely negotiating a £3 fee (but more importantly retaining his good health). The vehicle was eventually returned after a fashion, which left the band's transport problem still on the agenda. . . The early evening news was full of that afternoon's theft of a Royal Mail van. When Spry rendezvoused with vocalist Ranald Rennie (affectionately dubbed Rembrandt Remould by his peers, but not to his face) prior to a Cult gig that evening, RR excitedly gushed forth with his inside story. His father, a Post Office employee, narrowly avoided death as the stolen van roared out of the yard. The two impressionable musicians discussed the incident in shocked tones as they awaited the arrival of transport for the date. . . screaming around the corner at some 60 mph came the vehicle: a red van, upon which the words 'Royal Mail' had been hastily and ineffectually painted over. . .

Nonetheless, they found themselves playing out at the Culter Community Centre with two guest vocalists whom we shall for sub judice reasons call Mr Velocity and the Faithful Indian Companion. Not fey, dilettante middle class students playing at being pop stars, their time was spent equally between trawlers, singing and. . . doing time. When they were freedom-side of the grey walls of Butlins By The Dee their party trick of opening beer bottles with their teeth was regular show-stopper. It was rumoured that drummers, starting the year with a two-piece biscuit-tin kit, could soon be equipped to 1997 Pink Floyd standards, due to the low cost acquisition techniques employed by the duo: veritable rain forests of drumsticks sprouted overnight.

Procedure dictated that the worst act were the first on stage, as related by a reliable-ish witness. "The Deadbeats were first up, they were truly appalling. Then it was The Cult, they were only terrible. Then came The Patter Merchants, a University group along the lines of The Misfits, they were almost competent. Finally, top of the bill were the long-awaited Delinquents: after the audience enduring hours of torture and an agonising build-up, the electricity failed. . . not a flicker. The un-plugged Delinquents were reduced to Stewart Kemp giving it big licks on that drummer's eternal standby, Sandy Nelson's Let There Be Drums. What a fiasco.'

The Cult's guest singers declined to travel back to Aberdeen with the rest of the musicians, opting instead to make their own way home in the early hours of the morning. As they passed through the environs of Cults. . . hhmm, is it just a coincidence, or are there a right load of cults in this story?. . . they concluded that they really fancied some chocolate.

Hence a convenient brick was launched through a shop window that was then liberated of its Cadbury's and NestlÈ goodies. The sweet-toothed larcenists legged it down to the banks of the river Dee, to consume their illegal Bounty in safety. As later reported by Mr Velocity, events took the following intellect-free course. FIC: "Ken ess, ess f———g chocolate's f———g rotten, it must be aff, a canna get ma f———g teeth through it.' Much molar destroying mastication occurred before Mr V diagnosed the cause of Jay Silver Heels' problem. "Ye daft winkle, 'at's 'at mackie oan chocolate ye've pinched.' Indeed, it was a slab of wooden-cardboardy-plasticy display Dairy Milk the Commanche was trying heroically to consume. The fast man further elaborated that "It wis f———-g murder, it wis freezin' doon 'err an' a couldna get a tune oot o' ma guitar cos the daft bastard filled it up wi' Easter eggs.'

With all that sophisticated Culture getting too much for him, Spry graduated to The Born 5, effectively second incarnation of The Tsars. In their original format they were baby rockers, an early template for The Bay City Rollers. But now they had Billy Riddoch in tow providing a gratuitious dramatic sideshow. For the rest of Aberdeenshire, memories of Lord Sutch's Inverurie extravaganza soon faded: not so for the aspiring thespian Riddoch. Back at the Aberdeen Academy, he raided the theatrical society's Friday Frantics props cupboard; at home he raked his mother's pantry; at his father's King Street butchers shop he investigated the offal bucket with awful diligence.

With demonic fervour he set to concocting an abdominal abominable blood bomb, containing tomato ketchup, strawberry jam and any other red matter that came to his satanic hand. In a mad Frankensteinesque twist, breasts were fabricated and placed over a thin plywood shield secreted under the top layer of clothing of the Ripper's victim. Bill's piece de resistance was a bag of turkey intestines filling the stomach area. Aye, out of control, big style. Thus at the succeeding Born 5 gig at Belmont Street's Philomen Club, the audience watched aghast as Jack repeatedly and bloodily plunged a 10-inch butchers knife into some wretched lady of the night, expelling gore over the entire stage area. Thrilled at the crowd's shocked reaction, Riddoch went doo-lally, throwing handfuls of poultry intestines at them. . . much horror from female fans turkey-trotting for the exit, much "For f—k sake' from the males. As the aroma-sensitive Spry says "I hope they all went straight home for a bath. I set my drum kit up for a gig the next night, and it smelled absolutely rancid on account of just a wee bit of turkey guts stuck underneath it.'

The stunt was soon repeated in a modified form at the small Sea Cadets' hut on Pocra Quay: this time, joy of joys, Bill had an axe of his own to play with. With the sheddie's lights off, he dramatically made his candle-lit, heavily made-up entrance. One smart-arse sea scout cheekily blew out Bill's candle, and left the premises on a stretcher, having been nearly decapitated in the darkness by Riddoch in grim reaper mode.

His career as a rock drummer was short-lived (the lads getting him so drunk one evening that his ma wouldn't let him out to play anymore) but Bill subsequently enjoyed much greater success as a professional actor. With an important BBC script to learn on the train that carried Bill to a victorious career in television, theatre and radio, he said a fond adieu to his rocking colleagues in Aberdeen. The devil-may-care Spry cautioned imploringly in his ear "Don't do it Bill, you'll regret it.'

The time was a-coming. Things were stirring on the soul front, and Spry would soon hear the righteous call. . . . Following his conversion (with Kevin Henderson) to North Sea Stax, the duo were in on the start of Aberdeen's inaugural brass-driven ensemble, The Hyland League. Al Hyland himself denies any responsibility for the name, claiming the idea came from the other guys: Stewart 'Otis' Kemp fronted a horn section of Al and Alisdair McKenzie, with Rossi on guitar, and a back line of Kevin on bass and Spry on drums. At The Place on Albyn Terrace, the band's repertoire gob-smacked the young, spectating Gogsie Lemon. "I wasn't too familiar with the music, but it knocked me over. Up until then, I hadn't done any singing in public. But I thought I would give it a go.' He soon replaced Otis as the HL became immensely popular purveyors of their own brand of Atlantic-Stax and Spencer Davis material, on the North East student dance circuit. The seeds were sown for the second soul spasm: within the year, The Lemon Soul kicked into action.

As Hyland blew for jazzier fields, the horn section was consolidated by trumpeter Graham Smith and trombonist Eddie McGovern (Pete's big brother). With a repertoire familiar to owners of theThis Is Soul sampler, LS primarily covered popular material from Sam and Dave, Otis Redding and Wilson Pickett. Packed houses ensued during 1967 and 1968 at the Beach Ballroom, the Four Mile at Kingswells, city student dances and throughout the NE. Their Caucasian soul shared the same frequency as Winwood and Cocker, a generation before the likes of Michael Bolton gave the genre a bad name. Graham Spry recalls that it was "great to dance to and it was intelligent music. . . and we dropped in other good time stuff, C'Mon Everybody and Charlie Brown for sure.' As they brought the Memphis message to Fraserburgh, the band's roadie disappeared up a close with a local wench. She was, however, already spoken for. Word soon spread amongst the crowd that she had been coerced by one of the Aberdeen soul posse, although it was unknown who the foolhardy Romeo specifically was. "The next thing we knew we are being chased out of the place by a horde of demented Brochers led by the lassie's steady boyfriend. Mic stands to the fore, we battered our way to the van but couldna get away, the roadie had the keys and he was roon somebody's backie wi' this dame. At the last minute he came to the rescue as fast as he could. Which was not very fast at all. He was running like a penguin, it's nae so easy to sprint wi' your jeans roon your ankles.'

We've all heard that everyone has a double somewhere in the world. At the Douglas Hotel in 1968, Rod Stewart had the fright of his life when his doppelganger sat next to him. Having gone over his ankle kicking a ball about the beach in the afternoon, Stewart rested his injury during a break in his set with The Jeff Beck Group. As he turned to pick up a drink (which someone else had paid for), he dropped into the first stage of a catatonic fit when confronted by Gordon Lemon. Having come out of his Denis Law phase, Stewart's coiffure and clothes mirrored exactly those of his gravel-voiced Aberdeen soul brother: witnesses say that they resembled a pair of proboscisally-gifted bookends. How bloody sad that Rod had a fixation with Gordon. . . perish the thought that it could possibly have been the other way around. As always, our sources remain confidential, so special thanks to AH for that juicy snippet.

Whilst Lemon Soul endured only for two years, there was something special happening. . . on stage as well as doon back closies. Either the band were exceptional, or the times were - probably both. Certainly their scene stays ever fresh in the memory of cognoscente of that period. Gordon had now unwittingly adopted the mantle of Aberdeen's own godfather of soul - the Flying Dutchman of funk, damned to eternally proclaim Hold On I'm Coming in the Midnight Hour of innumerable pubs and clubs.

. . . .

Meanwhile, Kevin Henderson, Howie Stewart and Graham Spry were ensconced at the high specific gravity end of things with their new group Def Ted. Following Howie's summer holiday visit to The Marquee in London, they selected the densest bits of Vanilla Fudge, King Crimson, Yes and The Nice, then mixed it all with some self-composed thixapropica: it certainly wasn't background music. A stray Cockney, having stumbled upon their set at the Black Dog, wasn't over impressed with either the 'fizzy Scotch beer' or the band's performance. His cheeky chirpy luvaduck request between numbers "Blimey, turn it up mate' saw Howie gleefully crank up the volume through his Selmer Hammond speaker yet another notch - witness blood exploding from ruptured audience eardrums. . . Def Ted after all.

One waitress in particular was unhelpful in such moments of crisis (she was concurrently physically attractive and deformed: she had external lungs) but her language and manners were fish market porter blush-making. The band developed a routine whereby, when she harangued a customer particularly virulently, a pre-agreed nod stopped the music instantaneously. . . Complete silence broken only by the waitress from hell loudly effing and blinding, suddenly the focus of attention for everyone in the room. Eventually realising that she was providing a floor show, she wiggled her way back to the bar, affa embarrassed. . . until the next time.

Def Ted's regular spots at The Black Dog were followed on the next night by Lennie Albiston, (debonair doyen of the blue rinse set), who did a piano and vocal act after the fashion of Liberace, backed by trio. As DT packed up their gear at the end of their evening someone had a bright carpenteresque idea. They somehow sourced a saw to partially cut through the leg of Lennie's piano stool - the dastardly deed was then deviously camouflaged using clear sellotape. Lennie may have been surprised the next night so see the rock group in attendance: maybe they had come to pick up some tricks of the trade?

Albiston's trio pumped up the atmosphere and he made his dramatic Las Vegas-inspired entrance. With his post-menopausal audience going bananas, he milked it in a big way. . . his black leather gloves had been slowly and seductively peeled off by the time he reached the piano. Eventually came the big moment as Lennie sat down to tickle the ivories and heart strings. The stool explosively collapsed, sending the singer trajecting across the stage area like a Polaris missile towards his aghast followers. Exit Def Ted, giggling like schoolgirls. "We had thought about sawing through the leg of the piano instead of the stool, but that would have killed Lennie rather than just maiming him.'

The trio's name was the subject of philosophical debate by would-be intellectual student followers. "Tell me, is it a reference to a skilled artisan, as in Deft Ed?' Which was greeted with the response it deserved: "Awa ye feel, its one o' Lennon's daft poems.' Coming from John Winston's doggerel Stanley Unwinish poetry, Def Ted followed on from Spiggy Topes as being the second Lennonesque name on the NE scene.

Graham: "We took existing very heavy material and turned it inside out, to the extent that it finally bore no resemblance to the original. We spent a lot of time working out arrangements and rehearsing. So it was demoralising at places like the University Union to be grudgingly and indifferently tolerated, as we earnestly went through these complicated routines. Then we only had to thump out those easy-to-play opening chords of Smoke On The Water for everyone to come alive and fill the dance floor within a few head-banging seconds. How we suffered for our art. . . '

Despite being the only teetotal and non-smoking drummer in the universe, Graham heard on the grapevine that his name appeared on the Grampian drugs squad's 'most wanted' list. The Sweeney included an acquaintance from school in their ranks. Graham challenged Plod about the rumour. "Why are you efter me, I dinna even drink?' Some lengthy mental process later, the aspiring Popeye Doyle confided "Well, yer in a band, ye've got to be deein' something.'

Whilst other rockers engaged in alcohol and substance abuse, Spry was into his grub in a big way. His new 20-inch tom-tom was much envied by rival percussionists. Little did they know that its prime purpose was to provide a suitable table for bowls of All Bran, Sugar Puffs and tattie crisps. At the top of The Blue Lampie's stairs one evening, Graham was approached by a dopey character who asked "Hiv ye goat oany grass?' The nutritiously equipped Spry retorted "No, but I've got two epples and a packet o' Polo mints.'

In his capacity of the Granite City's spokesman for the genre, Lemon's next stop on the soul train was Another Camel's 1970 jazz-funk. These additional ships of the desert (who also had the Texan albino Edgar Winter blues) humped their equipment (and God knows what else) into student dances throughout Aberdeen. Another Camel included some well-kent faces in drummer Harry McFarlane, bassist Hugh Falconer, Robert Wilson on guitar, Al Hyland on sax and trumpet, Dick Osborne on flute, and Gavin Stark on sax. Gav later became a jazz presenter on Northsound Radio.

1972 meant Once Upon a Band where-in Trevor Hart was later to replace Gordon. But first time round the Once Uponers were Graham 'Crisp and Dry', Rossi on bass, Davie's 'On The Road Again' Flett on guitar and Bill Michael on keyboards. Hyland and Osborne saxed and flauted.

The train standing at platform rhythm and blues in 1974 was Jock, the band's first appearance in Aberdeen, but its creation harked back to London. The Granite City version had Spry on drums, Hughie Falconer on bass, with Keith Milne and Ian Michael on guitar and vox. Jock moved on to funk central, with new hands on board (Andy Dalgarno on bass and Bob 'Parko' Parkinson on keyboards). . . All aboard! for Jock's reversal back into the R 'n' B siding: Neil Findlay succeeded the Jive Bombing Spry, and George Cheyne vocalised with Lemon. Jock played the Aberdeen Technical College, RGIT, the University Union, and filled Ma Cameron's before taking up a weekend ABC Bowl residency. Gordon said "When the band first got together, we performed mostly simple rock 'n' roll type songs. But as time progressed, we strove to bring more subtle and sophisticated material into our repertoire'. . . which they played to good effect at their biggest gig, supporting Cado Belle at Fusion.

. . . .

In July of 1974 Kevin Henderson had packed his guitar and headed for Europe on what was planned to be a six-week holiday. In France, a costly operation left him without either appendix or money, and in need of work. His search took him and his acoustic to Spain, where he secured employment at an American air base club close to Zaragoza. This provided sufficient pesetas for Kevin to live in a caravan on a nearby campsite, as the month-and-a-half drifted into a year. Airmen on the base suggested that he try his luck in Germany's multitudinious clubs.

Taking their advice, he was fortunate in immediately pulling a two-month, five nights-weekly contract . . . he was to continue playing the Ami clubs for the next eight years. Kevin slowly grasped the language and crossed over to playing non-military pubs and clubs throughout the country. As his career picked up momentum, Hendo acquired a manager and released his first album Somewhere In The

Country in 1982. Thereafter he recorded various types of music, including disco and Schlager, "a music peculiar to the multitude of Tanz-cafes here, good fox-trot music but unfortunately not very original or exciting to play.' But with his first album he effectively hitched his wagon to the rocketing 'new country' movement. Swapping his Aberdeen soul shoes for German cowboy boots, in 1992 his second country album Kentucky Bound gained him music business awards. Kevin played throughout Scandinavia and both Western and Eastern Europe.

. . . .

Back in sunny Aberdeen the bashful Spry had swopped Jock for The Jive Bombers, led by David Stroud, who showed no aptitude for music in his early days: ("It shows') apart from singing in the school choir. Nonetheless, at 14 he got together with Arthur Watson in a Ban The Bomb duo, during the Campaign For Nuclear Disarmament craze. So it was all denim jackets and nifty wee Bob Dylan peaked caps, Pete Seeger and Dirty Old Town. After treating the Shortloanings Spiritualist Church to innumerable Blowing In The Wind type dirges, this protest-bluesome twosome furtively roamed the corridors and wards of Foresterhill hospital.

These were the days before hospital radio, when Dave and Artie dodged medical staff, allegedly entertaining patients, supposedly cheering them up to accelarate their return to fitness. "It didnae work, they dropped like flies.' Dave did a wee solo thing at the Beach prom Gaiety, and Watson became a legend in his own lunchtime in the folk field. Stroud strode into art college. To put this into historical perspective, classes involved drawing hunting scenes onto cave walls. This was his makie-on bohemian phase. If you happened to climb the stairs to the lounge at The Harriet Street Bar, you would have heard his folk-rock band Daddy Stove Pipe in action. Their sobriquet originated with an old Chicago blueser who wore a tall black hat: their audience was half-arsed beatniky with polo-necked woolly jumpers, brown Jesus sandals and "Hoos yer doos, lay some skin on me, maaan.'

DSP had the colourful Ian Crighton on vocals, John Canavan on ragtime guitar, and Stroud on rhythm guitar and harp. . . or moothie. Frightening Crighton moved on to play with Johnny Lawson and Ian 'Woolly' Wolstenholme. . . there are people leaving the bar, they think it's all over. . . time gentlemen please: it is now. The Canavan rolled on to Johnny Sutherland's hobbit-forming Gollum The Underdog. In a mid-period Once Upon A Band (post Lemon-pre-Hart), 'Sing it loud and Stroud' found himself inveigled with Graham 'No comment' Spry on skins, Keithy Milne on bass, Dick Osborne on sax and Al 'Hae a wee toot' Hyland on trumpet. . . (Al had learned his instrument on his father's rag-mannie round, hence his early dress style pre-dating the Oxfam shop look). This was also where DS came into contact with guitarist Davie Flett. Playing venues like the Uni Union and TC College, Bill Innes demonstrated his sax appeal and Harry McFarlane sneaked a shottie of the drums when Spry was out buying Aztec bars, and Old English flavour Spangles.

The day job had that wee gem Stroud working in the jewellery design and manufacturing business. Someone told him that the streets of London were paved with 18 carat hall-marked gold, and off he went. The lady who owned the Blackheath premises where his workshop was located ran an arty-crafty Nova-ish crockery, nick-nacks and artefacts outlet upstairs and was married to a South African Rolf Harris look-alike keyboards player named Manfred Mann. T'was Goldfinger who fixed up MM with a new guitarist, but that nugget comes later. . .

His trade brought him up to Edinburgh and eventually back to Aberdeen in 1980. Welcomed back into the Silver City's rock clique, he got into The Big Dipper Band, knocking out Elmore James licks. . . (well, that one Elmore James lick actually) and some rocky stuff, at the Albyn, the Uni and The Bobbin Mill. The Big Dippers were Stroud on vox, Al Hyland on sax, wee brother Peter Stroud on bass (having fallen off Sitting On The Fence), ex-Parts rhythm guitarist Keith Garden, and Kenny McIssac on guitar. Kenny later started feeling a bit Sikh. . . he later practiced homeopathic massage from the Mastrick ashram. The man with the urban turban.

All good things come to an end, and Stroud fell in once again with the admirably colourful Crighton in 1981. In the beginning The Jive Bombers were "a bit like country blues'. . . just a bit you will note. The JBs were to structured music what Davie Robb was to cultured football: the Marx Brothers bumping into The Pogues in a dark room full of LSD-crazed chimpanzees. Cri's frightenin' vocals reappeared on the scene, with Stroud on mandolin and singing, Woolly on various things, and brother Pete on bass and guitar. Particularly full of jive was Spry on drums, he really calmed things down. . . putting out fire with gasoline. The Jive Bombers was actually the second choice of name. The original nomenclature, Laughing Gravy, was considered too daft even for this crowd. . . Laughing Gravy was a dog in a Laurel and Hardy movie.

Hold tight at the back of the bus. . . the louder you scream, the faster we go. . . Rossi in and Woolly out; Paul Massey and Frank Morgan horn their way in; Rossi shoots the craw and Kevin Dow enlists; Crighton goes offshore to become a North Sea tiger. Personnel vacillations notwithstanding, they were Aberdeen's fun rocky-bluesey outfit, which the band certainly enjoyed if not their audiences. If Keef Richard(s) got annoyed with Chuck Berry when the latter, not giving a shit, frequently lost the place, it is a testament to the individual and collective talents of the Jive Bombers that the whole band were able to cope with Crighton going unintentionally, repeatedly on and off the beat. Even worse, Cri would start singing a totally different song, maybe a slow number when the band were rocking, but persisted to the end. At the Albyn Lounge and on a support gig to Hank Wangford (the singing gynaecologist who likes to keep his hand in), they played some eccentric stuff, like my da's favourite He'll Have To Go done Cajun style, and The King's That's Alright Mama. Great banter between the guys in the band: anyone who deigned to tune up before playing would immediately be branded "a big jessie.'

Bill Alexander had a brief spell in the JB madhouse but relocated to Holland to work in graphic design for Enigma Records. Coincidentally Stroud had first met Bill down by the Amsterdam canals 14 years before. . . he didn't know him before then, but recognised him as a fellow Aberdonian, by the way he asked scantily-clad hookers where he could find a sheep. Stroud let himself calm down for about a year before entering the Land Of A Thousand Dances with Paul Massey's gargantuan Aberdeen Soul Revue. . . 1989 saw the re-birth of The JBs, this time welcoming into their fold Kevin Oliphant (one of 1997's Beatles re-creationist Billy Shears Band) on drums, Brisie Clark on guitar and Gerry Dawson in the horn section. Alan Bruce from Banff came in on bass (such were his experiences with the band that he was last seen baying at the moon as he scampered to Ohio in the USA: his personal Letter From America reads Chalmers steak pies no moarrrr), Willie Milne slid in on trombone; Mikey Rae had a couple of years on bass before Dennis McKenzie took over; Careful With That Sax, Eddie Reid; Kevin Dow again on guitar; Doctor Tommy Finlay pays a house call. . . straight out of The Temperance Seven or The Bonzo Dog Doodah Band came, on trumpet and monocle, the Right Honourable Angus Moncreif. . . from Croydon.

In 1992 The JBs were strapped into straight jackets and driven out to Steve Gibb's 16-track basement Production House studio in Kintore, where the Sock It To 'Em JBs CDEP was crafted. Material comes from Chuck, Otis, Mitch Ryder and Dobie Gray: further hints as to the spirit of this release come from the sleeve credits. Worthy of mention are "Easy Jeans for the fuller man, Cossack hair spray for men, the Right On Surgical Appliance Company, all the staff at Glenburn Wing', and finally, that long-time fully paid-up member of the Gully Foyle fan club "the king of Morocco'. This Bouncing Bomb opens with the JBs irreverent take on Run Run Rudolph. This is just what you need after Christmas dinner instead of Noddy Holder or The Great Escape. Sit immobile, stuffed (in a strange role-reversal revenge scenario) with turkey, as you feverishly rip open your Oor Wullie annual and your Spice Girls selection box. "It was just a stab at a novelty thing for Christmas, a bit left-field. It actually came out a bit late but we still sold a few hundred copies. The whole thing took a couple of days to record, and it was great fun to do.'

December of 1978 saw Gordon Lemon's vinyl debut on Oily Records, the Aberdeen independent record label. Gordon sang Dave Baird's compositions and R n' B standards with The Squibs, having replaced their original vocalist, Dougie 'Fuggie' Brown. We discuss their On The Line / Satisfy Me elsewhere. According to Oily's Jim Allardice, Gordon left because "The band preferred to concentrate on original material, but he wanted to introduce more soul stuff.'. . . now there's a surprise.

A year later Previous Convictions were taken into consideration, as the band of this name played pub and student gigs, supporting Ian Dury and the Blockheads at Fusion. In 1982, Lemon's tree branched out with Airtight, a guitar based rock band. . . things heated up at city pubs including Dizzy's, where it was 90 Degrees In The Shade. This was a funk, soul and blues amalgam that included Davie Keay on bass, John Rogerson on guitar, Mike Forbes on keyboards, with Tom Findlay as sex cymbal. The temperature remained high with the Hot Shots in 1986 and 1987. The band had originally decided on the name Hot Spots but a printing error on early posters changed it for them.

The Aberdeen Soul Revue was formed in November 1987 for a one-off gig as part of the Aberdeen Alternative Festival. Paul Massey's concept, these sanguinettes amalgamated The Hot Shots with those other rhythm aces The Jive Bombers. The line-up fluctuated throughout the band's existence (Aberdeen's Alternative Festival for five years and hotel gigs, offering a welcome alternative to Agadoo and Hi Ho Silver Lining at weddings and private functions) until ASR's final extravaganza in December of 1993. Al Hyland made a welcome guest re-appearance on sax, right at ASR's death.

There were plans for the Soul Revue to reform the following year, with new material and fresh personnel - but the small matter of Lemon Soul was destined to get in the way. . .

Kevin Henderson's chance telephone call from his home in Frankfurt to the Dutch Mill in Queens Road just after Christmas 1993 caught the ex-Lemon Soul coterie in seasonal bonhomie. The guys got to talking about the old days - their last gig together had taken place at the Cowdray Hall in 1968. Hence was born the idea of their first performance in 26 long years. After preliminary planning, the venue and date was fixed, appropriately enough, for the Lemon Tree on April 3, 1994. Word hit the street well in advance of any advertising or ticket arrangements: Lemon Soul are back together, lock up your grannies!

Fortunately, the original line-up committed to making themselves available - this involved Alisdair McKenzie travelling up from London, whilst Kevin returned to Aberdeen from Germany. Therefore, the home-boy contingent of these grizzled Caledonian soul veterans commenced rehearsals at the Arts Centre - with Pete McGovern and Joe Leonard drafted into the horn section and David McKenzie on keyboards. The set was to be pretty much as they had last played - not much change out of Otis, Sam and Dave, the Wicked Pickett, and The Purify Brothers. The sound check on the afternoon of the gig. . . Gordon nervous as a turkey before Christmas. . . final arrangements as he prowled the floor incessantly smoking Gitanes. . . yes, that's where the voice comes from, hoarser than Shergar. . . (the French tobacco company's Marlboro-targeted advertising translates as 'The cigarettes that make the cowboys cough.')

Kevin's colleague and record producer Dave Bell accompanied him from Germany to run the mixing desk and make a digital recording of the show. So with the stage set, for the first time since 1968 - live on stage, Lemon Soul. "Good evening ladies and gentlemen - we've been away for a long time - but now we're back!' To a capacity audience, they kicked straight into Respect - in your face like a Glesca' kiss. Fundamental coolness in a room of rain-forest humidity levels from be-suited acolytes of the Memphis message. Twenty-two peaches. From Muscle Shoals to Mastrick without a second of dead time, despite Lemon's voice cracking mid-set as les cigarettes Francais took their revenge.

And then it's over. Amen. "See you all in another 26 years, good night.'

. . . .

This chapter on Aberdeen's rock dynasty was designed to end when the curtain came down at the Lemon Tree that April night. Fortunately for the city's music public, events took a synchronistic turn as this saga turned full circle after nearly 30 years.

Graham Spry's enthusiasm was the principal factor in the band deciding to capitalise on 1994's momentum. Gigs were therefore planned for July, October and December, but with a new member on board. Trevor Hart's name and number appeared in Gordon's filofax (or perhaps on the back of a fag packet), when he had kindly tracked down Trev on behalf of your correspondent. When the need arose for someone to consolidate Gordon's efforts (a lengthy soul set makes amazing demands on the vocalist) and to play keyboards, the choice was therefore fairly obvious. Trevor's recruitment filled out the band's sound and subtly modified its canon. . . controlled evolution, ensuring that the founding fathers of Aberdeen's soul and blues movements continued to thrive. Publicity photographs of the band concentrated on Ross, Hart and Lemon. According to Graham Spry, these present an image of vibrant R 'n' B experts at the peak of their powers. Graham himself is noticeably missing from such pictures. "The image I present is more of the Westburn Park bowling green on a Sunday afternoon.'

For aural gourmets with eardrums jaded through over exposure to grotty fish suppers, a cordon-bleu combination seafood platter, using ingredients Lemon Soul and Albert Fish, was a mouth-watering prospect. The revamped Lemons put Aberdeen's 1994 rock year to bed and kicked off the New Year celebrations with a headlining, blizzard-conditions Union Terrace Gardens spot. They paused only to shout up to the Gardens' treetop crows' nests "Have you bred any good rooks lately?'

As for that crusty old council jobsworth who disconnected Albert Fish at the same venue in the Sixties - his ghost hovered around the snow-covered arena, itching to again pull the plug on Trevor Hart. Not that the latter was scared, telling the spirit "Go ahead spectre, fill your boots.' The band couldn't attract Phil Spector, but they did get spectre fill. . . another ghostly apparition has since returned, this time to haunt TV and cinema audiences, in the shape of one Bill Riddoch. A lavatorial appearance in Shallow Grave, parts in Rab C. Nesbitt, Lachie Senior in Hamish McBeath, he was also a rotund, rosy-cheeked, middle-aged farmer advertising a gardening centre and its products in a decidedly Teuchterist fashion. This harks back to his teenage Doric infatuation with a scratchy old 78 of Aikey Brae with which he bored the pants off anyone daft enough to listen. But ask yourself, would you go within a lupin-length of this latter-day Raving Monster Loony, a chill gleam in his eye as the sun glints off that razor-sharp scythe resting against the garden shed wall?

LEMON SOUL
1968

WESTBURN PARK BOWLING GREEN
1995

82

Chapter 9

They made the heavens bright: the Sixties

The joys of one's golden youth in the late Sixties: drinking, fighting, falling in lust. The surreptitious sliding of your da's suit jacket out of his wardrobe on its hanger, to which you tie a length of string to enable its subsequent lowering out of the back window. Sleekitly bidding your parents a nonchalant "I'm just off to play fitba' wi' the boys', as you rescue said jacket and leg it into town for the forbidden fruits of the pub. Demanding a pint of 'beer' draped in Pop's Sunday best with a black sock tucked into the top pocket as a makie-on hankie, shoulders burying you like a parachute. When a plain clothes policeman on under-age drinking assignment enquires what you are drinking, innocently replying "That's affa nice o' ye, I'll hae a Newkie Broon.' Luckily getting sprung out of the Diamond Street nick as your uncles Archie and Bob happen to be on special constable duty. . .

Buying scratched Little Richard and Fats Domino 78s at a Saturday jumble sale in the hall next to the Prince Of Wales. Gate crashing parties team-handed at parent-less houses in the West end on the basis that someone who kind of knows one of your posse, who isn't with you anyway, might have maybe had an invitation. Carting mega carry-outs right across town, changing busses twice, instead of buying your hooch at the licensed grocer nearest to the party. Well, you might not get served even using your deepest voice - such was logic.

Experimenting with the delights of Don Cortez in three litre screw top bottles, oh how well it complemented a refined glass of Scotsmac! Immediately ditching Ravi Shankar's greatest hits from the aghast host's turntable before whacking on Long Tall Sally, Blueberry Hill and your ma's Chubby Checker. Hiding the cairry-oot in what you think is a safe place, bogarting that joint which you pinched in the first place, before running a twist train through the ever-so-posh house. Over the beds, occupied or not, in and out of the bath taking the shower curtain with you.

As the electric soup takes a hold, trying to chat up any crumpet regardless of its physical appearance or its relationship to male attendees. Last minute panics trying to locate the fabled final can of lager, before at least someone does a technicolour yawn in some inappropriate spot. Having your state-ment read out in court when appearing for breach of the peace, after some maniac came at you outside Woolies with a knife and fork (which he lifted from the Peacock Cafe). "Well fit did ye expect me to dee, jump on a plate?'

Faced with the frosty mid-January financial choice of one last pint then walking home, or a bag of chips then the last bus - ah well, it's nae that cold the night. . . Midnight barbecues at the Brig O' Don beach where cremated sausages are drunkenly tipped onto the unlit sand, to remain lost until they become breakfast for the crabs on the bright new morning still to come. Your drunken mate Alfie disap-pearing head first off a sand dune and not responding to your shouted "Far are ye, are you a' right ?' Until, after ten minutes of feverish-ish searching he is located in a six-foot deep WW II anti-tank hole, mumbling contentedly that he is "Warm as a kipper.'. . . Listening stoically, eyes raised skywards as your da explains authoritatively that Donovan has been around for years. "That's him that did My Old Man's A Dustman. Lonnie Donovan.'

Pinching a keg of lager from the Brig O' Don barracks and rolling it as far as the nearest phone box, from whence a taxi is summoned. Travelling over to seagull island with the taxi's nose pointing sky-wards due to the weight of beer in the boot. Stashing the barrel in Alfie's da's shed covered with an old carpet before wheel-barrowing it up to the Grumps the next night. Attacking it ineffectually with hammers and screwdrivers before storing it in disgust in a Corporation grit bunker by the side of the road. Liberating a proper keg key from the pub and then discovering that some bastard has pinched the booty from its hidey-hole. Cursing the fact that you can't trust anyone.

We have covered a lot of ground and many talented musicians so far. Just when you, dear reader, started musing triumphantly that your favourites from the groovy decade have been overlooked, our rock 'n' roll clock now starts ticking. . . Hank Marvin asks Jennings Music in London to build him an amp with two speakers instead of only one. They come up with the AC30, a 30w tube amplifier with two celestion speakers. Things would never be the same again. . .

Pop chart wise it actually begins in 1958 with Lord Rockingham's XI, led by Henry 'Harry' Robinson, a musician who had contracted tuberculosis in Elgin. Whilst his health improved after treatment at Gray's Hospital, he wrote for The Elgin Courant, encountering local entrepreneur Albert Bonici when filing a report on the latter's dance promotions. Albert's connections prove productive for Harry, who relocates to London where he resides with Bonici's sister. Through Albert's business and family contact Tito Burns, Robinson goes up for the position of musical director of Jack Good's Oh Boy! television show, the definitive rock 'n' roll document of the era.

With the Lord Rockingham name being lifted from an actual historical character, the band perform novelty spots on the programme. With respected musicians Chery Wainer (organ), Red Price (sax) and Rory Blackwell (drums) in his line-up, Harry is almost told "that's shallot' in May with the failure of The XI's inaugural single Fried Onions. Four months later, his surreal re-working of A Thousand Pipers, the honking Hoots Mon! on the Decca label reeled its way to number one in the hit-parade, with the follow up Wee Tom reaching number 16. Subsequently Ra Ra Rockingham and the Chubby Checker cash-in Newcastle Twist/Rockingham Twist find the novelty wear thin. (The moose was loose aboot the hoose again 36 years later when a Lauderish pastiche of Harry's chart-topper appeared on national television in 1994, advertising a new brand of fruit pastilles.) The Crackerjacks become resident band at The Argosy in Bucksburn. Vocalist Ronnie Green looks more like Elvis than Elvis does, and he is a great singer. Their drummer is Hamish McHardy and the others are ex-Alligators Alan Payton and Jimmy Gray. The latter meets vocalist Francis Main and they eventually marry. The unlicensed venue is constantly packed and band-members are sighted in the Staging Post and the Auchmill Inn having a fly pint. "The money isna' that bad' says Gray "and the owner Councillor Burns has given me the keys to the premises. I've persuaded him to get the baby grand piano painted sparkly-white, Liberace-style.' The West End garage in Aberdeen wants £560 for a four-year-old Mark II Consul. The Equitable's price for a set of groovy mens' interlocking singlet and matching trunks is 6/3d whilst Molly Sugden look-alikes at Isaac Benzies are selling ladies nylons at 3/11d. Trad-jazz up in the Buckie area is virtually cornered by Bill Geddes.

December sees Tommy Dene and The Tremors win the North of Scotland rock band championships in Dundee - they turn pro the following June. Inverness group The Beatsters are approached by London-based American Jeff Maxwell, hinting that he wants to take the band to London and America. Ron Mackay, Charles Masson, Michael Shanks and James Macbeath are, naturally, very excited at the prospect. Eddie Leppard and The Leopards are formed in Elgin in September. . . Wearing pink suits were The Diamonds (Freddie Ellis, Sonny Pearce, Brian Nicholson and guitarist Davie Whyte "the guitarists' guitarist). In May, Freddie and The Dreamers hit number three in the national chart with If You Gotta Make A Fool Of Somebody. His management crib from an old Aberdeenshire song when advertising his gigs: you musr remember Come Up An' See My Garetty.

1964 rolls into life with an announcement that The Georgians had found a 'fairy godfather' in Inverurie impresario Bert Ewen. Bapper provides the band with musical equipment valued at £350 to allow the boys to continue their rehearsals at the Banks O' Ury Hotel. These Garioch groovers adopted their name because the majority of their members lived in Inverurie's George Square. Bert has only recently recovered from a severe illness. . . he and his wife Hilda May were professional dancers in their younger days, Bert being a Charleston champ in the 1920s. A press-release from The Apaches allows us to savour what was on the menu in Buckie. Vocalist Kenny Lawson can't get enough liver, peas and tatties. . . bassist Bill McKenzie goes daft for eggs and chips and lead guitarist Doug Maclennan has the hots for steak and chips. Rhythm guitarist John Rennie never says no to boiled ham, and Ian Young has little chance with the women as he continually scoffs pickled onions. The Scottish Records label, based at 52 Bon Accord Street, release two gems from Duncan Macrae. Me and Shakespeare is bettered only by the classic The Wee Cock Sparrer.

Later in the month Barry Wayne and The Strangers appeal to the public to invent a new name for them. Derek Freeland and Norman Shearer having left to form The Facells, The Strangers were now led by Johnny Johnson. Their agent Gordon Hardie offers two tickets for a Beach Ballroom appearance by Johnny Kidd and The Pirates as a prize for the best suggestion. The successful entrants turn out to be Linda Grant and Edna Massie. Their name Mod and The Trends (now we know why Johnny Johnson emigrated to Australia) is judged to be the "most up to date, original and catchy.' Second placed Malcolm McCalley comes up with Ebb Tide and The Sound Waves. A copy of the teen weekly Fabulous features "World pop stars in colour, colour, colour' and costs a whole shilling but you do get 11 full size colour pin-ups for your money. As The Rave-Ons are raving on with Sandy and The Sandstormers kicking up a storm, Syd Weaver gets the award for the most surreal name on the circuit for El Cid and The Commancheros, which is well up to his other brammer, Sheriff Syd Weaver and The Deputies. . . lovely stuff. Further North, The Badenoch Eagles are tips for the top. When organist Alistair Maclean and lead guitarist Alistair Meade leave Kingussie Secondary School, it's all systems go for them and their co-musicians, bassist Ewan 'Crow' Munro and drummer Rab Smillie. Manager, Londoner Pete Wicker, gets them into audition for the inscrutable Joe Meek, and records demos in Edinburgh. The resultant tracks This And That, Haggis Stomp, Spanish and Sleepy bring them into contact with Aberdonian disc jockey and music biz impressario George Elrick. Under their new name of Eagles Combo d'Ecosse they set the heather on fire in Devon, Cornwall and Soho. With the addition of female vocalist Bobbi Jean there are ambitious plans for trips to South Africa, and to appear on Japanese TV. On the MacDuff circuit, such as it is, are Billy Little and The Giants who appear at the same venues as Gordon Urquhart and The Bluebeats.

At the Thurso Town Hall (mainland Britain's most Northerly dance venue) Decca's English recording artist Robby Hood, leader of The Merrie Men, says "Yeah man, it's like the moon way up here.' Was he referring to the landscape or the lack of atmosphere? Membership of the Tommy Dene and The Tremors fan club nears the 2,000 mark, as they are voted Scotland's most popular group in February's Scottish Beat magazine, coincidentally edited and published by the band's manager Andy Lothian Jnr. Second placed are Johnny and The Copycats who turned pro in January. Dennis Kyte and The Wildkats tape It's Beginning To Tell On You, co-composed by bass player Johnny Denoon and rhythm guitarist Harry Davidson. The Inverness band say "We will send it to a recording company then we'll just keep our fingers crossed.' Braemar-born Peter Waller begins his chart career with Peter and Gordon. A World Without Love hits number one.

A catastrophic typhoid epidemic severely curtails entertainment in Aberdeen, gatherings of more than a handful of people being temporarily banned. In the first days before the veto came into force, guitarist Brian Youngson experiences what would soon become the norm: musicians appearing at Inverurie town hall are usually treated to post-performance hospitality in the shape of cups of tea, sandwiches, sausage rolls and the like. On this occasion, the catering wifies wear white gloves as they serve the food and drink using disposable paper plates and cups, all of which go in the bin for incineration. On the lighter side, kids throughout the North East are overheard singing, to the tune of The Red Flag: Where 'er we go we'll fear no foe, we buy corned beef from William Low. The Tartan Dive in Market Street (later to become the Looking Glass) hosts a trio of Jimmy Gray, Alan Payton and Sharkey the drummer. The latter would join The Barron Knights.

Former Midnighters' vocalist June Cowie collaborates with Robbie Benzies, Alex McRobb, Jim Walker and Alex Brands. This pre-dates a residency at The Palace Ballroom with Roy Pinder's band, in which June co-vocalises with Ian Dowbekin. Later she was to be active on the country scene with Chris Sellars and The Corvettes and Can Do. Later, June was to renew her dialogue with ex-Tsar Robbie in Can Do 2.

STV producer Liam Hood arrives in Aberdeen in March to audition acts for his One Night Stand television show. . . Those hopefuls who turn up at the Music Hall include Buckie's The Apaches, Frankie and The Strollers, Jerry and The Sunsets, The Facells, The Playboys, and Eddie Leppard and The Leopards. The latter-named are soon crossing the North Sea for Germany on a trip organised by their manager Sonny Rogers, and Albert Bonici. The manager's brother Rae plays bass for the band, Chick Ralph is the lead guitarist, drummer is Sonny Johnson and Fraser Armstrong plays organ. Eddie himself is the vocalist and rhythm guitarist in this Morayshire combo, citing Peggy Lee, John Lee Hooker and Sonny Boy Williamson as their musical influences.

As The Strollers also leave for Germany, a typical Friday night at the bottom of the Beach Boulevard stars The Battle 3, resident band Johnny Scott and The Scottsmen, The Phantom Sounds, The Misfits and The Beachies, part time spot operators at the Beach Ballroom. Their mickey-taking mime performances at private parties have developed into public novelty turns. They are Joss Greig, David Ballantyne, Ronnie Riddell and Robert Keith. In May, former Elgin journalist Harry Robinson returns to the big time as musical director for Millie Small's My Boy Lollipop. We herewith blow away that old pub quiz chestnut about the harmonica player on this number two hit on the Fontana label: no, it isn't Rod Stewart. Right from the horse's moothie I can tell you it is one Pete Hogman, a member of Jimmy Powell's Five Dimensions, Stewart having left the band some weeks before. Pete now resides on the Isle Of Wight where he plays occasional blues gigs with his own band and with Pretty Things' guitarist Dick Taylor. Robinson also scores the music for those dreadful Hammer horror movies so beloved by the macabre Bill Riddoch. . .

Sponsored by Aberdeen Corporation and JT Forbes, voting in the August beat band showdown on Aberdeen Links goes The Daltons 105, The Out 97 and The Gravediggers 91. The Daltons, from Tarves, are Peter Whimster on bass, John Thompson on drums and Alex Wallace on guitar. Their prize is £30 and a professional gig a few yards away at the Beach Ballroom.

Dennis Kyte splits from The Wildkats in Inverness in September: their replacement unruly feline is North Nicholls, former lead guitarist with The Four Winds. They visit Elgin to record four of the new man's compositions. "We are sending the tapes to EMI and we are pretty hopeful that they will put a couple of the songs on a disc.' After a dance at Tain, they are pursued to Dingwall by a carload of autograph-hunting fans. Deposed guitarist Dennis Kyte is as high as his surname when he claims "I was sacked from my own group and I wasn't given any explanation.' The other Wildkats counter that he was put outside because he was not attending practice sessions. Dennis defends himself by stating "That's not true. . . I missed only one rehearsal. I might have been five or ten minutes late for some sessions.' His girlfriend, pretty Pamela Connell, pitches in with "I think it was pretty rotten.' Back in Aberdeen The Playboys are one of the happening acts with Eddie Keith on drums, Mal Strachan on bass, Mike Wallace on guitar, and Ian Dowbekin on vocals. Eddie would later pulsate with The Throb, Mal was to join Albert Fish. Ian and Mike were to be mainstays of the local scene for many years.

The Outsiders win October's North East beat championship at Kemnay's Burnett Arms Hall. Runners-up are Peterhead's Stepping Stones and The Phantoms from Buckie. Individual awards go to drummer Reg Christie and rhythm guitarist G. McDonald from the winning group, bassist Gogs Cran from Inverurie's Z Guitars, The Phantoms' vocalist Frank Hay, and Gordon Ross - guitarist with The Triads. Rossi subsequently came a Steve Cropper with The Lemon Soul.

In 1964 it took five people to dig a hole. . . Neil Gibbons, Mo Butler, Ross Baird, Murray Hughes and Iain Cobb were The Gravediggers. Where was Paul Bearer? Up in Invergordon, Don Bremner joins The Dynamic Jetblacks replacing drummer Robert Munro, who has gone to university in Aberdeen. Fellow Northerners Size Four from Inverness win the Buckie beat contest despite experiencing PA problems. Their bassist is Ian Douglas McKay (years later he would become a QC) and vocalist Ally Gerrie "kept things bouncing along with an impromptu kick session.' The second-placed group are the 18-year-old Rebel Sounds from Keith, with lead guitarist Benton Green, drummer Jimmy Shand and Sandy Petrie on bass. They apparently have their eyes on a saxophone player to strengthen their sound. Buckie's own Bambis are third although vocalist Frank Hay is at times inaudible to the judges due the loud backing behind him. Those decibel-loving Bambis are Dave Simpson, Brian Davidson, Graham Falconer and George Campbell.

The year ends with The Symbols reminding Aberdeen that the devil doesn't have all the best tunes - they are members of the Salvation Army. Major Holmes at the Castlegate Citadel gives them his blessing and a monetary gift which has been donated by a sympathetic (and deaf?) old man.

Eagle Force Seven begin a two-month Scottish tour in January of 1965. Formed while the Royal Scots Greys were stationed in Aden the previous year, they were then resident band in a Hildesheim, Germany night club. The group's leader is drummer Eddie Hall from Bucksburn, who was the regiment's butcher. We make no comments about unsavoury habits involving beat and meat. Also from Aberdeen is rhythm guitarist John Murray - John Steven from Wick, Graham Noble from Arbroath, and Bill Farthing from Edinburgh completed the group's instrumental line-up. Vocalists are Andy McKay from Dumfries and Glaswegian Jimmy Burnett: apparently both are able to sing in the German language. Also in January, The Jaguars return to Inverness from London having stolen the show at the National Camping and Outdoor Life Exhibition at Olympia, where the Metropolitan police charge them with loitering within tent. . . In Banff, The Deveronaires have "the old-age pensioners of Macduff clapping and stamping.' A few nights later, they receive "a similar reception from a teenage club at Banff.'

Out of the Broch come The Beathovens, later to retitle themselves to avoid confusion with the Aberdeen group of the same name. As of February their engagements are limited to local Fraserburgh record shops, but they are optimistic about expanding their gigging potential. Claiming to "bridge the gap between R 'n' B and The Shadows', they are lead guitarist Doug Baillie, rhythm guitarist Brian Williams, drummer John Noble, bassist Alex Smith and vocalist Sandy Buchan. The Aberdeen combo operating under the same title play regularly at the Kaimhill Community Centre. Four of their five members are devout Mormons who decline to perform on Sundays on religious grounds. Lead guitarist Graeme Smith was later a member of The Facells - singer Stan Fraser continues forever on the city's entertainment scene. The others are Don Mackenzie on bass, George Esson on drums and second guitarist Bill Dunbar. Bill is also the group's principal songwriter.

Fronted by Tommy Dene's compadre, The Alex Harvey Soul Band are playing in Stonehaven just after Valentine's Day for the highly respectable fee of £50. . . Albert Bonici is fined £2 in March for allowing boys under 15 to play without the requisite license from the education authorities. Parents of the boys, who form The Phantoms, are admonished. The gig had taken place in Nairn the previous October. The Ian Campbell Folk Group's version of Bob Dylan's The Times They Are A-Changing hits number 42 chartwise. Formed in Birmingham in 1956 as The Clarion Skiffle Group (changing name two years later), they are led by Ian and his sister Lorna, who had flitted South in 1946. Their Ceilidh At The Crown is the first ever live folk LP, one of their ten albums during the Sixties alone. Prestigious British concerts take place at the Royal Albert Hall and the Royal Festival Hall in London. Across the pond, they perform at the Newport Folk Festival and appear on US TV shows Barn Dance, Hullabaloo and The Hootenanny Show. Fifteen years after his hit record Ian's sons Robin and Ali were to give chart compilers Food For Thought. . . May brings a change of name for The Jaguars who are packing them in at Doc's Club in Inverness. They become The Individuals, with a line-up of Chris Hughes on bass, Graham Hepburn on drums, John Urquhart on rhythm and vocals, and former Wildkat Dennis Kyte on lead guitar. Harry 'Lord Rockingham' Robinson is back in May as producer of The Spencer Davis Group's single Strong Love.

In the wake of fresh seaside resort battles between mods and rockers (the latter are now calling themselves greasers), The Rolling Stones play two shows at the Capitol in June. . . 18-year-old Brian Cameron is revealed as the man who tends The Flock from Inverness. As he washes their van for the third time that month, cleaning off lipstick and crayon messages from female fans, he says "It was getting dangerous. I have to be able to see out to drive.' Once he has set up the group's gear and they are playing, he finds somewhere comfy (the side of the stage or a vacant balcony seat) to have a snooze. The Flock are Tom Torrance, Alistair 'Beenz' MacBean, Sandy Johnston, Dave McKay and Drew Ross. Does their repertoire include I'll Never Find Another Ewe?

Evelyn Glennie is born in Aberdeen in July and is described as 'the monkey' by her mother. Fifteen months later in Iceland Gudmund also has a dottir, named Björk. Later the whole world would describe her as a bizarre. A few months on again, Aberdeen FC meet KR Reykjavìk in the preliminary round of the European Cup Winners Cup. Following a cruel 10-0 blitz at Pittodrie, the Dons are comfortably coasting 4-0 in the second leg in Iceland. The home 1,500 crowd go doo-lally when Hafsteinsson nearly bursts Bobby Clark's net, reducing the deficit to 14-1.

The entertainment scene in Aberdeen gives a cinematic choice of the Majestic, Playhouse, Cinema House, Queens Cinema, Grand Central, Torry Cinema, Odeon, Gaumont, ABC (previously the Regal) and Cosmo 2. In a state of close-down or conversion were the Kingsway and the Belmont. . . the latter is known colloquially as The Scratcher. The Gaumont has the added cachet of a double 'love seats' in the balcony, the location of much x-rated activity. . . If a night at the jigging is what you are after, the Douglas will cost you six bob and runs from 7.30 to 11.30 with a late supper licence. . . entry to The Palais is also six bob and down at The Beach you can see the Johnny Scott band and The Mighty Avengers. The Brig 'O Dee Stadium runs greyhound racing on Wednesdays and Saturdays. . . if you are a grappling fan, the Music Hall is the place to be. The good guys are the ballet dancing Ricki Starr, Gentleman George Kidd, Bert Royal and Vic Faulkener, and Les Kellett. The latter's dying swan act, in which he drunkenly reels around the ring, only to recover miraculously at the last moment to win the bout, is a thing of breathtaking beauty. . . even if he does use it every time. The baddies who old wifies attack with brollies and handbags are Mick McManus, Jackie 'Mr TV' Pallo, Kendo Nagasaki, 'Cry Baby' Jim Breaks, Alan Dennison and Steve Logan. . . "ask 'im ref, ask 'im.' Half an hour after these savage gladiatorial battles the combatants are to be found across the road in The Grill bar, having a friendly pint together and inviting each other round for Sunday lunch. Fixed? Wresting? Get out of here!

The Sorrows get to number 21 in the British singles chart in September with Take A Heart. Drummer on this disc is 20-year-old Neil Finlay from Huntly. After leaving the Gordon Schools, Neil worked at the music shop run by his father, where he tried out all the instruments before settling on the drums. His dad sent him off to join a pipe band when he was 15. . . he stayed there for two years before playing in his father's dance band. The Take A Heart LP, which was to become worth £100 on the 1997 collectors' market, claims it "will make your feet very, very tired long before the last track.' Re-released on CD in 1994, it certainly catches the zeitgeist: it's all there, a lumpy Stones-ish R 'n' B track, a couple of Pretties' type rave-ups, even a Beatley Merseysound-alike. Actually Neil's drumming is the highlight of the LP. The Sorrows' vocalist Don Maughn returned to the hit parade in 1968 as Don Fardon with Indian Reservation, basically a revamp of Take A Heart. . . In November, Union hassles and a fine for The Facells.

March 1966 has 100 teenagers twisting and shaking at Westerton School to The Beasts. At this venue, 14-year-old drummer Ronald Smith, 15-year-old bass player John Kain and lead guitarist John Morrison, also 15 - are joined by the fish worker James Peacock. The latter doubtless brings the wisdom of his 16 long years to the group, and would soon replace Robbie Benzies in The Tsars. Rumours abound in Aberdeen that Morgan Adams has been sacked from The Sunsets because he is too good-looking. The other Sunsetters, brothers Johnny Barclay and Bobby Vincent, are not available for comment. . . After attempting unsuccessfully to book firstly Manfred Mann and then The Barron Knights (both proving too expensive), the Students' Charities Campaign secure the services of The Steam Packet. They play the beginning-of-term hop at the Mitchell Hall and the Beatnik Ball the following night at the Beach Ballroom. Steam Packet are Long John Baldry, Julie Driscoll, Rod Stewart, and The Brian Auger Trinity. Also contributing to the charities campaign is Aberdeen's first indie single, The Misfits' cover of The Beatles' You Won't See Me. The Misfits carry the reputation of being a students' band, their natural habitat being the Mitchell Hall where they play to captive Saturday night university audiences. They have expanded both their repertoire and confidence sufficiently to venture out in to the big world of Aberdeen's Beach Ballroom, Cullen, Montrose, and Keith. They perform either to a dozen paying customers and a disgruntled caretaker, or to a place that is jumping because someone has told imaginative lies about which group is appearing that night. The historic recording takes place at Grampian's Queen's Cross studio, where Robin McKenzie on lead guitar, Dave Lunney on drums, Gerry O'Regan on rhythm and Alistair Simpson cut You Won't See Me and its flipside Hanging Around, written by Gerry.

Later that year, Aberdeen's Young Oxfam Group are also chasing the North East's spare cash through their YOG walk. . . In May, Stonehaven group The Yellb (aged between 15 and 17) find a place to jam and rehearse when Mrs Alice Blacklaws offers them the use of the empty wash-house at the rear of her shop. "If it keeps the young people off the street I am very happy. I am pleased to be able to help in any way.' This is the month when under-age drinking at 'discotheque sessions' in Aberdeen is considered a major threat to Western civilisation. Leader of country rock band The Corsairs Chris Sellars is killed en-route to a US miltary base gig at Edzell. Their van smashes into an unlit tractor bogie that has been parked on the road-side.

The Oldmeldrum Sports beat competition in June is won by The Georgians. The Inverurie group have Mike Foote playing lead guitar, Donald Young on bass, Alan Young on rhythm, and Sandy Ogston on vocals. The Fraserburgh Beathovens finally capitulate in the name game, re-titling themselves Wing Ding Dikets. . . what? From Shetland comes a burst of record releases on the Thule label. The Islands of Home is Elizabeth Barclay's first single, on which she is backed by Jim Halcrow, Willie Johnson and Jackie Robertson. Last year, Thule issued Sheltie group The Hamefarers' St Ninian's Isle and have plans for solo vocalist/guitarist Gordon Smith.

The Phantoms return to Buckie in September from a six-week, 35 concert tour of Poland. William Smith, Steve Coull, Stewart Geddes, Eric Farquhar and Stephen Wojcik also appeared on Polish television and radio. The trip was organised by Stephen's father Emil Wojcik, who is The Phantoms' manager. . . The North of Scotland pop-song writing contest in Thurso brings joy for 17-year-old Andy Munro, a member of The Talismen. Second and third places go to Ben MacDonald (from Wick's The Dynamos) and 12 year old Lorna Humphries. Fourth comes The Revelations' John Stewart, and a joint effort from another Talisman, Ian Sinclair. Inverness journalist Brian Swanson takes fifth place. . . In Aberdeen, Roger Daltrey has a lot to answer for when the exhibitionist Stewart Kemp overdoes his imitative swinging of microphone-on-its-lead act: the mic makes explosive contact with Gordon Ross' face. Gingerly spitting blood and teeth, Rossi moans something along the lines of "Oh heavens, how unfortunate. My oral and nasal features seem to have been badly smashed, necessitating painful and complicated surgery. But what ho! Happy New Year, Stewart old chap.'

Phase Five from Fraserburgh tell the world in February of 1967 that they prefer playing outside of their home town. "There's a certain section here who just don't dig us at all.' In the same month The Messengers make the long journey from Peterhead to Aberdeen. They are a young Christian group who perform "gospel songs and Negro spirituals to a big turn-out of teenagers' at Ronnie Ferrari's Marischal Street cafe. As the UK's gutter press fills its boots when reporting on a drugs bust at Keith Richards' Redlands home, sniggering teenagers leave sweetie shop assistants baffled as they ask for "a Marianne Faithfull', when what they actually want is a bar of chocolate to fill the gap (astrologically, Mars in Venus). . . Kurt Cobain is born in Aberdeen. . . Washington State, USA.

The Out travel on the blue canoe to Shetland, the whole trip costing £50. Drummer Ross Baird was formerly with The Gravediggers and The Outsiders from Banchory. Vocalist Johnny McKeand has been one of Elgin's Tearaways, whilst bassist Mike Marshall and rhythm guitarist Ian Fraser are both ex -members of Force X, a combo from Inverness-shire - where Mike also played with Johnny and The Diamonds. Ken Whitcombe is The Out's lone Sassenach. . . they are being tipped to "pose a serious problem for the main groups in Aberdeen: The Throb, The Cult, The Quantrells and The Royal Teens.'

Colour comes to British TV in July on BBC 2 only. . . and The Out are back in the news as qualifiers through the first heat of the Aberdeen and North East beat contest. Their mode of transporting equipment to and from engagements is getting them noticed: Whitcombe, a Scouser who is studying at Aberdeen University, explains that their black Rolls Royce hearse is ideal for the job. By now, Mike Wallace is on lead guitar: future C & W star in Germany Kevin Henderson is on rhythm. Fellow qualifiers through this heat were The Quantrells and The (Aberdeen) Beathovens. The latter earned the name at school because of their love of music. Stan Fraser and Graeme Smith were playing alongside Russell Milne on drums and Jim Pike on bass. Formed back in 1964, The Quantrells line-up now includes lead guitarist and vocalist Leslie Cumming. He lives in Kingswells, as does bass player Bryson Kemp. Organist Gus McLellan is a Newburgh loon. Raymond Ross plays drums and the Quantrells are completed by young guitarist Billy Spratt (a former Tsar and future Facell). Treble Chance, Chapel Street and The Knod are performing locally.

Three Blind Mice arrive home in Inverness after a disastrous trip to Sweden. Rod McKenzie, Don Cumming and Douglas McKay had ditched their jobs and pooled their savings to pay the travel costs. Despite having a "fantastic fortnight playing to packed club audiences', they run into work permit difficulties. They borrow money from the British vice-consul to get themselves repatriated, and leave their van and instruments behind in Stockholm. Three Blind Mice. . . see how they run. They plan a change of name to BB and D: "broke, bitter and disillusioned.' The Beathovens win the Aberdeen and NE beat championship final in August at the Beach Ballroom, with 431 votes. There is no use in crying over spilt milk for The Facells and Rhubarb, who score 273 and 224 votes respectively. After each group plays for 45 minutes, guest disc jockey Alan 'Fluff' Freeman presented the winners with their trophy and a cheque for £50 - a lot of money. . . not arf. The competition is sponsored by Aberdeen and District Milk Marketing Board, in conjunction with the local branch of the Musicians' Union. The event causes bad feeling in the local group community: amid allegations that The Beathovens' victory was fixed by busing in hordes of young Mormons from throughout the North East, The Facell's vocalist Sonny Pearce "wraps one of The Beathovens around a lamppost outside the Beach.'

Also in August, the Marine Offences Bill, outlawing radio stations from broadcasting to the UK from offshore, comes into effect. This sank Radio Scotland, Caroline, and most of the pirate fleet. . . In San Francisco, underground paper The Berkeley Barb suggests the possibility of getting high by smoking banana skins. . . bewildered staff at Knowles fruit and veg shop at the top of Market Street are baffled by the daily queue of optimistic hippies. These long-hairs are digging such Aberdeen bands as The Inset, Purple Amber, Perfect Alibi, Liquid Stone and Syn of the Tymes. Flings aint wot they used to be. . . Wing Ding Dikets take to wearing mini kilts on stage. . . shapes of flings to come. . . ? What's the difference between Sandie Shaw and Denis Law? Sandie stopped wearing shoes in her teens. . . Denis didn't have shoes until he was 14.

The hit parade is assailed by such as Strawberry Fields Forever, Mellow Yellow, Arnold Layne, I Can Hear The Grass Grow, Itchycoo Park and People Are Strange. Jimi Hendrix singles this year include The Wind Cries Mary and Burning Of The Midnight Lamp. By now, long-playing records (albums in the new parlance, LPs were old-hat) are all-important at the expense of seven-inch singles which are becoming much-derided pop candy-floss, with a similar shelf-life. We now have 33-and-a-third revolutions-per-minute instead of the previous 45 but the real revolution is altogether more durable and seriously important. Prior to this transition, LPs were basically collections of unrelated individual songs, but now young musicians are getting to grips with joined-up writing. Hence the truly defining stuff is Are You Experienced, Axis Bold As Love, Sgt Pepper's Lonely Hearts Club Band, Disraeli Gears, Forever Changes, Their Satanic Majesties Request and Mr Fantasy. In Aberdeen the flower power message gets through to Trevor Hart, who says to his ma "Love and peace, man.' Not hearing him properly, Mrs H glances at the clock and replies "Maybe you would, but you'll just have to wait half an hour, the stovies are nearly ready.' Trevor's local gig competitors include The Hellcats, Alcatraz, Dr Marigold's Prescription, Eskimo Blue and Masada.

Things are buzzing at the Beehive in September as 'a bottle-throwing mob of teenagers' chase The Out. . . Back in Inverurie, Twinkle's People are getting most of their work from twinkle-toed Bert Ewen. The band's leader is vocalist Mike McRae - he also plays alto sax and does a bit of dance band work on the accordion. His people are Mike Strachan on Premier drums, Les Pratt on Fender Stratocaster, Billy Wright on guitar and Vox Jaguar organ, Gogs Cran on Hofner bass, and Robbie Spence on tenor sax. They are playing throughout the North East and South to Brechin and Edzell, travelling originally in an Austin J2 and then a Commer van. At these venues, Twinkle's People play soul and pop on 'first half' work for the likes of Chris McClure, Dean Ford and The Gaylords, Pete Kelly's Solution and The Yardbirds. They rehearse every Sunday afternoon in the Inverurie Railway Hall, which was previously a popular Saturday night venue for old time dancing. . . it was later to be demolished, its place to be taken by the current Health Centre. Twinkle's People came from members of The Georgians, The Z Guitars and Seteque. Also in Inverurie, The Steele Combo issue their Good Times LP. With the encouragement and help of Bert Ewen, the band and their popular road manager wee Sandy Meldrum appear all over Scotland from John O' Groats to the borders. Their album includes John Fogerty's Lodi, The Drifters' Down At The Club, Macca's Let It Be and Johnny Stewart's Elusive Face. The Combo are led by Billy Steele (sax and piano) and include Eddie Douglas (sax and trumpet), Gogs Wilson (drums), Jim Walker (lead guitar), Johnny Smith (bass) and Jim McKenzie (lead vocals). . . Jim later joins Mr Fantasy. Later Inverurie supernovas are Jolson. Amazingly popular locally, they are Alan Robertson on organ and vocals, the same Jim Walker, John Smith on bass and vocals, and drummer Brian Hosie. BBC radio finally pull the plug on Housewives' Choice, a show which had been presented since 1946 by one-time Beach Ballroom bandleader wee George Elrick. The Middle Earth record label is launched at the end of October, 1969. First releases are albums from Arcadium and Wooden O, together with a single from female folkie Sweet Plum, from Inverness. Also from the the highlands are The Lite Brigade, and Aberlour is home to Rising Sun. Aberdeen pop-rockers Blizzard are Mike McCombie on vocals, Bill Sutherland and Charlie Adams on dual lead guitars, Jim Anderson on bass and Bill Adams on drums. Whilst folkie Ian MacDonald is making a name for himself oot the road, an alternative venue for Aberdeen youngsters, desperate to get into clinches with those of the opposite gender, is Madame's at the Cowdray Hall. This is the place where nervous, plooky, sap-arising adolescents are taught the Palais Glide by Madame Isobel Murray.

Chapter 10

"Gie us some Jimi Hendrix'

The Frank Robb experience can be somewhat of an acquired taste. Some seeing him for the first time get themselves in a right huff when he shines the light in their faces and brings out the rubber truncheons. For those audience members in the know, the whole thing is a hoot. Combine his unique caustic style of humour with his highly original compositions, and you've found yourself the best night out that a few pints can buy.

His musical career started in the mid Sixties with traditional folk group The Crofters, co-existing with the final throes of the old variety theatre circuit. Treading the boards with a dying breed of vaudevillean veteran turns, Frank absorbed an entertainment ethos, which has remained fundamental to his act. Crofters' television appearances and an eponymous album (on Decca's Beltona subsidiary label) led on to the founding an Aberdeen institution when Frank, Archie Buchanan and Tony Duguid got together as Hedgehog Pie (not to be confused with the same-named Tyneside band). Initially an acoustic guitars, harmonica, mandolin, banjo and vocal trio, their repertoire hung on traditional folk and Frank's original material. Archie's departure to fresh fields (including Wallop) saw Ronnie Nicol join, as the set progressed towards the contemporary electrified end of the spectrum.

Frank's association with drummer Ian Milne, bassist Dave Hepburn and guitarist Mike Bowyer saw him drift away from pure folk treatments towards upbeat, kicking rock interpretations of his distinctive compositions. This heralded Superklute, perchance Aberdeen's best rock band of the period.

Davie Hepburn was succeeded on bass by Hugh Falconer - the latter's subsequent move to the USA left a gap for Bob Wilson to fill on guitar. With the mid-Seventies recruitment of bassist Dallas Munro and with Glaswegian John Madden sharing dual lead guitar with Wilson, they transformed into country-rock diablos: record bar takings coursed through the ABC Bowl's till as Superklute attracted droves of cowboy-booted, pressed-jeaned topers, dopers and no-hopers. Frank didn't take any shit from the crowd. "I don't come yapping in your ears when you're laying bricks so shut up when I'm working.' Early reconstructed adaptations of Brown Eyed Girl and Big Yellow Taxi apart, original material predominated: a mix of Madden's guitar oriented epics and Frank's skilfully-crafted and often hard-faced numbers. Some of his compositions were already familiar to Aberdeen audiences from his HP and solo pub appearances. Painted Lady, The Mercenary, I See You and the vitriolic Mouse Killed The Minstrel were toughened-up by Superklute's tight, punchy readings: as Frank says "If a song is any good, it doesn't matter if it is performed in a five-piece rock band context, or in a solo acoustic situation. The song is the thing.' One popular finale was a showbiz extravaganza The Rock 'n' Rock Suicide Show, dedicated to the ultimate supergroup in the sky (Buddy, Jimi, Janis et al). Wonderful, irreverent entertainment, signed off by such audience-endearing barbs as "To a musician, applause is a banquet. Thank you for that spam sandwich.'

February 1979: a shakedown of band members. "Are you sufficiently committed to the cause to abandoned the day job?' A revamped conglomeration named Middle East resulted, where-in Mike Haywood picked up Dallas Munro's bass spot, and Dave Kinneburgh substituted for Bob Wilson on guitar, keyboards and vocals. Dave's enforced and unfortunate withdrawal later opened the door for keyboard-meister Mike Stobbie, a defector from Aberdeen's heavy metal supremos Pallas. The two Middle Eastern beardies Frank and Ian told Granite City fanzine: "This band formed for the sole reason of pulling a record deal. This (ABC Bowl) gig is bread and butter, no more. We're ready any time for the road, but not without record company backing. . . pointless to hawk ourselves around the club and pub circuit down South, for probably less cash than we get here.' Hopes for a recording deal rested on material taped at studios owned by those Scottish rock legends, Middle Of The Road. . . Last night I heard Frankie Robb singing this song. . . In a positive vein, Frank stated "For the first time I feel I'm playing in a band without passengers. Everyone contributes and has their part to play.' All the more unfortunate then, that when the recording aspirations floundered, Middle East went their own separate ways.

Frank had no intention of playing with another band (preferring instead to work in a solo environment) citing financial short-falls and his dissatisfaction with the group's non-progression.

Frustration in not pulling that elusive recording contract was evident: "We've been at the ABC for about eight years now, but we're no further on. I simply have to make a living from my music, and there is no way I could do it with the band. The guys have proposed a move to London, but it's simply not on for me. I can see what will happen. . . I'm not into performing for free and I'm definitely not interested in having to pay someone for the privilege of letting me play.'

Superklute's concluding gig together was "one of the few occasions when you really did feel that they could have played all night. Frank was in good voice throughout the evening - though most of his insulting banter with the crowd was gone, replaced with thanks to audience and staff for putting up with so much abuse over the years. Many departures from bands seem to be surrounded by bad feeling, but this was obviously not one of them.'

Frank's subsequent nationwide 'have guitar, will travel' career has taken in the Edinburgh Fringe and many other festivals. Highlights include compering Aberdeen's Alternative Festival Club, composing music for BBC radio's The State of Scotland series and his his own self-composed albums Life Lines and Silver City. He also scribed the occasional guest column for the Evening Express However, it's not all glitz and glamour: does anyone remember him banging on meaningfully about Flowers by Sadie on an early Northsound jingle?

By way of an introduction to Singing In A Bar, one of his older numbers, Frank recalls being on-stage with his five piece electric rock band: he had punters asking for Flower Of Scotland. Conversely, when playing a solo acoustic gig, the same species of moron will shout up "Gie us some Jimi Hendrix'.

Not surprising, then, that Frank's philosophy is to get his heckle in first. "I don't really slag the audience, I make observations about them. Occasionally they get annoyed, some folk think they are too important to take part. When I hit them with the punch line, sometimes they actually laugh. What I won't do is sacrifice someone's night out for the show. I don't think I have ever gone for a genuinely shy person. Comedy is the big test. If half the audience applaud a song, you get by. But if only half of them get the joke, it's a disaster.' Recently he has been in good spirits through a distillery-sponsored string of club and cabaret dates in London, which he performed as Watching Time, his third album of original material, was completed. Recorded at the RSD studio near Fyvie, with a supergroup (virtually Frank's Fairports), the line-up and instrumentation reflects a tangential direction for him. Former 30 Footer Ross Donald plays electric guitar with Ray Stewart on banjo, Steve Ranson on piano, keyboards and percussion, Alan Clark on accordion, Peter Hawkey on whistle and flute, with Shirley Peterson providing additional vocals and harmonies. Watching Time opens with North Sea Tiger, Frank reflects upon two decades of change since oil first darkened North East doors, when we used to raise hell at the alley. . . now they call me pussycat. And Wild Weekend In Dublin Upstairs At O'Donahues is a hooch-and-dirl brammer that would cheer up Private Fraser in Dads Army.

Frank reveals his career master-plan. "I will continue doing what I do until I retire at 65. I realised early on that there was little point in being a star at 30 and a has-been at 35. Or indeed, what's the sense in shooting up like a rocket at 40 and coming down like a stick at 42? As an entertainer, I am improving as time goes by. The target is to hit my peak at 60, then I won't have to sustain my success for too long.'

. . . .

As Frank left the Middle East, John Madden spoke for the remaining members. "I think we will lose some fans, but we're more than just a backing band. We plan to continue playing at the ABC as a four piece.' A flying start. . . Milne and Stobbie were in a road accident, en-route to Buckie. Mike came out of it lightly but Ian's injuries were more serious, incapacitating him over Christmas 1979 and New Year of 1980.

Reflecting their new start, the name Rue de Remarx was adopted in March of 1980. A month later, they advanced to the final six of the Scottish finals of a Daily Mirror and Arctic Lite lager sponsored rock contest. Co-candidates were another Aberdeen outfit, Horizon (featuring Jacqui Copland on vocals and later to become Private ID). Rue de Remarx didn't win the competition, but magnanimous in defeat, they donated their consolation case of lager to fans in the audience. Stobbie's verdict that the beer 'tasted rancid' probably influenced their generosity.

In June, they were off the Venue in London to contest, along with Aberdeen's The Shapiros, the final of the Melody Maker Rock '80 tournament. Their score-card was healthy enough until the votes from the ex-Aberdeen jury (in the person of Annie Lennox) came in. Perhaps she was still throwing aside her Aberdeen roots? Despite failure in the MM event, RdR sensed sufficient enthusiasm from London's recording cartel to justify a major push from the band themselves. Lindsay Adam, a sound engineer who had previously worked with Pallas, was recruited to handle a £5,000, 1500w PA system (bought on the never-never. . . it never was paid for). November first, 1980 saw Rue de Remarx bring their Aberdeen ABC Bowl residency to a finale, before relocating to London. . . is this starting to sound familiar?

Quite a final night by all accounts. "The floor in front of the stage was never empty, the sheer delight and enthusiasm of the dancers was something special. Few local groups could boast such popularity. When they had completed their act, including encores, Archie Carroll, manager of the ABC Bowl, had to plead with the audience to let the band go. It was only when Mike Haywood came onstage to convince the fans of the pointlessness of their persistence, that the shouting and clapping stopped.' A stunned John Madden said "I just can't believe it. When you've got the crowd behind you in here, there's nothing like the Bowl for atmosphere. But this was just terrific.'

So yet again an Aberdeen band found themselves pegging away in London, but only three months later, Ian Milne had changed his mind: "The idea had been niggling me for some time, and one morning I just woke up and decided - this is it. Although I enjoyed myself in London I decided I had to get out because my roots are in country music. The band were really surprised about it. I came back on Hogmanay and I've already sold my drum kit. I have no regrets about leaving the band - I just want to concentrate on working for a living now.' The band were fortunate in locating a replacement in London-based Aberdonian Peter Buchan (ex of home-town combos Crescendo and Manray). Rue de Remarx were being well received at Dingwalls and The Greyhound, bill-sharing with Frankie Miller. The London music press came sniffing.

Melody Maker's feature Beacon From the North touched upon the band's difficulties in finding gigs, a situation described by Stobbie: "A classic Catch 22, 'cos no recording contract meant no gig. No gigs meant no recording contract.' Even after securing work they found precious little gold in the London streets. Having hauled their own PA and lights all the way from Aberdeen, they brought their set-up into their first gig on Boxing Day, 1980. "Sorry lads, you've got to use the house lighting rig, non-negotiable condition of your contract.' This ripped a fiver off the top of the £15 fee. . . then came van hire at £12. Basic arithmetic identifies a two-quid hole for the privilege of working on a statutory holiday. Frank Robb's prophetic words must surely have begun to haunt them: does he have crystal balls? MM's scribe optimistically signed off his article "Their competence and professionalism is heavily marinated with freshly squeezed enthusiasm. And, given the somnambulant quality of current chart popsters, Rue de Remarx offer a beacon of hope for music.'

Under the wing of Jonathon Cook's Fatcat Productions agency, the gig quota began to improve. Manager Richard Lawler proved ultimately to be inexperienced and of limited usefulness. . . but the impressive single One Way Trip / Full Circle, produced by ex-Nice guitarist David O'List, provided a succinct snap-shot of John Madden's undiscovered guitar prowess. Finding a suitable drummer was proving problematic as Peter's jazz inclinations didn't sit comfortably with RdR's rounded AOR sound. Drummers came and went, including another London based Aberdonian Ron MacIntosh (formerly with Horizon), Welshman Mike Slocombe and the 19-year-old Englishman Phil Butson (where's the Irishman?) who eventually made the drum stool his own. Also indicative of the band's ambition was the involvement of 'image consultant' Heather Mensa, costumier for the dance-recording troupe Hot Gossip. Further recording was undertaken with the Oakwood International organisation, and interest in the band began frothing. Until. . . those nasty gremlins had been too-long dormant, and now inevitably attacked yet another London-based Aberdeen band.

John's prized guitar was stolen, although he eventually recovered it from a Tin Pan Alley second-hand music shop thanks to a friendly London bobby. The electric company then ripped the power supply out the boys' flat, followed by the first recorded incident of a landlord doing a moonlight flit, taking the band's gear with him. Ensuing searches for affordable accommodation marginalised them out of central London to Barking, where despised day-jobs were reluctantly resumed to pay the rent. Commuting left precious little time available for musical development (which was, after all, the reason for being there in the first place). Finally, the record producer insisted on depping a session drummer for Phil Butson, who decided to beat it. This catalogue of calamity proved too much for John - he returned home to Glasgow, totally scunnered of the music business. Rock thus lost Madden's major talent. He had written and performed many a startlingly original guitar Meisterwerke. He was the main writer and front man and when he went tatties o'er the side, the band saw no way forward.

Mike Haywood became resident in France, dividing his time between skiing and playing in a band called Contraband, entertaining a sur la piste glitterati set, including Peter Gabriel and Richard Branson We follow the fortunes of pizza king Mike Stobbie elsewhere in this treatise.

A deplorable ending for an excellent band: if that's justice, then the Graham Souness gets Christmas cards from Siggi Jonsson, George McCluskey, Peter Nicholas, Brian Irvine and that gadgie from Steaua Bucharest.

. . . .

Concurrent with Frank Robb's folk rock efforts in Aberdeen, Iain and Gavin Sutherland were ploughing similar fields, rooted in Peterhead. Their father George Sutherland ran a Blue Toon dance band in the late 1940s and 1950s. Usually a five or seven-piece, they played jazz, swing, and hits of the day: reels and strathspeys were thrown in as required. According to Iain, George "had a good record collection, mainly jazz. This was the first music Gav and I heard.' When he relocated the family to Staffordshire in 1958, Mr S bought guitars for his sons, and teaching them to play accompanyment to his jazz fiddle, 'à la Stephane Grappelli'. Later, the brothers worked out Shads and early Beatles numbers.

Iain formed a school band (later joined by Gavin), playing mid-Sixties beat and R 'n' B. On leaving school they played the Midlands and North West England for a couple of years "without making much headway'. In 1971, they moved to part-time jobs in London. Through a music publisher friend-of-a-friend a demo studio was made available. Auditions took place for Warner Brothers and Island, with Chris Blackwell firming up a deal first. The debut album The Sutherland Brothers Band introduced Iain and Gavin to the music public at large, their distinctive vocal harmony and guitar sound filled out by session musicians.

Establishing a more stable line-up and paying off the hired hands, the brothers aligned themselves in 1973 with English guitar-led quartet Quiver, already with a couple of Warner Brothers albums under their belts. Iain remembers "We were obviously unable to perform our recorded work live in a 'folk duo' format.' The Suthbros needed a band at a time when Quiver needed songs and a vocalist. The Peterhead loons got on well with Quiver (Tim Renwick on guitar, Bruce Thomas on bass, Willie Wilson on drums, and Pete Woods on keyboards) both musically and socially. "The impetus of the amalgamation gave us our first American top-20 hit You Got Me Anyway and a correspondingly successful LP Lifeboat. We toured this album throughout the States, supporting Elton John. Suddenly playing to between fifteen and twenty thousand people instead of UK college gigs was a real baptism of fire, and a great experience for us'. Bruce Thomas left the band prior to the 1974 Beat Of The Street album (later he joined Elvis Costello's Attractions, mysteriously to ghost into Aberdeen some years later, but that episode is still to come). Thomas was temporarily replaced by Tex Comer from Ace (before Gavin moved to bass), an episode inspiring Paul Carrack to write the enduringly immaculate How Long. "We did need a bass player at the time and Ace were on the verge of splitting up. Tex did several gigs and some recordings with us, Paul naturally felt insecure and bitter at the time. However, we've been friends ever since'. So, another exclusive for you: How Long is not about a deceitful woman, as is commonly thought.

In August of 1975 a smile crept across the face of Iain's bank manager when Rod Stewart's version of Sailing topped the British chart. It would re-enter the hit parade a further twice and was an unqualified international hit. Stewart's choice surprised Iain at the time. "He had talked to us about recording another of our songs The Fire so we weren't expecting it when his cover of Sailing came out instead. For us, the song is a 'spiritual', probably inspired by our North East roots because the sea and the fishing industry in our blood. Other associations cropped up, like the Sailor TV series and so it caught on. Whether or not Rod understood the lyrics (as I meant them) I don't know, but he covered it sincerely. He obviously popularised the song, helping us a lot at the time.'

The following April saw The Sutherland Brothers and Quiver score a top-five hit under their own steam with the sublime Arms of Mary from the album Reach For The Sky. But as the next album Down

To Earth album appeared in 1977 the boys concurred that the SBQ amalgamation had run its course, Iain comments that "it felt like we had reached a natural conclusion.' Henceforth they reverted to The Sutherland Brothers title for When The Night Comes Down.

The quality of the disbanded SBQ musicians is beyond debate. . . Renwick initially went solo under the guise of Lazy Racer, before becoming a top session hand for Elton John, The Bee Gees, Dionne Warwick, Eric Clapton, Pink Floyd and Tom Jones. Willie Wilson did some work with his schoolmate Dave Gilmour, and was a member of the shadow Pink Floyd which toured The Wall in 1979 and 1980. He subsequently did the rounds with Lonnie Donegan, Joe Brown and Hank Wangford before forming The Dolphins (a sometime blues band numbering Renwick, Clem Clemson and Snowy White amongst its members). Bruce Thomas has continued his association with Elvis Costello. Pete Woods, after working with Wilson on The Wall tour, died in sad circumstances in New York in December 1993.

Since then Iain has recorded two solo albums, 1983's Mixed Emotions and Fandango a couple of years later: "As a natural songwriter, the records were really put down to get those latest batches of songs out of my system. I still write quite a lot and intend doing another LP soon, having built up a long list of unrecorded stuff.' Other than Rod Stewart, many major artists have covered his songs: "Fortunately I've had quite a lot of success as a writer' - including Paul Young, Bonnie Tyler, The Everley Brothers, Merle Haggard and John Travolta. Iain's self-built a 16-track studio at his Staffordshire home has hosted sessions by Mickey Jupp, Clive Gregson, Christine Collister and Paul Carrack. "I'm not really interested in running it as a commercial venture, it has mainly been friends using the studio.' Iain's son (recently graduated from university) is monopolising the facility: "He wants to have a crack at the music business.'

Gavin recorded a Dutch-label folk-rock album in 1982 before immersing himself in computers and electronics. Iain tells us "He returned to the North East about seven years back. He is a published author with The Whaling Years about the Peterhead whalers, he edited diaries of a descendant of Christian Watt and is involved in heritage projects in Peterhead and Banff.' Gavin, who still returns to music but only when the muse takes him, has "re-acquired a bit of the old accent which we lost a long time ago.'

When royalty cheques have slowed, work locations became more mundane: bakeries, chicken-processing factories and the like. Perhaps not a bad thing, according to Gavin: "The chicken factory was like being in hell, but everybody has to do things they don't like. It keeps your feet on the ground.'

Iain again: "I look back on the Seventies with mostly fond memories of working with SBQ. As far as I know, Tim, Willie, Gavin and myself have been more satisfied on our own separate projects and music, but we have discussed recently the idea of a reunion: a few gigs and some recording. Because of commitments, this can't happen immediately, so it's only a possibility. I still get most satisfaction from writing and recording a new song.' What is his biggest regret? "Like most naive young musicians we signed bits of paper and contracts without really knowing or considering the long-term consequences. As usual, learning the hard way.' But what of the highs? "The biggest kick was probably when Arms Of Mary was a big hit in the UK, a breakthrough we had been working towards for four or five years. . .Although I left the NE a long time ago, I still have a lot of family connections there and a cottage in Gamrie. That's where I feel most relaxed and at peace with things. I'm very aware and proud of my roots, and find that my best songs are inspired by the feel of the place. . . Arms Of Mary was originally called Walking In The Hills Of Gamrie.'

. . . .

As we are now about four days into country-folk music land, let's just hold on a tattie-pickin' minute to reflect upon a close encounter of the sweaty, bespectacled variety. July 30th, 1981 dawned like any other hot, dusty summer day at Aberdeen's Country and Western ranch. Throughout the territory, hombres and hombresses were already preparing for that evening's hoedown at the Mean Machine down at the Metro Hotel in Market Street.

Spurs were shone in Summerhill, boots were burnished in Bucksburn, ten gallon hats were tilted in Torry. The backing track to this feverish activity, We were so poor that our dog had no legs, every day I'd take him out for a drag, typifies this upbeat, cheery musical genre. (Aberdeen guitar-meister Billy Bremner reckons that if you play a country song backwards, you get your kids back and they release you from prison.) That night's band of hired hands would be led by a black-clothed stranger, riding into town unannounced and unaccredited. Born Declan McManus, the kid achieved infamy as the fastest sneer in the West under his nom de guerre Elvis Costello.

Elvis' affection for country ballads pre-dated his uninvited arrival on the British rock scene, having played Hank Williams numbers in folk clubs and pubs. A country number Stranger In The House was dropped by Stiff Records from Costello's inaugural 1977 album My Aim Is True. They also chucked his personal cassette The Best Of George Jones out of the Stiff tour-bus window. Having contributed guitar and vocals to Jones' own version of Stranger In The House at CBS in Nashville, Elvis recalls that his country association was strengthened by the marriage of his producer Nick Lowe to Carlene Carter. The latter is a product of The Carter Family dynasty (June Carter's daughter and Johnny Cash's step-daughter). . . Aberdonian Sultan of Sessions Billy Bremner contributed his distinctive guitar licks to her Musical Shapes album, some time before Carlene shocked The Grand Old Opry in general and her step-father in particular, when she proudly claimed that her music put "the c—t back in country.'

Following the disappointing sales of 1980's emotive and classic LP Trust, Elvis stood back from song-writing. "Having developed the strong conviction that I could better express my current feelings through other people's songs, I started to collect material to record.' Prior to the Nashville arrival of Elvis and his band in May of 1981, producer Billy Sherill canvassed publishing houses for locally written material for the forthcoming album. Binliners full of demo tapes were sifted before commencement of the sessions for what became Almost Blue. The entire project was filmed by a television crew under the direction of Peter Carr, for later transmission on LWT's South Bank Show.

The Attractions who recorded the album at CBS's Nashville studio A, and performed local live club dates (filmed for inclusion in the television arts programme), were Steve Nieve on keyboards, John McFee on guest lead and pedal steel guitars, Pete Thomas on drums, and Bruce Thomas on bass. The latter previously worked with Blue Tooners Iain and Gavin Sutherland.

Elvis's dramatic change of musical direction was popular with the British record buying public. The principal single from these sessions, Jerry Chestnut's Good Year For The Roses hit number six in the charts, preparing the way for Almost Blue to achieve tenth spot in the album ratings.

Whilst Stiff Records brought the recording project in on-time to commercial success, the South Bank Show team struggled. Vital film of live performances was lost, rendering their programme incomplete. Hence it was decided to tape a specially-staged show to enable LWT to replace the lost footage. The location for this live performance had to be remote from the London-based music press. Which was how the Aberdeen Country and Western Club came to be unsuspecting hosts to Elvis Costello, The Attractions, and the South Bank Show that July night of 1981.

On this occasion the filming proceeded without a hitch as the Metro hootenanny climaxed the televised documentary. At the end of the night cowpokes and cowgals moseyed off home to relate excitedly to their family and friends of the dark, horn-rimmed stranger. As The Bi-focal Kid and his posse left town with a cloud of dust and a mighty "Hi Yo, Attractions - away!', the saloon doors swung closed on this episode of Aberdeen rock history. . . or did they?

Thirteen years later Demon Records (the company's directors include Stiff founder Jake Riviera and Elvis himself), engaged in an important celebratory re-appraisal of the optically-challenged one's back catalogue. His entire repertoire was lovingly remastered and augmented by the addition of appropriate previously-unreleased versions and live material. September 1994 therefore heralded the arrival of a revamped and revitalised Almost Blue on CD, consolidated by a handful of live gems from that Market Street shit-kickers' ball all those years ago. This album provides a snap shot of a fascinating, but largely unremembered event. It also has Elvis bridging the years back to boozed-up uncles murdering those wonderful Jim Reeves songs at New Year parties.

. . . .

OK, so maybe country music doesn't fry your own particular bacon, and if not, who can blame you. For many, the genre has been irredeemably polluted by the cloying, sickly Scottish-Irish pap saturating MOR airwaves. . . (the author's father-in-law came up with a real doozie: The Indians, an Irish country band who wear full Apache get-up. Truly awful. . . well done Albert). If you are able to identify anything of artistic credibility in the Devine Sydney or those loveable broths of boys Daniel and Dominic, please pick up a pen and let the author know. On the other hand, you probably aren't allowed to use sharp instruments.

But before we finally say that the music has lost its flavour, let's do ourselves a favour. . . (thanks, Adam). Revisit the harrowing country blues of Hank Williams, the chillingly introspective Nick Lowe Brit pop-country album The Impossible Bird and a whole body of Billy Bremner's work (the alternative Nashville take of Kirsty McColl's There's A Guy on her Desperate Character album is a down-home joy). There's a whole world of dynamite pedal steel guitar out there so give it a try. . . you could do a lot worse than starting with Aberdeen expat Kevin Henderson's 'coming of age' Kentucky Bound CD on the Gnoth label. By the time it was released in Germany in 1993, Kev had steadily built up a reputation as one of Europe's leading exponents of yee-hah cowboy songs. Now just slow down a mite there, partners. . . don't go getting all sniffy at the concept of non-Americans singing this stuff. After all, nobody has blinked an eye at white Brit jazzers, bluesers or R 'n' B shouters.

The more pulsating tracks on Kevin's Dave Bell-produced could easily be taken aside, and with new lyrics, would constitute straight-ahead, up-beat, banging rock. Title track Kentucky Bound is whole-some, mama's chicken dumplings and g'night John Boy fare, (nice banjo, though), but serves as a gentle introduction to Kevin's own composition Caught In A Corner. It really starts to happen here. . . the stylish acoustic overture deviates into T. Rexian Jeepster electric licks (I kid you not. . . and it works), country boogie par excellence: just luuurv that honky tonk piano.

As the amps cool, the beguiling Franklin has Kevin's vocals dropping an octave or six. . . Tequila, Chilli and You is a menuesque Tex-Mex tale of a con being released from the slammer. . . followed by a monstrously macho take on High Noon (you know, the one Bert Ewen used to sing out in Inverurie. . . Doughnut Forsake Me Oh My Darlin'). The Mississippi gambling tale Steamboat leads into the incredibly poppy balladeering of The Message, devoid of obvious country references. Then comes more amazement. Ignore the corny title: Cowgirls Cry must the very first country-reggae tune (Skank Williams ?) Yep, reggae in the ol' cantina, and unbelievably, it fits. Graduating from the same up-tempo contemporary country school as Timbuk3's Future's So Bright comes Hard Driving Man, a trucking saga made luminescent by Dave's superb guitar picking. So far Kevin has given us Marc Bolan in Nashville, Bob Marley in Houston, and now we get Ritchie Blackmore in Alabama as Rebel Highway delivers ballsy metal-country rock.

Congrats to Hendo on his vocal performance throughout. Dave Bell's production is faultless and non-clichéd. . . and the guys in the band are damn fine musicians. The album is a prime example of how country can be valid, contemporary and innovative. The follow-up Gnoth label album Lights Of Heaven sustained Kevin's ever-improving quality music.

On his Sunday radio show Roy Rhodes does his best to maximise plays of just such modern, immediate country music, although it's a damn hard fight against the conservative tastes of the majority of his listeners. Lowest common denominator rules, OK? Such take-the-easy-route programming only serves to alienate potential new country fans. Some 15 years ago we left Rhodes as Roy Foreman, dropping out of the city's pub rock circuit to go it alone after years in combos like The East Coast Flames, Mr Fantasy and The Throb. "When you are playing solo, it kind of limits you to either folk or country music. I had always been a fan of hillbilly rock, Elvis and Carl Perkins sort of stuff. So country it was, and as Roy Rhodes I played at various places in the town, including the Old World Inn. I sent a demo of my stuff to labels I thought might be sympathetic to my music, and it was picked up by Canon Records in Chester. They released my first LP, The Country Side Of Roy Rhodes.'

Canon went into liquidation. "Not my fault, honest', with Roy's second album already in the can. Having left his regular job at Telemech, he went into repping, selling records all over the UK and into Ireland. There, he took an acetate of the bankrupt disc into Emerald Records subsidiary Mint, who liked what they heard and issued it as Bright Lights And Country Music. "My stuff has also come out on Country House Records in Scotland. So, what with England, Ireland and Scotland, I'll have to do something in Wales to complete the set.'

The baying, pining white man's laments of the poverty-ridden American Appalacian region can be substantially traced back to Scotland's Buchan area: witness Bob Dylan's arrival with his eponymous 1962 CBS folk-blues album. Of its half-dozen traditional songs re-arranged and re-interpreted by the Zim,

Pretty Peggy-O (at least) was blatantly born in the North East. Keeping the fires of such heritage alight today are the Ian F Benzie-led Old Blind Dogs, the name deriving from old Appalachian blues sources. A veteran of the pub scene and perpetrator of a million Dylan dirges over the years, his vocal style equidistances Archie Fisher and a grinding machine: granite itself. Formerly one half of the progressive folk duo Alian with Alistair Clark, he went to Wallop with one time spiky snack Archie Buchanan and later with Davie Hepburn. 1985 brought Ian to Mabel Meldrum's Band, meeting Buzzby McMillen and recording the albums Limited Edition and Brownie Snaps.

Theatrical work saw Ian as musical director for The Invisible Bouncers company productions Fit A Turnoot and Tenements and Sentiments. An invitation to tour Northern Sweden with The Auchertby Band came in 1990: in the land of ABBA, Roxette, Bjorn Borg, Volvo and the £5 pint, concerts and workshops on Scottish music, dance and song were undertaken. That same year he co-founded Old Blind Dogs with Jonny Hardie and Buzzby, with whom he toured in concert and ceilidh, complementing the play Pinkybrae. A supposed one-off gig with Dave Francis (of The Desperate Danz Band and later of Edinburgh's Ceilidh Collective) in Portland Oregon expanded day-by-day into an ad-hoc three-week tour of the US West.

Buzzby had migrated from Aberdeen to London, sound engineering for ex-Small Face Ronnie Lane amongst others (Jonny also ran Plonk's recording studio). Back in Aberdeen he ran into Davy Cattenach in the manic reggae outfit The 30 Footers before collaborating with Ian Benzie in Mabel Meldrum's Band. A talented actor and musician, McMillen buzzed around Scotland with The Apple Tree/Carob Ann Ubhal, a Doric-Gaelic language play.

Percussionist Cattenach originally learned his left-hand independence in the school jazz band but most visibly floated to the top of Aberdeen's post-punk sea with The Squibs in 1978. They kick-started Oily Records' charge into the indie market, effectively laying the lines on which APB's grand funk would railroad all the way to Manhattan. That first Oily single evidences Cat's reggae and driving rock styles. . . The Squibs burned out, Davy collaborated with Buzzby in London before their founding The 30 Footers in their home town. A performance-oriented high energy reggae combo, they came damned close, but no cigar. . .

In London once again, Davy developed his skills in the areas of writing, production and engineering through his employment by Lambeth Council as a music technician. This involved him in such projects as Cultures In Exile, exposing him to South American and African music and musicians. Back in the Silver City, Davy then dipped into R 'n' B with Gerry Jablonski's Mojo Pep, appearing on their 1990 CD Pep Talk.

Then came The Dogs' polycultural instrumentation: A Cajun version of Bennachie (Gin I were where Gadie rins). . . gumbo sharing the same plate as stovies; German Lairdie at breakneck speed with African style drumming. Fresh life infused into songs long-asleep in the NE's consciousness: for the author (saturated to overflow with R 'n' B, blues, rock, punk, the whole nine yards) The Dogs' arrangement of The Barnyards O' Delgaty (a song forgotten years since) saw yours truley sping-heeled and sparkle-eyed unable to expel it from the cranium. The lilting Banks O' Sicily and the haunting ballad Lay Ye Doon Love rest easily with a distictive take on Pills Of White Mercury, reinforcing our earlier rant about the North East's contribution to American music. For Streets Of Laredo (or Only The Heartaches) read Pills Of White Mercury (or The Road And The Miles To Dundee). It's all so inter-related. Reviews of their work range from the adulatory to the orgasmic: "the traditional is still alive and well, moving towards the 21st century. . . they have a dark hued, with a nervy feel, edgy fast and furious set of reels and sweetly-keening slow airs.' The Dogs toured the USA four times in 1995 alone and headlined Europe's biggest folk fest at Tonder in Denmark. Ian briefly stepped aside for his solo album So Far, the very essence of rural Aberdeenshire, sharny dubs on a fairm-chiel's beets. Twenty-six years in the coming, but worth the wait.

Not too far outside Aberdeen's city limits we find Marc Ellington. For all his dedicated teuchterism, his accent is decidedly untroubled by Fit-like-the-day-isms. If an Englishman's home is his castle, then for Ellington (a Canadian of Scottish and English ancestry), home is his Towie Barclay Castle. Born in Vancouver, British Columbia, Marc came to the UK at the age of 14. Prior to returning to his roots here in the cosy corner of the British Isles that is forever Aberdeenshire (his maternal family are from the North East) he recorded an eponymous album in London on the Philips label.

Towie Barclay had been empty and derelict for 200 years before he acquired the estate in 1969. His loving and devoted reconstruction work has been accredited by five different international restoration awards. It now constitutes his home, recording studio and the epicentre of his frantically busy film and video business. Whilst the studio primarily services his film enterprise, it has also supported some of a handful of solo contemporary folk albums: Rains/Reins Of Change, A Question of Roads, Restoration, Marc Time and Border Skipping. Between 1967 and 1974, Marc also issued a handful of singles. This adopted Auchterless chiel took to our heritage and tradition with a vengeance, achieving a board position with Grampian Initiative and sitting on the Scottish Heritage Commission. His business expertise has brought him many major industry communications consultancies.

A close personal friend of Richard Thompson (only recently being accorded the global appreciation his talent warrants), Ian Matthews and the Sutherland Brothers, the visitors book at Towie Barclay is a veritable who's-who of contemorary folkies. In addition to those already mentioned, Marc's recording studio has been utilised by Bat McGrath, Henry Keijser, Dave Swarbrick (check out his Smiddyburn LP), Simon Nicol, Dave Pegg, our own Charlie Allen, and the late Sandy Denny. This prestigious hall of names falls into place when balanced alongside el Ellington's session work with The Fairports, Linda Thompson, and Matthews Southern Comfort. Whilst the studio is not actively pushed as a commercial facility in its own right, châtelain Marc confirms "it has been made available to the occasional local act and to people that we know.' A case in point was Aberdeen's jazz-fusionists Manray and their Duke's Den pub-promo jingle single several years back. We should be fair chuffed that such an enthusiastic and talented protector of our indigenous culture has come home to roost.

MIDDLE EAST
ABC Bowl
L-R Mike Haywood, Ian Milne, Frank Robb,
John Madden (Stobbie's Hiding)

OLD BLIND DOGS

Chapter 11

Smiffy, Plug and the Greek Goddess of War

One of the most distinctive bands to emerge during the late 1970s were The Bash Street Kids: not Smiffy, Plug, Cuthbert and their mith-making chums, but Greg Brechin on drums, Mike Wood on lead guitar, Ralphie Greig on bass and Brian Crombie on vocals and catapult.

Greg's report card shows he had picked up his drumsticks at the start of the decade, learning the backbeat whilst messing about with fellow engineering and music apprentices at a Bucksburn paper mill. "I come from a musical family and my dad was running the entertainment at the local social club, so I suppose it was natural that we started playing there.' Initially with Pyramid (in the company of Billy Sutherland, Bob Baxter and Chas Adams) Greg became Bash Street classmates with other expellees from other Aberdeen rock schools.

BSK were a hally-rackit, professional garage rock outfit, kicking-out a high-decibel, no-nonsense uncompromising guitar driven heavy rock show with unapologetic AC/DC leanings.

Brian Crombie's suspect dress sense manifested itself as early as their second gig together, as Greg explains "He told us he had found an old pair of shorts from somewhere - we geed him up and talked him into wearing them, just for a laugh. We started the first number without Brian on stage, and when he ran in with these shorts on, the whole place collapsed. A short while later we were playing at a hotel surrounded by trees where he spied a branch shaped like a catapult. He ripped it down, and that was his next prop. Then somehow we got hold of an old school blazer and we were away.'

Background music is was not, leaving the ears ringing, if not bleeding, for hours. Brian performed an Angus Young-ish act (complete with school cap, blazer and shorts) way out in front of the rest of the band, often amongst the audience. Their early repertoire at the Argo Lounge, the ABC Bowl and the Crescent Hotel included frantic covers of material by The Who, Bad Company and Ted Nugent - along with a complete range of punk-metal material, encompassing The Sex Pistols, The Clash and The Stranglers. Obligatory AC/DC noise pollution naturally remained the integral, focal component of their set. Now working full-time pro four nights of the week in Aberdeen (with residencies at the Argo and the Treetops' Croft bar), each weekend they were on the road to other parts of Scotland, followed by busloads of fans. Playing support to pop acts as diverse as Shakin' Stevens, Slik, Marmalade and Chris McClure, their material increasingly became self-composed. Song-writing ideas sprung primarilly from Ralphie and Mike.

The result was fabulous entertainment, that the band attempted to replicate on the self-financed 1979 single Travellin' Man/C'Mon Kids. Having come into contact with Jim Hunter, who had links with Decca label and the BBC, the band utilised his recording facility in Forres. Guitar and drums were recorded on a Sunday afternoon at the band's natural habitat, The Argo, on a mobile four-track unit. Vocals and mixing then took place in Forres with the resultant product being released on the Agenda label, a Decca subsidiary. This single was credited to The Kids, highlighting an interesting conflict of interests at that time for the band. The most comprehensive media coverage of the contemporary Aberdeen and NE rock scene came from The Peoples' Journal, a D.C. Thomson weekly. They also publish the enlightened Weekly News, Sunday Post and The Beano.

The Oor Wullie/Broons conglomerate therefore reported on the progress of a band using a name owned by Thomsons themselves. Touchy about such matters, they had already red-carded Glasgow's Desperate Dan restaurant. Hence The Peoples' Journal fudged the issue, terming the band The Kids, though it was common knowledge on Aberdeen's music scene that it was really The Bashers causing mayhem in the local pubs and clubs. For Travellin' Man Greg wrote to Dundee, politely requesting permission to use the name on the single. Jings, crivvens and help ma boab! Richter-scale panic tremors throughout Dandy mansions' corridors of power. . . Greg's phone rings itself off the table with a ballistic call from Keyhole Kate's legal advisors: under no circumstances whatsoever could the name be used on the record. Bet your bottom dollar that The Bunty annual was removed from the band's Christmas shopping list, PDQ.

A popular crowd-pleaser Travellin' Man stood out as the choice of first single. Radio One (including good old Peelie) got on the case. Nationwide promotional appearances ensued as the track was chosen 'single of the week' by local radio station in Leeds. The entire 2,000 copies shifted, sold at most of Aberdeen's record stores and at gigs. Jim Watt (stalwart of Aberdeen legends The Throb, Mr Fantasy and Grit) joined the band in 1984 when Mike Wood left, with live sets metamorphosising away from conventional rock gig formats and theatrical props becoming increasingly central to the show. A roadie with carpentry and electrical skills constructed a convincing replica of an electric chair, a pivotal part of their homage to Alex Harvey's They're No Lights On The Xmas Tree Mother, They're Burning Big Louie Tonight. The Bashers' version ended with bursts of machine gun fire sampled from Georgie Fame's Bonnie And Clyde as a Chicago gangster-attired Brian blasted away with a wooden tommy gun. In 1986, this track was their most popular live number and was selected as the topside of the second single, with the B side Sky Jive being written by Jim Watt.

Greg considers that this effort was far and away more professional than its predecessor. "We were in tow with Niall and the guys from Pallas who had a real recording contract with EMI - what I mean is real compared to the loose arrangement we had with Agenda/Decca. We taped Louie at their studio where their experience and skill really helped us a lot.' Brian became the recipient of an unscheduled, undesired frizzy hair-do, when the faultily-wired electric chair nearly fried him one night. 'Jesus', thought the band and audience, "He's really giving it the big one the night.' For the singed singer, the three minutes until the hot-seat was unplugged seemed like an eternity.

As with Travellin' Man seven years earlier, this 4,000-selling release was self-financed. Greg explains that the funds for the record were generated by the punishing gigging schedule to which the band was committed. "We had no time off for ages - I think our booking diary showed 346 gigs one year, and 333 in the next. BP invited us up to Shetland a few times - they went wild for us up there, they had never seen anything like Brian before. They looked after us really well . . . it's not often you have a helicopter at your disposal.'

Come the late Eighties Greg decided he had been at Bash Street long enough. "We were playing places like golf clubs doing material that really wasn't my sort of stuff any more.' Greg, my sympathies are with you: it just aint rock 'n' roll when the band opens with "Onay luck at the bingo the night?' One of these golf club gigs didn't get past the first green. "Because it was our first appearance at the place, we decided to start our set with Burning Big Louie - it was normally our closer, but the idea was to make our supposed residency there start with a bang. However just as Brian exploded into the lounge, raking the room with machine gun fire, an old fella came back from the bar with a tray of drinks. The next thing we knew he was on the floor having a heart attack. An ambulance was called to cart him away to Foresterhill - they kicked us out and told us not to come back. So I left the Kids and have been playing with Gerry Jablonski in Rough And Ready, and in other bands Shogun and Snakebite.'

Whilst the Bashers are pupils of a school that exists only in Beanoville, in the real world that is Bucksburn, The Northern Lights shone from Bankhead Academy. Hot-shot musical students and precocious pets of the mannie Addison (he kept them in a cage at the back of the class) they won the TSB Rockschool competition in 1985. The NLs (vocalist Glen Brechin, saxophonist/vocalist Alison Christie, keyboardist Karen Addison, guitarist Steve Proctor, bass player Kenny Hutchison, drummer Kenny McCabe and synth-bassist Gillian Esson) came up with two original compositions in Numero Uno and The Big Black Cloak. These were released on the Mysterious Publishing Company label, prompting the heedie's end-of-term report "It's about time that these Boxy boogie merchants realised that the three rs are 'readin', 'riting and 'rithmetic, not rhythm, rock 'n' roll. In 1986 Bankhead's The Thieves were edged into second TSB place, the following year's swots Phaze 3 were triumphant in the Scottish final.

Back to the reptile house and Snakebite: the band also featured vocalist Teresa Moir and Greg's fellow FPs Mike Wood and Ralphie Greig. Their The Angel And The Devil album (produced by Mike Allan at Mill Of Hirn in 1990) is a nine-track dose of heavy rock joy. Kicking off with a shot of melodic, Dylanesque Texas rock, Every Day Now leads with Teresa's gutsy vocal and guest harp work from Eddie Burnett. Tobacco Road has Mike Wood booting up John Loudermilk's classic at unrelenting boogie pace, leaving The Nashville Teens standing. Mike and Teresa's Silver Blue And Distant (showcasing Mike's beguiling acoustic guitar, squeaking strings and all, and warm vocals from his co-writer) is reminiscent of the quieter passages of Zeppelin's Stairway To Heaven. No surprise that these ex-Bash Streeters found it irresistable: hey, we are straight into a Quasi-Ozzie blitzkrieg with Let There Be Rock, segueing, in good-time live-gig fashion through She Wore A Yellow Ribbon, Bonnie Lassie O' Fyvie Oh, Marie's Wedding, Alouete, and Deutchland Deutchland Uber Alles. . . The second Wood-Moir cut Blue Eyed Lady is an up-beat bouncy Thin Lizzyesque rocker with a chorus catchier than HIV on Regent Quay. Pick of the crop is the title track Angel And The Devil, weirdly subterranean FX giving way to Greg's militaristic tattoo beat and then Teresa's expressive vocal. An anti-war paean, it breaks into a jazzy finale: exceptional stuff indeed. Pete Ham and Tony Evans' Without You (best remembered for Harry Nilsson's defining performance), is a difficult one to cover. . . but the album closes with a blistering take on Steppenwolf's Born To Be Wild, cutting to The Hall of the Mountain King, returning Edvard Greig's music to its ancestral origins in the Scottish North East.

As these talented rockers are frenetically hissing and rattling around Aberdeen, the current version of the Bashers is still terrorising audiences and teecher. No longer Kids, The Bash Street Mannies of late have been Jim Watt on guitar, ex-Superklute bassist Dallas Munro, drummer Phil Ritchie and perennial vocalist Brian Crombie. The latter's fetish for the clothes of 13-year-old schoolboys still surfaces in moments of weakness.

Little Pleasures, the first vinyl from Mojo Pep, appeared in 1988: recorded at Airtight Studios in Aberdeen's Crown Terrace, it captured the band's live vigour and power. Produced by vocalist/guitarist Stewart Todd, the others on this LP were former Standard Issue and Shapiros drummer Adi Addison, lead guitarist John Lamb, bassist and vocalist Dave Wright and Scotland's premier blues harpist Spider McKenzie. The cover shot fixes the Mojos' locale as Dobies pub, one of their favoured venues. When Gerry Jablonski later arrived in Aberdeen from his native Banff, he had returned to his regular work as a chef. On the first of his infrequent weekends off, he sniffed around the pubs to see what was cooking. In Dobies he found an a la carte live blues-rock scene with afters at a Davie Hepburn-organised bluesey jam at Oh Henrys in The Shiprow. Gerry's own tasty jam recipe soon had the city's blues players and punters turning up at Cousins Lounge (formerly operated under the control of Dons heroes Jimmy Wilson and Willie Miller) in Exchange Street.

Successive relocations took the venture firstly to Caesar's Palace and then to Radars, where the jam format became a Sunday institution. Musicians are welcome to sit in and do their thing with Gerry's house band: Scottish vet rocker Tam White, The Blues Burglars and former Black Abbots drummer Russ Abbot have all done their party pieces at different times.

This was happening in parallel with Gerry's work with Mojo Pep, whom he had joined in time for 1990's Pep Talk CD. With Adi Addison moving to Edinburgh, the Peps needed a drummer, and who better than that "human rhythm machine, he even talks in perfect beat' Davy Cattenach. The former Squibs-30 Footers skin beater had been demo-ing some material with Gerry, who describes the sessions as "nae bad at all, but I don't suppose they will ever see the light of day.' Recorded at Jeep's private 16-track studio in The Hardgate, Pep Talk also includes The Marijuana Brass (Gerry Dawson, Frank Morgan and the Dorain Grayish Al Hyland). ''Aye, we had a wee toot' confirms the latter.

Davy Cattenach sadly began ageing, his eyesight failed him, he began peeing against lampposts and mounting strangers' legs at the most inopportune moments: the poor bugger became an Old Blind Dog. Stewart Ritchie, another highly rated drummer, took his place. Between 1987 and 1992, Mojo Pep was one of Scotland's hardest-working bands, their subsequent slowing down in pace being attributed by Gerry to his extensive non-Popular activities. The way the band were enthusiastically accepted and received during a German tour "took the shine off the Aberdeen scene a bit' for him, setting the over-familiar local pub circuit into perspective against the more unreserved European live market.

Nevertheless he continues to foster the jam venture and to play with both Mojo Pep and rock covers band Rough and Ready, with Ralphie Milne and Greg Brechin. The original format of R&R had been a much-travelled Rory Gallagher style blues outfit, the name was retained thereafter to maximise booking opportunities. Spring of 1995 saw him working with a new song writing and performing talent Karen Shun, with bassist Pete Duncan and drummer Hugh Burk, a fellow Banffer. Karen's mellow AOR material is a welcome change for Gerry, getting him away from the blues, heavy rock, and associated on-the-road scrapes. He encountered many hair-raising episodes, but his band got into a real lather trying to return to the mainland from a Western Isles tour. A fatal booking cock-up had resulted in a death of a thousand cuts, their Seventies and Eighties heavy rock set falling on deaf ears: the crowd were expecting a country and western show. "I remember thinking as soon as we arrived 'They hate us already'. The hall was totally empty, and when I peeped through into the bar it was choc-a-bloc. Then they wouldnae pay us the full money, so that was another fight.'

The morning after the non-gig the van was loaded and ready to leave from the digs for the nine AM ferry from Benbecula, a drive of about an hour: the next sailing was not scheduled until six PM that evening. Realising at the last moment that Greg Brechin was missing, a search party re-entered the guest house to chase up the errant percussionist. Much door-banging and agitated shouts of "Get your arse in gear or we'll miss the boat' were drowned out by the high pitched whoosh of a hair drier, before the reply came "I'm deein' my hair, I winna be long.' Thirty minutes later, with the perfectly-coiffured syncopater finally on board, the van set off on a sheep-squashing kamikaze dash across narrow Hebridean dirt roads for the ferry terminal. To no avail. . . as they crested the hill overlooking the quayside, the boat's doors closed and it prepared to sail. Screeching to a dramatic halt along side the still-moored vessel, the band's protests were brushed aside by the onshore 'more than my jobsworth' ferry official. Bringing Dock Of The Bay to mind, the guys were left stranded as the boat glided majestically away with a crew-member giving them a permanent wave. Nine interminable hours in Benbecula, an x-rated episode subtitled The Longest Day II starring Greg Brechin pulling his hair out and vowing "I'm never (back) combing back here again.'

. . . .

Whilst one brand of heavy metal blasted out on Bash Street, down the road at the Pallas something else was cooking. In 1974 Aberdeen Grammar School pupils Mike Stobbie and Graeme Murray founded a five-piece rock amalgam entitled Rainbow. Graeme's inspiration came from seeing Genesis play a support spot to Lindisfarne: saving up his paper round money, he bought a bass guitar from Woolworths, and acquired a cheap amp. Months of playing along with records in his bedroom cumlinated in his stage debut at the age of 15. His premiere appearance at Aberdeen University (with Stewart Kemp's hot-rockin' Levi) was shocking: he was electrocuted by a badly earthed PA system.

Murray apart, the primary colours of Rainbow had already shone in previous city combos - Mike Stobbie with Lynx, Dave Taylor with Mr Fantasy, and George Gibson with Pyramid. Colin Rae briefly occupied the drummer's stool, before being replaced by Ali Milne and then Derek Foreman - the latter having previously been with Profile. Dave Holt played guitar, with vocals the domain successively of Brian Wood and Craig Anderson.

The story jumps to 1977 when an unknown, struggling English guitarist named Ritchie Blackmore (one-time Hamburg-based Mandrake Root co-member with Aberdonian drummer Ricky Munro and Northern bassist Jimmy Bain), pinches the name Rainbow from the Aberdeen lads. Hence their change of name to Pallas, its exotic source being Pallas Athena, the Greek goddess of war. Mike Stobbie says that, in the city itself, they were "very much a student's band, playing at the university union and RGIT, supporting Thin Lizzy at a Freshers' Ball.' Then came regular Saturday lunch-time spots at the Treetops Hotel Croft bar, and at Ruffles. Pallas at the Palais. Shame that they were too young to have appeared at the Place. Pallas at the Place. Or at the Palace. Pallas at the Palace. Shame the were not invited to the Queen's London residence. Pallas at the. . . Stop it, now.

From gigs at RAF bases, a smoke canister (designed for stunt parachutists) had been chorred. The boys thought it could add flare to a Union Terrace Gardens show. However when the roadie pulled the ring out of the canister, it exploded out of his hands onto the grass in front of the stage. It was gingerly retrieved and lobbed towards the band, immediately obliterating them: stinging eyes, choking throats and generally toxifying the locale. Gradually the band were forced to abandon the stage to the delight of the crowd who thought this fiasco was intentional. The bright orange cloud slowly drifted to Union Street where it came to a halt against the C & A building, causing severe bafflement for wifies doing their shopping.

Through the Grammar School old boys' network they secured a gig at a sixth year end-of-term dance. The afternoon school-hall sound check was invaded by the wifie McDearmid (head of the music department), shouting, in a most educational fashion "Stop that incessant racket at once!' Such an enlightened tutorial viewpoint, 20 years after Chuck Berry pleaded Roll Over Beethoven. Soon advancing from such rudimentary gigs, Pallas penetrated an Edinburgh studio. The resultant thousand copies of the self-financed four-track EP surfaced the week before Christmas, 1977 on the Sue-I-Cide label. Reds Under The Bed (directed at those from the Soviet block rather than Pittodrie) was a McCarthyite Why Don't You Get Back To Moscow prog-rock hybrid, dementedly strangled vocal punctuated by punkoid shouts of Oi! Sure, it sounds dated now, but construction of Italy's capital city wasn't acheived in 24 hours. With its uneven changes of pace, Thought Police blended Kafka, Huxley and The Mothers Of Invention.

Personnel changed constantly over the next couple of years. June 1978 brought the departure of Dave Holt who was succeeded by the awesome guitarist Niall Mathewson from local heavy rock outfit Pryer. Three months later vocalist Craig Anderson flew the nest due to 'external pressures', replaced by chemistry and biology student Euan Lowson who had previously exercised his tonsils with Balrog. In September of 1979, Mike Stobbie also abandoned ship (albeit temporarily) for pastures new with Middle East, Rue de Remarx, and Private ID/Vera Cruz. Keyboards were thereafter calimed by Ronnie Brown, hanging up the shiny jacket and bow tie he previously wore on Aberdeen's cabaret and club circuit.

1980 was marked by an appearance at the Glasgow Apollo in the final of the Battle of The Bands contest in November before the Arrive Alive album (recorded live at Paisley's Bungalow Bar in March of 1981) appeared on their own Granite Wax label on cassette. Encouragingly, it ran to three pressings: people were obviously beginning to take notice. Arrive Alive/Stranger At The End Of Time was pushed by arduous live work, extending, for the first time down to London. Sympathetic Scottish rock venues such as Glasgow's Dial Inn, Edinburgh's Astoria, Bannockburn's Tam Dhu and the Rothes Arms in Glenrothes all saw much of the semi-pro Aberdonians. Rock/metal magazines Kerrang and Sounds carried features on the band, now being pigeon-holed as part of the 'progressive rock revival.' Further afield, 1,000 mile round trips to play at the Marquee in London became frequent, with February 1982's 'Over The Wall Tour' returning Pallas yet again to England.

1983's Cool King label re-issue of Arrive Alive lodged itself in the national heavy metal charts for several months. Relentless club touring continued, the Marquee becoming a regular booking. The second Pallas single Paris Is Burning/The Hammer Falls hit the shops in May of the same year in both seven-inch and 12-inch formats. A support spot on Uli Roth's tour saw the boys appear at the Hammersmith Odeon for the first time. . . All positive signs but crunch time was fast approaching. Struggling financially, most of their non-essential possessions had been sold to finance their musical aspirations. Then, at the last moment, salvation galloped over the horizon. EMI (heroic burnished armour glinting in the sunlight, banners a-flipping in the breeze) signed Pallas to a major contract.

Now that they were middle-league recording artists, the woodwork divested itself of enthusiastic fans, as Graham Murray wryly commented. "To be honest, Aberdeen was one of our least successful places until we got the EMI deal. Then it started to pick up, perhaps everyone's proud of us all of a sudden.' This explemplified just how difficult it can be for local loons and quines to win respect: the old "you canna be any good, I ken your father' kick. Think back to the bollockings Johnny Hewitt used to get from the harder-to-please sections of the Pittodrie crowd. No doubt they are happier nowadays watching Coronation Street on Wdnesday nights). The summer months of 1983 were spent writing material for their forthcoming album The Sentinel, triumphantly previewed at the prestigious Reading Rock Festival. Next stop on their inexorable rise in the echelons of heavy rock was Atlanta, recording The Sentinel with producer Eddie Offord (renowned for his work with Yes). On the downside, the Brave New World promotional UK tour was aborted due to vocalist Euan Lawson's throat infection.

Video, seven-inch and 12-inch mixes of the precursory Eyes In The Night/East West single came the following January ahead of the much-awaited appearance of The Sentinel, with its incredible Patrick Woodroffe art work. The Sentinel: defending the world against impending armageddon. A brave, inspiring album, which overtures to the grandiose keyboard chords of Shock Treatment. . . Cut And Run is the dramatic theme for the great movie Hitchcock never made. . . Arrive Alive is substantially reworked from its original conception, in this incarnation a passing, red-eye flash-bulb shot of a band frantically on the run. Incredibly for Pallas, this time the riff gets down, dirty, and funky. . . the panoramic East West, one of the most immense anthems generated by the rock genre. . .

A major tour, headlining in their own right for the first time, brought them to Israel and in the UK the Hammersmith Odeon hosted a substantial concert triumph. Euan reputedly wasn't fitting in and found himself the unwilling possessor of a P45: he subsequently became vocalist with Minas Tirith (later renamed ERG). Pallas found themselves Alan Reed: the guy sings like an angel, descending from the same celestial choral supernova as Terry Reid, Robert Plant, Jim Diamond and Andrew Montgomery. Previously with Glasgow's Abel Ganz, Reed was onboard for The Knightmoves EP released early in 1985. Hardware freaks pay attention: by this stage, Ronnie Brown's accoutrements included Fairlight CMI, synthesisers and a grand piano; Niall was on 'real' guitars and Roland guitar synths; Derek used Premier and Simmons drums. This kit was used supporting Uriah Heep, the ex-Toe Fat guys sacked by Cliff Bennett in favour of Spiggy Topes.

The succeeding, Mick Glossop-produced album The Wedge was unveiled on UFO-support shows. An impressive mainstream rock hot biscuit. . . mainstream yet at the same time distinctively Pallas: their time had come. Alan's warm, sympathetic vocals. . . the sublime riff of Throwing Stones At The Wind. . . punchy, commercial, rocky and bouncy. . . Got To Fight That Monday Morning Feeling moves its oh-so familiar sentiment along superbly with a jump into Van Halen territory. . . Imagination, Takes Me Where I Want To Go virally invades the lugs at first listen, and stays there forever. The boys must have been delighted with this, their best work thus far. . . Notwithstanding The Wedge attaining a highly-meritorious second position in the heavy metal charts, the band felt this had been acheived despite poor promotion on EMI's behalf. A parting of the ways after only two albums.

Still the merciless touring regime didn't let up, bringing with it the first of many Dutch dates. Inevitably something had to give and 1987 found the band taking a much-needed rest. It was October before a revitalised Pallas (with original keyboards player Mike Stobbie back in the fray in place of Ronnie Brown, who gave up the music business), re-entered the Scottish prog-rock circuit, concurrent with writing material for the next album. Early in 1988 they revisited Amsterdam's Paradiso and the London Marquee before signing a new contract with Artisan Records. Under the producership of Owen Davies the band settled into recording studios at Great Linford Manor in Milton Keynes.

Blaming management problems Alan Reed left, the band continuing to work on the album and auditioning new vocalists. However the group soon split from manager Harry Maloney and in August of 1989 they mailed out a cassette fanclub-only postcard, entitled Sketches, demos and ideas designed to keep Pallasites up-dated on the band's activities. The prodigal Alan Reed and his prodigious voice were back: he and Stobbie were resident in London with the rest of the crew still Aberdeen-based. Rehearsals and travelling became problematic to the extent that Pallas (as a live performing concern) effectively went on hold. Each of Members diversified into other musical activities. Niall Mathewson, together with Mike Allan, set up their recording studio at Crathes, where local bands have since queued up to make use of their ever-expanding facilities. The Mill studio has made the recording aspirations of many up-and-coming local combos realisable.

Stobbie's guest solo work on Clive Nolan and Geoff Mann's prog-rock album Casino in 1992, together with the re-emergence of Pallas' track War Of Words on a Dutch SI label compilation, precipitated fresh interest in the band. Invitations were received for a Dutch stadium gig and to headline at a summer festival at Whitechurch, both events during 1993. A good bit of business with EMI licensed both previous albums for CD release: the re-mastered shiny beer mats emerged on the Centaur label through Dave Shoesmith's specialist CD Services in Dundee. Dave deserves a pey and a pent for his valiant efforts. The Sentinel re-appeared, its uplifting bravura underpinned with additional tracks. Holding its hand was the titularly-unifying Knightsmoves To Wedge. Make no mistake about it; this was BIG music: B for brave, I for invigourating and G for grandiose.

So in May of 1993, Pallas blew away their cobwebs at a warm-up gig at Aberdeen's Lemon Tree. This audience was largely new to the band, but nonetheless received them enthusiastically. Hot on the heels of their Aberdeen rebirth came their top of the bill performance at July's Whitechurch Musicians' Convention. Amongst the 11 support acts that weekend was Sonja Kristina, hitherto Curved Air vocalist, wife of Stewart Copeland, and ex-regulaire of Spiggy Topes' bassist Johnny Gray. . . Dutch interest increased when the track Never Too Late featured on another SI Music compilation CD: late in the year, gigs were undertaken at Utrecht's Tivoli and at the Norderlicht, Tilburg. Word spread throughout European prog-rock grapevine of their return, and invites arrived from France, Italy, Germany and Poland. Concentrating instead on recording a new album during 1994, the boys were unable to accept these offers. In the meantime, a solitary track Refugee surfaced on Audio Directory Cassettes, as work progresses on the new LP.

. . . .

After the sad denouement of Rue de Remarx, Stobbie played with Aberdeen band Private ID, which featured the eye-friendly vocalist Jacqui Copland. Originally formed in October 1977 as Horizon, premiering at the Craigmile Lounge in Kinellar, their original line-up included French-born Bernard Andre Alexandre Rose (more manageably known as Ben Rose) on guitar, vocals and song-writing. Ben, Graeme Black on drums, Colin Smith on lead guitar, and bassist Colin Millum were initially fronted by vocalist Clark Whitly. As they served their apprenticeship on the time-honoured NE country circuit, they mixed Ben's songs with covers of chart pop hits.

Ian Moore (a former member of The Afro-Gaelic Ensemble) briefly added sax before Ron McIntosh replaced Black, adding a funkier edge to drums. With original songs increasing proportionally in the repertoire, the band were placed third in the Artic Lite/Daily Mirror rock contest (Rue de Remarx were also finalists). Falling out of this lager-tabloid episode came an invite to visit State Records' recording studios, with Bob Seivwright as keyboards player. WEA sent an A & R rep to check them out in August of 1980. The pop-oriented name Horizon was dropped in favour of the more secretive Private ID, as Seivwright left and McIntosh made way for Alan Stuart, drummer with contemporaneous Aberdeen combo Dirty Weekend. This phase marked a move into a Police-influenced white reggae. . . Regatta de Blackburn? Despite qualifying for the Scottish final of The Battle Of The Bands rock competition, it was felt that contractual obligations imposed by the organisers were onerous. The band instead concentrated on demo-ing their work at Highland Studios in Inverness: Chrysalis showed interest in Private ID as they opened for Tenpole Tudor and The Supremes. . . (On different occaisions, we hasten to add. Eddie doing a medley of Baby Love and Who Killed Bambi in a tight, sequinned dress surely can't be right).

PID's first single appeared in 1981 on their own Dodo label, inspired by the Guild Street pub, the band's local). A Little Fun (produced at Highland Studios by David Baker), sold out both runs of 1,000 copies, helped along by a Grampian TV spot at, unbelievably, a Beach Ballroom heat of the World Disco Dancing Championship. The singles' airplay on Radio One reached ID's expanding fan-base in Glasgow and Aberdeen. Again entering the Battle Of The Bands fray, they outstripped a thousand rival groups, making it to the London Dominion Theatre finals. Fans travelled down from Aberdeen to witness ID being voted second by a panel of Phil Lynott, Hazel O'Connor, Suzi Quatro, John Entwhistle and Noddy Holder (the velvet-voiced Slade crooner was still wondering why Spiggy Topes hadn't shown up at his party).

In the wake of this came the Dave Lee Travis show on Radio One: you know, the hairy cornflake from up the M1 or somewhere, banging on ad nauseam about his farm and ducks and horses: why it took the Beeb 50 years or whatever it was to get wise to his boring drivel is a great mystery. Amid copious yawning and blood pouring from ears, the band crawled out of his studio, to find their number From The Top included on a Battle Of The Bands compilation album. When Jacqui developed vocal-chord problems a virus was diagnosed, requiring surgery. Her subsequent recuperation and voice-resting resulted in the derailment of Private ID.

It was Christmas 1982 before they reconvened, back down at a snake's arse-end: the pop business has a short memory and nine months away left lots of ladders to climb. Throwing a six straight away, they were joined by Mike Stobbie, just home after the dispertion of Rue de Remarx. His input enlivened things such that within four months, BBC's Street Buzz had PID doing a ten-minute spot (live numbers Turn Back The Tears, You Can't Go On Without Me and a video for The Bombay Song). Smithy flew the coop just before the band played support to Kajagoogoo in June, blowing the headliners off the stage in the process. Again on BBC TV, in August they performed live on Aberdeen beach for The Untied Shoelaces Show. It was Odyssey's turn next to be upstaged by the soaring Aberdeen ensemble, ever-present on the Scottish university circuit since their re-launch.

The time came to cut a representative demo to re-appraise the London market of the band's latest material and style. Members personally came up with £1,000 to finance the recording and flew Stobbie's English contact Graham Quinton-Jones to Edinburgh to produce the sessions. With money running out fast, Gabriel's horn sounded as Aberdeen club proprietors George Tester and George Stewart came to the financial rescue. The result was the impressive contemporary pop of Cold Cold Sweat/Dreams Of You, 200 copies of which were pressed (in recognition of ID's benefactors), on the Gabriel's label. This established a precedent for ID's confident pushy Eighties padded-shoulders pop. Concurrent with the single's readiness for distribution, Stobbie's younger sister Jennifer was introduced to songwriter Paul Cousins 9,000 miles away in Los Angeles. Paul suggested that the demo should be submitted to his London address at Trident Studios. . . upon getting an earful, Trident themselves broke out in a cold sweat, immediately issuing an invite to the big city.

Returning to Aberdeen from an Inverness gig in the early hours of a cold February morning, the car in which Alan and Jacqui were travelling hit black ice and landed upside down in a ditch. Luckily Alan was unhurt and Jacqui sustained only face cuts and superficial injuries. When this shock had worn off, Paul Cousins signed up as manager. . . and had soon arranged a three album deal.

Jacqui was the life and Seoul of the party when, as a sideline from her Private ID work, she represented the UK in a Korean song festival in April 1984. Despite her song being un-placed, she made valuable modelling contacts before returning to Blighty, where things were hotting up on the ID front. John Freida's London agency worked on a new image, £100 hairstyles and all (they should have phoned Greg Brechin: not the fastest, but much cheaper), as the first legit single was recorded. The demo Cold Cold Sweat was reworked for the seven-inch version under the producership of Stephen Short (his track record included Genesis and Kim Wilde). Former Rich Kid Rusty Eagan, the guy who tipped off John Peel about APB's popularity on the NY dance floors, produced the twelve-inch mix.

Not a chart success, but it proved catalystic in the band's decision to move en-bloc to London: frequent trips to and from Aberdeen were proving inconvenient and costly. Ben Rose could only hack London for a month before he packed up and came home to move into production at the new Airlines studio. . . he was recently playing with veteran Aberdeen rocker Stan Fraser at The Metro Hotel in Market Street. Ben's place in the group was taken by Edinburgh born Keith More.

With prestigious dates at The Marquee and the London Hippodrome, a revitalised image and personnel, new management and improved material, it was felt opportune to adopt a new name, hence the arrival of Vera Cruz (a Mexican town: pronunciation guidance from our consultant Glaswegian Spanish-speaking roadie, Paco Ra Van. It's Vera as in there-a, not Vera as in Duckworth). The band's healthy London reputation brought a performance on Radio One's Richard Skinner show: an unnerving experience, playing live to eight million listeners. Alan froze on the count-in, but off they went to finish a storm. An enormous buzz. . . but not enough for founder member Colin Millum, who decided he had enough of the music business and headed home to Aberdeen. . . to be replaced on bass by another expat Aberdonian, Dave Williamson. Former David Bowie and Duran Duran producer Colin Thurston took VC under his wing, recording demos with a view to securing a major deal.

All the bricks were in place by April of 1986 for the band to finally hit the big time. A specially staged showcase at The Mean Fiddler was attended by an audience heavily salted with music and show biz faces. Supported by pre-hit Calling All The Heroes It Bites, Vera Cruz played their socks off, to the delight of executives of 10 Records (a Virgin subsidiary), who were due to sign the band the next morning. Agency company Wasted Talent also had a contract waiting for signature - they had promoted tours by U2 and Bowie. After a triumphant gig, everyone went home elated and excited in the early hours of the morning as the big moment loomed. And so to bed. . .

At eight AM Alan Stuart drove off to collect Jacqui, to bring her to 10 Records' office for the signature of a four album deal. . . figuratively speaking the icka-wicka fluffy bunny wabbits were hopping playfully around a sun-bathed, flowery spring-time meadow with the birdies singing fit to burst. Within the hour it had become a black, slime-coated subterranean cavern inhabited by hellacious, scaly, slithering reptiles. Alan returned bearing bad tidings. Miss Copeland had decided to leave the band and go solo. Disaster with a D bigger than their home-town river. An already-committed high profile Greenbelt Festival appearance was cancelled as the band struggled unsuccessfully to find a replacement. Horizon/Private ID/Vera Cruz were cruelly defeated by an inexcusable own-goal, seconds before the final whistle. Yet another London debacle for an Aberdeen group.

The eloping Copeland became a backing singer, appearing with Duran Duran and Climie Fisher. Bassist Dave Williamson subsequently played with chart act Heatwave; Alan Stuart moved into session work and currently pursues a solo career under the name Anton; sessions also attracted Keith More, he played with Jackie Graham, Five Star and toured with Asia, before recording his own album Guitar Stories (on which Stobbie also appears). The latter re-joined Pallas, the band he had co-founded in Aberdeen.

. . . .

A childhood musical prodigy, Stobbie's precocity was marked by several awards during his formative years. The bane of Redcoats' lives, he won a junior talent contest at Butlins in 1970 and has been chasing the lost chord ever since. Filling in the gaps in his career outside of Pallas, Private ID and Rue de Remarx, we find him in the strangest of circumstances. Following the untimely collapse of Vera Cruz he played piano for ballet dance classes before he became involved with Five Star, darlings of 1986's pop charts. Having played on their Rain Or Shine chart-topper (and co-written the B side Summer Groove) he was scheduled to commence rehearsals for their world tour that July. However, when song writing credits for Summer Groove were not forthcoming, he recognised an unfair situation. Three months later he was in Port Stanley, entertaining British troops, penguins and seals.

Between 1986 and 1987 Stobs was with such London-based bands as Hoorah Boys Hoorah, Temper Temper, Back To New York and Archer. Concurrent with his rejoining Pallas in 1987 he travelled to both Stockholm and Los Angeles to produce 123. He was then musical director for the Grotbags television show before producing jingles for Radio One's Steve Wright In The Afternoon and releasing an album with Wozani. His telly commercial music has sold deodorants, beer and his greatest success: Pizza Hut - Hit The Huuut. Mike kept busy making pesonal appearances, autographing the twelve-inch pepperoni mix.

During 1994 his music appeared on Paul McKenna's hypnotic cassette tapes. These covered self confidence improvement, stress elimination (don't start writing rock 'n' roll books, that helps), stopping smoking (don't start writing. . .) and sleeping like a log (I woke up in the fireplace after that one). Of late, the energetic Mike produced the album Songs From The Lion's Cage for Arena, a band fronted by original Marillion's drummer Mick Pointer: all concerned with the project were delighted with its 18,000 presales. In yet another quantum leap Mike was off to the Philippines, Indonesia and Singapore with The Real Thing. . . Can't Get By Without You, No Way. . . (Chris Amoo, Crufts champion breeder. . . Mike did Radio Two with them). All hands to the pumps of late for the new Pallas LP with the working title Beat The Drum again on the Centaur label from CDS in Dundee.

Mike plans to sometime finalise his solo project Exordium, entirely keyboard-generated with what appears to be, at first hearing, the tastiest acoustic guitar piece this side of Jimi's Hear My Train A-Comin'. Freddie Mercury proudly proclaimed "There will never be synthesisers on our albums.' The contrary Stobbie laughs when he says 'there ain't no guitars or drums on my album, so there.' The foresight of those Butlins' talent contest judges 25 years ago is borne out by the ambiently panoramic Exordium, a non-narcotic antidote to the pressures and stresses of modern life. In an early version, the title track appeared in 1994 on the cassette British Progressive Audio Directory Part 3. Demos of other highly original tracks for his project suggest that this is a sweeping majestic work, deserving of major commercial success.

. . . .

Rivalling The Bashers and Pallas in the metal-progressive business were Freebird (the name sourced from that defining, wrist-breaking guitar track from Lynyrd Skynyrd). Current Gaelic rock icons Run Rig are managed, of course, by Aberdeen's Marlene Ross. Long time supporter of the live music cause in the city, Marlene and her husband Graeme ran Abbotsford Acoustics for many years. Freebird were the first group to come under her protective wing, with their gutsy rock canon encompassing UFO and Rory Gallagher at The Croft, RGIT and the University Union. Despite being immensely popular on a local level the birds essentially never really took off into a bigger sky despite recording for the BBC and at Glasgow's Cava Studios. Set on a foundation of dual lead guitarists/vocalists Gareth Davies and Nods Graham, a variety of bassists (Graham Watson, Colin Buchan, Stuart Tait and Mike Bonner) and drummers (Phil Anderson, Zander Ruxton) played their part through to Freebird's fall from the stratosphere in 1980.

Five years on, a quartet of Davies, Graham, Bonner and Anderson had recreated themselves as Tour de Force. First inklings of Bon Jovi, (a then largely-unknown proposition) provided inspiration, but original material was well to the fore, as Zander and ex-Airtight vocalist/bassist Ian Benzie came to the party. Colin Chapman, a 17-year-old drummer auditioned. TDF gigged and ligged ad infinitum, supporting the ascending Run Rig via the Marlene Ross connection. Prestigious as they were, warm-up spots to

Big Country were arranged at such short notice that the band were unable to capitalise on such exposure. By 1989 Nods was writing keyboards material, although Wishbone Ash and Thin Lizzy continued in the set. Keyboardist/vocalist Deanne Munro (daughter of Sixties Royal Teens' keyboardist George Munro) completed the jigsaw on her arrival from Heads And Hearts. UK and European adult oriented rock fanzines lauded TDF as hot prospects but despite the valiant efforts of Greg Bannerman (a handful of demos and tours of Italy, Belgium and Australia) TDF failed in the recording contract stakes. Disappointing then, for these guys: years of dedicated hard graft vinylly came to nothing.

Gareth was made redundant from his day job and, under the circumstances, thought "Bugger it', took the money and went off on an around-the-world trip. A fortnight after his return to Aberdeen late in 1993 came a call from Mark Ashton, co-editor with Bruce Mee of Boulevard, a melodic rock publication. Mark apparently had been attempting to round-up TDF unaware that the band were defunct. Demos had continued circulating throughout European fan circles: each fanzine review was more enthusiastic than its predecessor. . . "Keep a firm eye on the band for the future' (Kerrang); "Immaculate. . . music for hot Julys' (Metal Forces); "Lip smackin' eargasms' (Raw). Tour de Force's work warranted a proper release but major label rosters were replete with Seattle-inspired grunge acts, displacing now-unfashionable heavy-to-melodic rock exponents. Even some big hit-record names found themselves floundering and contract-less. Against this background, Ashton established his own record company directed at profiling his favoured bands (which may not otherwise be made available to the CD-buying public). At the time of Mark's call-to-arms Tour de Force hadn't been a working unit for some time: Colin was in Australia.

They had endured endless false dawns and a corresponding magnitude of disappointments: scepticism and caution at Mark's approach was therefore understandable. However in July of 1994 they were back together, recording the album at Mill of Hirn, with the skill and cosetting influence of Niall in evidence. According to Gareth, Niall has "a real ear for it.' Tracks consisted of a dozen Tour de Force numbers and three new originals. It became known that an American band were also using the TDF name, hence the Aberdonian band (and the CD) being re-dubbed The Promise. "None of us were particularly pleased with the name but you've got to be called something.' The sleeve notes name-check 95% of the Granite City's rockers over the last 15 years, the band's way of thanking everyone for the support during the TDF era. Demos were well-received in Japan, where The Promise was up for issue on the Alpha label.

1995 brought the major London Astoria 'Gods' AOR event, Aberdeen Lemon Tree gigs, features in Kerrang! and European dates in advance of hitting Tokyo later in the year. "We all know it will be a hard slog and we have no pretensions that we will ever be major league players. Nevertheless, it is all ultimately satisfying after such a long haul.' Even good old Northsound came to the party, selecting the track Don't Keep Me Waiting for steady airplay. As Lynryd Skynryd asked us in 1976 If I leave here tomorrow, will you still remember me? Course we will. . . Japan is a long way from Freebird's first noisy pub gigs, let's hope they fulfil The Promise.

PALLAS
L-R Derek Foreman (Drums), Niall Mathewson (Guitar),
Alan Reed (Vox), Mike Stobbie (KB),
Graeme Murray (Bass)

VERA CRUZ
1986
L-R Alan Stuart (Drums), Colin Millum (Bass),
Jaqui Copland (Vox), Mike Stobbie (KB),
Keith More (Guitar)

BASH STREET KIDS

Chapter 12

There's a guy works down the chipshop swears he's young at heart

Back in the early Sixties, The Strangers' rhythm guitarist Derek Freeland was injured in a road accident. Fifteen-year-old substitute Billy Bremner, already streets ahead of the competition, was in the Saturday crowd hanging around Harry Lord's guitar shop in George Street. He was the one attentively watching, and listening to what was going on. Self-taught, he first got to grips with the guitar by watching people playing on the TV, simply copying what he saw them doing with their fingers. Billy was an avid record buyer. "Everything the Everly Brothers turned out had great guitars and harmonies, and I thought that James Burton's work with Rickie Nelson was terrific.'

Norman and Derek came out of the shadows to form The Facells, leaving The Strangers to continue under the leadership of bassist Johnny Johnson. His new format included 'Barry Wayne' on vocals, future Stroller Bob Milne on drums, with Billy and Joe Kelman on guitars. Thirty years after the event Billy remembers that Kelman was "one of the best musicians in town at the time but there were many great players around. They were doing the same as I was at the start, copying guitar lines off the records. I suppose the only difference is that I committed myself to making a living from my music. I went after it where I could find it. . . you've got to be determined and make your own chances.' Kenny Taylor (Royal Teens leader and vocalist) figures that his line-up which included Bill and Speedy King was the best he ever had.

With his original Tremors moving to Hamburg, Tommy Dene drafted in Billy on guitar along with bassist Speedy King and drummer Jim Lunan, later replaced by 'Aberdeen's beatiest drummer' Freddie Ellis. Tommy recalls that Billy was a touch immature during this period. "In London, we were really struggling for money but he would come in carrying magazines that cost two or three quid. Which would have been fine if we had known where our next meal was coming from, but we didn't. So later the same night, having read his magazines he would come bumming a quid to get something to eat.' Tommy demonstrates a talent for recalling domestic minutiae of 30 years ago, revealing that Billy was also a socks maniac. "We were biding in some grotty digs and I would be raking about without success for semi-presentable clothes... "Has onybody seen my last clean pair o' socks ?' No takers of course. . . then hours later I spied them on Billy's feet. That lad had no sense of responsibility.' Attempts to attract interest from Tin Pan Alley met with sufficient apathy for Tom to pack his last pair of socks and catch the train home from Kings Cross. Syd Weaver moved to vocals as The Tremors strove to carve out their own destiny in London. They were ''very green, and our struggles had nothing to do with musical abilities.' Pat King remembers how they shared a dicey Chelsea bedsit and blagged their way onto gigs. Freddie's wife visited and was appalled at their domestic surroundings, telling him "You can't live like this' before hauling him back to Aberdeen, clean clothes and decent food. The Tremors' roadie Arnold Scott, affectionately dubbed 'fat Arnie fae Mintla' became a very competent replacement drummer. His previous claim to fame was rescueing The Royal Teens' van the morning after it had killed the coo. Bottom of the bill tours with Mike Berry, The Roulettes, Frank Ifield, The Small Faces and The Paramounts (later to become Procol Harum) ultimately led nowhere, and the theft of their equipment proved too much for Syd and Arnie. Weaver went back to Press and Journal country, and Arnie eventually became a theatrical agent, booking strippers in the Peterborough area. That left Billy and Speedy toughing it out in London on the bones of their arses: desperate times.

In 1964 Kris Ife was a member of The Quiet Five, who, together with The Tremors, opened for The Walker Brothers. Hence he met Bill on the American trio's national UK tour. When the Walkers' guitarist was sacked ("I wouldnae say he was bad, but he used to swing like a eunuch's bollocks') Billy was offered the job, a spot he was to keep for a couple of years. Thereafter, as one the post-Lulu Luvvers Billy appeared on Ready Steady Go and made two singles which he describes as "bloody awful - the drummer didnae know a crotchet from a hatchet.' Bill went on to join Johnny B Great and The Quotations (with Johnny Goodison subsequently of Brotherhood Of Man) and played on many demos and on later releases by Nirvana They were not the Seattle grunge rockers but the act which first came to prominence in the Sixties on the Island label. Anyone who owned a copy of Island's seminal You Can All Join In sampler will be familiar with their exquisite Rainbow Chaser which Mojo magazine succinctly sums up "phased orchestra rips through the speakers like a jet fighter.' Strange to relate that for a band which produced such a quintessentially English sound - Tiny Goddess, Girl In The Park and Pentecost Hotel - Nirvana were the Greek Alex Spyropoulos and the Irish Patrick Campell-Lyons. Pat: "I met Billy next door to Central Studios in Denmark Street - Tin Pan Alley - at La Gioconda a cafe popular with musicians, studio people and publishers. The first thing he said to me was "will you lend me a fiver?' He did a lot of the early Nirvana demos with us, Alex and I both also used him on some other solo recordings. Our sound wasn't really that up-tempo or rocky so Billy didn't fit on the final, issued versions of our early stuff, but he did a lot of work on our later LP Black Flower and my own albums.'

Then working on sessions (so numerous that he long since lost track of which records he played on), Bill nonetheless was up aginst it financially. "The money was criminal, but it was how I made my living, regardless of how poor it was. I didn't know anything else.' Indeed, Cousin Norman Shearer recalls family gossip of Bill fainting through malnutrition. Such struggles continued through to the mid-Seventies, when Ife signed Billy to Heath Levy Music, an offshoot of ATV making demos of writers' songs. Kris later produced two solo Bremner singles. Downtown Hoedown/Rhyme And Reason, released on Polydor in 1977 featured Huey Lewis (then a member of Clover) on harp. A year later The Heart and The Stone/I Don't Want To Be A Hero appeared on the State record label. Collectors please note: no matter how comprehensively one might search through boxes of vinyl heaven at record fairs and car boot sales, copies of neither release credited to Billy Bremner will be unearthed. Kris explains "He was worried that people might somehow think that his work had something to do with the other Billy Bremner, the Leeds United and Scottish football captain. So he used his middle name and the singles came out under the name Billy Murray. He didn't want to be known as the singing footballer.'

In the company of steel guitar player Roger Rettig, bassist Brian Hodgson and drummer Peter Kircher, Billy then constituted the Northerly part of Compass. This line-up mutated into Fatso and was soon in a rut, thanks to the BBC, Eric Idle and Neil Innes. The latter named renegade Monty Python/Bonzo Dog duo were responsible for the Beeb's Rutland Weekend Television, an off-the-wall scrapbook of comedic sketches and parodic skits on Sixties beat music. Enter The Rutles, soon to cause international youth hysteria Rutlemania. Classic songs All You Need Is Rot and The Long and Winding Rut were publicly attributed to band members Dirk, Stig, Nasty and Kevin. But away from paparazzi attention and fan frenzy, the unacclaimed guys who actually committed Rutlebeat to vinyl were anonymously sessioning away. Following in the tradition of manufactured non-musician bands such as The Monkees, the TV show's accompanying album The Rutland Weekend Songbook was in reality the work of Innes on piano and vocals, John Halsey on drums, and former Compass members Bremner, Hodgson, and Rettig.

Following the album of the TV series came the book of the album of the TV series, which whilst having no specific association with Billy, certainly touch upon the Aberdeen area. The Rutland Dirty Weekend Book includes a spoof rock magazine Rutland Stone featuring an illustration of an LP cover. The record in question bears the suspect title Cocks of the North, allegedly the work of the Gay Gordons and bringing to mind a certain cosy cause celebre at the Bridge Of Don Gordon Highlanders barracks. Of further local interest are Neil Innes' family roots in the North East. His dad is from the Cullen area where the paternal side of the family still reside. His cousin is in the taxi business and reflected Cullen's diminutive dimensions by telling a boozy telephone customer seeking a cab in the village: "You dinna need a taxi jist fall o'er twice and you're there.' Neil himself was an army baby, born whilst his father was on a posting with the Black Watch.

Whilst The Rutles were fab in their own pastichesque, cultish way (as one would expect from a member of the Innes clan) Billy's subsequent work with Nick Lowe and Dave Edmunds moved him into a situation which was much more. . . well. . . rock 'n' roll. He finally began to reap the rewards which his skills so richly deserved. Lowe had decompressed from a pub-rock hangover after a lengthy residency at the Tally Ho in London's Kentish Town with his former band, Brinsley Schwarz. Although their allotted 15 minutes of fame dragged on to six years of medium fame, the Brinsleys had been a terrific rock outfit. For his part Edmunds had deservedly acquired a reputation as the country's premier defender and exponent of traditional rock 'n' roll and rockabilly, most noticeably marked in the pop charts by I Hear You Knocking, name-checking many of the genre's primal screamers.

Lowe, one of Britain's most consistently under-rated and naturally talented rockers, didn't get where he was in 1977 without knowing a superb guitarist when he heard one. He was brought by Edmunds, producer of the first Brinsley's LP, to check out Billy's guitar and vocal work at Fatso's regular Monday night slot at London's Nashville Rooms. Nick was thoroughly impressed with what he saw and NME soon reported on a short British and European tour by 'Dave Edmunds and Rockpile' that February. Slap-bang in the middle of the punk eruption this combo fused the considerable talents of the self pro-claimed Jesus Of Cool Lowe (who had recently launched his post-Brinsley solo career with So It Goes) and future Dire Straits drummer Terry Williams, together with guitarists Bremner and Edmunds. The lat-ter had long hankered after a band in which he could share equal status with other members. Rockpile was his stated dream-ticket with Lowe and Bremner sharing the vocal load with the oft stage-nervous Edmunds, who said "This band is formed with the idea of playing smelly rock 'n' roll bars and clubs.'

A contractual conundrum saw Edmunds already signed to Led Zeppelin's Swan Song label and Lowe tied to Radar: issuance of the band's recordings under the Rockpile flag was impossible. Hence half-a-dozen albums featuring the hot quartet were to appear credited to either Lowe or Edmunds. For live work however, Rockpile gigged prolifically throughout the international rock market-place. April marked the commencement of a monumental 54-date US tour with Edmunds' Swan Song stable-mates Bad Company. That summer Granada filmed a Rockpile support spot to Elvis Costello in Liverpool for a TV special, whilst October passed in a blur of hectic shows. Somehow in between all this stage work Lowe's debut album Jesus Of Cool, with its hit single I Love The Sound Of Breaking Glass, came to fruition. Certified rockaholics, the following year also saw Rockpile cutting Mickey Jupp's inaugural album for Stiff and Edmund's LP Trax On Wax 4, promoted at September's Knebworth Festival. From the album came the Bremner-composed Trouble Boys, an American single (with Edmunds handling vocals instead of Billy, who sang this number on stage). Trouble Boys became a much-covered track, Thin Lizzy's ver-sion amongst the most notable.

No respite in 1979: as a precursor of the new Edmunds' LP Repeat When Necessary, Rockpile's version of Elvis Costello's Girls Talk hit the top-five. Its concurrent success in the USA was later noted by Billy as being "the turning point in my musical career. After Girls Talk, I had more work than I could han-dle and finally began to make a decent living.' Queen Of Hearts followed into the chart. In tandem with these Edmunds releases came Lowe's Labour Of Lust album, recorded at London's Eden Studios and Helsinki's Love Studios. Profiled in the singles market by Crackin' Up and Cruel To Be Kind, this LP is a shining example of Lowe's idiosyncratic writing skills - complemented perfectly by the intuitive perfor-mances of Williams on drums, the massed Celtic chords of Edmunds and Bremner, with Lowe himself on bass. Flawless British pop-rock at its best, but Labour Of Lust stalled at number 43. In mitigation of this failure, it should be remembered that this was a year in which the tasteful UK record-buying public placed both The Bee Gees and Boney M top of the long player charts.

The guys who had laboured and lusted were back in 1980, at last being able to record openly as Rockpile (Edmunds and Lowe now being being free of their respective Swan Song and Radar obligations) for the Seconds Of Pleasure album. An uncomplicated fun collection of numbers, it followed the histori-cal rock 'n' roll ethic (written by Lowe, Chuck Berry, Difford and Tilbrook, Joe Tex. . . get the picture?) It sounds as if they simply plugged in and set the tape running, deceptively straight forward and direct. Any listener unable to dig this good-time rock 'n' roll celebration (and there were many such Philistines with the album peaking at number 34) should have got themselves down to B & Q to buy a new spade. Sounds described Rockpile as "simply the best firmly traditional UK rock 'n' roll band in existence bar none save The Rolling Stones on a good night.' Later the same year came the Musical Shapes LP from Lowe's wife Carlene Carter, backed by Rockpile.

February of 1981 brought the announcement that the group was disbanding with individual members concentrating on solo careers. Despite the decision to split being 'joint and amicable' rumour was rife that personal differences underlay Rockpile's demise. Already in the can from the line-up was Edmunds' parting Swan Song album Twangin' (its plug single was John Fogerty's Almost Saturday Night). Billy continued his association with Edmunds for the latter's Arista LP DE 7th in March of 1982 and the Spectorish Baby I Love You single in May.

During a visit home Northsound Radio hauled in Billy for a live interview. The guitarist had been mixing with the grown-ups for years, whilst the radio station was still toddling around in trainer pants.

Anxious to establish the street-cred tone of the programme, the presenter hit Billy with "Dave Edmunds rates you as one of the best rock guitarists in the world. Is there any one thing in particular to which you would attribute your musical talent?' Striking faster than Frank McDougall against the Old Firm Bill replied "Aye, Aitkens' rowies.' Not so much a rock 'n' roll answer, more a morning roll answer. He also used Northsound as his personal broadcasting service: Tommy Dene was driving down the road one day and heard DJ Damien McLeod announce "And now, here's a message for Tommy from Billy. I'm back in town so give me a ring at Marilyn's and we'll go and get drunk.'

Reputation bolstered by his Rockpile work, the Eighties brought a flurry of activity, both under his own name and as one of the busiest session hands in the business. By the author's reckoning six solo singles (all attributed to Bremner, Murray having been dropped as had the Leeds United skipper) were created between 1981 and 1985. The first of these was the superb Will Birch-produced Loud Music In Cars on the Stiff label, later efforts appearing on Rock City and Arista, including the wonderful Bash LP with its home-town related track North Sea Tigers. The ever-modest Billy bemoans that "Loud Music In Cars wasnae that great as a record, but we did a shit-hot live version of the same number with a group I had later in Los Angeles, with Ian McClagen. Pity that band never recorded it.'

Following the untimely deaths of Jim Honeyman-Scott and Pete Farndon, Chrissie Hynde turned to Billy to fill the Pretenders' guitar void. Jim had been a mate of Billy's, so he felt honoured to do the job. The result was his classic performance on Chrissie's elegy to Honeyman-Scott Back On The Chain Gang. Bill's sometime co-writer and producer Will Birch perfectly described this as "A highlight of Eighties guitar rock.' Check out The Pretenders' stunning My City Was Gone whilst you are it. Bill remained with Chrissie for the Packed album.

Whilst Bremner's name may not be immediately familiar to the average pop fan, it is certain that his work is. Focus your aural memory - hear the guitar link between Kirsty McColl's There's A Guy Works Down The Chipshop and The Bluebells' Young At Heart ? His distinctive touch can be found on a myriad country rock material, including Phil Everly's 1987 solo album Louise and releases by Rosie Flores, an American artist. Billy blew his rock 'n' roll cred however, when he hesitantly whispered that he also plays on Billy Connolly's Supergran: "I'm nae so sure that's one I'm affa proud of. . . "

Plaudits from his peers are plentiful and are generously given, typified by Patrick Campbell-Lyons. "He was highly rated as a session player and I continued to use him on many projects over the years. The best compliment I could pay Billy would be that I immediately recognise his playing, either on some-one's demo, a master recording or on a live performance. I felt that he sounded happiest playing with Rockpile, it was a real pity that they didn't continue to greater success.' On the social side of things, our Billy carries the reputation of being a gregarious and outgoing character, a party animal of reknown. Patrick hazily recalls how he "spent many lost days and nights with Billy in various London drinking establishments. He is one of the best story tellers I know, and that says a lot coming from an Irishman.'

Having already played lengthy American engagements with Rockpile, Bill returned to the US in 1986 as musical director for a Nicol Williamson one-man stage show in New York. At the end of the run, Bill still had a few months left on his work permit and many friends Stateside. So he stayed and picked up a few gigs. When that first green card expired, he applied for another. . . ten years on he is still resident in the US. Having been based in California for six years, he moved down to Nashville - the home of both traditional and 'new' country music. Life in Los Angeles was "nasty - and I didnae like the earthquakes much.' Nashville is apparently much quieter and has increasingly become a centre for rock music. When he is not recording, Bill fronts his own band and guests with local clubs groups.

Asked (without any advance warning that the question was coming) who his favourite guitarists are, he responded "Well, that's a really difficult one, even if I'd had some time to think about it. Trouble is, there are so many different styles and just as many ways of playing. Buuuutttt. . . if I'm going to be nailed down, I would have to say. . . I think. . . that Albert Lee and Mark Knofler are the best I have worked with. And there is a British guy living here in Nashville, Ray Flack: he is simply a great, great player. As for vocalists, before I came over to Scandinavia at the start of 1995, I was playing on a new album (Mr Moonlight) for Foreigner, who are back together again. Their singer Lou Gramm has the most terrific voice I have come across. . . I am always into music but it's not as if the very first thing I do in the morning is switch on the radio. It's nae too bad up in New York or in LA, where the radio is pretty rocky, and there's plenty to choose from. . . . in Nashville, there's four choices on the local stations: country, western, take it, leave it. And in the UK, I think the radio is really sad. But really, my time is better spent writing and playing - sometimes if you listen to other peoples' stuff too much, you can become over influenced, even if you aren't aware of it at the time.'

Perhaps surprisingly for someone in his situation, he doesn't possess a CD player (can we detect a 'hear-hear' echoing from you vinyl luddites, led by Aberdeen plastic fetishist Bob Spence ?) "I just never bothered buying one,' says Bill "you can imagine that I often have CDs given to me but they finish up getting stuck away in a cupboard at home. They will be shifted along with the rest of my stuff when I get back to Nashville. I'm moving to a place nearer to town. At present, I live about five miles out in the sticks and it's nae like living in Mastrick wi' a bus every half hour. If you're lucky, you might see one every four days or so.'

In 1995 he was producing a young Swedish rockabilly band (the tribal name for such acts is Fjord Cowboys) in Javla, a small town outside of Stockholm. Billy and The Bjorns performed up at the Arctic Circle and regularly played at ski-slope clubs where thousands of entertainment-starved Swedes turned out for the dancing. He wasn't looking forward to flying back to the States at the end of the Scandinavian gig. "The flying disna bother me. It's crashing that I don't like.'

He emphasises that Nashville aint all yee-ha cowboy music. "It's less traditional than people would think, it really is thriving as far as top studios, producers and musicians are concerned - the Grand Old Opry is a much smaller deal than it appears to outsiders. It's only really in Summertime, when the town is crawling with tourists that you really notice it at all.' His residency in Tennessee offers him the opportunity to maximise his session and gigging potential, playing music which Billy (one of our greatest rock 'n' roll champions), understands and loves. He has more work than he can handle and that's all he wants. "When I'm playing or even when I'm on a tour bus, that's fine by me. I can handle one or two weeks off as well as long as I know there's a gig coming up at the end of it.' Plenty work then, and a great standard of living in the American South. But one wonders if, instead of a breakfast menu of grits and Dunkin' Donuts he occasionally craves for an Aitken's rowie? Toodle-oo Bill!

. . . .

If Billy was destined to be Aberdeen's most succesful rock guitarist, his bass-playing colleague Pat Speedy King from The Tremors and Royal Teens wasn't slow either. Pat's big-time rock career saw him crossing paths with Davie Flett, another hot-shot Granite City guitarist. To track the progress of Speedy and Dave, we begin by retro-checking the British pop charts of the Sixties in the bearded company of Manfred Mann. The group and its eponymous leader enjoyed a run of 17 quality chart singles, from 1964's 5-4-3-2-1 to Ragamuffin Man in 1969. As the latter record disappeared from the pop chart, Manfred's men went their different ways. Between 1969 and 1975 Manfred and Mike Hugg developed (in contrast with their successful pop careers), an adult, albumcentric fusion of jazz-rock styles. Operating under the title Chapter Three, the new direction brought greater appreciation on continental Europe than at home in the UK. Manfred, having popularised obscure Bob Dylan material in the previous decade, now turned his focus towards New Jersey in the obscure persona of Bruce Springsteen. He wasn't yet The Boss, still several E Streets distant from the packed stadia which would become his future international domain. Fundamentally, Manfred endeavoured to construct an escape tunnel away from unfaithful, transient pop singles buyers. If all went well, the tunnel would surface well beyond the wire at the other side, safely in the territory of mature LPs, musical expertise and instrumental eclat. The initial Chapter Three amalgamation which Mann and Hugg created was succeeded by the prolific Earthband which by 1975 had released its seventh album Bombers and Nightingales.

Singer-guitarist Mick Rogers skipped back to his native Australia, leaving Manfred to employ the considerable vocal talents of Chris Thompson and the guitar dexterity of Dave Flett. The incoming guitarist had made his public debut at 15 in Aberdeen with one of Trevor Hart's bands (skulking at the rear of the stage, hiding from the audience behind Harry McFarlane's drums). Graham Spry remembers that Davie was "great to play with: he was soaked in music - immersed in it. Looking back on it his move away from the local scene was inevitable. He wanted to play every night and the best we could come up with was, more or less, Ma Cameron's once a fortnight. There just wasn't enough scope for him on the Aberdeen semi-pro circuit.'

London-based Aberdonian jeweller (and former Daddy Stove Pipe) Dave 'Ratner' Stroud had been speaking on the phone with Bill Innes back in Aiberdeen. Binner raved on about a new Hendrix from the Isle Of Skye. Apparently this guy was the best thing since second helpings at school dinners, but didn't want the commitment of playing in a steady band. Manfred's wife (Stroudfinger's landlady) happened to mention to him that Manfred had vacancies for a crooner and an axe man. . . his policy apparently was to recruit unknown cheap talent. . . "reputedly a bit of a bread head').

First off, Stroud thought about Binner's new find but then remembered that he wasn't a band man. Flett was still in London, having arrived full of expectation with Trevor Hart and Keithy Milne. Pursuing their own pot of gold, no amount of gigging or demo tapes would secure that slippery recording deal. . . Just when Stroud had stopped thinking about a guitarist for Manfred's Earthband, who should he see driving an Initial Towels van down Blackheath High Street? None other than Davie Flett. Apparently he took a lot of persuasion before gathering sufficient audition-day nerve. Flettie's fretwork flattered and he got the job, allowing him to throw in the towel. Quoth the embittered (but un-emlagered) Stroud. "And the bastard never even bought me a pint.'

Mrs. Mann had actually suggested that Stroud went up for the vacant vocalist's position himself, but he had taken such a shine to the bangles, baubles and beads biz that he didn't bother. "My tonsils were a touch rusty anyway, I hadn't sung seriously for a while', he recalls.

This reworked version of The Earthband was completed by Chris Slade on drums and Colin Pattenden on bass. Davie brought his guitar talents to Manfred's sublime interpretation of Springsteen's Blinded By The Light with its lengthy, spacey instrumental introduction, a number six single in the UK in the summer of 1976. It also topped the American chart the following February, and has been a fixture on AOR radio's playlist ever since with international sales exceeding two million. Its host album The Roaring Silence hit number ten in the British chart.

After their Tremors days in London Billy Bremner joined The Walker Brothers band and telephoned Pat King at his fill-in day job in a menswear shop, telling him that The Luvvers were looking for a guitarist. Bill brushed aside Speedy's protestations that he was actually a bass player, telling him 'You can do it, its easy.' Pat fulfilled engagements with The Luvvers (London based, but playing as far North as Lerwick) but didn't feel too comfortable on guitar. Dundonian Jim Kelly was ' A shit-hot guitarist and vocalist, with all the talent of Stevie Winwood.' Jim was involved in an unfortunate and talent restricting accident. Session work beckoned for Speedy, playing on Eurovision songs and records by artists of the calibre of Paul Raven (several years before the tin foil suits and hairy chest wig) and. . . Tony Blackburn (not long before Blackburn began wearing the rug that he bought in a Cosy Carpets sale).

A move into The George Bean Group, with its highly talented musicians, proved to be an important step for Pat. "Until then, I had basically been a chancer, but now I was involved with theory and arrangements.' The Beans played a club and cabaret circuit, but also recorded the sound track music for the Paul Jones movie Privilege. Drummer Rod Coombes was around at this point, and was to continue his association with NE music with Trevor Hart's The Lasers. Rod, of course, also played with The Jeff Beck Band, Brian Auger, The Strawbs, and Stealers Wheel. Gradually the quality of Pat's session work improved (titter ye not at Champagne, The Dooleys or Billy Ocean, work is work) and he played with Cat Stevens at the latter's final live gig at Weston Supermare. Pat's next outfit was Trifle, who recorded their First Meeting LP in 1971 at Pye's Marble Arch studios, produced by the label's renowned John Shroeder. The band "Went through various styles from soul music into a Blood Sweat and Tears/early Chicago heavy brass format.' Trifle's personnel were George Bean (vocals), Dick Cuthell (trumpet and flugel horn), Barrie Martin (tenor and alto sax), Alan Fealdman (piano and organ), John Hitchin (guitars), Chico Greenwood (drums), and of course, Pat King on bass. If you are into brassy rock, First Meeting is a necesity.

Soon Pat was a croupier at the Playboy Club and co-incidentally "behaving like a rabbit' himself outside of working hours, before becoming involved, in July of 1975, with Pete Kirsher, Cliff Bennett (erstwhile Rebellion vocalist) and peerless guitarist Mick Green in Shanghai. Their original American bass player and male/female vocalists returned to the US, with Speedy and Bennett filling the vacancies. He already knew Green from the Dalrymple Hall in Fraserburgh, having bailed him out of a no-equipment situation. Bennett recalls Shanghai was "an R 'n' B-soul-rock stew, encompassing all combined career elements of Cliff himself, King, Green, Kircher, Alterman. Powerful and accomplished but too professional and polished for the time.' Their sole LP was February 1976's Fallen Heroes, released on Green's Thunderbird label (of Thanet House in West London's Craven Road) amid the question "Is Fulham ready for Shanghai?'. Regular punters at the Greyhound in Fulham Palace Road had been "getting into the band' for months, winessing Bennett blasting away on vocals, with Mick "The Guitar' Green duelling with his nearest challenger for the title, Brian Alterman. Londoners crossed the river from Putney just to say they were "there' as Speedy King played bass, and drummer Pete Kircher had his own fan club in Tottenham . . . or so they said. In the USA, CBS jumped in with both feet, releasing two singles, Candy Eyes and Shakin' All Over, in the same month (Thunderbird also issued them as UK singles). Fallen Heroes featured an impressive gangster-idiom cover-painting by David Dragon, styling the guys as gun-toting Chicago hard-men leaning on a bullet-slattered automobile. However, Green's money was soon eaten by the label's set-up costs. . . it folded and the contracts were sold on to President Records, who expected the band to work under unrealistic conditions. Bennett recalls the band was "They had toured heavily in England, Holland and Germany but in December of 1976 Shanghai ended 'a bit distastefully.'

Then. . . uh hu, it was The Manfreds. . . Pat found himself sitting around as a paid spectator in his capacity of UK MU sanctioned shadow as Roy Harper's band played a televised gig with an American bassist. The show was managed by someone from Manfred Mann's Workhouse Studio. Soon afterwards, Manfred quizzed his Workhouse posse about a possible new bass player for the Earthband, and the bassist frae the Broch was suggested. Manfred called Pat and two weeks later, he passed the audition and was in. "I'm sure that he sounded out better guys than me, but they were probably playing a style that was over-typical of the current slap and tickle stuff, whereas my style was a bit more old-fashioned and that suited better.'

A new version of Springsteen's Spirits In The Night (which the band had already issued two years previously) was the first emanation of the Flett/King-enhanced Earthband. Not a hit but it was a taster for 1978's album Watch. This spawned some terrific singles as it rose to number 33 in the LP chart. The FM friendly single California was wonderfully evocative of great distances between yearning, parted lovers. . . saudade: sorrow, longing, nostalgia, hope, all rolled into one. The song featured Thomas' superb vocals stretching languidly through Dave's fluid, relaxed guitar work. The B side, the jazzy Chicago Institute jointly composed by Mann, Thomas and Flett, was a considerable radio hit which unfortunately didn't enhance their bank balances as disc jockeys don't buy records.

The second extract from the LP returned the Earthband to singles heaven: written by John Simon (he had previously penned Manfred's 1968 pop hit My Name Is Jack) and The Band's Robbie Robertson, Davy's On The Road Again drove on to number six in the hit parade of May 1978, and to eternal rock popularity. Nothing to say about about this glorious number: if you don't know it intimately and love the hell out of it, then maybe you picked up this book by mistake? A live rendition of Dylan's Mighty Quinn also a Sixties hit for Manfred, concluded the singles from what should essentially have been a massive album. Then the perpetually restless Manfred then decided to split his Earthband.

Chris Slade humbly went on to join Uriah Heep before his subsequent work with Gary Numan, Dave Gilmour, The Firm (Jimmy Page), and AC/DC. Davie Flett formed Special Branch along with future MMEB bassist Matt Irving and recorded a lone eponymous Zaine Grigg album. He operated a small recording studio in Blackheath, collaborating with ex-Winkies front man Philip Rambo. Music press rumours on September 5, 1979 about a major move for Flettie came to fruition a fortnight later when he left for Japan with Thin Lizzy, pairing with Californian Scott Gorham in Lizzy's trade-mark dual guitar sound. Midge Ure played keyboards on the tour of sell-out gigs, with the band based at the Keio Plaza Hotel in Tokyo.

Sets featured 15 numbers, and were played successively at Osaka Festival Hall, Tokyo Nakano Sun Plaza Hall, Nagoya-shi Kokaido, and Tokyo Korakuen Hall. Flettie suffered from food poisoning during the first two dates but was on top form by the time Lizzy returned to Nakano Sun Plaza for their final gig on September 30th. Gorham's guitar cut out during Jailbreak and Davie held the floor alone. Lizzy's charasmatic leader Phil Lynott was delighted. "What I really liked was that this was Dave's gig. For me, it was the first time where he came into his own. . . I could see that he was thinking, I have nothing to lose now, I'm going for it.' Flettie later confirmed "It was the last day of my dream. Even if there were no strings on that guitar, I would have been out there throwing shapes.'

Back in the UK in November, Flett became one of the few Aberdonians to appear on Top Of The Pops (an appearance which was repeated on UK Gold during 1993). That same month he guested with Manfred's Earthband five-a-side football team at a Wembley Arena Sun/Goaldiggers celeb event. The week before Christmas of 1979, Davie played his final shows with Lizzy at the Manchester Apollo and Bingley Hall, Stafford. Scott Gorham summed up Davie and Lizzy "The only problem was that his guitar style didn't really fit in. I would have loved to continue playing alongside him but you have to be truthful with yourself and everyone else. . . I had to be honest with Dave. I had to say that his attitude and everything else was right, but his actual style wasn't right for Lizzy. I think he pretty much agreed with that, even though he did want to be in the band. I wish him all the luck in the world.' Brian Downey remembers that 'Dave Flett was the most nervous guy I ever met in my life. He used to puke up all over the shop before going on stage. He was a great guy and a brilliant guitar player but Jesus, he'd be a bag of nerves every night.' Latterly Flettie played the live circuit with Rory Gallagher's erstwhile bassist Gerry McAvoy, before disappearing from the UK rock business. He apparently now resides in Florida, where he maintains a low profile. . . do Initial Towels have a branch in Miami?

As Davie was Waiting For An Alibi with Lizzy in Japan, Manfred unveiled a restructured Earthband. Geoff Britton (previously drummer with East Of Eden, The Wild Angels and Wings) was joined by Steve Waller, a veteran of London's pub rock circuit. Chris Thompson and Speedy King remained on vocals and bass respectively for the Angel Station album. This generated two minor hits, Bob Dylan's You Angel You and Don't Kill It Carol, an incredibly-stringed Mike Heron composition. Illness prevented Britton from touring the album and his place on-stage was taken by John Lingwood. This live format recorded former Albert Y Lost Trios Paranois vocalist Jimmy Hibbert's Heavy Duty LP in 1980 at Manfred's Workhouse Studios in London's Old Kent Road. Other than Hibbert, Lingwood, King and Mann, Geoff Whitehorn (guitars), Graham Prescott (piano and string synths) also appeared on the Logo label album, produced by Hibbert and Laurie Latham. It is a superb effort: any time you need cheering up, have a listen, beginning with the dead-pan vocalised Mr. Wonderful. Heavy Duty was one that went undeservedly unrecognised.

Minus Waller and with a variety of vocalists these personnel created The Earthband's 1980 album Chance, with its stand-out Springsteen-penned track For You, proving to be Speedy's final recorded work with Manfred. The following year he put his bass into retirement, his spot being filled by Matt Irving and his track-record stretching back to the heady Sixties Scottish beat scene.

Speedy moved into tour management and agency work with Alec Leslie's company. His client list included Elkie Brooks, Europe, Joan Armatrading and continued with Toto, Roger Chapman, Protocol . . . and Manfred Mann's Earthband, a relationship which endures to the present day and Manfred's latest album Soft Vengeance. Pat hasn't played for more than 15 years, but maybe one day soon, when the itch gets unbearable, he'll plug in again. "Nothing pretentious though' he hastens to add, as if you could expect anything else from yet another down-to-earth, unassuming success story from the Granite City.

Let's now spend a few seconds in the fantasy music league. . . our championship contenders have splashed out on the transfer market making some big-money singings. Dual lead guitars: Billy Bremner and Davie Flett. Bass: Speedy King. Not a bad start, probably about 20 million records sold between them. . . if we made the right offer for former Spiggy Topes drummer Graham Walker, he could bring his five million sales from Gary Moore's Midnight Blues Band albums to the side. Mind you, he would have to fight off chunky ex-ruggerist Spry and deft wing-wizard Billy Allardyce. There aint no way in the world I am going to upset or offend any of our angelic-voiced tonsilular technicians: so you, dear reader, are permitted to select our singer. And what about an Aberdonian name for the band. . . drawing inspiration from previous mega-status acts we could look at The Fa?, Aye, Tak 'At, The Jienners, or Wiz Wizna.

ROCKPILE
L-R Nick Lowe, Dave Edmunds, Billy Bremner,
Terry Williams

MANFRED MANN'S EARTHBAND
Davie Flett *centre*

Chapter 13

Kincorth Cockneys

It is 1978 and shock waves from the Sex Pistols' earthquake, classically hyped by manager Talcy Malcy McClaren, have eventually reached Aberdeen.

The supposed anti-rock negativism broadcast in the Pistols' propaganda was blatantly belied by their retention of, and dependence upon, songs composed by their sacked bassist Glen Matlock. However, in the songs, Cookie's power drumming and Jones' awsomely malevolent metal guitar work lay an integral truth within McClaren's bullshit. The out-of-tune psychotically paced God Save The Queen induced that cold shiver and hair rising at the back of the head for thousands across the UK: the biggest pop thrill since Alice Cooper and his snake on TOTP in 1972. That same thrill cascaded North to the crop of punk bands which festered in Aberdeen over the next few years.

The bastard offspring of this aesthetic maelstrom incongriously mutated into Kincorth kids with cockney accents. Hence the city's low budget venues were plagued by hordes of pogo-ing baby rockers, endearing themselves to cleaning staff by gobbing affectionately at enthusiastic, rudimentary bands. The prime source of publicity for these be-spittled groups was Colin Murray's Granite City fanzine, faithful in itself to the punk Sniffin' Glue ethic, and eclectic in its coverage of what went down.

Three-gig Barlinnie took their name from Peter McMillen's brother, pardoned and awarded £2,000 two years into a four-year stretch at the Bar-L. Led by the unique Bobby Equus (who began applying his make-up at eight in the morning for a gig 12 hours away, Barlinnie were undefinably different. It all began for The Miscreants when they first heard The Pistols' Anarchy In The UK - guitarist Ian Harrower worked out the chords and days later they were playing their first gig at the Drumlithie Village Hall in December of 1977. The venue was unlicensed but did remain open until one am, so attracting local kids of a bored Kincardineshire nature. The other band that night, Duty Free, played Status Quo numbers all night before The Miscreants' shambolic set was met with a stunned silence. The bemused organisers pulled the plug on the group, a green light for the baffled crowd to wreck the toilets: Harrower, bassist Kenny Thomson, vocalist Sinclair Lamb and drummer Neil McCallum were landed with the blame for the vandalism, banned eternally from Drumlithie. The band complained that it was thereafter inexplicably difficult to find gigs. Grand derring-do plans emerged to record a single by the end of September 1978: smelling like punk spirit, they claimed that they would decline the Top Of The Pops invitation that was certain to come their way. They had seven songs for which they knew words and music, with another seven incomplete. One Aberdeen venue which did take them on was the East Neuk in King Street. "That was terrible' said the new wavers, sadly. Their unstoppable slide to ignominy continued at the University Union where they supported a disco. . . no, not the other way around. "How low can you get?' cried Harrower "Mind you, it was a good night especially when my amp blew up.'

Without either a single or TOTP invite to their credit, The Miscreants were among a spike of punko-combos which turned out at the Kincorth Community Centre. Organised as a fund-raiser for one Mike Stopper (he had been injured in a shooting accident), the event epitomised the genre's anti-ego fundamentalism. Various bands swopped instruments and musicians, hence The Miscreants playing each of their three numbers with a different bass player. At various times during their short, sharp existence they had Alan Tyler on guitar, Jake Davidson on bass and Ernie Morrison on drums battering hell out of the echoing You're So Explicit, Memo From Control and We Will Never Surrender Wir Chibs. A common moan from them was "Nobody wants to talk to us 'cause we never play anywhere that people like us.' When the band finally ran out of pubs naive enough to let them destroy their bar trade, Harrower returned to his native Inverness and Tyler was seduced by the bright lights of London. Also on that Stopper benefit bill was Bobby Equus, breaking out of Barlinnie.

Tipped for stardom, he appeared in a £75 white suit (specially purchased for the occaision) and wrap-around slit shades. With slashing, fierce guitar chords and screamed lyrics, he performed Killer Bomb and Black Equus totally immobile but for Mad Ludwig he was off on a mutated Chuck Berry duck-walk at the front of the stage. From Hilton came The Bored, a trio of 14-year-olds and a BOF of 16. Vocalist Keith Westbrook had already mastered the art of looking disinterested. . . they were followed by

The Generators for whom drummer Paul Clark gave a virtuoso performance as they powered through covers of Rip Off, Pure Mania, Dot Dash and Anarchy In The UK. No sycophantic entourage, designer drugs or stretch limos waiting for these Kincorth cockneys. Ladies and gentlemen Bobby Equus has left the building and is now waiting for the last bus home. Described as a "latter-day Clash' were The Parts. Bruce Mills (vocals), Keith Garden (rhythm guitar), Alison Robb (keyboards), Peter Stephen (lead guitar), Paul Turner (bass) and John Watson (drums) punked-up such Chuck Berry classics as Around and Around, (Oh) Carol and Bye Bye Johnny.

The 62 Club had found new life as a punk rock venue, where Brigade were really hacked-off about the sparce attendance at their gig. . . much bewildered scratching of spiky heads took place before they realised that not only were The Undertones playing in Aberdeen that night, but the students' Torcher parade was tootling its charitable, can-shaking way down Union Street. Brigade also claimed to be Aberdeen's very first punk combo, having started their rudimentary fumbling through three chords after being smacked between their safety-pinned ears by The Ramones' 1976 debut LP. They were rated as being "highly deserving of a recording contract, a great band on a great Music Hall night.' Super-charged power chords cocophanied through Destroy, Attack, Burglar, Psycho and Bomb Berlin. Their intermeshing guitars, solid drums and rock-steady bass attracted praise as "the most accomplished punk band.' This apparently contradictory adulation (did punk and accomplished ever belong together ?) was directed at Pete Clark (vocals, influences The Vibrators and Chris Spedding), Kevin Anderson (bass, influenced by Sid Vicious, a guy who couldn't play), Paul Clark (drums, impressed initially by The Glitter Band and Showaddywaddy before punk grabbed him) and Hest (guitar, his mentors were Bill Nelson, Bob Andrews of Gen X and Mick Jones of The Clash). The aggressive intensity of these be-zipped and be-leathered young guns was offset by the be-army Sid Ozalid. His only musical accompaniment was the tambourine which he banged frantically on his thigh, exorcising surreal poems such as that old favourite My Tortoise Can Burst Into Flames. Not so much Johnny Cooper Clarke, more Rabbie Burns on mescaline. . . stage props included a Mr Punch puppet as he read extracts from The Topper annual, and claimed that his father was a redundant caveman and his mother was a transvestite Egyptian monkey. If Sid was a Marxist after Groucho's example, The Chaos Brothers took their anarchy more seriously. However, with their music being weaker than their political stance, prospects of ever becoming stars were nullified by their policy of changing the band's name and line-up every fortnight. The Enormis Snakes lasted six months before shedding their skins and heading for London. They were soon back on their home turf, giving it another slither.

At the Noo Yoyk Dolls end of the spectrum Standard Issue's vocalist was Bennie Duthie (aka Ben Galaxy), a David Bowie clone dancing around the stage in leopard skin strides. Their original guitarist was sacked for being 'stuck in a mid-1968 time warp'. Admittedly the new drummer Addi Addison was an ex-Shapiro with sideboards and long hair, but he was grudgingly accepted nonetheless because he could play really well. Despite playing many gigs in Keith, Elgin and Echt, Standard Issue preferred down-town venues such as Ruffles and Fusion. Outside of Aberdeen's city limits (where they played straight covers purely for monetary reasons) they received the rough end of the pineapple from agrarian audiences. A rural riot at Echt was blamed on the locals' non-appreciation of musicians with green, blue and pink hair: a new experience out in the sticks. With an early-Seventies Stones/Bowie feel they played, in Aberdeen, largely original material which included Schooldays, Don't Let The Music Stop and How Do You Feel. The plan was to record a single "half way between Boney M and Abba so we can get to the top of the charts.' Ben Galaxy's rival as Aberdeen's most outrageous singer was Peter Thompson of The Resistors, rated as the city's toughest punk outfit. Thompson's stage chic involved peroxide hair and eye make-up. The other Resistors: Stan Smith on guitar, Tony Cheyne on bass and Stewart on drums, developed the knack of animating their audiences. At the ABC Bowl they even had punters dancing to their punky, rousing versions of primal Chuck and Beatles material (No Particular Place To Go, I Wanna Be Your Man).

With their name reminiscent of seedy shop-window postcards, French Lessons had a good front-man in Graham Barclay and a full bass/vocal sound from Andy Harthill. Granite City predicted "Once they have more songs they will be a force in the land.'. The Adaptorz (Colin Pope on vocals, Charlie Sullivan on drums and Geoff Steele on guitar) assailed their audiences with City Of Terror and The Velvets' Waitin' For My Man before they poached Mark 'Hest' Westbrook from Brigade.

Splitting Headache, later to devolve into Oily recording artists, were boosted by the arrival of the impressive Jeremy Thoms but already had a strong visual identity in Kenny Barnet and a retro-guitar whizz-kid Roy Ingram. Bondage played material split 50/50 between cover versions and their own compositions. Surely George Gershwin would have envied such memorable melodies as best For Adolfs Only, Jet Set, and Suzie Is A Headbanger. . . The Ramones comes to Rosemount? Drummer Tommy Reid, guitarist/vocalist Jim Shepherd, rhythm guitarist Adam Sanderson and bassist Steve Wilson played Tillydrone School and Linksfield Academy. They were destined for London and Creation Records, but that was still in the future. . . The Vicar's Children, The Robots, The Tools and The Outsiders were all on the circuit. Bobby Equus was back, this time revealed as James Tully. With Neale Gordon, Peter McMillen and Keith Miller this was Stereo Exit, a more musical version of Tully's madness with a set-list of The Chimes, Middle Class Daughters and Young Scientists. "Maybe we could play for the troops. . . nuclear war Vera Lynns.' Iggy and The Stooges were alive and as well as they ever gonna be. . . vocalist Dave Elliot Loch Ness led Burnt Remains through No Fun, Raw Power and I Wanna be your Dog.

Formed coincidentally the day after that fine upstanding figure of a man Sid Vicious went to the great glue-bag in the sky, The Abductors were Powis schoolboys venting their anti-establishment frustration in ways other than writing on their rucksacks. The originals were Gary 'Wee Eck' Dawson on vocals, Keith Thompson on skins, Stephen 'Steppe' Dempster and Fred 'Inspector Blake' Wilkinson on geetaar. The Inspector apparently earned his name by bossily taking charge of a bus en-route to Banchory: not quite hijacking a jumbo jet and forcing it down in Havana, but we are, efter all, talking Aiberdeen here. Jimmy Sim soon came in as new drummer with Trouper on bass, as The Abs terrorised any venue daft enough to accommodate them. Playing stuff like Football Violence 'a rant about terracing mayhem' (nothing to do with Pittodrie's sleepy hollow south stand, knee-deep in sweetie papers) and a selective set of Pistols' covers Blakey says that they were "pretty wild but quite naff really.'

By September of 1980 the band's noxious reputation, combined with tragic, unconnected events elsewhere in Aberdeen, precipitated a change of name from The Abductors. With Blakey working as a pharmacy technician, the Alternate Title of Toxik Ephex filled the prescription. And off they went, pogo-ing their way to an illustrious recording career overshadowed and under-achieved only by the impressive failures enjoyed by John Otway (self-proclaimed biggest loser in rock music and proud of it.) Never mind your Abbey Roads, the 62 Club was good enough for The Toxiks as they taped Police Brutality in all its angry glory on a reel-to-reel machine.

Much wheeking of cassette tapes through the mail to hopefully sympathetic record companies, and even more telephone hassling of these labels on the phone, and eventually Crass Records took the bait. On the face of it Crass were the UK's prime champions of anarchic, counter-culture music. So lo and behold the much exited Ephexers saw their song appear on the 40-track double-LP Bullshit Detector Two. The record climbed dizzy heights to top the punk chart on October 8, 1982, and to fourth place in the national indie chart. Selling around 15,000 copies, BD2 earned the boys the astonishing royalty of £135, paid incrementally over two years.

Despite having become major recording artists of inter-galactic mega status (well, their mas and das were fairly, if suspiciously, pleased and the wifie in the chipper asked "kin ye get Rod Stewart's autograph for me ?) 1982 was with typical Toxik logic, their quietest year with only three promoters putting the lads to work. Inactivity resulted in Jimmy Sim wishing the squad arrivaderci. Well, what actually happened was that Blakey found out that Simmy had sold his drum kit. Blakey got to thinking "oh f—k, maybe I should get another drum person.' Another Powis FP Chiz was just the boy and was welcomed with open arms before Mikey Smith beamed down in 1984. As well as mellow fruitfulness September 1985 brought a valuable addition in Dod Copeland, coinciding with Wee Eck jumping ship. Blakey's brother Dave Wilkinson filled in on second guitar, taking time off from his own combo Baroque before a gadgie named Steve Anderson becomes the regular rythmic strummer. Frank Benzie jumps onboard in 1987.

Blakey wanted another vinyl orgasm but thought "Bugger this, I'm fed up of making loads of money for multi-national conglomorate record companies.' This was typical ahead-of-his-time thinking, pre-dating those hard-done-by, hard-up pop trade serfs George Michael and The Artist Previously Known As Prince. "If a geek like Richard Branson can make millions with his own record label then surely someone like myself. . . better looking and more intelligent. . . can make even more.' Such capitalist day-dreaming came to fruition with Green Vomit Records.

The money for Toxik's first EP was raised through live gigs with valuable advice coming from one Andy Kirk (a church in a convenient location?). On his say so, they went down to the Pierhouse Studio in

Leith where the EP Punk As Fuck was recorded in a day. The lads gleefully skeedaddled their way home, clutching the prized tape, taking turns to hold, touch, stroke and caress it: "C'mon, it's my shottie you've had your go.'

It was duly despatched to Cops in London who soon returned a box of seven-inch black biscuits to Toxik Towers in Aberdeen. "Pretty much a DIY job as far as the rest of it went' says Freddie "We did the covers ourselves with spray glue and sticky labels all over the place. We punted most of them at our gigs and on the street. Sometimes we only got 50p a shot but at least it covered our petrol money. Fast Forward distribution told us first off they would take as many as we could send them, which naturally chuffed us at the time and they took a canny few. But then one day we were in Edinburgh anyway so we dropped in past for a natter with them. Then they said, Oh, whilst you're here, take this lot wi' you' And they gave us back boxes of the records. Smashing.' Their idiosyncratic brand of spikey punk had never-theless been captured on vinyl. The song titles themselves summarise Toxik's view of contemporary life: Always Skint, Nothing's Permissive and Fallout Shelter offer an alternative opinion of Maggie's let-them-eat-cake arrogance.

Let's now head off in the Punk As Fuck van, perchance to experience on-the-road commonalities between the retro-punkoid Toxiks, their dads (late-Sixties prog-rockers Gully Foyle and Spiggy Topes) and their grandads (winkle-pickered Brylcreemed, DA-sporting beatsters The Strollers).

For some reason or no reason, Toxiks toured extensively in West Yorkshire where those rock 'n' roll cities of Leeds, Bradford and Barnsley fair trip off the tongue. After one gig in the pulsating metropo-lis of Huddersfield, the boys had reserved a four-star floor for the night when local promoter Toddy said is was cool for them to kip in his kitchen. More than cool, actually is was freezing. As the post-gig party quietened down in the late hours of the morning, he told them he would organise a string of dates for them. Here we go, here we go, etc, etc!

The PAF van had definitely seen better days (perhaps it was the same vehicle that would-be bus conductor Jim Diamond painted all those years before) but somehow it got through its MOT. First port of call was Toxik Towers to pick up too many boxes of their records, and then on to collect the group, groupies, gropees, and gear. Then they were away. . . crash bang wallop. . . smoke everywhere in the middle of nowhere. Luckily and untypically the van was registered with the AA. . . however when the break-down vehicle turned up, the driver informed the stranded spikys that he could carry only five pas-sengers as he towed the kaput PAF-mobile. A wee bit of a problem then, as there were ten of them onboard half of whom hitched their way to the gig, shared with Edinburgh thrash exponents Oi Polloi. A whip-round generated enough money to hire a replacement van. . . they finished up with £36 each profit for the tour, which took them on to Bradford. . . who needs Madison Square Gardens anyway?

Meteoric success continued on Green Vomit with the Mad As Fuck LP, shared with Oi Polloi. The album defined TE's music as an equitable balance of politically-driven protest and aural cartoon pop-punk, encompassing such gems as Akanamynathingawizbleezin and a mad take on The Wild Side Of Life. The latter was your ma's Alexander Brothers' cheapo Marble Arch label version played through a food blender at 78 rpm.

Kelvingrove in Glasgow is probably best forgotten. Nazi skinheads wrecked the punk party, giving the polis an excuse for clobbering all and sundry. Replacement impromptu gigs were picked up in Paisley and Clydebank as the band headed South again, turning up on spec at the Dutchess Of York in Leeds where the UK Subs uhesitatingly added the boys to their bill. The two bands were already friendly from shows in Aberdeen.

Today West Yorkshire, tomorrow the world. . . starting with Germany. A promoter arranged a seven gig tourette of the Fatherland, promising transportation for the band. . . . fine in principle, 'cept it didn't show. So a replacement was hurredly pressed into action and they departed in Son Of The PAF Van. As it shoogled through the Angus roads it may have heard horror stories about eingangs and einfarts from its grandad, The Strollers' van. Yep, you're ahead of me here: it broke down just after Laurencekirk, prompting The Inspector to bawl at the driver "No, no, Steve. . . we want Bremen, nae Brechin.' Eventually in Germany, youth clubs and community centres in Mannheim and Bonn were aurally demolished by the band's idiosyncratic Aberdonian politico-alcoholocaust. Audiences were apparently very mixed (up?) and more appreciative than British crowds. The venture left the boys in a £400 hole. "Worth it for the experience' quoth Das Inspektor. Once again the P & J filled its front page with blazing headlines: "North East iconoclasts lose their shirts in Germany', "Theycannamynathingtheywizbleezin' and "Toxik Ephex puzzled by border guards' demands for Old Spice.' In Newport Wales they got pally with the proprietor of the Words Of Warning indie label, resulting in a shared WOW EP with Welsh pogoists Shrapnel in 1988

The 1 Up-funded album The Adventures Of Nobby Porthole Cock Of The North, recorded in five Leith days in 1989, saw the band getting ripped into contemporary problems as unemployment, with a pointedly barbed reworking of the traditional Irish air Maggie, directed at the wicked witch of Downing Street. . . The Other Half Lives, an impassioned diatribe on the inequalities of life, rocket-fuelled with demented, twiddly guitar: The bright lights of London are glowing, that's where all the profits must be going, In restaurants the prices are rising, outside on the pavement someone's dying. They have created a jungle where the law says the fattest survive. Caring, sharing and musically appealing but not the stuff of mainstream record contracts. Nobby Porthole set the scene for a soon-to-develop Aberdeen folk-punk movement, but local gigs at the East Neuk and the Venue became repetitively unchallenging. So when Fred was asked to dep in Frantik Zimmer and then took the spot full time, he was soon followed by Chiz. Before long the Ephex wore off. . . de-toxified.

Nobby Porthole was made possible by 1 Up records. If anyone is deserving of support from Aberdeen's music buyers, it is Fred Craig and Ray Bird, who have put their money where their 1 Up mouths are over the years. Fred first set up a record stall within the Happy Trails jeans shop in 1973 starting with his own record collection, along with a miscellany of neo-hippy jewellery and head accessories. With his sub-let rent rocketing, five years on, it was cheaper to move into his own premises a few blocks up in Rosemount, (conveniently located next door to the Masada Bar).

Still with a hefty stock of second-hand vinyl and a leaning towards punk-indie material, Bird flew in as a partner. By 1981, an upturn in trade justified a second unit in George Street specialising in youth clothing, catching the tail end of punk anti-fashion and the eye of the mod revival craze (dodgy adverts in NME, Melody Maker and Sounds hitherto were the source of such merchandise). However, when redevelopment for Norco's new supermarket destroyed business for smaller shops in the middle George Street area, 1 Up consolidated their operation with a move to Diamond Street in 1986.

They have consistently catered for non-Cliff and Sydney Devine buyers, and have done their admirable best for the city's indigeneous bands and live music scene. Their policy of stocking local groups' releases on a sale-or-return basis developed into the sponsorship of Adventures of Nobby in 1989. The £2,000 invested in this project paid for studio time, pressing and art costs: a commendable punt from this small local business. The album sold a massive two copies, leaving 2,000 still lying in Fred's loft. Here's a tip for you Fred: cremate 1,800 to create instant mythology about this fabled, epochal Pict-punk LP which then becomes massively collectable. Gradually leak the 'last' copy into the market 200 times at 20 quid a hit, with 10% for your truley. You know it makes sense. 1 Up have sunk £10,000 over two years to help fund the Lemon Tree's live programme. "Well, it was a new club providing opportunities for native Aberdeen bands to perform. We thought it was well worthwhile to put something back into the scene and help it keep developing. The groups need all the encouragement they can get.'

With the opening of indoor concrete-jungle shopping malls, I Up was "on the wrong side of Union Street. In May of 1995 we moved to Belmont Street into two floors, each of which is bigger than our previous space. We should pick up more passing trade at our new location.' Best of luck guys and keep up the good work.

. . . .

The Siouxsie and The Banshees road-show, with support acts The Scars and the pre-Mick Kluczynski Cure in tow, rolled into Aberdeen in the first week in September 1979. This was an early gig on a 24-date UK tour scheduled as the first leg of a global expedition covering Japan, Australia, Canada and the USA.

Sioux had progressed in the business from inauspicious beginnings as one of the self-styled Bromley Contingent ligging and hanging-out with The Sex Pistols at the dawning of the new age. In this guise she was a member of the London punk posse which so outraged the nation's television audience during their appearance on Bill Grundy's Granada show, much to the scuzzy delight of Grundy himself.

By the time The Banshees hit Aberdeen Sioux was a well-established artiste of note herself. With vampiric compulsion she attracted hordes of raven-haired, white faced kids through her funereal Gothic image and dark gloomy music. Her '79 British odyssey began badly and progressively got worse. . . as a reaction to audience violence, the vocalist trashed an already malfunctioning PA system. Due to logistics cock-ups, borrowed equipment had to be used in Belfast. . . the situation was destined to degenerate further in Aberdeen.

In the Granite City, Sioux and the band were booked for a personal appearance at The Other Record Shop on Union Street, prior to their sound check later that day. The idea was to meet with their local fans, several of whom inhabited the city's punk groups. Copies of the latest Banshees' album Join Hands would be signed as a PR exercise, the first time that the band had acquiesced to perform such a show-bizzy chore. However, Polydor delivered only 50 LPs to the shop instead of the 250 ordered. The band's manager Nils Stevenson took the opportunity to personally sell 30 promo not-for-sale copies to the retailer. With promos having a greater cachet, TORS could then have sold them on at a tidy profit to Aberdonian Goths who packed the premises. . . This blatantly capitalist transaction contradicted the group's apparent philosophy: from their inception, The Banshees claimed to debunk what they perceived as unsavoury duplicity in the rock music business.

Eye witness Bill E Wizz from local punko outfit The Toppers reports that "Their guitarist John McKay and the drummer Kenny Morris widna autograph the albums and then they dished them oot as freebies to the crowd. Me and our bass player got one each. Then they took their own record off the shop's stereo deck and slapped on The Slits' LP Cut, I think that was new into the shop as well.' Having enraged both their own manager and that of TORS, McKay and Morris body-swerved a path through the teeming customers and out of the building. First stop on their great escape was the Caledonian Hotel, where the band had checked in earlier that day. They made dummies of themselves with pillows on which they pinned their personalised backstage passes, before tucking the impostors cosily in bed. Carrying hastily-packed kit-bags, the errant Banshees jumped into a passing taxi which they impulsively decided would take them to Stonehaven. A change of heart saw them command the driver to go instead to Aberdeen rail station. At some point Stevenson intercepted them and attempted to placate his abscon-dees. Kenny Morris was having none of it, almost trapping the would-be peace-maker's hand as he wound up the window of the departing taxi.

Optimistically, the remaining Banshees felt that their guitarist and drummer would return to the fold in time for The Capitol sound-check and performance. Once it sank in that the escapees were not to re-appear, the surviving band members were distraught. "I just wouldn't want to live through that again, I've never had so much trauma in my life' moaned Steve Severin, "It was horrible.' The band's management pre-empted any possible future volte-face by the deserters with a rapidly-concocted state-of-the-union epistle. "Nils Stevenson and Pure Noise Limited wish to make it known that, as from Friday September Seven 1979, of their own violition, John Gareth McKay and Kenneth Ian Morris ceased to perform with the group professionally known as Siouxsie and The Banshees.'

The storm whipped up by the performances of The Scars and The Cure that night faded into insignificance compared to the vitriolic retribution soon to be unleashed by Sioux. Announcing that The Banshee's set was cancelled (with a money-back sweetener added), she addressed the theatre's stunned audience. "Two art college students f——d off out of it. If you've got one-percent of the aggres-sion we feel towards them, if you ever see them, you have my blessings to beat shit out of them' quoth the gentile Sioux: "Next time you see them - Pow!' Rather than finish the night's proceedings with this bombshell, The Cure returned for a couple of numbers before being joined by Sioux and Severin for The Banshees' mandatory Lord's Prayer. A final derogatory jibe "John and Kenny were doing it for the money. . . we'll be back !' and it was over.

In retrospect Sioux's latter remark bears little similarity to the truth. Inasmuch as the band were well and truly a-spin in rock's money-making vortex, a cancelled tour date would have cost around £5,000 in gig deposit money. Stevenson's earlier unsuccessful pleas to those jumping ship alledgedly focused on financial, rather than artistic, priorities. Accusations that McKay and Morris were cash oriented were thus diversionary and inaccurate. Nonetheless this was history in the making at The Capitol and it kept Aberdeen's scary punks gossiping like Torry fishwives for weeks.

Chapter 14

"Fit Like, New York?'

From the fallout of the punk-generated indie explosion oozed Aberdeen's own indigenous label, fostering and promoting abundant local talent. Oily Records was all about doing it here, without needing to prove anything to anyone else. Ghosts of Aberdeen bands scuffling ineffectually around Tin Pan Alley would soon be excorcised.

Since moving to Aberdeen from Edinburgh, Jim Allardice had admiringly watched various local bands and in 1978 he was working with The Squibs' guitarist Murray Hadden. Jim thought that the arrival of Gordon Lemon on vocals in place of Dougie 'Fuggie' Brown, coupled with Dave Baird's original material, lifted The Squibs above their contemporaries.

As part of Kid Jensen's Battle Of The Bands on Radio One, they demoed tracks (including Dirty Lie and No Defences) at REL in Edinburgh. Fairly successful in reaching the quarter finals of the contest, further recordings took place in Manchester, but that was the end of it. Jim took a copy of their tape to Bruce Findlay's Zoom label in Edinburgh, hoping to generate some interest. However, Zoom faced a demo mountain of such magnitude that Jim didn't consider it worthwhile even leaving the tape. On the return journey to Aberdeen he discussed the thing with his wife. He had some vague idea that it was possible to press up 500 singles for about £200 or £300, but it was Linda who suggested he should run the project himself.

A friend, Howard Gemmell, shared Jim's interest in local Aberdeen bands, and expressed an interest in getting involved. They were both heavily into the Scottish Labour Party (which had broken away from the Labour Party, under Jim Sillars), and the whole Scottish Assembly referendum issue. Their altruistic political rationale for Oily was to establish a platform for NE bands, negating the trek to London to prove themselves to an unsympathetic and hostile market.

Another associate Mike Craig had been running a mail-order business for a number of years, specialising in bluegrass, Cajun, and the less commercial side of contemporary and traditional country music. He had experience in marketing, distribution and promotion world-wide and had released an instrumental bluegrass album by Red Rector and Bill Clifton on Breakdown Records. He was therefore the logical person to ask for advice about pressing plants and associated problems. Mike went one better, and said he wanted to participate. With capital of £600, they were up and running, with an initial target of releasing three or four singles until the money ran out.

The Squibs' line up which recorded the inaugural Oily single were the aforementioned Baird, Lemon and Hadden with Dave Cattenach on drums, Colin Garden on keyboards, trombone and vocals, and ranking Jim Rankin on sax and vocals. Their intensive gigging campaign in Aberdeen during the summer of 1978 sound-tracked disgrace for Scotland on the football fields of Argentina. Whilst The Squibs worked up their set and developed their sound, deserters from Ally's tartan army rioted at the Kincorth Covenanter pub and threw TV sets out of the windows of George Street tenements.

A thousand copies of On The Line/Satisfy Me (cut at Craighall Studios, Edinburgh) were pressed. Scotia (owners of the Other Record Shop) accepted 300, Rough Trade took 50, and about 500 copies were sold at the band's gigs. Before the single hit the streets, Dave Baird was surely symptomatic of small town blues. "It's totally out of the way up here and there's nowhere to play. We're getting pissed off playing around Aberdeen so we will move away, probably to London.' Melody Maker granted the single a review but airplay was scant, although the record broke even financially. Dave sounded happier after release. "We are very pleased with the way the record has turned out. We think the numbers are a good enough choice, a nice contrast.' On The Line is a hooky piece of staccato white reggae, its choppy rhythm maintained by Dave The Cat's skank drumming, although a more dynamic production might have sharpened the parping horns and Gordon's vocal. A muffled mix all but spoiled the debut but the vibrant rocker Satisfy Me saved the day, its brass riff complemented by Murray's rock guitar fills. A terrific groove develops, allowing Lemon to go for it in an exhausting work-out. Band and label were justifiably made up with Slick 1, both sides written by Baird the bard.

The Squibs decided that Gordon's style was a shade on the soulful side for them. . . he was hot for R & B and soul covers in the set, whilst the rest of the band were addicted to original material. Thus when Oily were ready for another bang from The Squibs, they were auditioning new vocalists and reworking their material. Having lit the blue touch paper, Gordon retired diplomatically to continue his enduring career elsewhere. . .

Smart money was on Scottish bands The Skids, Simple Minds, and The Tools to crossover into the big league. Granite City tipped the latter to make a massive album and to undertake a smash US tour. . . so it was a surprised Oily who took a call from The Tools' manager Robin Murray. He asked if a single from his band would be of interest. Although based in the North (Alness, What A Mess) The Tools had become very popular in Aberdeen. Depping for the Stranglers at Ruffles with great success, they went from strength to strength. They recorded something for Zoom, but with Bruce Findlay concentrating on breaking Simple Minds, The Tools remained unreleased thus far.

Oily immediately ran into problems with the delusional Murray, seemingly believing that his boys were superstars and that Oily's financial coffers were deeper and wider than Rubislaw Quarry. His unrealistic demands for royalty payments and promotional budgets led Oily to thinking Murray was simply wasting everyone's time. The Aberdeen label operated on the basic principle that, after recouping costs, any profits were split evenly with the artists. When The Tools eventually conceded to those terms, Craighall Studios was again selected as the venue for recording the appropriately titled Gotta Make Some Money/TV Eyes. A substantial and expensive indie run of 5,000 were pressed despite Murray's paranoiac demands for an amazing 15,000. Reviews and early sales were healthy, Uncle John Peel was again supportive. Then trouble poured on to Oily waters.

In what could only have been a scam to attract attention from a major label, Murray decreed "No more gigging.' In effect they downed Tools and without live appearances the single died overnight, leaving Oily with about 2,500 copies on their shelves and with half of their capital up in smoke due to these time-wasters. A calamitous and most unsavoury episode. The Tools were last heard of doing session work and commercials for David Balfe (Daniel Boone. . . Sunday morning, up with the lark. . .) at Highland Studios, not quite matching the stadium-filling glacial Northern rock triumphs of their supposed co-equals, Simple Minds and The Skids/Big Country.

The Squibs were finally back on the line with a new vocalist Cliff Taylor and a fresh set. Jim and his fellow Oilers were still stoonin' following The Tools fiasco but they forced a public smile as they sank more money into their dream.

Whilst they were fairly happy with Craighall Studios, Oily felt that the 32-track facility produced an 'over-clean' sound. Tony Pilley ran Barclay Towers studio in Edinburgh from a top- floor tenement flat overlooking Bruntsfield Links, where he had recorded the early Rezillos and their later re-incarnation The Revillos. The Oily crew were big fans of Tony's production of Another Pretty Face's All The Boys Love Carrie, just the rough excitement to complement The Squibs' sound. Barclay Towers was an eight-track facility that promised a more immediate 'live' feel. Out of this first session came Parades/Out on the Town. With the music press enthusing and John Peel plugging hard, things were on the up with all 1,500 selling out. Nation-wide distribution came through Fast Product in Scotland, Red Rhino in Yorkshire and Rough Trade in London, accessing most of the alternative shops in the UK. Considering that the novelty of the indie release was wearing off, sales of the Joe Jacksonesque Parades were encouraging. The market was saturated and had developed into the survival of the fittest. Given Peel's stalwart support (you can imagine that it was a real kick for Allardice, in an Aberdeen pub, to hear Parades come across national radio), it was surprising that The Squibs didn't make an even bigger detonation. Majors did show some interest but it was the same old story about "come down to London, and we'll see what you can do down here'.

The band did actually catch The Rip Off Train to freedom, but second rate treatment knocked the stuffing out of them and The Squibs fizzled out. Their singles had, however, given the label credibility with the music press, radio DJs, and the music business generally. It opened doors for Oily and credit is due to The Squibs for their part in this achievement. The band's manager had been Duncan Hendry who was now expanding his promotional network. Oily formed a relationship with him facilitating the promotion of their artists at his local venues including the Copper Beech and Valhallas. He was also to act as agent for Oily's bands, fixing worthwhile credible gigs throughout Scotland (and later with APB all over the UK). Duncan, currently director of Aberdeen's Alternative Music Festival, provided invaluable support for local bands in the late Seventies and early Eighties.

Parades had taken a small loss but a re-enthused Oily moved quickly on to Aberdeen band Splitting Headache. They split before Oily was ready for them but re-assembled as The Escorts, and a deal was struck. To avoid confusion with another combo of the same name, they re-christened themselves The President's Men. The label liked their "really good guitar sound and nice little pop songs.' The Presidents Men's Out In The Open/State Of Mind/When Someone Says No became Slick 4. More Castlegate than Watergate, The PMs were Donald MacDonald on bass, John Watson on drums, Jeremy Thoms on vocals, and (with a 20-year Hank Marvin and Brian Kennedy echo) Roy Ingram on guitar. Fast Product were keen again, distributing to the entire UK market. Plentiful airplay left few of the 1,000 copies unsold. . . NME featured Out In The Open as the lead item in their Garageland column, prompting a letter from Philadelphia college radio station WKDU. In response to this American enquiry, Jim shipped Slick 4 over and within days OITO featured in the Philly station's top-30 playlist. It stayed in their chart for six weeks, broadcast to a catchment listening audience of about one million people. By this time, perhaps 90 percent of Oily's product was being sold outwith Aberdeen. The Presidents Men were better known in Philly than in the Granite City. The PMs had previously cut a demo at Barclay Towers for a London label, subsequently sussed as being actually interested in the band doing covers for its publishing catalogue. Rather than waste the excellent demo effort, it was released as Slick 5, Reasons For Leaving /Cry/Best Suit.

Fast Product now awaited each Slick with bated breath and actively courted Oily's every issuance. Distribution headaches vanished: the catalogue was certain to get into the right shops, and Fast was now a crucial consideration in Oily's game plan. Notwithstanding much critical acclaim and Peter Easton's frequent playing of Reasons For Leaving on his Radio Scotland show, sales totalled only 750. A disappointing surprise to Oily who felt it had under-performed, but it came cheap and more-or-less balanced financially. The up-side was that Oily returned to WKDU's play-list.

Granite City oozed praise over another local band APB, despite them having played only a single public gig at the time. "This band has potential with a capital P.' Early material Monsieur Marceau, Blessed Are The Pure Of Heart, Last Chance and No Scene In Aberdeen inspired GC's editor and publishing tycoon Colin Murray to recommend APB enthusiastically to Oily. Rehearsing out in Ellon, such was the impression made by Iain Slater (bass and vocals), Glenn Roberts (guitar), and George Cheyne (drums), they were signed up on the spot.

Jim, on the early days of APB: "With the benefit of hindsight, I think we moved them into the studio too rapidly - they were still in a punk phase, and it was to be another couple of months before their own characteristic funk style began to take over.' Chain Reaction/Power Crisis was recorded again at Barclay Towers - it didn't go down too well and received mixed reviews. However, I am still really proud of Iain's broad Buchan dialect in the spoken middle of Chain Reaction. It was more or less ridiculed as being parochial, but personally I thought Iain showed a confidence in what he was doing. It would be three or four years before The Proclaimers and Jesse Rae were accepted singing in dialect.'

So, Chain Reaction: first release from APB: an opening rumble redolent of PIL's debut Public Image, fuzz guitar, driving drumming, plaintive vox: easily as direct, charming and funny as anything The Undertones ever created. I need employment I need some cash, to get my girlfriend down on the grass - a parallel universe would have da Ramones brudders brought up on an Aberdeenshire fairm: Gabba Gabba Hay? And check out the echoed fade, a wonderful production job from Tony Pilley. The flip, Power Crisis: minimalist guitar (Jim's punk reservations?), but within that sparse mix, Iain's bass has begun its inexorable, funky bubbling to the surface and that I-don't-give-a-fuck vocal style was almost there. Upon release, Slick 6 only moved about 500 units, although after the subsequent success of Shoot You Down the balance of the 1,000 pressing sold out. At one point, copies were selling in New York for $50 each - but Oily decided not to re-press, keeping the rarity value intact.

Sounds journo Johnny Waller came to Aberdeen to write up The PMs and APB, the first expression of national rock music press curiosity. Crowd response for APB became increasingly manic, particularly with their set closer Shoot You Down, a natural single. Those three or four releases that Jim originally targeted were long gone. . . we were now on Slick 7, another Pilley peach from the Towers.

"We were all really chuffed with the way it sounded, reviews were reassuring but after a few radio plays sales fizzled out and stalled at 700. Fast were perplexed, on the same lines as us: it was a great record, deserving of good sales. We pushed it through various stations but a month later it was dead. Through our contact at WKDU, I learned about a New York organisation called Rockpool, an agency issuing records to FM radio stations, college stations, and club DJs. Thereafter, they compiled a chart based on the number of plays each record logged. I sent them 25 copies of Shoot You Down but got no feedback.'

A few weeks on Jim had a phone call from John Peel. He had been out on the town with Rusty Eagan. Rusty (a former member of The Skids and Rich Kids), had just returned from New York, raving about a huge dance floor hit record in the clubs over there. . . none other than APB with Shoot You Down. What was all the fuss about? It was all about the freshest, most invigorating slice of power dance funk with intentionally mumbled lyric and virtuoso performances from Slater, Cheyne and Roberts, playing as men possessed. Had they followed Robert Johnson to the crossroads just for this fleeting, untouchable moment of perfection in 1981, had they sold their souls to Old Nick? Music to die for, that's what all the fuss was about, and it took the Americans to recognise what had been largely ignored in APB's back yard: we had diamonds in our hands and treated them like lumps of nutty slack.

Peely booked the band for a Radio One session (a first for an Aberdeen group?), played the single two or three times a week, and broadcast a live interview with Slater, (in all probability, Iain shocking many listeners by saying that APB were not interested in travelling to London, as Ellon was a nicer place to stay).

As more copies were pressed, New York wanted anything and everything - Rockpool took another 75 copies to push, Fast Product exported to the New York indie record stores, Big Apple agents hustled after the band. Out of the blue one Saturday night, Jim's much-valued quality time Beechgrove Garden hour was interrupted by a transatlantic phone call from Mark Beavan, who ran the Advanced Alternative Media agency. A Belgian band had cancelled at the last minute and he wanted APB Stateside within the week for dates in NY, Washington, Boston and New Jersey.

Naturally jumping at the chance they were stunned on arrival to find SYD playing incessantly on dance floors at trendy joints like the Mudd Club. . . instant celebrities in every night spot in the city that never sleeps, a helluva culture shock for three Ellon guys who had only played a handful of gigs outside Aberdeenshire. Indeed, they had thus far never performed outside of Scotland. As the East coast tour ended APB signed a management deal with Beavan, who generated extensive work in the States for several years. Back to reality in Aberdeen, the band filled out their sound by adding John Watson, former drummer with the President's Men, (an interim measure; John soon moved on to concentrate on his talent as a cartoonist for NME, The Face and Oily sleeves). His replacement was Nick Jones from Tarves, that noised-up epicentre of rock 'n' roll. National radio sessions continued on the Peel and Kid Jensen shows.

For Slick 8 they went to Edinburgh's Planet Studio and its magical producer, Wilf Smarties, who recorded Palace Filled With Love/All Your Life With Me on his 16-track facility. The first 3,000 went faster than Ian Donald passing a gang of Dons fans and it eventually ran to three pressings. Laudatory reviews, indie chart for the first time, a TV appearance on BBC 2's Riverside. Returning to the US East coast, this time with advance publicity and a new single to promote, venues from Chicago down to Washington DC succumbed one by one to the APB virus. Valuable contacts were established with club DJs and FM stations, particularly WLIR on Long Island, which during a later visit was to broadcast a gig live from the Ritz in Manhattan.

Undoubtedly, the highlight of this second tour came from a second on the bill spot to funk-incarnate Mr James Brown. The locale for this historic episode was the Brooklyn Zoo (incidentally, where much of Saturday Night Fever was filmed. . . Rumour has it that Slater couldn't resist it: when he thought he was alone, he gave it big licks with the shirt opened to the waist, medallion like a cocoa-tin lid, jecket oer the shooder and hand in the air.

Wilf's Planet yielded Rainy Day/From You And Back To You, another indie chart entrant. Oily were now inundated with calls from agents, record companies and other predators after a piece of the action. Mark Beavan's AAM fielded record company deals from the US, with Oily dealing with agents in the UK.

Chaos at Oily's corporate HQ in Aberdeen with daily enquires from A & R departments in NY and LA. . . It seemed only a matter of time before a major six figure deal would come to fruition. Oily had requests from radio DJs in Spain, Portugal, Poland and then came a deal to gig in the Bergen area of Norway. Unwittingly, APB then re-traced the path of Edvard Grieg, one of Norway's pre-eminent classical composers: his grandfather had fled to Bergen from Aberdeen area to escape persecution at the end of the 1745 rebellion. APB returned to Norway's rainy city on future occasions with great success.

Rocketing stature or not, the band were happy to stay with Oily who decided that the next single should be something special. As far back as Slick 4, they had established their own music publishing company as a vehicle for publishing songs they released and which gained exposure on radio and TV sessions. This proved fairly lucrative, and Oily decided to plough that kitty into APB's next. Fast Product distribution now flying high through the massive success of The Human League, managed by Fast's main man Bob Last. A Fast/Oily meeting in Edinburgh brought pledges of substantial financial promotion for the ensuing Aberdeen release. Fast also promised assistance with credit in the event it was needed (panic record pressings, or similar emergencies).

APB's creative muse was now in overdrive, writing new material faster than they could record it. Mainly working and hanging-out in New York, Radio City studio in Manhattan was a logical location to record the new single. To produce Slick 10 the boys used their new chum DJ Ivan Ivan. The pressing plant worked overtime to cut 10,000 copies (seven inch and twelve inch) of One day/Help Yourself, released amid abundant hype. Oily felt at last, this was the big one and it made the indie top-ten, even gaining day-time Radio One plays from Simon Bates of all people. . . (during his childhood days, he was nick-named Master. . . some habits never change). The London based Mafia had been in a meeting for the previous three years, blanking the band. . . but they now wet themselves for a piece of APB. Jim Allardice recalls "The funniest was Peter Powell who booked APB for a session on his show. We gave him a roasting about his failure to play any of their earlier singles, prompting him to claim he had never been sent any. That was a load of bollocks, I had run up a postage bill of more than £25 sending material to him.'

Twenty years earlier Aberdeen promoter Gordon Hardie experienced English ignorance and indifference to things Scottish and Jim confirms that the attitude was still there. "We had a London A & R man calling us up to grandly announce he had arrived at Edinburgh Waverley train station. He basically demanded that we collect him there. I patiently explained to him that Aberdeen is just a wee bit further up the line. After thinking for a moment, he then suggested Haymarket as being more convenient for us. Such was their geographical understanding of Scotland. And they say that the Scots are parochial.'

One Day was stirringly launched to great brouhaha but suddenly all went deathly silent: something was drastically and irrevocably amiss. A fiscal Scud missile zapped through the window of Oily Mansions, its detonation lighting up the Aberdeen sky... Bob Last pulled the plug on Fast Product, because the distribution side of his business had made a disappointing return for the year. In comparison to the vast financial bonanza created by his management of The Human League, he was probably right. But having put about £7,000 into One Day mainly on the strength of Fast's promised financial sponsorship, Oily were distraught. The situation worsened when Last put his company into receivership. Fast Product had grown from being a small indie label itself and knew better than most about precarious financial tight-rope walking and narrow margins. Oily regarded the winding up of Fast Product as being an unwarranted kick in the teeth: Don't you want me baby? In retrospect they escaped from the situation comparatively lightly; Fast Product were into them for a few hundred pounds, when it could have easily have been thousands. More serious was the fact that Oily's promotional budget was gone. Bob Last's quote "The way you build power relationships into contracts is something that fascinates me' says much.

A guy called Sandy McLean had run Fast Product's distribution and he now picked up where FP left off with his newly-established company Fast Forward, through The Cartel. Under the worrying circumstances Oily were only too pleased to give Sandy the rights to Slick 10. He shifted a credible 7,000 copies, which promo budget-less Oily considered was good going. Oily spilled £3,000 on the single, directly attributable to Fast Product.

The band were still receiving attractive offers from major record labels, but manager Mark Beavan probably felt he could keep pushing for a better deal: this was APB's 15 minutes. they were hot and marketable. Bands like The Stranglers could barely fill one show at the Ritz in New York whilst APB sold out two nights easily. They also broke out of the US East Coast, playing from California to Texas to Florida. Shoot You Down was nominated record of the year by American radio DJs.

The scale and locale of the operation had changed, calling for greater resources and money appropriate to the new situation.. No animosity on either side, APB had simply out-grown Oily's capabilities. . . the band agreed on one concluding single before it was tatties 'oer the side. Now a regular fixture on Rockpool's play-based chart, APB's final funky Oily slick would be targeted at US club dance floors, rather than at radio. Danceability, recorded at Castle Sound in Edinburgh and produced by the boys themselves, was expanded to a four track, twelve inch release.

One of the many labels chasing licensing deals from Oily was Albion Records, run by Dai Davies who had worked with Dave Edmunds, Hazel O'Connor, and Joe Jackson. Whilst Oily were unempowered to deal with him long term for APB, they licensed Danceability to him. . . the band went on to release another single on Albion, 1985's What Kind Of Girl, cut at Unique Recording studio in NY. Oily acknowledged that they couldn't progress much further with the Ellon funkateers, having taken them to the brink of major success. Mark Beavan tried really hard in the belief that he could pull off a really big one. Maybe Mark pushed the ante just too high, at the wrong time?

APB were a great live band and were also Buchan loons through and through with absolutely no pretensions. They were always themselves, ambivalent to trends and image at a time when the promo-video carried more importance than the quality of the music. In their post-Oily phase APB continued to make some great singles and an excellent album released on their own Red River Records label. Mike Craighead replaced the departing Nick Jones, and subsequent guitarist/keyboardists were Kenny Williams and Neil no not that one Innes. They were frequent visitors to the USA but four years back George Cheyne hung up his drumsticks, effectively signalling the band's demise. Iain and Glen continued with a new drummer, Dundonian John Russell, under the name The Loveless and continued their American exploits with indie labels Sleeping Bag and Link. The latter issued the career-summarising album Something To Believe In, which is still on catalogue.

Oily were now in a quandary because a £600 single in 1978 now cost £6,000 and bands now turned their noses up at an eight hour session at an eight-track facility. The new standard was a 36-track studio with mandatory promo video. Changed days.

Aberdeen band Alone Again Or (later to mushroom into The Shamen) had recorded with Wilf Smarties and thought that working with Oily might benefit their profile-enhancing campaign. When their Smartie-produced demos dropped onto Oily's doormat, the label felt that Alone Again warranted a total commitment that Oily couldn't in honesty offer at that specific time. Oily were also offered tracks by New York and Canadian bands. Mike Craig had become increasingly involved with country music mail-order imports and was introducing the UK to Dwight Yoakum, with 'new country' a growth market here (as it was in Germany much to the delight of Lemon Soul's emigrant bassist Kevin Henderson).

Oily had simply run out of momentum after the highs of APB. The longer they left it, the more difficult it became to get motivated again. Family and other commitments took over. Today they look back on the label as being terrific fun, from The Squibs' first gig at the Bobbin Mill onwards. Sleeves for the first six releases were designed by friends and were printed and assembled communally by Oily moguls, families and musicians. Which made it all the more rewarding, according to Jim, when they heard a Slick on the radio or saw a copy in the shop. Overall the venture was a success and exceeded their original targets. Despite investing more personal cash, the account finished slightly ahead. Few genuinely indie companies financed and released 11 singles and made a small profit. Naturally disappointed that they never broke a local band on a really big scale, they nevertheless achieved much in capturing airplay and positive reviews for The Squibs and The President's Men. This was something new, perhaps giving other Aberdeen bands some incentive. The American success of APB (the degree of which was not fully appreciated locally in Aberdeen) justified their original belief that London is not essential in the business. New York or Los Angeles can be reached just as easily from Aberdeen. The States had no preconceived ideas about Aberdeen bands: if the music was right they would play it. The opposite applied when trying to deal with the majority of London people, who considered that Aberdeen was somewhere up near the North Pole, and about as interesting. Oily found it easier, and more rewarding, to do business with New York rather than London.

Once they had publishing rights sorted out, they were able to distribute several thousands of pounds of royalties to the respective songwriters. This enabled them to educate later bands on securing, and protecting proper publishing rights. In his Sounds article Johnny Waller opined that the Aberdeen people he met were too nice and polite. He missed the point that, during an era of rampant Thatcherism in England, this decency was a strength and not a weakness. With the sole exception of the manager of The Tools, Oily remain on good terms with everyone they dealt with. When they came across genuinely sympathetic people like David Jensen and John Peel, relationships negated any music business hype. Major labels, paying record pluggers £200 per day, asked how Oily garnered their bountiful harvest of air-plays and radio sessions. They were incredulous and seemingly uncomprehending that the music itself could communicate, with scant regard being paid to style, hooplah and bullshit.

Oily latterly developed music press and radio station contacts on the US East and West coasts, Canada, France, Belgium, Scandinavia, Poland, Spain, Portugal, Eire - and even had an enquiry about distribution in Africa. However, notwithstanding this impressive international dialogue, daytime airplay from our local station Northsound was extremely sparse. The Other Record Shop and 1 Up were supportive, but mainstream Aberdeen shops showed a lack of interest in stocking indigenous material. Had Shoot You Down appeared on import white label, purporting to be by an American band, it would have created a massive stir: certainly Northsound would have paid more attention.

Undoubtedly, Oily promoted the self confidence of local bands and encouraged them to broaden their horizons. It was the first, concerted tilt at showing the world that Aberdeen could rock with the best of them. Can you imagine the buzz at Oily Towers to see APB come on-stage at The Ritz New York to a crowd of 1,800 screaming, shouting hipsters, and to hear Iain Slater greet them with those immortal words. . . "Fit like, New York?'

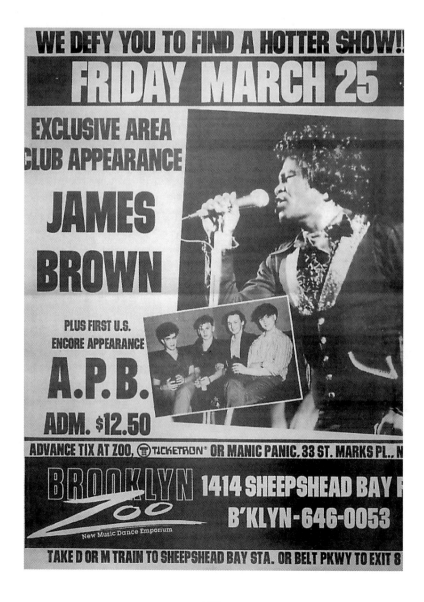

APB

PRESIDENTS MEN

THE SQUIBS

Chapter 15

"It's difficult to read when it's going round so fast'

When the Oily boom started to recede, the fates of their recording artist roster were cast to the bone-chilling Aberdeen wind. From the detritus of The Squibs, Gordon Lemon and Jim Rankin re-collaborated in Previous Convictions. Lemon peeled off to Airtight and Tooter Jim went into The 30 Footers, who made an initial impact at private parties with performance-art an important part of their shows. On-stage they adorned themselves in heavy make-up and white perriot hats, bodies swathed in Egyptian mummy-style bandages. "The stage show is an integral part of what we do. It's terrific dance music. If people love danc-ing, then that's just the sort of music we play.' They bore typically Aberdonian names like Chief How Dee Doo Drum, King Stubbah, Crown Prince Rankin, The Duke Of Bone A Parp, Count Imin and Tin Pannee. Exactly who was who is a bit clouded now, but Buzz McMillen and Davie Cattenach were there (at the time, both were young pups with good eyesight).

Behind the humour and good-time ethos The 30 Footers were startlingly hard-working and dedicated. A rigorous three-nights-a-week practice regime bore fruit during a lengthy exile in London, headlining a three band show at Dingwalls and undertaking support spots to The Mighty Wah and Spear Of Destiny. Extensive studio time was available through the band's promotions company. Jim Rankin recalls "At the time it looked like we could make it.' Reggae became the band's forte and the rhythm sec-tion were sold on pan-Caribbean music with its calypso, ska, blue-beat and soca heritage. Jim ruefully recalls how they lost that sharp, fresh edge. "It was going well in London until the music stylists got a hold of us. It became less of a home-grown thing and I personally took a right scunner wi' it all.' The 30 Footers' spirit (invincible during the embryonic Aberdeen days) waned, ultimately seeing the disintegration of this talented and innovative combo.

Presidents Men guitarist/vocalist Jeremy Thoms moved to Edinburgh. With Dave Baird's wee brother Ewen he baked up The Strawberry Tarts: their delicate material appeared on various compilation albums and tapes but they couldn't cook up a decent deal. He moved on to the wacky world of The Revillos, spending a year with Fay, Eugene and Rocky. With A Girl Called Johnny he recorded Hello It Isn't Me/Shallow for Ten Records in 1986. After a couple of years behind the scenes with MCA records and in publishing, he returned to the live scene in 1990 with The Naturals. Described by a London record company scout as "the weirdest band I've ever seen', their music was dubbed a "sophisticated, swaying pop sound, with brass and epic sentiments.' A seven piece line-up, The Naturals produced a lush orches-trated sound, which whilst harking back to certain classic Sixties music, was, according to Jeremy, "very much a product of the hi-tech Nineties.' They looked to an Eden-like past of free love and psychedelia for inspiration, taking the beat spirit by its long shaggy hair and shaking it around in a modern-age mael-strom. Formed August 1990, they showed no regard for the current grunge musical climate, instead draw-ing on The Small Faces, The Monkees and The Byrds. They came close to a deal but not close enough. Jeremy's 1994 band New Leaf recorded their strangely unsettling, so straight that it's weird, album On Safari at Mighty Reel in Edinburgh. Released well before the easy music boom, Mike Flowers Pops 'n' all, Safari's inspiration comes from Jimmy Webb (the author's favourite composer) and Sixties unhip MOR pop tunes dismissed offhand at the time by us rockers. Jeremy has broken into the TV music scene (his themes featured on Channel 4's Short Stories where Discworld creator Terry Pratchett visited orang-utans in Borneo).

The biggest Oily reservoir was APB. Renamed The Loveless, they capitulated in July of 1994 by making the dreaded move to London. Iain Slater says "We had taken it as far as we could in Aberdeen. The frequency with which we can play the Lemon Tree is finite. Once every four months is about all that the market will stand. And then what? There are only pubs. . . after you play to 300 people at the LT who are paying four quid to see you, are they going to return there if they can see you at the Malt Mill for noth-ing. . . for this band it would be a backwards move.'

An early set-back was John's defection to fellow London based Aberdonians Coast. Iain and Glen were then "taking it easier, concentrating on writing' using a midi-studio set-up in their flat. "For some reason, we seemed to be getting noisier and noisier but now we are getting back into dance music.'

Regardless of knocks they have taken, Iain is adamant that The Loveless will never take the easy way out by becoming a covers band. "Sure, you can get plenty work and probably make a lot of money. For us though its the same as asking a guy,who has worked outside all his life, to come and work nine-to-five in an office. It's simply not on'

Oily captured the top-of-the-milk from Aberdeen's post-punk circuit, but in fact very few strollers on late-Seventies rock street wore bondage strides, striped furry jumpers and safety pins through their bodily extremities. 1976 brought us Manray, named after the American photographer, painter and film maker, one of the founders of New York's Dadaist movement. Just as well that this jazz fusion ensemble, which wrote much of their own material, didn't use Ray's real name, the somewhat less catchy Emanuel Rabinovich. Regularly appearing at The Albyn, the owner asked the band to record something to publicise another of his licensed premises. The Duke's Den/Baked Alaska was cut at Marc Ellington's Towie Barclay studio in 1980. The personnel involved in the single were Al Hyland, Stuart Cordiner (guitar), Eric Anderson (drums), Barney Mackie (keyboards) and Brian Hill (bass). Manray's original drummer Steve Harvey is now a top flight producer for acts like Kenny G. Other members were drummer Pete Buchan (ex-Crescendo and Rue de Remarx) and Bobby Fyfe on keyboards.

The Shapiros (previously Nightshift), created a distinctive soul-pop sound: vocalist John Innes, saxophonist Jon Smith and keyboards player Malcolm Cornwell featured on Waitress In A Hotel, a 1979 single on the North Of Watford label. At other times their "crisp pop-soul, devoid of frills or ego trips and commercial as hell' was created by vocalist John Bisset, bassist Eric Grant and drummer Dave Scott. With a live set including Won't You Let Me In Your Garden, the catchy Money Honey and an irresistable Fall Guy, they should have gone places (other than down the dumper, which was Helen's actual destination).

If Ferryhill funk or Rosemount reggae in the live environment didn't toss your pancake, the delights of local radio were there at the flick of a switch. Does anyone remember how we survived in the long cold winters before Northsound began surfing across our Grampian regional airwaves in 1981? Life was surely intolerable without Damien, Nicky and Robin. It was near-impossible to drag our un-enlightened bodies from our dreary pits of a morning, without the joys of Radio Fit Like to freshen the step and gladden the heart. Northsound switched on the Aurora borealis for us, with their AA (affa amateur) road reports and cringe-making commercials, presented by DJs using accents located somewhere between New York and New Pitsligo. Reporting techniques were clearly a mystery to the early Kingsgate communicators: Joe Buchan (a big fan of the bedside manner of morning TV's Doctor Gorgeous) filed a live traffic update from the old Brig O' Dee: "It's still very busy here. . . beep beep beep. . . oh hell, I've run out of change.' The concept of a script was seemingly also too complicated to be tackled - perhaps performing the concurrent tasks of reading and speaking was too demanding. The author was part of the sheepish Bucksburn party posse which flocked Southwards on innumerable Saturday mornings, following the unstoppable Dons. It was not unusual to be tuned to Northsound - anything for a laugh until Tom Jones and Gary Hackett ran out on to the pitch.

The DJ very professionally talked over the intro to his next record "and this is the new one from ZZ Top - it's called. . . " Long seconds of silence from the presenter were finally broken by the confession "It's difficult to read when it's going round so fast.'

With Oily oozing throughout the US and Europe, Jim Allardice had good reason to be dissatisfied with Northsound's poor support of his fledgling starlets. Despite subsequent indie shows and the station's Hip Factor programme infrequently playing token local bands, it is only recently that the situation has improved. It is important to realise that the station has never actively aided Aberdeen bands as a matter of management policy: rather, individual presenters and DJs have provided such sustenance. Previous programmes which at least gave (due to the jocks' efforts) some support were Karen Davidson's Street Beat and Bryan Burnett's show. A recent case in point is Jim Gellatly, in whom the Kingsgate broadcasters have found a DJ who is genuinely supportive of the local cause. With obvious enthusiasm he plays local tracks back-to-back with more familiar, mainstream music. Hence instead of a cosy sycophantic "Here's the new single from so-and-so who I drink with doon the pub every night' format, the city's indigenous music is allowed to stand or fall on its own merits. Jim achieved this by negotiating 'free time' within his play list, allowing him to do his own thing free of pressure from the station. He gives airplay to demos and official releases, as well as inviting combos into the studio to do informal acoustic sessions. More power to Jim's spiky alternative wavelengthual elbow.

North East football fans were left out to dry when control of Northsound moved to the West of Scotland following its acquisition by Radio Clyde. Before NS2's recent inauguration, locally irrelevant and unsupportive Saturday afternoon broadcasts from the pride of Aberdeen featured no other than Archie McOldFirm (even the BBC eventually got wise to him). Archie waxed orgasmically and ungrammatically over Glasgow's finest. . . Northsound featured Rangers and Celtic only when they were at home or away. Assuming that Granite City sporting stomachs were still full after such irresponsible programming, the coup de grace of Chic Young and Derek Johnstone's football phone-in was surely the icing on this inedible cake. Welcome then, to Fittie loon and Old Trafford strarlet-as-was Johnny Fitzpatrick: what with Scot FM exclusively covering the Premier League, NE armchair fans (and those exiled in England) were in for a quiet time of it. But save us from the indignant drum-banging, petition-signing, how-unfair-that-we-canna-commentate-from-ittodrie fiasco: when you had the chance to give us chicken salad, all we got was chicken shit.

Northsound 2: easy listening, Sixties and Seventies music and that's just dandy, 'aint got the slightest problem with that. What does leave a nippy taste in the bum is Saturday night DJs who tell us "No, I've never heard of The Pretty Things either but apparently this record was top-ten in 1964.' If the guy isn't into the job he should quit, or get the sack. If you genuinely don't know such things, bloody find out. Surely 20 quid for a couple of reference books wouldn't break the bank and would at least give the impression you care two hoots about your subject? NS2's coat is hanging on a shakey nail with such amateurs: after all these years, it still stands out a mile that some of these chancers love themselves to the exclusion of all else, particularly the music. Thus endeth the rant.

Mind you a gadgie like John McRuvie deserves a pat on the back: a local presenter, speaking in a local accent, nae pretentious bullshit or ego to get in the way. The common man whose natural sense of humour shines through - absolute drivel, but it's funny drivel. You are a balloon of the biggest and reddest variety. I, a mere mortal, bow before thee, oh Great Creator of Ye Canna Beat Us.

It is perhaps unfair to lambast Northsound alone for their sometimes dire efforts, as they had a helluva act to follow in their televisual media muckers further up the West end. Since its inception Grampian Television pioneered local pop and rock music. Witness radical, on-the-pulse happenings such as Bothy Nichts and Aye Yours. As far as the Queens Cross cultural gurus were concerned, seventy years, as well as the Dee and the Don, separated Aberdeen from the rest of civilisation. Grampian's concept of youth telly was to throw on such dynamic presenters as Jimmy Spankie, James Cosmo's dad Jimmy Copeland and the Torry Quine herself, June Imray. While the rest of the world was being set alight by youth revolution, Grampian was giving us John Mearns and his cornkirsters wearing galluses, dungarees and shite-catchers. One thinks that the latter term is not inappropriate when applied to Grampian itself. When one considers the programming which was available on local television, the exodus of beat musicians from Aberdeen to London, Germany, Australia, anywhere - is all the more understandable.

Let's now have a bash at Northsound's first cousins, mobile discos. By 1969 a new phenomenon emerged on the Aberdeen dance hall scene. Big bands in the traditional Johnny Scott, Derek Sanderson, Roy Pinder and George Lawrie mould were decomposing. The void was filled by 'pop' groups, which (whilst being self-evidently popular), didn't have the resources to fill out an entire evening's worth of dance music. The resultant gap was padded with the emergent bane of professional musicians' lives: the disco. We have already shared a pint of snakebite under UV and stroboscopic lighting at the Holburn Disc, but at least that particular venue was dedicated to disco experience specifically. More insidious was the spread of the mobile discotheque. A few quid got a promoter a van-load of non-dues paying flashing lights, dodgey turntables, beer crates full of the 'latest sounds' and more rabbit than the combined contents of the city's butcher shops. Thus ensued a car sticker campaign with one side extolling the virtues of XYZ Disco and the other righteously demanding 'Keep Music Live.'

Tom Waller probably goes as far back as anyone in the annals of disco in the North East. He secured his first booking in the then West Germany at the salubrious environs of the NAAFI of 13 Signal Regiment. In Aberdeen late 1969 saw Tom doing the rounds of church and scout halls, before breaking into the expanding lounge and night-spot market. Short spins at such diverse venues as the Beachcomber Lounge (on the bottom floor of the Gloucester Hotel), the ABC Lounge, and the Copper Beech preceded a long-term residency at the Royal Hotel in Bath Street. The latter engagement imposed a seven nights per week workload, leading Tom to recruit Bruce Kennedy to share the burden for the next year. There were only three mobiles of note in the city. Tom remembers his contemporaries as being Jeff Jones, Brian Youngson and Tom Sillers. From the Royal Hotel, Tom and Bruce went off on separate tracks. The latter got together with Fergus Watt as Purple Helix, providing someone else's music to open the Carousel discotheque at the Caley. Local listeners will have realised by now that Bruce Kennedy was to progress on to radio work at a station named...Northsound...ah hah!

Tom began DJing full time, immediately vanishing into the Market Street triangle, moving those crates repeatedly between the Guild Hotel, the Lunar Seven, the Bon Accord and the Imperial Hotel. We are now in the era of flared trousers, ridiculously dimensioned collars and lapels and boots with platform soles thicker than Joe Harper's belly. The concept of the private function was by now well- established, complete with sausage rolls, egg mayonnaise sandwiches, bowls of crisps and nuts and, at the posher end of the spectrum, chicken legs. The latter were however the only drum sticks present on such occasions, invariably taking pride of place on the next table along from the now accepted - nay - the now obligatory. . . mobile disco. Either provided by the management of the function venue as part of a package deal or organised by personal contact. "It's jist a disco but it's somebody that Willie kens fae work. He's got a' the latest records but he plays a bit o' a'thing, and he's nae dear.'

This burgeoning market begat a plague of disc-spinners that included Easy Disco, Group Three, Jason King (now there's a realistic Aberdeen name for you) and the punningly, cunningly-titled Sanfran Disco. Mike Hannet also brought us a hybrid from hell, the country and western disco. In 1978 Waller returned to college to train as a marine radio officer, so it was 1986 before he began to style us again. Having helped out Downtown Discos in Edinburgh he did a local gig for them at Aberdeen's Don View lounge. Stints for Top Cat Discos preceded his reactivation of TW Discotheque but he has also worked for Atmosphere Sound and Light on their Rainbow Chaser-Shamona operations. Gigs throughout the North East in the late Eighties and early Nineties took him to Kippie Lodge, the Udny Arms in Newburgh, the Gordons Hotel and the Five Star Truck Inn. A lengthy engagement at Murdo's Bar, and more specifically the equipment he used there, brought Tom to the attention of BBC Acorn User magazine.

Which brings us to a logical point to run over - oh, please God! - the hardware which our highly respected jocks have employed over the years. One doubts whether dancers knew or cared how many woofers or tweeters were being used to hammer out Hi Ho Silver Lining and the DJ's insurance policy, Allright Now. There were many things we neither were aware of, nor appreciated - so let us enlighten ourselves. The original TW set-up didn't use vinyl at all: instead, three open-reel tape recorders were employed. The mixer was an Eagle four channel battery unit, with rotary controls housed along with the PA system, a home made Sinclair Z30 amplifier in a shoe box. Tom reports that he had the first all solid-state disco system, which kept him in gainful employment during 1973's winter of discontent (when Nick fell into the cellar) thanks to a pair of car batteries.

Stereo came to the Aberdeen disco scene in 1972 when Tom had two, 100w H & H slave amps built into his unit: glass-topped belt-driven turntables, magnetic cartridges, and Electrovoice eliminator speakers. By all accounts, expensive hardware with the speakers alone costing £800 in 1974. Current hardware includes quick-start turntables, broadcast quality cartridges, seven channel mixer with CD input, carbon fibre slip mats and an H &H 150 watt stereo slave amp which feeds Mordaunt-Short hi-fi speakers. Indexing of Tom's 5,000-plus collection of records, fast being invaded by CD in place of vinyl, was computerised in 1988. Invaluable as it searches by artist or title within seconds. Tom's original BBC B computer was replaced by a 32-bit Acorn Archimedes which, having been rigged with a sound sampler, also acts as a digital tape machine as a contingency against any problem with the CD or vinyl players.

Let's now disconnect the flashing lights, pack the records back into their boxes, load up the van and return our accents to Union Street Aberdeen (rather than any other USA) and take contemporary view of the DJ situation. A late-night stroll down Market Street takes us to the Pelican Club where Titch shouts at us over the noise. He more or less fell into jocking at the Torry Community Centre (birthplace of The Facells). The DJ there never seemed to have the right sounds, so Titch brought his own records: after a while, it seemed logical for him to play them himself. Initially a punk afficionado his ensuing one-off gigs in the town saw the blossoming of a blend of punk and dance. "It was quite new at the time, I don't think anyone else was doing that type of mix.'

Paz and Mark Burnett, then on the threshold of opening their new Pelican Club, happened to catch Titch's performance at a pub gig. Mightily impressed, they made him an offer he couldn't understand. That was ten years ago. . . nowadays, a typical Pelican weeks offers a reggae/jazz/hip-hop Thursday, underground techno Friday, more accessible house/garage Saturday and a live band Sunday. Each event attracts its own identifiably different 200-capacity crowd although there are also crossover punters, nine-to-fivers and out-of-towners. Titch says "The jock is there to give the customers a good time.' That sure 'aint acheived by following already-established trends. "I play music first and foremost, true to my own taste. . . I wouldnae dream of playing stuff that I don't personally enjoy. It always has to give you that kick, that buzz. In my position, you must have faith in our own judgement.'

Titch was fortunate in being one of Fred Craig's 1 Up commandoes: "It saves the grief of being on dozens of mailing lists. I get the stuff on pre-release up to four weeks before it is officially on sale, a good edge on what's hot.' Such One-Upmanship continually brings out Aberdeen's dance freaks, although his amigo, techno-electro boffin Kev Gunn says "Titch has been playing there for a few years now, and is paid a pittance. Numerous offers have come his way to play elsewhere outside Aberdeen - he could probably have made ten times the money but has turned it all down on a matter of principle.' That principle is quite simple: Titch is loyal to his crowd, and the crowd are loyal to him. Despite the longevity of his residency, he keeps it fresh. "If I thought it was stagnating, I would pack it in. I wouldnae be seen dead playing at weddings or discos. Or maybe I would, 'cos I would shoot mysel'.

Chapter 16

Loons in loons: the Seventies

So another decade, another million detours on the rocky roads from Northfield to North Africa, from Bash Street to Brooklyn. . . lest we forget, other things were occurring during the Seventies. . .

Standing at the bus stop with King Crimson's latest under your arm - never mind why, it was just something that had to be done. As if you hadn't had enough of 21st Century Schizoid Man tapping you up for the price of a cup of tea in Market Street. Eking out your one pint in the Douglas Hotel, it being a Sunday lunchtime, as the same tapping wino comes in to order himself a half of heavy and a double Watsons.

Buying a white Royal Navy surplus jacket from McKays in Queen Street and thinking you are Erchie as you strut your long-haired platform-soled stuff up Union Strasse at shutting time. . . and then getting kicked in the face by a giant tattooed skinhead monster called Yankee. Getting into rumbles (for reasons unrecalled but certainly not differences of opinion on the relative artistic merits of Claude Monet and Henri Matisse) with those affable chaps from the Torry Derry and The Crew.

Going to Tannadice to witness the Dons slaughter United five-nil in the Scottish Cup with Bertie Miller sliding across the muddy penalty box to score a goal with his arse. Watching a police dog being sent over the wall behind the goal to quell crowd trouble. . . Rover is stabbed before being thrown back onto the track. . . being chased out of the ground by the Arabs into the welcoming arms of the crombie-zombie Dundee skinhead fans (their team having already been knocked out of the competition), obviously intent upon filling in their free afternoon with a bit of timber-felling or rock-breaking. Why else were they carrying axes and hammers?

Travelling to Edinburgh to see The Who and crashing six to a room at Alan Dawson's house. . . when asked fragrantly if he never uses a deodorant, Davie answers: "No, I always make sure she's on the pill.'. . . Showing solidarity with your mate Barney when he is thrown out of the Nineteenth Hole for whistling by a fascist red-necked Torry mannie, when the off-key pianist and his off-key piano are making noises more painful than a centipede with sore feet. Barney's waist length hair and Chairman Mao tee-shirt might have had something to do with it.

This one falls into the 'why do I always get the nutter?' category. . . nine o'clock on a getting-busy Prince Of Wales Saturday night, waiting for the rest of the boys to arrive. Cogitating over a pint of Guinness and for the second time, the Green Final. . . not over bored, just relaxing. You are approached by a nervous obviously out-of-towner who is desperately seeking something. With much paranoid glancing over his shoulder, in a hushed conspiratorial tone eventually comes the much rehearsed question "D'ye think I could get some dope in here?' Dismissing the obvious answer "Well you've managed OK so far' and being keen to get back to the crucial primary schools football results, one maximises one's man-of-the-worldliness before replying. "If you get yoursel' through the back o' the bar, some o' that student crowd might fix you up.' With the twitchy teuchter still hovering, one's curiosity comes to the fore. Realising even as the words leave your lips that this is a mistake. . . "How much dope are you looking for?' Having re-checked the terrain for the twentieth time, one's acquaintance malgre lui comes out with a real doozie when he takes a stab at "About half a stone.' Suddenly, the Wee Alickie cartoon takes on vital importance. . . Later that evening our financial analysis of the nutter's shopping list comes up with a touch over three grand at prevailing (Union) Street prices.

In 1970 Peter Innes leaves the Aberdeen Academy. Making appropriate recognition of the departing pupil's outstanding performance at the school, rector Alex Goldie says "Adios, whoever you are.' In May Aberdeen win the Scottish Cup with goals from 'Cup-tie' Derek McKay and The King. September brings a representative of Phonographic Performances Limited to Aberdeen to investigate pirate mobile discotheques on behalf of the Musicians Union. It costs between 7/6d and 10/-d to enter the 600-capacity Mothers in Beauly, a progressive rock happening on Saturday nights between 8.30 and 11.45. Soft drinks only, but there are colour projectors. Eight bob gets you into The Ballerina in Nairn, which boasts ultra-mod decor and room for a thousand customers: its Friday blues/prog rock club stays open until 1.30 on Saturday mornings. The King's Grange in Banffshire runs a Saturday pop club through to 1.00 am which costs 6/6d. Hogmanay night 1970 at the Palace Ballroom features The D Men with Sandra, the TW Discotheque and the Caledonian Pipe Band.

The American tribal love-rock musical Hair is touring Scottish theatres. Gully Foyle's tenth German tour in October has been extended through into December. The eleventh edition of Scotland's teenage magazine Transplant is on sale with a cover price of two bob. ATV casting director Alex Fyne approaches George Elrick, inviting him on the panel of New Faces. He is henceforth to shoulder part of the blame for unleashing Jim Davidson, Lenny Henry, Marti Caine and Roger de Courcey with Nookie the Bear upon an unsuspecting television audience.

Out in the Garioch BMG are continuing their careers that we last touched on with Twinkle's People. BMG are Billy, Mike and Gogs. . . Derek Bisset and Terry Rickard leave Lewis Kane, an Inverurie-based heavy rock band in July of 1971. They are replaced by toonsers Jeff Stuart and Raymond Bruce, on guitar and bass respectively. Lewis Kane's other members are vocalist Charlie Fraser and drummer Norman Gillanders. According to Helen Gauld in her letter to Shout magazine, they were "A definite rock band with a hard danceable beat to their music and The Billy Steele Combo is the most commercially-minded in the town. . . Julian's Garden also feature mainly commercial material with a few heavier numbers thrown in.' A strong keyboard emphasis was evident in the latter's sound, which is the work of Ron Tawse: Alec Reid on vocals, Gary Horn on lead guitar, Michael Phillip on bass, and Brian Hosie on drums are the other gardeners. Brian also played with Jolson.

The following month, Grit call it a day. A fine heavy rock band led by brother and sister Dave and Dianne Kinneburgh, they come close to big-time success. After local television and press attention, they take the well-travelled London audition road. Other original members include Mike Gordon on bass, Denny Alexander on drums, and vocalist Phil Sinkins. The later phase of Grit's career was marked by frequent personnel changes. Mike Gordon was replaced in turn by Dave Hunt and Dennis Thompson, whilst Dave was succeeded by Mr Fantasy's Jim Watt on guitar - he goes on to enrol as one of The Bash Street Kids. Out of Grit come Age Of Kali - Bill McRae on drums, Jim Smith on guitar, Dave Smith on bass and Phil Sinkins on vox.

Changes also for progressive rock band Warlock, who settle into a format of Kenny McKenzie on lead guitar and vocals, Gordon Edmond on rhythm guitar and vocals, Dave Laing on bass, and Eric Smith on drums. Previous incarnations of this outfit saw Graham McKenzie, Murray Cowie, Colin Smith, Pauline Anderson and Doug Smith Jnr. all move through the ranks. The Ronnie Deans Quartet are amongst the first adventurous bands to blend traditional Celtic Caledonian music with progressive rock, as evidenced by the instruments they play. Ronnie handles vocals, lead electric and acoustic guitars, Ragnar Fagervold squeezes the electric accordion, Bill McRae plays drums, and Raymond Mitchell handles bass guitar. Quality pop-rock comes from Atlas who are Charlie Bruce (vocals), Johnny Riddoch (lead guitar), Bill Henderson (bass) and Bill Jolly on drums.

Lizard King undergo changes in December. Taking their name from Jim Morrison of The Doors, they play mainly their own rock-blues material. Bassist Ainslie Macleod and rhythm guitarist/keyboards player Neil Ross shed their skins and leave guitarist/vocalist Tony Paxton and drummer Colin Rae behind. Vocalist Fiona Bullock and bass player Elliot Morrison become the new reptilian royalty. At the Cabaret Cafe in April 1972 Levi play a very loud but varied set that includes Speed King, Albatross and Hold Your Head Up, featuring unfeasibly stratospheric vocals from keyboardist Rickie Postgate (Demis Roussos' long lost cousin, a singing yeti), incredibly tasty guitar from Mike Bowyer and resolute rhythm sectioning from Hugh Falconer and Stewart Kemp, a competent vocalist himself. Levi's track record includes The Delinquents, The Hyland League, Hedgehog Pie and Superklute amongst innumerable others.

The bill for the students' charities Pre-Torcher dance this month features The Montanas and Mr Fantasy, who rose Phoenix-style from the ashes of The East Coast Flames and The Children. Up Elgin way stay-press and stay-go gangs cause aggravation for fans of Morayshire groups Summerset, Windy Miller and The T Set. August is a time of transition for The Royal Teens. Howie Stewart has completed his post graduate course in ceramics and is off to Greece on a working holiday, before he continues his education at a London college. Former Time Machine member Bill King replaces Howie, joining vocalist Kenny Taylor, saxophonist and vocalist Dod Leonard, bassist Andy Willox and drummer John Gibson.

The Edgar Broughton Band is supported at their Music Hall gig in April of 1973 by the second Once Upon A Band line-up that includes Trevor Hart and Dave Flett. In a cubby-hole at the Grosvenor Club in Loch Street, Bobby Vincent is interrupted whilst changing into his stage clothes - the intruder is unsuccessfully sworn to secrecy on the taboo subject of Bobby's long johns. . . Aberdonian brass player of renown Pete McGovern is playing on cruise liners and in holiday camps - In a letter home to brother Eddie, also a horny individual, he whinges "I want to be a yellow coat' as he pushes his cleaning trolley around Butlins at Skeggie. . . Progressive rockers operating in the early-to-mid Seventies in Aberdeen include Hotnostril from Cults. These warm nasal cavities are trumpeter Andy Young, lead guitarist and vocalist Tim Grant, organist and vocalist Al Graham, Gogs MacCallum on bass and Butch Helm on drums. . . old trouper Stewart Kemp is drumming for One Way Glass who are led by husband and wife team Laurie and Ray Hamilton. . . Chronos are an acoustic based band who feature Alan Newbigging and Alan Dick on guitars and vocals with Jim Masson on percussion. On the jazz-rock-funk front, we have the heavyweight Mama Lu. Their supergroup personnel boasts Al Hyland from soul pioneers The Hyland League on trumpet, Bill Binner Innes on tenor sax, Robert Wilson on guitar, Dave Stroud on acoustic guitar and vocals, Mal Strachan on bass, and Harry MacFarlane on drums. They feature Sly and The Family Stone in their repertoire, unlike heavy rock specialists Dusty Hill: Zander Ruxton on drums, John Fitzgerald on bass, John Richards on guitar and Dennis Smith on vocals.

The drummer who makes Keith Moon look like a pussycat and gives Viv Prince a run for his money is playing with Ragoop. Of course it is Albert Ricky Wild Willie Munro, the guy who parted company with The Royal Teens ten years ago because of his "I hate everyone' philosophy. Keith Fraser is the band's guitarist and keyboards player, and Johnny McKeand is their bassist and vocalist. First degree Mordor from 16-year-olds Gandalf. . . these young blues-rockers are Eric Leslie on vocals, Trevor Wood and Johnny Riddoch on guitars, Bill Henderson on bass and Bill Jolly on drums. . . Sounding like a genital wash is required, Dirty Dick have Dennis Thompson (ex-Grit) on vocals, John Fitzgerald on guitar, Ian Cooper on bass and David Ritchie on drums.

January of 1974 sees Charlie 'Iron Man' Sinclair from Shetland succeed Humphrey Ocean and Jerome Lucas as bassist with Kilburn and The High Roads. Charlie deserts the land of horizontal rain (where he had been a member of The Sons Of Darkness with guitarist Mike Smith) to record an album for the Raft label with various sooth-moothers including lyricist and vocalist Ian Dury. Parent company WEA decide to sink Raft in April and offer alternative contracts with other WEA labels to all ex-Raftees. . . apart from KATHR. Five years later after Ian and The Blockheads hit the top-five with their New Boots And Panties LP, WEA suddenly re-consider that the Raft material is worth releasing after all, hence 1978's Wotabunch. Charlie remained with The High Roads to cut the album Handsome and the singles Rough Kids and Crippled With Nerves, all for Pye. . . Jerry O'Regan surfaces again in August on Seaside Ladies, the debut single by Bright Red Tandem. A lecturer at Moray House in Edinburgh, Jerry was one of The Misfits on 1965's students' charities single Hanging Around. . . Later in 1974, 28-year-old Eric Clapton is rescued from his three-year heroin oblivion by Dr Meg Patterson, using her pioneering neuro-electric therapy technique. A medical graduate of Aberdeen University and a Fellow of the Royal College of Surgeons, Meg had been awarded an MBE for her medical work in India. . . In a Market Street pub, Freddie Ellis is having difficulty enjoying his quiet pint, being bugged to high doh by some American oilfield trash banging on about the size of his spread back in Texas. Eventually the exasperated Freddie tells JR "Well, here's another two acres for you' before launching a well-aimed, genital-destined kick. A number 11 hit in November for Pilot with Magic, pre-dating their chart-topper January by three months. Pilot's guitarist is Shetlander Ian Bairnson and their drummer is 23-year-old Aberdonian Stuart Tosh, who was destined to join the Things We Do For Love and Dreadlock Holiday era 10cc. Country rockers Hennesseys are Billy Milne (lead guitar), Hugh McKenzie (rhythm guitar) and Ernie Beaton (bass).

Just because you need a letter from your ma doesn't mean you can't rock 'n' roll. . . Mertia are 15-year-olds from Hazlehead Academy. . . instead of swotting for exams, Murray and John McCormick, Ross Logie, and Dave Reid are the youngest rockers in town. . . and not much older are Hazzard, starring 17-year-old lead guitarist Mike Alexander. They don't come any rasher than Pigg, an impressive heavy rock combo. Bringing home the bacon are vocalist Satch Harper, guitarist Bruce MacPherson and bassist Mike Rae. Drummer is one Monty Python. . . and now for something completely different. . . Fraserburgh gives birth to Fractured Ham Sandwich. Their Broch 'n' roll is created by vocalist George Burnett, guitarist Jimmy Cheyne, bass player Peter Geddes and drummer Ian Brown.

Jazz combo Crescendo feature Fifties rockin' trombonist Colin Fraser, Munce Angus on keyboards, Jim McDonald on vox, and Aberdeen's Gene Krupa, Peter Buchan. Out of Mother Hubbard's cupboard come Cody High. . . drummer Ian Milne would later form part of Frank Robb's Hedgehog Pie, Superklute and Middle East combos, bass player Jim Tytler may be Jim Watt hiding from East Kilbride's nosy Parkers, John Morrison is their vocalist, and Billy Walker plays a punchy guitar. Another Frank Robb connection with Pick Up, in the person of bassist Hughie Falconer. Bill King on guitar and Dave Russell on vox complete this line-up. In the charmingly-titled contemporary folk trio Squeezewart, all three members Derek Stewart, Donald Duncan and Ronnie Nicol sing and play guitar. . . Still on a hand-knitted jumper and hand over one lug folk kick, Alian are Alistair Clark and Ian Benzie, who seemingly played the pub circuit eternally before it came good for him with Old Blind Dogs. Anticipating a cooling-down in the pop-package tour business, Albert Bonici converts the Two Red Shoes to a freezer centre.

In March of 1975 Jeannie Robertson dies at the age of 67. She had been awarded the MBE in 1968, in recognition of her services to traditional music. Jeannie learned a great deal of her repertoire from her mother, Marie Stewart from Ballater. Both parents were travelling folk, from the Stewart and Robertson dynasties. Her captivating voice was featured on the 1959 LP Jeannie Robertson, The Great Traditional Ballad Singer.

Les Rothmer, Robert Wilson and Tom Reid are joined by future Northsound jazz presenter Gavin Stark in Gabriel Oake, a progressive jazzy splinter combo from Septimus and Another Camel. On the pre-Bash Street Kids scene are Pyramid (Greg Brechin, Billy Sutherland, Bob Baxter and Chas Adams) and Shegra (Jim Watt and Ralphie Greig). These Klondike, oil rush years of the mid-Seventies see local men desert the paper mills and trawling en-masse, heading instead for the burgeoning offshore drilling rigs and the support industry which fast develops around them. Suddenly people in the pubs are talking about BOPs and casing as they down copious pints on their fortnight ashore: droves of young men with surplus money and lots of free time: the fear factor in our city centre escalated dramatically. Steve Gibbons will have good reason to remember these hectic, often confused days when walking the mat is just as likely to bring you a Glesca kiss as a friendly 'Fit Like'. Hot on the heels of his top-twenty hit Tulane, he brings the Steve Gibbons Band to The Capitol. "I think we were sharing the bill with Be Bop Deluxe that night, and it had been a great gig for us. We were feeling very pleased with ourselves. There was a nearby party we had been invited to, so several of the band and crew left The Capitol and walked off down Union Street. I've been in some rough places over the years but Union Street at ten o'clock that Saturday night took some beating' An unfortunate choice of phrase from Steve Gibbons, an icon of rock 'n' roll cool and an absolute gentleman to boot.

"Somewhat bemused by the whole scene, I had let myself fall behind the rest of our crowd who were twenty or thirty yards ahead of me. My feeling of well being was probably enhanced by having consumed a fair proportion of the tequila and brandy which was always on our rider in those days, so I sauntered on oblivious. Ahead of me a bunch of young guys were punching hell out of each other and as I deftly stepped around them I made a comment - a big mistake. All I said was 'Come on lads, sort yourselves out.' Like a red rag to a bull, my English accent penetrated their drunken fury. About fifteen seconds later I stopped in a shop doorway to light up. I felt a tap on my shoulder, and as I turned I was hit in the mouth by something akin to a slab of granite, although it was probably only an Aberdonian fist. I slumped on the floor under a hail of boot leather and at the end of the holocaust I caught a glimpse of my assailants disappearing down the street, united again. We had to cancel our gig the following night in Dundee. A real pity, as SGB had never missed a gig until then. With my fat lip I couldn't even speak, let alone sing. At the end of the day I counted myself lucky. Careless talk costs lives.'

At the Waterton Hotel in Bucksburn, Vincent pack them in with their quality dance and chart music. They share their Sunday lunchtime spot with various boilers taking their clothes off and coming on about as sexy as your granny slipping you the tongue when you give her a birthday kiss. The diving and marine crews from the Oregis and the Smit Lloyd 112 draw up ice-skating style score cards using squares of shiny toilet paper and a black marker pen. When one allegedly erotic dancer is half way through her routine, she is aghast when scores of 0, 0, 1, 1, 0, and 0 are held aloft. . . it all ends in a tearful exit. In the town, Abba facsimiles Sunny Sound are giving Mamma Mia and Waterloo laldie upstairs at Jimmy Wilson's. They are apparently very fond of Indian food, singing Ckicken Tikka. . . Following a lead, Aberdeen's health inspectors give birth to the expression 'wokking the dog' with their discovery of the contents of the freezer at Crown Street's Great Wall Chinese restaurant. It certainly puts a new slant on Pekinese cuisine.

The Ramones start making waves in the USA. Their name is inspired by a certain Paul Ramon, a member of The Silver Beetles who moonlight-flitted out of Aberdeenshire hotels in 1960. Trevor Hart pays a flying visit to the area in December 1976 as part of The Glasgow Works Band, performing in Aberdeen, Huntly, Kintore and Ellon. . . One of Aberdeen's big mysteries comes to light when King Edward VII loses his knob. This refers, of course, to the statue opposite the Monkey Hoose and the old C & A building - the bulbous bottom end of his sceptre disappeared. This puts an end to giggling passers-by stepping on winos and looking at Eddie from a certain angle, which gave the impression that he was in a state of some excitement. Where did the hard royal appendage go? Another as-yet unexplained mystery was the disappearance of that icon of childhood Christmas stockings, the tangerine. Where did it go and why was it replaced overnight by exotic impostors like the satsuma and the clementine? And while we are in this shady, twighlight area of curious X Files happenings, what happened to penny whoppers, black sugar aley, those rooty things you chewed and, worst of all, souricks? We herewith demand a govenmental inquiry.

A week after supporting Cado Belle at Fusion, Jock split up just before Christmas. Like shite to a blanket, Michaels, Spry, and Dalgarno plan to stick together. Lemon and Parko are off to pastures new, the working title for their proposed new band is Larko. 1976 also brings us Busco, which ultimately produces two big names in the music business. For four years their repertoire concentrates on Average White Band, Fatback, and Brass Construction. At venues like The Douglas Hotel, The Metro, and Ruffles, Busco fast become one of Aberdeen's most popular attractions, with Dilys Cooper on vocals in front of a horn section which includes Geoff Innes Neil Ferguson, and the evergreen Al Hyland. Andy Scott and Graham Edwards handle guitar and bass respectively with Steve Harvey on drums. Edwards and Harvey subsequently hit the big time with The Foundations, and Janet Jackson. 1977 sees the end of popular Banff group Benny's Dream. . . for 14 years anyway.

Amongst those sitting in and jamming with The Shapiros at their Croft appearances in July and August of 1978 are members of The Squibs and Hedgehog Pie's Ronnie Nicol. . . Former leader of The Leopards Eddie Leppard is playing as LM Express, along with Neil Milne. After engagements at the Croft in Aberdeen and at Lossiemouth's Silver Sands holiday camp, they are off to play pub dates in London. Bunion perform Gift Of A Brand New Day on Grampian Television. Mike Keavey and Eddie Ross were to continue playing together for 20 years, touring Germany in 1976 and 1977. The first band to play on an offshore platform, Bunion's gig at the Malt Mill in Holburn Street saw them play there every week for 16 years. The landlord says "I suppose you could call them regulars.' Both Bunioneers also played in Quillon. Graeme Smith, whose last band was Ded Strait, joins Sound 'n' Vision. . . At the Bobbin Mill, Twang are playing - the name goes back to an itinerant wino type who played banjo around the city centre in the Fifties: another such character was Bubbly Snitch.

The Stiff Records Pullman special pulls into Strathpeffer, Wick, Aberdeen and Dundee in October. All aboard are the second wave of Stiff odd-balls - including Wreckless Eric, Mickey Jupp, Jona Lewie, Lene Lovich and the 16-year-old Rachel Sweet. They are the first live pop act to visit Wick in ten years. In November, it all starts paling into insignificance when Sitting On The Fence fall off due to unmanageable debts, a disappearing PA and members also going missing. . . United Artists ask The Shapiros for a second demo tape. At Bruce Miller's Loch Street shop, Fender Stratocaster guitars are priced at £375, Rickenbacker basses at £450 and 100w Marshall amps at £255. A Premier B4000 drum kit with cream finish will set you back £530 and orders are being taken for Peavey's new T60 electric guitars at £299.

Boleskine House on the shores of Loch Ness is purchased by Led Zeppelin's guitarist Jimmy Page. Formerly owned by Aleister Crowley, a warlock-magician who proudly claimed to be "the wickedest man alive', the property was the eerie setting for many occultist ceremonies, most notoriously when Crowley ('The Beast') summoned the devil, in a ritualistic face-to-face encounter. Expelled from the Order of The Golden Dawn for extreme practices, his own Silver Star cult attracted rumours of drugs, orgies, magical ceremonies and baby sacrifice. Many who associated with him died in tragic circumstances, including his wife and child. . . Page's reason for acquiring Boleskine is his fascination with such dark practices. Zeppelin are, for a time, reputed to be jinxed. . . a security man is badly beaten up during a US tour, Robert Plant's child dies from a sudden stomach infection, John Bonham is injured in a car smash.

Chapter 17

So good to be back home again

Billy Bremner's infinite session work apart, pop chart success was almost virgin territory for acts from Aberdeen until Annie Lennox's hit parade career began with The Tourists in 1979. Soon afterwards a one-hit-wonder emerged with Jimmy The Hoover's annoyingly catchy African influenced Tantalise (We Wo Eee Yeh Yeh), which hit number 18 in 1982. He was in fact one Derek Dunbar, a 24-year-old North East loon who was also a male model. The band which backed him included musicians from Zambia, Malta, Los Angeles and London, and were adopted by Malcolm McLaren during his Bow Wow Wow phase. He gave them the daft name and put them on as support act to Annabel Lu Win et al on a national tour. Within the time it takes to vaccuum your carpet, Jimmy The Hoover disappeared again (in common with fellow Innervision label-mates Wham! and Animal Nightlife, they encountered legal problems, in the Hoovers' case, preventing them from promoting their follow up single Kill Me Quick).   Tantalise was Jackson Browne's favourite pop tune at the time. Jimmy's mum Mrs Hoover still lives in Huntly, but he was last rumoured to be in South Africa. Which is not West Africa but it does move our rock 'n' roll safari along again. . .

Douala on the coast of Cameroon, a world away from Bucksburn, in the middle of the rainy season, unsteady and dizzy through some strange anti-malarial drugs side-effect. Having already been away from home for months before travelling to West Africa, it was getting to me. The job was a nightmare due to a combination of fuck ups, my mistakes, and a project superintendent who detested me - as the client was fond of reminding all concerned as often as possible, le travail ne marche bien. I had already once decided to drag up and get myself out of it (the worst crime in the offshore game) but a couple of the other hands talked me out of acting rashly. I resolved to grit my teeth, deflect the flak as best as possible, and to stay with it.

Although she was unaware of it, Annie Lennox caused the author to throw in his job. In an attempt to improve on the non-existent team spirit, the boss took the entire crew out for dinner to a local restaurant. Things were passably bearable: one of our divers, Pat O'Mahoney (he occasionally sat in with a local African rock band) played a set of local drums he rooted out from somewhere. The fried chicken and plantain were pretty good, and the 33 was cold. Fine, I was getting my head into its best shape for several days - the sole Aberdonian amongst a crew that included French, English, Irish, and Africans (both black and white). As we talked about anything except work (I vaguely recall Big Brother and The Holding Company came into to the conversation) lizards ate food scraps off our trainers under the open-air tables. Through the restaurant's rudimentary PA, speakers hanging off the bamboo poles supporting the grass roof, came piped music. No, not Manu Dibango, Youssou N'Dour or anything remotely African, but Annie Lennox. So Good to be Back Home Again. I found it hard to take: the odds against the situation were incredible - I let it sink in for a wee while and then thought "Bugger this for a game of soldiers.' I was on the first available Air Cameroun silver bird back to Aberdeen via CDG and Heathrow: Skintsville for three months till the next job came up.

No such worries for Annie herself - even before her solo albums Diva and Medusa became international best sellers, her finances were fantastically healthy. With co-Eurythmic Dave Stewart she established a company to handle their performance fees and royalties. The turnover of DnA Limited increased from £151,160 for fiscal year ended March 1983 to £5,307,795 for year ended March 1988. Canny accounting practices resulted in a corresponding pre-tax loss for 1982 of £157,301 - and a pre-tax profit in for 1987 of only £19,592. The sums paid to both Annie and Dave in respect of directors' emoluments in 1982 were £12,500, whilst each drew £1,020,000 in 1985.

Accountants were installed as nominee directors of a complicated myriad other companies that protected and managed incomes from Eurythmics' creative efforts. These companies - owned either jointly or individually - included Anxious Music Ltd, Anxious Records Ltd, Fundamental Music Ltd, TVP Ltd, Famous Castle Ltd, Double Feature Productions Ltd, and Punclose Ltd. Other group companies with obvious direct links to Annie herself included La Lennoxa Ltd, and 26 Warwick Avenue Ltd - the latter company owned the house in which she lived. Another cog in the corporate wheel, Eligible Music Ltd (which turned over £253,257 for year ended 1987) allowed 45% depreciation on the company's houseboat and 33.3% depreciation on its musical and houseboat equipment. Such assets are obviously essential for a bloke and lassie who write and sing songs. It is worth mentioning that the above network of companies represented the UK situation only.

Annie was reported as being Britain's fifth highest female earner in 1992 with an income of £3,100,000. As my da used to say "nae much if you say it quick'. Her personal fortune has been estimated at a minimum of £15,000,000 which is an affa lot of money to keep in the Christmas club at Ellon's Spar shoppie. She maintains abodes in Majorca, Paris, New York and London. Having researched the above financial information, you will understand my amusement at a somewhat stern but typically canny Scottish request from Annie's mum. "Mind and send a stamped addressed envelope if you want a reply when you write to her.'

Annie was born on Christmas Day 1954, in a month that saw cat burglar, master safe-blower and war-time commando hero Johnny Ramensky released yet again from Peterhead prison. At the time of her birth, her mother (from Speyside) and her father (a Communist shipyard and railway worker), lodged at 169 Gairn Terrace. Annie was brought up in a Hutcheon Street tenement flat to which the family moved, opposite the Richards textile mill. Lacking in basic amenities, the kitchen served also as dining room, sitting room and the adults' bedroom. An only child, Annie slept on a studio couch in the flat's only other room, with communal toilet facilities located in the tenement hallway.

However, by all accounts, these were happy times for the young quine despite her father's strict protective disciplinarianism. When she was eight, the family moved to a flat in the Mastrickland high rise block, replete with the modern amenities missing from the previous home. At the High School For Girls she took piano lessons from Mrs Murray and played in school concerts. Whilst her efforts in other subjects brought moderate success, it became clear early on that music was to be her best card. The school's individualistic dance tutor Marguerite Feltges taught a sound and movement mime technique named Eurhythmics, in its original form. The system's modern antecedents lay in turn-of-the-century France, where it was developed from its Greek origins.

When she was 12 music teacher Bill Spittle introduced her to the flute, an instrument she would persevere with beyond leaving school at 17. Spittle had been a theatre-pit orchestra player who re-trained as a teacher, bringing his appreciation of theatrical show music and the value of personal performance with him to his new career.

The young Annie was reputedly singing constantly, finishing second at a Butlin's holiday camp talent show with Marie's Wedding. It was music all the way: military bands, school choir, British Youth Wind Orchestra. . . until puberty brought other things to think about. Hoary old Aberdeen jokes about the sexual happenings at the Girls' High come to mind when Annie described the school's regime. With female-only pupils and a scarcity of male teaching staff, she became "totally boy mad by the time I was 14.' Her interest in contemporary music also began during this period as one the city's self-appointed creme de la creme: come the typically problematic teenage years of 15 and 16, Annie was a self-confessed rebel, reacting against the strict upbringing of her father. From early teens dancing to Tamla Motown at the Beach Ballroom, she followed an established pattern by graduating to digging rock acts at the Students' Union and local progressive bands at smoky dens such as the Silver Slipper. She hung out with Trevor Hart's band, playing flute at their rehearsals. Remembered by Aberdeen acquaintances as being a dreamer, she was also fiercely determined to succeed. Co-incidentally, she lived within 200 yards of Davie Flett, another musician whose dedicated commitment finally brought his music into the international rock arena.

At 17, La Lennox left the neo-Jean Brodie environs of Queen's Road behind to work at Findus, where she earned £9.50 for a fishy 40-hour-week. She saved the money for her future musical training, and had a good bath before leaving Aberdeen in September of 1971. Atop wind-buffeted cliffs at Cullen, with seabirds shrieking as they rode the air-currents Graham Spry told her "Don't do it Annie, you'll regret it.'

Auditioning in flute and piano at London's Royal Academy of Music, she targeted an eventual career as a professional classical musician. However, Annie soon regretted passing the gruelling, all-day entrance exam, being immediately disillusioned by what she felt were pretentious, negative pressures. .

. students were terrified of making mistakes for fear of being ridiculed by tutors and peers alike. She realised that, for her at least, classical music was over-restrictive, inflexible and prioritised the performance itself at the expense of the musician as an individual. Detesting what she considered was an inhuman atmosphere, she neglected her studies to the detriment of her exams. Causing great parental dismay, she walked out a week before her finals. When he heard the news back in Aberdeen, Graham Spry thought ruefully "I told you not to do it Annie. I said you would regret it.'

Alone in London in 1974, she drifted through a variety of going nowhere jobs. Living with a fellow book shop employee, Annie chanced upon his copy of Stevie Wonder's seminal album Talking Book: it blew her away. In what seemed to be a period of musical discovery, Joni Mitchell's Ladies Of The Canyon showed her what could be achieved by a female artist, a glimmer of what might be ultimately possible for Annie herself. Whilst paying the rent through another-day another-dollar jobs, she took a couple of alternative singing lessons from an Australian voice coach. He encouraged her to loosen up and to strive for a Negroid sound. Now sufficiently confident to write lyrics and music during her free time, waitressing by day kept her music dreams alive by night. . . but the dreams fast became nightmares.

Running a gauntlet of soul-destroying, low-budget music, three months was the most Annie could endure of being ignored in working mens' clubs with alleged folk-rockers Dragon's Playground. Red Brass was a slight improvement, but their national tour and potentially important London dates served only to put her off socialist jazz-rock. Club and cabaret venues in the South East cold-shouldered her efforts with the duo Stocking Tops (this name being accepted with great reluctance) in the company of co-equal no-hoper Joy Dey. Despair and depression were never far away, balanced on a razor's edge against the deeply-held belief that she did have something to offer. . .

With Annie going nowhere fast other than her Camden bedsit in 1976, an acquainted record-stall dealer named Paul Jacobs made the introduction that was to change her destiny. He brought a messed-up Dave Stewart to Pippin's Restaurant in Hampstead where Annie worked as a waitress: Stewart's first words to Annie were reputedly, "Will you marry me ?' Having also moved to London, in his case from Sunderland, Stewart had been a member of Longdancer. They signed to the Rocket label, owned by My Dear Watson's former session keyboards player Elton John. Poor sales of Longdancer's two albums in 1973 and 1974 killed the band off. With a serious LSD habit warping his career focus, Stewart was free-falling, busking the streets and playing beer-money session guitar. Notwithstanding his acid-induced disorientation, he was a technically excellent guitarist who, prior to meeting Annie, had been sketching out ideas on demos with fellow Mackam Peet Coombes. Annie recalls her first impression "He was a serious nutter and I was right. He did look a bit. . . strange.'

Despite (or perhaps because of) this strangeness, it was a cataclysmic moment: "For me it was love at first sight although all he wanted to do was talk about music.' They spent that first night together and within days shared a flat. Dave moved in his two carrier-bags containing all his worldly goods and possessions. Annie threw in the dish towel, leaving her waitressing job and with Coombes, they busked with acoustic guitars in record company offices throughout Tin Pan Alley. Lennox and Stewart were fellow lost souls adrift amongst London's anonymous flotsam and jetsam. In each other they found mutual sympathy and support, both physical and emotional. In their music they found their dreams made tangible. A demo tape of the trio's earliest efforts landed on the desk of Logo Records boss Geoff Hannington, who gleaned something of value in what he heard (particularly, he was to claim later, in the female vocals). When he waved cheques for £500 under each of their noses, the financially strapped trio bit his hand off. The haste with which they signed Logo's recording and publishing contracts was to haunt them later.

The combo released a sole single for Logo as The Catch in October of 1977, Borderline/Black Blood (currently worth a cool £50 a copy on the collectors' market). Despite Borderline flopping Logo maintained their interest as the trio expanded by recruiting a rhythm section. They now had a fully fledged five-piece band to play live, promoting future recordings. Abandoning their preliminary choice of name The Spheres of Celestial Influence for the more succinct Tourists, this new band began a steady progression up the precipitous face of chart recognition. Blind Among the Flowers and The Loneliest Man in the World reached number 52 and number 32 respectively. Flying in the face of late Seventies anti-professional punk stance, The Tourists hit their mark as power-pop progenesists par excellence, with a strident cover of Dusty Springfield's I Only Want to Be With You finally cracking it at number four in 1979.

Annie's immaculate and dynamically powerful voice was therefore brought into the public domain, and the band's off-their-faces appearance surely helped things along once their songs had hooked the listener. Stewart came across as D'Artagnan in a motorcycle jacket, Malaysian bassist Eddie Chin was Fu Man Chu in aviator shades and Annie, adorned in hard street threads, was. . . well, . . . weird. Those wildly staring, indecipherable searchlight eyes screamed "Don't even think about messing with me, buster' Even this early in the game she appreciated that image was a large proportion of the battle.

Despite the next single So Good to be Back Home Again (the one that sent yours truly scuttling home years later) hitting number eight, relationships were strained within the band. Neither Annie nor Dave had much say in decisions, Coombes being the principal songwriter. The Tourists were decried as being latter-day hippies hiding in drainpipe strides and new wave chic. Criticism that they were mere Sixties re-creationists, coupled with their non-adventurist material led to stand-up fights between Annie and Coombes. Their final release Don't Say I Told You So died at number 40, and whilst on tour in Bangkok in the autumn of 1980, they decided that the holiday was over for The Tourists.

Annie and Dave's collaboration continued, re-directed towards an avant garde electronic feel. Their new band structure concept was that of invited musicians working around a nucleus of the duo themselves. Rehearsals and jamming in Cologne with personnel from German bands DAF and Can at Conny Plank's studio yeilded a first release from their new creation, Eurythmics. This name derived from the mime and dance education technique taught to Annie by Marguerite Feltges. Six months on from the demise of The Tourists came Eurythmics' RCA single Never Gonna Cry Again, followed in October of 1981 by the album In the Garden. Their initial product can be described, with the benefit of hindsight, as being somewhat unfocused and indecisive, an interim phase between The Tourists as was and Eurythmics as would be.

The debut single did no better in the UK chart than number 63 but by January of 1983, with Sweet Dreams Are Made Of This peaking at number two and Love Is A Stranger achieving number six on its second chart appearance, they were unstoppable. According to Annie the objective had been a coalescence of punk energy, cold European synthetic mechanical rhythms and soul music sweetness. The latter influence she traces back to those Motown sounds she heard at the Beach Ballroom on Friday nights.

From the outset Eurythmics releases were complemented by memorable videos, broadcasting a unique Euro electro-swing dance style to a hitherto unsuspecting audience. These premiered Annie's spellbinding, intense performances together with Stewart's out-of-it, fa's the boy? mania. The sexual ambiguity of the earlier videos in which Annie cross-dressed in male clothing caused much furore, particularly in the USA where they didn't know what to make of her ever-changing androgynous image. True to their original personnel manifesto, collaborative musicians orbited around Eurythmics' core. From the conventional rock world came Clem Burke, Green Gartside, Billy McKenzie, Kiki Dee and future Fairground Attraction vocalist Eddi Reader, and the arty sphere was represented by Holger Czukay, Robert Crash and Jackie Leibzeit.

An eight-year UK track record included 32 top-50 singles and eight top-30 albums, four of which hit number one. However as Paul McCartney told the world in 1964 Money Can't Buy Me Love. Annie's professional success found few echoes in her off-stage life and the Lennox-Stewart personal dependency wained. Successive failed relationships and personal tragedies, obviously traumatic and painful, are reflected opaquely in her lyrics throughout her career. Sweet Dreams Are Made Of This dismisses the Eighties feeding frenzy which was Thatcherite commodity greed, reflecting Annie's success-happiness paradox, performed in her best dispassionate anti-star vocal with the smartest synth-pop lick, driven unremittingly into the floor like a tacket by Stewart. Missionary Man refers to her short-lived marriage to a German Hare Krishna devotee whose enormous sexual appetite totally contradicted his supposed religious beliefs. Would I Lie To You and Thorn In My Side also come glaringly from this unsuccessful relationship and Angel manifests the death of her great aunt, although the song took on new personal meaning following the still-birth of her first child.

On the sunny side When Tomorrow Comes and Right By Your Side are optimism crystalised on vinyl whilst You Have Placed A Chill In My Heart begins as a bleak and desolate portrait of betrayal and concludes in thrill and anticipation. The latter tells of the happiness she found with her husband and their two children.

By the end of Eurythmics both partners were eager to engage in other projects, Dave frustrated with what was often perceived as his supporting role, Annie needing space if they were to part on reasonable terms after 13 years together. They were no longer close friends although the split fortuitously came before terminal animosity set in. A fitting coda was the 1991 chart-topping Greatest Hits LP. They finished as the most successful male-female duo of all time, selling in excess of 23 million albums.

Since then Dave Stewart and The Spiritual Cowboys created lovely albums. . . the excellent first single Jack Talking only tickled the chart and the others were bombing until the 1994 Isley Brothers Summer Breeze-inspired single Heart Of Stone (and the Greetings From The Gutter album) at last brought overdue recognition. Dave was also responsible for the theme music to BBC's Jute City, a dark threatening drama set in Dundee plotted around toxic chemical dumping and Masonic corruption. As a producer he has collaborated with acts as diverse as The Freaks of Desire, Tom Petty, Mick Jagger, Bob Geldof and Candy Dulfer. Destined to be forever an extremely well-heeled rock 'n' roll gypsy, he needs more than two poly carriers now. The man is a genius, albeit a nutty one.

Annie took some time for herself, her family and to consolidate her personal life out of the demanding rock 'n' roll spotlight. Slowly, and for the first time without Stewart running the control desk, she embarked upon her first genuinely solo project, which became the album Diva.

In April of 1992, coming four years after the last bona fide Eurythmics release, Diva was unveiled to critical and popular acclaim, selling over five million copies world-wide. Annie steadfastly refused to partake in the hooplah and histrionics normally demanded of such an artist, leaving others to reap that particular harvest. In a considered, mature and confident fashion, she instead allowed her music, her videos and a memorably intense Top Of The Pops live performance of Why to speak for her. Further singles Walking On Broken Glass and Little Bird/Love Song For A Vampire were international hits, the latter featuring in Francis Ford Coppolla's movie Bram Stoker's Dracula. The music industry, as always brown-nosing after financial achievement, showered Annie with awards: Grammys, Brits, MTV and Rolling Stone magazine all jumped on the accolade band-wagon.

Her second album Medusa saw Annie under the covers performing material composed by other writers. "Medusa has arisen from the need to perform something different. . . from the early Eighties I've been writing and co-writing songs. I just wanted to break that pattern for a while.' Whilst parallels can be drawn between this March 1995 release and David Bowie's Pinups tribute LP, here Annie re-evaluates her favourites rather than recreate them. "Like old friends, these songs were drawn from memory or partial recall. For me, the challenge lay in the notion of interpretation.' Medusa was trailed in the singles chart by her spell-binding treatment of The Lover Speaks' No More I Love You's, sounding for all the world like something she may have composed herself - the mark of the great cover version. Encompassing material from Neil Young, Paul Simon and The Blue Nile at the respected song craftsman end of the spectrum, the album up-tempos with treatments of Al Green's Take Me To The River and The Tempts' Can't Get Next To You. In many ways the covers project was the bravest thing Annie has tackled to date, leaving herself open to criticism that her renditions are either to close to, or too far away from, the original cuts. As if she really has to worry: personal happiness, enough money to choke a horse, one of the world's top three female recording artists. Annie Lennox has everything, including an un-used stamped, addressed envelope.

. . . .

Fusion, the dance-hall previously known as the Palace, was a heaving mass of bodies for Annie's triumphant return to her own patch with The Tourists. On the heels of So Good To Be Back Home, the joint was a-hoppin'. The author stood atop two crates to catch sight of the band's storming set: they were dynamite. Whilst Eurythmics later became stadium-filling, platinum record, award-winning stratostars, there were developmental problems back in Annie's home town. Despite being a decade into oil boom-town territory, mid-Eighties Aberdeen suffered from an acute shortage of live music venues. Duncan Hendry described the situation as 'drastic', and he was probably the person best qualified to comment. Through his 50-act Moondance Entertainments Agency and Aberdeen Rock promotions companies, Duncan was the Silver City's guru of gigs.

A west coaster, he arrived in Aberdeen in 1974, bringing his Glasgow Apollo (Green's Playhouse) expertise and degree in psychology with him. The latter doubtless proved invaluable to him during his three year co-ownership of the Crazy Daisy pub on Commerce Street. He brought occasional live music (Freebird, Munce Angus) to that tiny but well-loved bar upstairs in the Cra's Nest. Dunc shone his torch into that dark no-man's land between The Capitol (which, in any case, was established on a formalised 'sit doon and behave regime'), and small pubs. The ABC Bowl and Valhallas had gone, and the city council seemingly were unprepared to allow the Beach Ballroom to get down and get with it. He bore glad tidings for Aberdeen's multitudinious spiky-tops, long-hairs and rockers when he instituted Friday and Saturday bashes at The Venue, based in the Douglas Hotel.

Admittedly certain aspects of the facility soon declined: unhealthy druggie toiletular episodes, foot-adhering carpeting, second mortgage prices for crappy Inde Coope brewed Red Stripe. All undesirable, but all constituent parts of large-scale rock experiences. Duncan opined that, notwithstanding the welcome breakthroughs of APB, Pallas and The Shamen, the scarcity of other live platforms effectively de-opportunised local upwardly-aspiring bands. Progress and experience only come from baring all in front of critical punters, screaming for fresh blood. How else to identify what works and what don't? The bedroom rehearsal gig only gets you so far, and your ma and da 'aint normally sufficiently cognisant to pass a constructive opinion: au contraire, when the amp is switched off, for them it's the end of an earache.

Despite his proclamation that promoting rock was "a high risk business' Hendry seldom reined himself in, repeatedly hanging his arse out the financial window. He gave us the opportunity to catch Big Country on their way up and Divine, as he was going down. A thousand people turned up for the weird experience that was Divine. His sole access to the stage out of the audience's view involved his clambering accross the roof, and down the fire escape. Not an easy task for this hefty individual, particularly as he wore high stiletto heels and a tight cocktail dress. Pity any poor Aiberdeen wifie who happened to glance out of her kitchen windae to espy such a manoevre. Divine, of course, presented an incongrious on-stage persona, but out of drag was also (apparently) unnerving. . . under the wig lay a short peroxide blonde Mr C-Gazza barnet. His show was probably the most bizarre that The Venue hosted, but the doors closed when The Douglas changed hands. . . the new management perceived the downstairs shenanigans as being incompatible with their hotel business. "A violent den of iniquity' located directly below guests' rooms just wasn't the thing.

When the city came looking for a director for its Alternative Music Festival, Duncan was therefore the pefect man for the job. Aberdeen Alternative Festival has been in existence for 14 years. A ten-day event, it primarily targets the promotion of NE culture within an international context. Thus it encompasses jazz, folk, rock and multi-arts. Without internationally known names, Duncan feels it would be like a movie without a star: to secure the financial viability of the event, the box office needs a cash infusion. . . Perhaps the biggest of the big names brought to Aberdeen by AAF was Mr James Brown, providing a logistical nightmare for Dunc and his small, harassed crew. . . no less than 33 JB personnel poured off the transatlantic flight in Glasgow at ten o'clock in the morning. They had to be flown to Aberdeen, hotelised, fed and watered and transported to the Bridge Of Don, all in time for the show that same night, un coup par excellence for AAF in securing Mr Brown's first-ever appearance in Scotland. Despite his recent PCP-induced paranoiac, jail-resulting traumas, JB was "impeccable' throughout his brief sojourn in the city. . . the gig itself was "excellent, just a shame that our hoped-for 6,000 attendance in reality only was 4,300'.

Van Morrison's AAF Music Hall show was stopped by a bomb scare: Van and the band adjourned to the Caley Hotel, assuming that it was all off. However, Duncan got the all clear from the bomb experts, and sped through Golden Square. Eventually, Van's posse were extracted from the hotel bar and escorted back to the venue where they played an unruffled, superb set. After the gig Van went in search of happening night clubs, with their attendant proliferation of feminine attendees. . . unfortunately for him, such cuddly individuals proved monastically scarce downstairs at The Lemon Tree. After an equally fruitless skite upstairs, he left in an exasperated huff. So much for the oil capital of Europe.

Along on King Street, Marlene and Graeme King presented an alternative vista of the promotions business. After abandoning their careers in nursing and medical physics they established Abbotsford Acoustics in May of 1977, developing it into one of Scotland's premier stage lighting and sound equipment set-ups. Graeme flexed his muscles and flex on the white light, white noise, white-man's magic of the venture. Marlene concentrated on hiring out the hardware and having cut her managerial teeth with Aberdeen AOR specialists Freebird, looked after the affairs of Hebridean/Isle Of Skye proto Gael-rock icons Run Rig. The Kings concurred with Duncan's bemoaning the North East's venue-starved predicament, correlating the upsurge in 'upmarket discotheques' with the arrival of that crude and nasty North Sea oil. Even the student market, traditionally guaranteed to turn out for even the most esoteric live music, had now in Marlene's estimation transferred its socialising to Aberdeen's burgeoning discos and night clubs. An unholy triumvirate of Thatcher, Duran Duran and Loadsamoney culture had a lot to answer for.

The shortage of venues appropriate to indigenous bands prompted the launch of the Music Support Group. Based at the Summer Street community centre, this collective's rationale was to shepherd new, young musicians through the wolf-plagued rock music forest. Developed from an Urban Aid Unemployment project, MSG's spokesperson was Pat Davies a former member of the band Hum that had been unsuccesful in finding anywhere to play.

Hum finally arrived at the community centre's senior youth club, attracting 160 to their first gig. The £23 profit was ploughed back into the scheme's PA fund, a first step towards the target of £1,300. A variety of local combos pitched into the battle which eventually bore fruit in the shape of a 900w PA system, an admirable achievement indeed. MSG hired the unit very cheaply to native groups, with financial surpluses again going back into the pot. Pat apparently had "a wealth of experience in running bands and putting on gigs.' However, he also bore "a fierce hatred of the established music business.'

Come 1990, the live circuit was in a healthier condition despite The Venue having closed its scarred doors the previous May. The Malt Mill never wavered, and a revitalisation of the indie music scene down-scaled the gig dimension but broadened its spectrum: smaller events but more of them. Hence pubs were better positioned to accommodate the 500-600 disenfranchised Venue attendees. Caesar's Palace typified a re-alignment back towards live groups: the premises' manager Ray Daniels was adamant that any decent band would get a fair tug of the toga at Caesar's. The disco concept was an anathema to Daniels, not a surprise when balanced against his own musical background as a member of Aberdeen bands Hustler and Hold The Frame during the Eighties. HTF included Mike Allen (he later joined The Persuaders and now co-manages The Mill recording studio) and bassist/vocalist Colin Davidson. Their single Against The Wind (produced by Niall at Crathes) on the CRM label was a stirring, heart-accelarating Scottish stomper, of equal value as anything from Big Country or Run Rig. The B side I Want You was a jumpily-tempoed rocker ripped out of Keith Richards' human riffology manual with a neo-Ric Ocasek vocal.

Another promotional maestro is Ian Middleton, who runs Ibis Productions from the environs of Royal Deeside. Born late into his family, he stumbled upon a pile of 78s left behind by his sisters when they flew the nest. . . hence his interest in music stirred early on in his life. After "messing about with a guitar, but not very successfully' he frequented Aberdeen's Platform Jazz venture as a punter. One of PJ's main men Chris Tauber moved out, leaving Ian to take over the secretary's position... Platform Jazz was a non profit-making Arts Council-funded enterprise, targeted towards promoting the jazz genre within a Network Scotland framework. Ian's initial involvement developed, as these things tend to, into his handling bookings and logistics. . . three years of hard work later, he decided that he was 'up to here' with his day job in the offshore business. In 1986, he downed oiltools and decamped into the music scene permanently. This brave step moved him into small time agency work, "scraping a living supplying bands for private functions and small venues.' Applied Jazz Services, also fostered by the Arts Council, then took Ian on in the capacity of Touring Officer, effectively exposing him to band selection and venue co-ordination. . . indeed, the whole nine yards of tour management. He recalls that for the next 18 months, he "really got stuck into it'. Now more experienced and confident, Middleton freelanced for the Glasgow International Jazz Festival, Mayfest and other major events. The heaviest hitters in modern jazz thus enter his domain, as he negotiated and handled John McLaughlin, Keith Jarrett, Herbie Hancock et al.

His personal jazz train choogled on with his establishing and running the Scottish Jazz Network in the early Nineties. . . funding problems brought SJN's collapse and Ian's return to artist management. Earlier activity on the GIJF justified his appointment as the event's Director. . . Ray Charles, Oscar Peterson and Tony Bennett all succumbed to Glesca's lure. Further development came with co-production of Stefan Gapelli and Carla Bley TV specials for BBC Scotland, and his consultant expertise coming to the Dunfermline and Dunoon jazz fests. After bringing the Jimi Hendrix Exhibition to Glasgow, Middleton returned to Aberdeen at Christmas of 1993. Since then Ibis has handled a diverse roster of artists. . . local folk protectionists/developmentalists Old Blind Dogs rub filing cabinet shoulders with Yes prog guitar magician Steve Howe, National steel guitar definitionist Bob Brozman and renowned jazz guitarist Martin Taylor.

So, the feasibilty of being a player in the contemporary music biz from a rural base many miles distant from London? A decade ago, Jim Allardice at Oily opined "Aye, of course it's possible.' Now that we are deep into the information technological revolution, Ian Middleton is able to run his globe-spanning operation across the telephone, telefax and E-mail waves. At present he has challenges enough to keep him working flat out but he says "At least I am working in a lovely part of the country where the quality of life can't be beat.' On a specifically Aberdeen level, he is keeping Old Blind Dogs barking up interesting trees throughout Europe and the USA. . . but we rattle their kennels elsewhere.

Chapter 18

Ee, they're good - funghis to be with

He is a graduate in microbiology (specialising in protozea, viruses and fungi) who roots amongst the country pancakes in fields around Aberdeen once or twice a year. Afterwards he may stop off to visit some of his former psychiatric nursing colleagues, before heading back down to London with an Asda poly bag full of red capped, white spotted fungi. When he arrives at his home in the big city, he sets down his crop of amanitas between the bookcase and the record rack.

A browse through his book collection reveals a collection of Aldous Huxley's writings on psychedelics, a heavy tome entitled The Anthropic Cosmological Principle, a volume of William Blake's paintings, and Richard Cooper's Guide To British Psilocybin Mushrooms. He purchased the latter from the long defunct Other Record Shop in Aberdeen's Union Street (currently occupied by yet another plastic monument to the Sol and Red Stripe poseur ethic). A spin through the diverse spectrum of vinyl and CD in the music pile will lay bare influential constituents of the techno-pagan cyberpunk that our mystery mushroom harvester produces. The Upsetters, Kraftwerk, Derrick May, Michael Nesmith and Steve Hillage: chilly Eurosynth meets JA scratch riddim, via hippy ambience on the Last Train To Clarksville.

If we have not yet deduced what this is all about, the arrival of his rapper- MC, a diamond geezer London boy with a daft Gazza blonde hairdo, might close the gap. A computer nightmare come to life, techno jesters: the bespectacled ex-indie guitar rocker and the gabby geek. Call them what you will, Eeh, they're good: they're The Shamen and they keep coming on

The early Eighties prototype which featured Colin Angus on bass and keyboards (with brothers Keith and Derek McKenzie on drums and vocals) gave no hints to the music's future direction. The inspiration for the band's name was the epochal track Alone Again Or from Love's 1967 landmark album Forever Changes, but any musical reference to Arthur Lee's laid-back Californian hippydom was well disguised.

Their early efforts uneasily grafted guitar-rock on to lame synth psychedelia, touted around on Scotland's college circuit. AAO dropped a batch of demos on Oily just as the Aberdeen label finally lifted the stylus off its exhausting APB spin: pushing those eloquent Elloners Slater, Roberts and Cheyne to the Brooklyn Zoo had taken its toll. The demos personified a disorientated band crying out for a St Bernard, equipped with a barrelful of direction, to come leaping through their poly-influenced snowdrift. I Only Live was melancholic, moping sub-Soft Cell bedsit angst, sultans of sulk feeling sorry for themselves over rudimentary synth percussion, kind of Kraftwerk-in-progess. Wonderful was a tad cheerier lyrically, but equally introverted musically; Floundering approached conventional pop, catchy in its own unhappy discordant way; Talk built on an understated guitar and echoed vocal with a transcendental hypnotic effect. Oily recognised an uneven promise but didn't feel able to do AAO justice.

Regretfully Oily were obliged to walk away leaving AAO to release their first single in December of 1984 on their own All One Label. The self-financed Drum The Beat (In My Soul) was produced in Edinburgh by Wilf Smarties. Of more importance than the first seven inch biscuit itself was the dialogue which was established between the band and Smarties. Firstly, AAO accessed Wilf's cornucopiac late Sixties psychedelic records, including Syd Barrett period Pink Floyd, and the LSD impregrated Californiania of The 13th Floor Elevators and The West Coast Pop Art Experimental Band. The second sweetie to come out of the Smartie tube was the Aberdeen trio's exposure to Wilf's studio electronic trickery. The spacious and spaced-out result was the single's B side Smartie Edit.

Drum The Beat showed sufficient potential to tempt Polydor, who issued the follow-up Dream Come True/Smarter Than The Average Bear in 1985. The twelve inch version continued the remix electronic experimentation shown on the flip of the first self-financed release: their future style was slowly finding itself. The commercial failure of this single made the band re-evaluate their music, and demos for the next release shifted towards synthesised techno-house. Polydor, however, had lost the thread, promptly terminating their short-lived agreement with AAO. Demos were re-directed to Zippo, an psychedelia specialist indie. Consequently a three track, twelve inch EP was issued on One Big Guitar, Zippo's subsidiary label.

Late in 1985 The Shamen came into being (the name originating from South American Indian magic men, who use hallucinogenic drugs in their quest for spiritual enlightenment). Copies of an exclusive flexidisc The Wayward Wednesday In May Affair were issued with the Skipping Kitten fanzine. Of the Wayward tracks, Four Letter Girl was later to re-appear on the Drop album. The One Big Guitar tracks surfaced in March of 1986 as the They Might Be Wrong, But They Certainly Aren't Wrong EP. The material had been revisited as fresh examples of contemporary psychedelia, gaining the accolade of Sounds single of the week. The release also marked The Shamen's first steps into the world of political comment: Happy Days diatribed against the greed of the Thatcher decade and the Malvinas incident (co-incidentally mirroring the beefs of those damn punko commies Toxik Ephex/Frantik Zimmer back in Aberdeen).

Radio Scotland had the band doing studio sessions that included a take on The Beatles' Baby You're A Rich Man. Alan Morrison joined briefly on keyboards, he was replaced by Peter Stephenson. The band's manager Charlie Cosh set up his own label to handle The Shamen. Taking its name Moksha from a collection of psychedelic essays by Aldous Huxley, releases carried the Soma prefix - another Huxley reference (Soma was a depressant drug used on the subverted proletariat in Brave New World). First off the Moksha blocks was Young Till Yesterday with a cover version of Syd Barrett's Golden Hair on the flip side. Barrett, idiosyncratic creator of the early Pink Floyd's quintessentially English pop-psychedelia, was flaunted as a crucial inspiration. Indeed the twelve-inch version included two blatant in-your-face swathes of such Sydisms: It's All Around, a facsimile of Barrett-era Floyd coupled with Strange Days Dream.

With the hyper-beat of 1987's follow-up Something About You, The Shamen laid young pretender claims to the techno-dance throne occupied by The KLF. Again wandering down Arnold Layne the B side was Syd's Do What You Will. The following month saw the release of the album Drop, drawing its title from the twin themes of nuclear warfare and mind-altering drugs. Drop also rolled-up previous A sides and thus was a staging post of a fast developing style, further demonstrated by the next single Christopher Mayhew Says, a dance rhythm drum-dominated track. Mayhew was an MP who in 1955 dropped mescaline in the presence of a psychiatrist and television cameras, to whom he described his experience. As the BBC deemed resultant footage too controversial for screening, it remained safely locked away for 30 years. The Rise And Fall Of LSD, a 1985 episode of Everyman screened this fabled film for the first time and hence into the arsenal of The Shamen. Their anti-Thatcher campaign continued with the single's B side Shitting on Britain. Derek McKenzie, thus far Colin's co-composer, left The Shamen, expressing his dissatisfaction with the direction the band was taking. Colin found a replacement in his former psychiatric nursing colleague Willie Sinnott (Will Sin) who took over bass guitar. Colin moved to guitar and vocals.

With their profile ascending, they were head-hunted by Scottish and Newcastle Breweries who commissioned a song as part of a McEwans lager advertising campaign that effectively used inventive video work and hip Scottish-connected backing tracks. The Shamen re-fried their earlier Happy Days which got past both the advertising agency and their clients Scottish and Newcastle, and made it to the nation's TV screens. Too late, the lager moguls twigged to the song's anti-Tory lyrics, and were forced to close the adverts down. The Shamen had already exchanged the cheque for readies, leaving S & N with egg on their faces (to the tune of a reputed total £1,000,000) for the aborted promotional debacle. With substantial beer money in their pockets, The Shamen's performances now moved away from a conventional rock or dance gig situation, incorporating samples, DJs, dancers and slide projections - it was now a live experience titled Progeny. 1988's Knature Of A Girl was a distinct hip-hop, skip and a jump into house territory but also brought with it the realisation that their own Moksha label lacked the financial promotional chutzpah to service the band's inexorably snowballing career. Hence the band lodged albeit temporarily with Red Rhino Records, who issued Jesus Loves Amerika on their subsidiary Ediesta label in the Summer of 1988. This tackled US evangelical religious fervour and sampled the sermons of fundamental preachers.

The onset of the UK's smiley-faced acid house phenomenon co-incided with both Peter Stephenson and Keith McKenzie quitting The Shamen: bad timing, as the big time was hiding just around the bend. Willie and Colin moved into a North London squat - getting themselves around the big city's nocturnal scene, they became exposed to the subterranean world of club culture. Effectively this moved the remaining Shamanic duo away from rock rhythms, towards beat dominated dance mentality. Red Rhino's hide proved not so thick as they went bankrupt in the Autumn of 1988, driving the band into the arms of Fiction Records. A collaboration with mix-master Bam Bam saw C 'n' W (Colin and Willie, not country and western) sitting at the mixing desk eyeballing and learning what was going down, rather than Bam Bam doing his electronic magic out of their sight.

When Fiction pushed out the single Transcendental on their Desire label, dance club jocks and punters were at last beginning to pay attention. But both Colin and Willie went back to day jobs as they ran out of money. Will succeeded, through a work acquaintance, in getting a copy of the tape into Demon Records (the parent company of Zippo, with whom they had already worked). The Brentford-based label picked up on the demo, subsequently issued as In Gorbachev We Trust in January of 1989. Again the band's radical political views found expression through tracks like War Prayer and Misinformation, but Gorbachev also saw their dance stall set out with Synergy, complete with Star Trek samples. The album was promoted through wide-spread live appearances on which they collaborated with a female vocalist and mixer Evil Ed. Live gigs culminated in their light-show-enhanced Collision extravaganza at Camden Town's Dingwalls, hitherto a bastion of traditional rock music. In retrospect the pairing of Demon with The Shamen was incongruous. Notwithstanding the intrinsic worth of Demon's support on Gorbachev, the band's fundamentally singles-orientated thrust fell into juxtaposition with the label's more staid AOR albums situation. Indeed Demon operates its own re-issue business through labels like Edsel, distributed through its Blackmail mail order operation.

Thus the band pushed out a bewildering canon of psychedelic synthesised dance material, much of it again subliminally celebratory of hallucinatory drugs, back on their own Moksha label. . . which is roughly where One Little Indian and the big time creep on to the screen. With surprise hits from Reykjavik's finest The Sugar Cubes under their belts, OLI were intimately familiar with The Shamen's work, having engineered In Gorbachev We Trust. This association ignited the band's trajectory to the top, beginning with a dip into de rigueur ambient music entitled Omega Amigo. The band had by now mutated their live work into a fundamentally unique experience bearing no resemblance to traditional rock or pop events. Synergy pulled in a plethora of DJs (including one Mr C, destined to figure centre-stage in the future), brain-bending light show effects, and wall-to-wall sampling seamlessly mixed with band performances. A heady concoction, mixing aural and visual stimuli into one disquieting happening, and all designed purposefully towards enhancing the drugs experience espoused through the music. Omega Amigo enjoyed success on the indie chart, and was bettered by the follow up, Pro>gen, The Shamen's inaugural dent in the national hit parade at number 55. Something was clearly happening, as evidenced by the single Make It Mine, improving their chart showing at number 42 and previewing the new En-Tact album. Dedication to the immediacy of the dance moment was clearly seen by the proliferation of more mixes than the average building site. A bewildering array of twelve inch and CD versions make The Shamen the most difficult artists for serious record collectors to track: one revolutionary idea was to record each live performance and to issue the audience with the tapes at the end of the night. On one such occasion, randomly selected fans were presented with CDs of the show they had just witnessed, hot off the pressing machine: the antithesis of major, copyright- protective acts and labels.

En-Tact marked The Shamen at last selling in commercially viable quantities, and was a cornucopiac multi-faceted collection of contemporary dance influences, encompassing reggae, house, rap and hip-hop aspects. It burst its way into the national LP chart to number 31. The band met with great popularity during a string of national tour dates following their triumphant return from equally manic European engagements. Eventually came the long-awaited summons from Top Of The Pops when Hyperreal, a reconstituted En-Tact cut eventually penetrated the top-30 in March of 1991. For TOTP the band featured Pavla, a black female soul prima-donna, further fuelling public interest in the ongoing national tour. Willie said "We wanted a hit. . . so we started making our pop song singles. When we heard Simon Bates playing Hyperreal every day, we knew we had cracked it.' A newly-spawned legion of Shamanites were desperate for new - nay, any product from their messiahs: thus Pro>gen was re-recorded as the more up-beat Move Any Mountain Pro>gen 91. With a salivating fan base anxiously anticipating its release, the single was a guaranteed smash after what had been a seven- year haul since the inception of Alone Again Or in Aberdeen. The obligatory accompanying promo video was shot in the white heat of Ibiza, the epicentre of European rave and club culture. Top Of The Pops, top of the mountain, top of the world. . . then the unbelievable news: Willie Sinnott was dead, drowned whilst swimming in a hazardous area off Gomera near Tenerife.

. . . .

In the emotionally confused aftermath of Will's untimely and shocking death, Colin was faced with the unenviable challenge of deciding what to do with his beloved Shamen. "Right in the wake of it, those first couple of days after I got the news I thought this is it, The Shamen are finished.' He had lost not only his musical and business partner, but more importantly, his long-time friend and soul mate. In a transparent catharsis, Colin's later song Space Time related how it was "hard living on since you've been gone, there'll always be a place for you in my space time.' Forget that we are talking about mega dance-rock stars. This was an Aiberdeen loon whose best mate had drowned. With the family of his deceased amigo expressing their desire for Colin to continue, he eventually realised that Pro>gen personified Will's hard work and aspirations, this culminating moment should not be discarded. "I realised that The Shamen meant too much to me, to the people who buy our records, and to Will.' The single gave Willie a predictable, albeit posthumous, top-five hit record. A particularly insensitive piece in the NME, concerning Willie's final few days alive, rightly disgusted Colin who swore he would not speak to the magazine again.

North London DJ Richard West (aka Mr C) had met the group in his capacity of host of the Klink Street club, had rapped on the original version of Move Any Mountain and worked on the Synergy project for 18 months. He was now welcomed into the combo's inner circle, becoming a full time Shaman. This move was to alter the band's image and product to the core as they went full-tilt for the dance throne lying vacant since The KLF left the building. Mandatory black vocals fell to Jhelisa Anderson, hitherto singer with Soul Family Sensation. An appropriate coda to the whole Move Any Mountain/Pro>gen episode was Progeny, consisting of no less than 19 remixes of the number and lasting over 100 minutes.

The on-going track record of subsequent singles confirmed that Shamenmania was now something tangible. LSI Love Sex Intelligence was followed into the chart by the band's 15th single, which had the country's entire workforce annoying the hell out of each other by unconsciously chanting Eezer Goode, e's Ebeneezer Goode. This tongue-in-cheeky piece of wordplay combined an obvious pun on the rave set's favoured drug with Mr C's music hall cockerney vocals and rhyming slang pastiche: "Has anybody got any Veras = Vera Lynn's = skins. The record had the desired effect in feeding the country's tabloid media its weekly ration of shock and outrage : is there really such a thing as bad publicity ? Colin made light of the furore. "It all happened in exactly the way we wanted it to - perhaps it wasn't very subtle but I would like to think it was funny.' No barrel of laughs for the parents of young Hanger 13 and Blue Monkey casualties, but the blame for such fatalities cannot be laid at the door of The Prof and The Prat. It was intended to be a piss-take, not 'a paean to Ectasy.' As to the cartoonic nature of Ebeneezer Goode as a song, Colin revealed that he was "re-reading The Pickwick Papers when I wrote it, so its distillation included a lot of Dickensian spirit.'

The groovy hit-laden Boss Drum album, a mongrel from a coupling of crucial happening dance and drug-espousing psychedelic mumbo-jumbo, sired Europe-wide anthems which crossed over into the pop mainstream. A real hodge-podge of mystical bullshit, psychedelia, and sing-along, in-yer-brain doggerel.

An American tour had The Shamen spreading their techno-pagan virus to such isolated and unlikely pockets of cyberpunk resistance as New Jersey, Austin, Dallas, San Antonio and Salt Lake City. Despite topping the US indie chart three times in succession, American club audiences had not quite got the joke. Mr C ticked them off for slam dancing and stage diving in Dallas. . . the next night, the Houston crowd were slow to warm up and scarpered mucho pronto even before the flight-crew of the Starship Shamen had a chance to log the computers off. That same week the Sixties psychedelic message was returned mutated to its birthplace slap in the middle of San Francisco's silicon valley, via the dunghills of Aberdeenshire. At these gigs, The Shamen wheeled on their extra special guest star "a considerable influence on the band. . . Mr Terence McKenna.' He had been the guru of yippie counter-culture, but as he shuffled on stage he came across as an ageing, bearded, suede-sandaled small town polytechnic lecturer. This ethno-botanist and psychedelic pioneer rolled his travelling medicine show into Youthville 30 years ago, proclaiming naturally occurring drugs as being a cure-for-all: old hippies never die, they only lose their hair. . . and most of their dazzies. If you are fond of hospital food, just play Re-evolution (with McKenna's eight minute hypnotically droning incantation) when you're driving.

The Boss Drum LP, issued in September of 1992, bulleted straight into the chart at number three, staying in the top-40 for 27 weeks. The techno-snowball rolled on with singles Boss Drum and

Phorever People at number four and five respectively. By the end of the year, they had racked four top-five smashes and sold over half a million albums world wide. Even the nine minute long Re-evolution, which appeared only on twelve-inch vinyl and limited edition CD (hence receiving virtually no airplay) still entered the pop chart at number 19. After many maverick years in the shadowy ghetto of uncommercial-ity and critical indifference, they became public property overnight on the strength of their translating and crossing over club-culture into mainstream pop.

The rest of 1993 was spent working up the next album and performing at European festivals. The remix EP SOS also lodged itself in the top-20 in October, a month before The Shamen headlined a Freedom Of The City concert in Glasgow's George Square in front of a 12,000 crowd. The event protest-ed against draconian killjoy club curfews introduced by Glesca's city fathers. The Different Drum album carried 'pop' remixes of all of the previous hit singles as well as live favourites, cut up by club and ambi-ent DJs. Keeping up with the information explosion, work commenced on an interactive CD.

Despite The Shamen's unstoppable domination of British dance music, the February 1993 Brit Awards vindictively ignored the band's achievements. After all they are an indie act and hence without the clout and lobbying power of the major international corporate labels. Pop's corporate hierarchic fat cats were mightily miffed that The Shamen succeeded (and how!) without compromise - and on a small label. The Shamen don't have mushroom for such sniping. Summer of 1995 saw the new single Destination Eschaton (the apocalypse and a new beginning) recorded at their Nematon studio. Premiered at Glastonbury in June (with a real drummer rather than the cousin of Frankie Milne's wee Japanese beat-box), and veteran soul diva Victoria Wilson-James on lead vocals, Eschaton came in advance of the Axis Mutatis album. Colin dropped teasing hints throughout Mutatis: depending upon your interpretation, The Shamen's days on this earth (and on their own particular planet) might be numbered. The album was also designed to return the duo's dance credibility, lost via the kiddie-pop, tabloid-fodder Ebeneezer Goode. C and C then hit the studio for 5 days, producing an ambient bass 'n' drums scrawl that is the Hempton Manor album. Your first suspicions after a quick skeg at this title with your pun-detective glasses on are soon confirmed by a listen at tracks like Cannebeo and El-Fin. Not then, a poptastic effort, more another underground-consiliatory measure at a time when the band's time with the label was running out. They fell out with One Little Indian over unauthorised remix releases and over perceived cack-handed promo-tion of the last two albums, both commercial failures. So the 1996 albums Collection and Remix Collection (such retrospection surely totally contradicts Colin's future-looking philosophy) mark the end of The Shamen's stay with OLI. With Colin ever-present on the internet and sponsoring a production of A Midsummer's Night's Dream, and Mr C busy with his clubs and his Plink Plonk label, they will be back. In their own way, in a place and a style and medium of their own chosing.

Alone Again Or-The Shamen ricocheted off half-a-dozen labels before eventually finding a spiritual home with One Little Indian. So their mega-selling populo-techno dance anthems appeared on a London-based label, albeit one of the most credible and success-worthy indies. After Oily stopped flow-ing in Aberdeen, the city was bereft of its own record label until dance music champions Eoan Pritchard and Chris Cowie came to the rescue with their Hook and Bellboy labels. Chris had done some record engineering and Eoan had played guitar in early Eighties bands Gillian Silver and The Hungry Freaks. These drew from Echo and The Bunnymen, The Teardrop Explodes and the jangly Rickenbacker Long Ryders as influences. Eventually Eoan (nicknamed Elvis) turned his attention to DJing, being caught up in the widespread post-Acid House DIY plague. "A lot of people suddenly twigged that the dance music flooding in from the USA and Europe could be done without expensive conventional recording studio equipment.' A boom in small-scale labels came through the realisation that (apart from talent and inno-vation), a conventional PC, keyboard, sampler, mixing desk and DAT machine constituted the total nec-essary hardware. "It's so basic you wouldn't believe it.'

Elvis put out signals on the Aberdeen club grapevine, seeking similar-minded enthusiasts to pool their ideas and resources, towards establishing a Granite City dance label. A resultant convention of some 50 interested musicians, DJs and musos established a discrete scene of its own making, co-operative and self-supportive. The duo struggled to interest a record company in the material they co-recorded, and so decided "We'll do it ourselves.' With Elvis working in an Aberdeen record shop, he was party to a plethora of indie distributors, although their first deal proved ill-advised. "Because we didn't have the cash to set things up under our own steam, we got into bed with Great Asset. The deal was that we sent them the DAT tape and they took care of pressing, distribution: in fact, the whole thing. We basically had no more to do, other than to help by spreading the word as best we could, and wait for the money to arrive.' Great Asset took Hook's first two releases: Give Myself To You by Party On Plastic (Elvis and Chris) and Barimba by Bubble Up (Andy Adams from Atmosphere Lighting and Sound). Unfortunately, it was Great Asset that went bubble up: they had shifted 2,000 Hooks by the time they went bankrupt, but none of the cash found its way back to Aberdeen. This set Elvis and Chris back on their heels for the next eight months.

Through a friend of a friend they found a manufacturing service prepared to extend some credit. So the finances of Keep On Pumping It Up by Brother Sledge (Chris Cowie's pun on Sister Sledge, geddit?) actually worked and brought in a few pounds. Tapes under consideration took a more experimental twist away from Hook's straight ahead dance direction. To offer a left-field arena, a second imprint (Bellboy) arrived, working hand-in-hand with Hook. Bellboy's first message came from underground techno-boffins Skintrade (Kev Gunn and Dave Dunbar). Their Uman/Subuman brought them a promising contract with the Glasgow-based Soma label.

Thus far, neither label has generated funds of any real substance but the guys keep the faith. Sales may only number a thousand or so, but Further Hooks and Bellboys starring dab-hands of dance dub have featured The Turnbull ACS, Canyon (Andy Atmosphere again), Wavelab and Inertia (Keith Nicholson, from Portlethen), The Scan Carriers (Cowie and Nicholson), Excabs, and Ian Elvis Pritchard himself. The current idea is to consolidate on a solid foundation of DJ support before (hopefully) progressing to a more wide-spread appeal. . . it would help initially if the paperwork had a filing cabinet to live in, rather than a shoe-box under Chris's bed. The releases so far already reflect great musical progress, and a July 1995 sales/distribution deal with RTM had the potential for curing the cash flow blues. Having already outstripped Oily's output, it may not be too long before we have an influential record syndicate here in Aberdeen.

Aberdeen band Bondage had formed part of the city's zillion-miles-per-hour punk sub-culture. Drummer Tommy Reid moved to London in 1980, soon to be followed by guitarist/vocalist Jim Shepherd and rhythm guitarist Adam Sanderson. They therefore strode different London streets concurrently with Alone Again Or/The Shamen, re-inventing themselves as The Jasmine Minks: a pop group name consummate in its exotica. . . but the romance evaporates when its source is known. The lads were (in their own opinions) minkers and Jim had lived in Jasmine Terrace. Hence they were reborn in the big city (where it would take a month to explain what a minker is) as The Jasmine Minks. Initially they rehearsed and messed about at Alaska Studios in Waterloo, sending their demo tape into NME's Playback feature. Alan McGee somehow laid hands on the tape and came to see the Minks going through their paces.

McGee relocated to London in 1982 from East Kilbride on a mission to replicate Postcard Records' hip, mobile, media smart and faultlessly cool chic: in short, he pursued the holy grail of the perfect pop single. At the time when McGee's Creation Records label was merely an un-realised, cherished ideal, his associate Dick Green ran a Wardorf Street club The Living Room. With the venue prospering, the record label concept transferred from McGee's mind to shiny black vinyl. . . it took its name and inspiration from Eddie Phillips' Sixties band Creation. Indeed McGee's own combo Biff Bang Pow were titled after a Creation LP.

Early recruits to Creation included Primal Scream, The Jesus And Mary Chain and the pre-KLF Bill Drummond. Londoner Martin Keener joined The Minks on bass as they cooked up an individualistic pop stew at studios in Kingston. Creation signed up the JMs as its third vinyl act with their single Think in 1984. An NME scribe also freelanced for rock publications in Los Angeles: her raving reviews led to frequent plays of Think on college radio stations, and to correspondingly healthy sales. However, Tom-Tom Reid admits to bafflement as to why, of all people, the Japanese record-buying public took such a shine to The Minks (who kept busy on the live performance scene, putting in over 200 gigs in a year throughout the UK and continental Europe). Adam left in 1986 after the second album Sunset, to be followed by a succession of guitarists. Aberdonian musicians were brought down to play on JM records (Foosky fae Torry, Derek Christie and Walter Duncan), not because they were superb technical players, rather because they were all known to the band.

Tommy honestly admits that they never made any money despite releasing four albums and four singles in a five year period with the final LP Another Age selling about 20,000 copies. "Sure we made enough to get by but we used mates from home as roadies, so a lot of the cash went on paying them and went back into the recordings.' Refreshing, straightforward talk: "No doubt about it, we could have done better if we were interested in licking up to certain people, but that just wisnae our thing. We just went in, made the records, and played our gigs. Certain bands were always hanging about the office but that wasna' the way we did things. Basically we were just a bunch of mates interested in playing music, getting drunk, and having a good time.'

The eponymous Jasmine Minks LP was recorded in Iain Slater's bedroom studio, another example of keeping it in the family. "Why not use somebody we knew, or at least knew of, from our own backyard? We were at Iain's for a fortnight, it was better that he got a little bit of money rather than it go to complete strangers.' The final JM gig, together with APB, took place at Aberdeen's Pelican Club at New Year of 1989. For London bassist Martin it was his Scottish hogmanay: he still hasn't recovered. A couple of years back Tommy and some mates played a few Paul Weller and Jam numbers at a company do, and were amazed at the rapturous response to their set. "It was just done for a laugh, but it went really well.' On the strength of that opening success, further gigs took place, each better received and more hansomely-paid than the previous. The rest of the guys began taking it a bit more seriously, talking about wearing re-creationist Jam-mod threads. "It was getting too strange for me so I bailed out.' Now operational as The Paul Weller Experience, the band don't have the Aberdonian on drums. "No way', says Tom, "I offered Weller a spot with The Tommy Reid Experience and he turned it down. I'm nae taking second best for naebody.'

THE SHAMEN
L-R Will, Colin

Chapter 19

Boom town brats

"Nelson Mandela, there's only one Nelson Mandela." He never scored four against Celtic or three against Rangers but Aberdeen's councillors saw fit to give the South African president the freedom of our city. Nothing against the guy, but this accolade was more than they ever did for Frankie 'Goes to Fusion' McDougall. To paraphrase Private Eye editor Ian Hislop, if that's justice I'm Canaan Banana.

Fortunately not all of the city fathers' decisions have been as bizarre and one of their most progressive ideas was the institution of the Woodside recording studio, with its related City Arts record label. Operating as a free facility under the auspices of GRC's library service, the studio's prime raison d'etre was the furtherance of the local spoken and musical word, fostering development of music, poetry and prose. To this admirable end, studio facilities (replete with the services of recording engineer Stewart Diack), were available to musicians with a will to develop their skills. The sole entry requisite is a basic level of competence and an evidenced desire to make the project work to the best of the performers' ability. The studio also lends guitars, keyboards and drum machines (Frankie Milne's little Japanese employee doing a homer?) to its recordees. The City Arts label came into play when recorded work was deemed worthy of exposure to the general public. Such releases were funded jointly by the artists and from the department. Subsequent distribution and marketing is accommodated through libraries and other council operated outlets. . . buy your jock 'n' roll as you furtively sneak your weekly Catherine Cookson fix out the door. Ever-supportive of local music, 1 Up have stocked City Arts material. . . however, Union Street majors HMV and Virgin 'aint shown much interest.

The City Arts catalogue is an eclectic mix encompassing country Doric material (Willie Kemp's King O' The Cornkirsters and Stanley Robertson's Nippit Fit) through the traditionalist music of The Guagers' The Fighting Scot and Aberdeen Folk Club's A Celebration, to contemporary rock music. The latter is represented by Blah!'s album Or What?, Sound Control's So Good EP and an eponymous release by She Said. On the Aberdeen Rock Volume One album the better participants in the city's 1991 Battle Of The Bands were afforded studio experience. A mixed bag and perhaps a once in a lifetime opportunity for Dreamworld, Satyr, Menage, Lower The Tone and Something Reasonable to commit their performances to tape.

City Arts panned two nuggets when prospecting through their Aberdeen Rock artists. The Other Side, with their track Got This Feeling are graduates of the Sutherland Brothers/Difford-Tilbrook/Crowded House school of glorious melodic pop. A Cinderella amongst numerous Ugly Sisters, they never did meet a Prince Charming major label A & R man. The Other Side's driving force was lead guitarist, vocalist and song-writer Steve Insch who took bassist Gary Bennett, dual lead guitarist Scott Butler and drummer Steven Mackie to places which other harmonic rock outfits cannot reach.

Blah!'s City Arts metal rock album . . . Or What? carries the self-effacing message "listening to this is only marginally preferable to eating your mother-in-law's occasional table.' Well. . . straddling an uneasy line between Ric/Ade's Bad News and St Hubbins/Tufnel/Smalls' Spinal Tap, it doesn't sit too comfortably on the lugs. Far be it from the author, who cannae carry a tune in a bucket, to cast (Rolling) stones at musicians of any description, buuuttt. . . Blah! would have been better-served if they had recruited a proper vocalist - singing in key is surely a pre-requisite egg in this omelette. Guitarist Steve 'High Tower' Quinn and bassist Steve 'The Shark' Jeffrey play some competent, if stereotyped, heavy rock-type shapes. Whichever way you slice it, their tonsilary efforts don't quite cut the cake. With yet another Steve on keyboards - 'El Kapitani' Davidson - and Dave 'The Hatt' Wilson on drums, the general result crosses early Pallas with Wayne's World. Never mind chaps, keep the faith and concentrate more on High Tower's bluesey guitar work which is outstanding on the track Big Vern. It is better to have rocked to the best of your rockability than not to have rocked at all.

Out of Aberdeen's Eighties punkos Toxik Ephex came Frantik Zimmer (worth a mention for the name alone) who went on from Aberdeen Rock Volume One to record Liars, Leaders and The Law, a stirring acoustic-electric-violin album. LLATL is home to Come on a' You Folk, an impassioned anti-poll tax rant with a beat to make a haddock tap its feet. The Zimmers' distinctly Scottish writing was shared between the Wilkinson bros, Dave and Fred (erstwhile Inspector Blake) and Bill Henderson. Their Frantik political stance finds expression in Determined In The South (a centralised London government tirade gutsier than anything ever emoted by the SNP) and Privatise The Army (an ironic comparison of the worth and resources of the Falklands and Scotland to the English parliament: oil reserves and livestock outweighing the value of the native peoples of these countries). The Military continues the theme of sabre-rattling, gung-ho vote-winning gunboat diplomacy (as experienced by the 250 British lads and four times that many young Argentinian conscripts who died in the South Atlantic. While generals sit in Easy Street, you all stand and weep. . . the bloody military. Not all plain sailing however during the recording process as the Zimmers waited in the queue until "some wifie had finished her accordion record'.

If London groups have difficulties in enticing record company A & R reps to come talent scouting, it has therefore been forever impossible for Aberdeen bands to compete. Oily Records in the late Seventies and early Eighties did much to raise the profile of Granite City rockers: for the same reason the Battle Of The Bands provided showcase gigs featuring as many city bands as possible. The idea was to maximise publicity for the event and educate the London music Mafia about the Aberdeen scene. As veteran agent Gordon Hardie related earlier "just head North after the Forth Bridge and you will find Aberdeen'. BOTB catalysed the vibrant band scene in Aberdeen, proportionally the most active and creative in the UK at that time.

The 1992 BOTB/Big Bang event took place at Bonkers where nine combos showed their worth in an ego-free running order being decided by drawing lots from a pub ashtray. One assumes it had been emptied first? Such was the response from Aberdeen's aspiring groups that overflow events swamped the Pelican Club and Cafe Drummond with no less than 19 combos appearing in one night: Andy Warhol's promised 15 minutes of fame, realised in Market Street and Belmont Street. Organised by Mea Culpa's Greg Herrera Battle Of The Bands became a kind of Opportunity Knocks without Greeny Hue's clapometer and insincerity. Those exposing themselves artistically included soul act The Big Blue, hefty indie guitar wielding One God Universe, rockers Living With Alice and hippy-jazz-rap dance exponents Greenblade. One gig by the latter at the Pelican Club saw them billed by promoter Pazz as "undertaking a prestigious tour of America, performing radio station PAs and live appearancess'. This totally untrue, complete hype generated more interest than "just returned from a tour of Fraserburgh and Peterhead.'

A discernable Aberdeen sound became detectable in 1993 with a crop of thrash-folk bands, and the smart money was on The Lorelei to cut the mustard. . . Geno Washington 1966: 'Hand clappin' foot stompin' funky butt - live!'. . . The Lorelei 1995: 'Ear bashin' brain scramblin' punky folk - Jive!'

Vocalist and guitarist Martin Watson got together with bass player Jonny Palmer around Easter of 1990 and was joined by guitar maestro Keith 'Beefy' Allardyce and William Leys on fiddle, mandolin, banjo, recorder and anything else he could get a tune out of. The following year saw The Lorelei complete when Keith Grant brought his drums and moothie and Diane Beattie her viola.

Following their Big Bang appearance a showcase gig at King Tut's in Glasgow brought the band to the attention of M8 magazine, picking up on the track Wendy Frenzy for their prestigious and selective cassette issue. Next to succumb to The Lorelei's spell was Radio One DJ Jackie Brambles who plugged Wendy regularly on her afternoon show. Glasgow record company KRL (boarding kennels also of Aberdeen folkies Old Blind Dogs) signed the band, cutting their debut album Headstrong at Glasgow's CaVa Studios (Linguistic guidance note for non-Francophiles amongst our readers: Cava = fit like en Francais. . . Merci = the tide has come in. . . Tomber le garcon? = Fa's the boy?. . . Aperitif = your granny's dentures. . . Oui = small).

Released on KRL's Lochshore label Headstrong is an ebulliently-performed collection of Martin's songs. Hell, what do these guys play? Rootsy Caledonian stomp. . . heavy metal folk. . . punk ceilidh? As if anyone gives two poops. . . if their Wendy and Perfect World don't get you a-heuching and a-teuching then you must be Nigel from Milton Keynes. Wendy is a hormonally-saturated plain daft girl-crazy spasm. . . which almost segues into the We'll Mak The Creel Row opening of Perfect World. . . an uproarious revelry, getting blootered with friends and strangers, with a beat that really kicks. Still on the upbeat comes Humour with its skanking rhythm and Martin telling us there's too much frownin' going on. The few eerie seconds of Last Leviathan brakes the pace for Hold; lyrically mature and musically both smooth and punchy, wandering into anthemic Caledonian stadium rock territory. Donny is the thought-provoking tale of a child escaping parental abuse. An all-round brammer of a debut. Live appearances played to an audience of Clangers (long-haired baggy tee-shirted grungeos and highly skilled human pyramid-builders) for whom sheeping out is the order of the day, rather than quiet, reverential listening. Seemingly having covered themselves with glue before running through their grannies' wardrobe, on stage The Lorelei come across as a freak show: Little Billy Goat Gruff meets Morticia Addams round at Hagar The Horrible's house. The barber-allergic Flossie had more hair than a truck-load of mattresses (if he ever went missing it would take the police months to comb the area. After a fortnight they might well find not only his school cap but also Shergar and Lord Lucan). Under Rob Swan's management their gig circuit encompassed Shetland, Skye and Arran. In December of 1994 The Lorelei were off to London with Covent Garden's Rock Garden, a starting showcase for innumerable bands over the years, on their itenarary. A second Lochshore CD Progression revealed a tangental 1996 direction, derived from songs being recorded immediately after their inception and from a different set of instruments being used, the last lot being stolen from the van.

Coming up fast on the inside rail behind them in the 1995 Aberdeen Music Stakes were The Dawntreaders. Formed late in 1991 they took their name from a C S Lewis Narnia book and began working up an original, category-defying set ('Cover versions are too difficult') at a farm in the Aberdeenshire hinterland, with only sheep and cows to decibely annoy (baa-roque moosic?) they debuted at Aberdeen's Caesar's Palace that November. Known to friends, associates and agents Active Events as the DTs, John Martin and Danny Hawthorn twanged and sang, Darren Alexander and Tony Stephen played drums and bass respectively.

After playing live on Radio Scotland's commendable Beat Patrol in May of 1993, and with copies of their debut single Today/Time (both later reprised on the self-financed ten-track eponomous cassette recorded at Crathes studio) in their hippers, they were off on the blue canoe to Shetland. There, they appeared at the North Star and the Brae Hall, that cauldron of sweaty bodies.

In tandem with these performances came The Cannonball, a locally-focused fanzine written by Tony. This developed into the Aberdeen band cooperative self-help project Cannonball Collective, which, in the face of apathetic Granite City promoters, staged two gigs at The Station Hotel. The Canonball survived as a newsletter, maintaining contact between band and fans.

A terrific support slot to Big Country at the Lemon Tree on May day of 1994 led to the DTs continue throughout the Highlands with Stewarty and the boys. The roll continued when Radio One jock Mark Goodier had them on his road show as part of the station's Glasgow Sound City event. An ecstatic reception from the 7,000 crowd saw Goodier go into print imploring the big labels to check out The Dawntreaders. The CD EP Talk released nation-wide in the spring of 1995 saw them in good stead for a final push for the premier league of British indie pop. Opening with Close Your Eyes . . . (and then you'll find, tomorrow will be beautiful) they hit a lovely riff and a superbly bouncy performance. Hell, there's even a false ending, just to hack off DJs. The second track, titled Save but lyrically hooked as We should talk about it is a 90 mph melodic cracker. Normally the author avoids cliches like the plague, but this one is a must for roaring down the Stonehaven road with the windows and sun roof open, keeping a wary eye out for Kincardine's finest in their jam sandwich. Leaving the best till last, with John Says The DTs come up with a pop record approaching perfection, the freshest sound for yonks. Understated and controlled, it builds to a mesmerising guitar riff. After demo-ing half a dozen new tracks which finished in the bin, The Dawntreaders hi-tailed it to the 200- capacity Cafe Au La Plage in a Paris arrondissement. This proved to be the first step in the group's European expansionist phase, soon heading into the former USSR (together with The Fabiens) to play a Chernobyl tenth anniversary remembrance gig in Gomel, Belarus. Danny's brother lives in Boston and fixed a solitary gig there for the band. The venue was a club owned by Aerosmith, and the trip developed into a handful of gigs. The guys' collective gang mentality and dedication has brought with it a maturity that makes their music sparkle. The highs of John Says are maintained with the remarkable Puppy album, a rounded coming-of-age that transcends their previous Aberdeen DIY situation. . . if I wore a hat, I would hang it on these boys making it to the next, well-deserved dimension. You'll do for me, DTs.

St Valentine's Day 1992, and the aptly-named guitarist Charlie Love sits down with long-time mucker and song-writing collaborator John Anderson, their previous work in self-confessed 'dodgy' heavy metal bands having ended a year hence. The duo's rough four track demos were sufficiently encouraging for Chas to assemble a band to perform the songs. With the recruitment of Red on bass, Keith Beacom on drums, Karen Hughes on fiddle, and Anna Towler on vocals, April '92 brought the premiere appearance by The Dreaming at Cannonball Two in Aberdeen's Station Hotel, first on stage before The Dawntreaders, Missing Jane and The Lorelei. (The latter band, admitted Charlie, were an inspiration to his own combo). Having gone down a bomb at this, their debut performance, they have ignited in everlouder detonations since. The follow-up show down at The Neptune Bar, packed tighter than Ian Donald's wallet: no room for dancing. . . the PA expired due to heat in the room. After a shower and a liberal scoosh of deodorant, The Dreaming trod the well-travelled road to Mathewson Mansions for a new demo.

John, feeling that he personally couldn't match the band's collective commitment, left at this point, being replaced by James Cree. The culmination of a year's perpetual gigging came at Glasgow King Tut's A & R showcase. . . which helped sell out the original run of 250 demo tapes, with a second batch of 250 also going before Christmas of 1992. (What the band's bewildered grannies and aunties thought of that year's personally-autographed presents, God only knows).

A live recording at The Lemon Tree filled one side of the album Let The Feast Of Fools Begin, instrumental in the biggest break thus far in their buoyant career. Exactly a year after their formation, someone tipped Charlie the wink that Runrig's manager was involved in booking acts for that year's Scottish Fleadh. The opportunist Chas dropped copies of the band's work through Marlene Ross' letterbox, and then accidentally (?) bumped into her that night at a gig. Once Marlene got her knowledgeable lugs around their tapes and caught them live, she pushed hard on the Fleadh's promoters Regular Music, and was able to offer the group a spot on the bill.

The Fleadh on Glasgow Green saw The Dreaming kicking up a storm, at the end of their set the crowd screamed for more and booed when it wasn't forthcoming. Schmoozzing backstage with the likes of Van Morrison, Aztec Camera, The Pogues, and of course Runrig, it was a helluva thing in terms of achievement for this group less than 18 months in the making. Marlene said "They're a local band, I was just trying to help them on to the next step of the ladder. They did the business on the day.'

Runrig now had the perfect support act: The Dreaming opened for them on the North of Scotland Castles And Canvas tour, which came to Aberdeen's Duthie Park with a crowd of 4,500 music fans and 80 terrified ducks.

A gig at The Venue in Elgin was marked by the return to the live arena of Waterboy Mike Scott, playing four numbers with the group. This was Scott's first rock show after a long period of inactivity, most of his time being spent at the Finhorn Foundation. Doubtless mixing in such exalted company broadened The Dreaming's horizons: the veritable Whole Of The Moon. . . and by now Feast Of Fools had shifted over 1,000 copies.

Whilst Charlie had registered the band's name with the Mechanical Copyright Protection Society, a Sassenach version had already signed a music publishing deal (as far back as 1988): welcome Tinderbox in place of The Dreaming. Important gigs at London's Mean Fiddler and on Radio One's Sound City '94 kept the momentum going, followed by an appearance at the Tarlair Festival in Macduff (in aid of The Big Issue magazine).

The 1995 CD The Haunting does the band proud: a well-conceived piece of work, from its thoughtful music to its packaging and art work. Kicking off with the drum driven Roads, Tinderbox rant about the inequities of life, taking in the Irish problem, black-white conflict, winos in Union Terrace and young squaddies sent off to war. Obvious targets perhaps, but, with Charlie's vocal and Carol's plaintive fiddle, it works. Killing Time is a feel-good, everything in the garden is rosy number. Sure, we could all be out there climbing bloody mountains, but what the hell, there's always tomorrow: I'm doing fine, I'm killing time, with a teuchter hoe-down groove. Neither folk nor blues, Shadows is a laconic introspective lonely, lonely beguiler. . . the mood of which is challenged immediately by Thorn In My Pride, a return to jig tempo traditionalist-ish Caledonian Aberdeen thrash-folk, and a sideways glance at Annie Lennox. For unfathomable reasons, Drowning Girl drags you into the undercurrent of 1983 (A Merman I Should Turn To Be). . . saturation decompression to surface from these deeps. . . for an instant Townsendesque chords threaten, but James admirably resists the temptation to give his guitar arm the full windmill effect. Connected but unconnected comes the Hendrix Seattle grunge blue noise feedback intro to I Want Out: yep, we've all been there Charlie, had enough of the whole thing. . . but as Tinderbox belt out hoodrum-hodrum rhythms, they've said it their own way. Parallel universe stuff next on Shelter, as Jerry Lee Lewis jams with Motorhead in a remote Highland loch full of whisky, where Aly Bain is having a dip: heads-down, no-nonsense Pictish boogie. . . for Jack And Diane read Martha And Johnny, at first glance a pleasant Mellencampist poppy thing until the lyrics hit. And on it goes to the end of a fine album. Charlie's beloved Tinderbox later underwent massive surgery with Jensen, Keith and Anna all firing bullets at the raven. Love stuck with it and the new band are a younger, more vibrant demonstration of his dream. Tinderbox, keep your powder dry and your vision as big as it obviously is, and who knows. . . ?

Aberdeen thrash-folk: "Oh no, not another fiddle band'. . . but other things were happening. A couple of blocks down from Aberdeen's guitar and fiddle rootsy stomp Mafia were those indie heavy grunge-punkos One God Universe, born at the same time as The DTs. Their self-financed maxi-EP/mini-LP six months later was hailed in Byrdian terms by M8 as being "Shrapnel-splintered, tension-twisted, seven songs long and eight miles high.' Two years progressed with a heavy live workload in the North East, Edinburgh and Glasgow. The new demo spurred M8 on again. "Total aural assault, mind blowing, man.' Come mid-1993 vocalist Matt Lynch was on board, soon to be joined by defecting Tinderbox/The Dreaming guitarist James Cree, taking Ru Seger's place.

OGU were on the Balmoral beat in 1994 to cut their Schiffer album under the protective gaze of Niall Mathewson. Metal magazine Raw rates Schiffer "A brooding scowl of a record, there is a musical literacy at play, keeping the whole collection sounding sussed.' Following a night club football hero-worship conversation with a band member, Aberdeen's favourite Yorkshire terrier Lee Richardson played drums on several jam sessions and dual-percussionist gigs. He was then booked to play on a couple of the album's tracks. Why not, he was accustomed to being booked every Saturday anyway. Must have been nice for Rico to get his kicks this way rather than from the likes of Peter Grant and Stuart McColl. One man Arts Council Jim Gellatly consistently play-listed OGU, who also pitched up on Radio Scotland and STV's Chartbite show.

These universal soldiers were a psychiatrist's dream. When his shopping at M & S was done, bassist Steve Morrison was rumoured to engage in S & M: amongst other things, he holds a first in English, specialising in the works of the Marquis de Sade. The others ran when he suggested a whip-round. Guitarist Ross Brockie's previous employment as a rat-catcher almost moved him to commit sewercide before his promotion to becoming a dishwasher in Greece. A most counter-productive venture - he intends to use hot water and Fairy Liquid next time. The tonsular Lynch was a certified schizophrenic: don't worry Matt, that makes four of us. Drummer Gordon Smith, reputedly Aberdeen's prime enthusiast of sunshine, cider and kebabs was a big fan of Doner Summer. Strange that such light-hearted player profiles fell out from a band making such unnerving music. The opening bars of lead track Orcadid welcomes us to OGU: a cavernous, tempestuous cacophany, its disturbed, claustrophobic total-guitar scream redolent of Hendrix himself. Sliding, Ugly Stick. . . scars, not songs. Shudder-making lyrics. . . Waste briefly deceives that the nightmare is over, Matt's vocals coming on like the bastard offspring of Ian McCulloch and Scott Walker. . . then the rage begins again, demento-madness undiminished. Impossible to catagorise, you had to listen and quake yourself. Since being forced out of Scottish football by the baying hyenas of Ibrox and Parkhead, Rico kept in touch with the band, organising gigs for them in England. Tragically it appears that the band's failure to secure a record label deal ultimately proved fatal. Guitarist Ross has gone on to pub-band Trousered with Martin Lorelei. Depressing, isn't it. . . One God Universe were great contenders, but finished up on the canvas.

With a line-up of Keith Gerrard, Iain Mutch, Mark Slater and the two Del boys, Millar and Butters (girlfriends, Marge and Flora), The Fabians retraced the glory days of Eighties funkateers APB, switching on West coast Norway to a new Aberdeen sound. Successful amped-up gigs were played in Bergen night-spots Hulen, The Garage and Trokkeriet, whilst an acoustic set went down well with the coffee at Cafe Opera. Keith Geddes says it was an enjoyable if expensive experience (notwithstanding a half litre of local ol at 40 NOKS a glass: 80/- ale in more ways than one) a subsequent date at Stavanger's Phoenix "is a bit of a blur.') Spring of 1995, The Fabs were again on the piste, this time in Albach Austria - their manager is a ski instructor who picked up on the band during his travels. A bad start to their relationship when he told the band he was a tobogganist: his confusion was profound when Keith gave him a fiver and asked for 20 Benson & Hedges.

Their March 1995 Crathes-recorded CD Locomotive saw the band becoming logo louts: it carries a band emblem to drive the Ford motor corporation's copyright lawyers apoplectic. The magic contained within the laser logic of their shiny silver beermat owes some to Americana: they can play country as in Texas, not Turriff. First stop down the trail, Come Undone will have you stompin' the dust off your shit-kickin' cowboy boots, somewhere equidistant between Poco and What Am I Doing Hanging Round) . . . .Dogs Day is a kennely-crafted gem, taking its lead again from a yee-hah ! head 'em up and move 'em out scenario. Then we are into the warm, melodic guitar rock (a riff that sticks like shite to a blanket) of Concentrate. Lovely indie guitar gives way to closing falsetto backing vox, and it dissolves into sub-Don't You Feel Like Crying pleas of Cry cry, baby baby, cry cry cry. She's All Mine is an exhilarating burst of Beep beep yeah pop nonsense and a mumbled vocal style (which Elvis Aaron Presley in his lean, mean Sun glory would have been proud of). Going Under and the unplugged Saturday morning ABC minors sing-along Sniffy's Last Stand are the final tracks on a fresh, uplifting debut. . . it all ends with an ultimately satisfying thump on the body of the acoustic guitar. Impressive musicianship, appealing honestly vulnerable vocals throughout, and terrific songs. The boys donned pointy horrible Hagar hats and set sail for Norway and Sweden, having already co-participated with The Dawntreaders in a short tour of the former Russia. The refreshing thing about The Fab Five is the realisation they bring that swathes of current young musicians have skipped the crap played on the radio during their formative years. Instead we are hearing dedicated, informed rock with precedents in classic Sixties music, (inspired by but not imitative of). They create something of sparkling articulacy in the process.

This applies to none more than it does to Coast, who are fighting the big fight in London. The band quote influences like The Beatles, Rachmaninov and Stravinski. NME waxed lyrical "As precise as they are reckless, their set is founded upon unflappable chord wizardry, topped off with tunes so startlingly attractive you wouldn't think twice about eloping with them'. . . weeelll. . . how long before Coast get themselves into the pop mainstream and the self same music paper starts throwing rocks at them? Originally formed on Christmas 1989, it was two years before their debut single Headlight shone out. M8 raved "A criminally neglected but highly recommended and bruisingly cool self-financed single.' The nucleus of Coast is lead guitarist Paul Fyfe and vocalist/guitarist Daniel Young: they found it difficult to settle on a fixed line-up over the next three years. Finally they suggested to bassist Mark Lawrence that he join them for their move to London, where the last piece of the jigsaw fell into place with the recruitment of Dundonian drummer John Russell (he left Iain Slater and Glenn Roberts even more Loveless.)

Under the sterling managership of Julian de Takats (you canna knock his credentials, having scored high with Deacon Blue: stick wi' me, loons, and yer tackets'll niver roost) they have concentrated on perfecting their live set from their Harringay base. Independent label Sugar beat off several majors to bring Coast into their roster, the historic signing taking place at a sub post office in Llanfair Caereinion. Their first lump of Sugar was Polly's Domain, recorded at Foel Studios in Wales by the hot team of Anjoli Dutt and Mark Coyle. Four-piece string section arrangements inevitably shadow prime Beatles but Polly is much, much more. Next out was Slugs/Shag Wild/Pretend, the middle track relating to a freaky on-the-beach sexification that resulted in Danny's hospitalisation (bloody sand gets everywhere). The headline track on Now That You Know Me/Tender Cage/She Wears A Frown is Dan's cleansing-of-the-soul after being a right bastard to a girl who ditched him. All the time these songs are deeply beautiful, sculpted modern music, with heavenly instrumental and vocal performances to break your heart. The Melody Maker 1996 Shaker Maker campaign saw Coast touring with Bawl, Puressence and The Gyres. The March 1997 single Do It Now and album Big Jet Rising might just provide lift-off, produced by Steve Brown (Manic Street Preachers) and Paul Schroeder (Stone Roses, The Verve and Dodgy). The band have denied that they are arrogant. They have been subject to physical violence back in Aberdeen, and that's a bloody disgrace. Its quite simply their inate confidence that attracts trouble from lesser intellects. Jealous or what?

With names out of Tales By The Riverbank, they didn't come any heavier than Fluff (bass), Taff (drums) and Sid (guitar): where's Bobtail? Korpse are a grind-metal experience like nuthin' you ever heard before. Drummer Taff says "When we first formed we wanted something brutally straightforward in a deathly sort of way. We progressed and couldn't really be classed as death metal (more Cloverleaf than cloven-hoofed), simply because our lyrics didn't go on about death or anything horrific.' Maybe not but I will tell you this, boy - this stuff is more intense than Billy Smart's Circus.

For live work they were complemented by second guitarist Graeme Crawford, formerly of fellow

Aberdeen combo Inextremis. Led by Nick Williams, Inextremis split up at the beginning of 1995, playing their final gig at Stonehaven Town Hall. OK, so its not farewell Cream at the Albert Hall.

Sid and Taff had been in Circle Of Tyrants, an Eighties thrash metal outfit. Korpse's inspiration came from the latter genre, and from the early Nineties grind and hardcore bands on the Earache label. They single out Voivod (relatively unknown despite having six albums to their credit) as spurring on their own efforts. Formed in Spring of 1990, Korpse's first gig took place at the Pinegrove in Elgin. Crathes conjuror Niall Mathewson produced their first demo Mauler in 1991 at the Mill Of Hirn studio, where Korpse returned the following year for the single XR/Rusted, leading in turn to the CD album Pull The Flood. Produced by Paul Johnston and the band at Rhythm Studios in Bideford-On-Avon, the album displays that, unusually for this morbid necrophantic mutancy, Korpse didn'tt rely solely upon one leaden repetitive riff. High density main guitar lines are the very nature of the beast, but melody was an integral part of their music. . . and they could actually play their instruments: (Taff on Pearl drums and Paiste / Zildjian cymbals, Fluff on BC Rich bass and Trace Elliot amps, and Sid on a traditional rock combination of Stratocaster and Marshall). I know your voice is supposed to be that way Fluff old chap, but caustic soda works a treat with the drains at home. Latest reports from the morgue suggest that Korpse are dead. But have they been interred forever?

Light years away from such guitar, bass and drums set-up were Skintrade with their keyboards and computer techno revisionism. Having begun amassing hardware six years ago, it is only since 1993 that Kev Gunn and Dave Dunbar have been in a position to produce their own work in one, self-contained operation. Coming originally from the dispassionate Eurosynth regime of Kraftwerk, it was the Detroit and Chicago house groove of 1987 which planted the germ of Skintrade's techno ethic, nurtured down at The Pelican Club in Market Street with the connivance of DJ Titch. Three years back, under their previous nom de musique Rejuvenate, their track Utopia appeared on Future Music magazine's CD, setting the pace for the inaugural Skintrade twelve inch single Subuman/Uman (on Elvis Pritchard and Chris Cowie's Bellboy label). From this they progressed to a two year contract with Glasgow's Soma label, calling for four singles and an album in each year.

Shape Shifter/Slither/Psalm had NME in near orgasm: "Rippling clarity, soothing arpeggios and pristine perfection.' (Didn't she sing I'd Rather Go Blind?) Within days the run of 3,000 were sold but Soma pressed no more, imparting a scarceability cachet to the release. Spring of 1995 brought with it a ten-date British and European tour, encompassing Dutch and German gigs at which Skintrade took the stage amid banks of state-of-the-art synthetic music hardware. They acquired Wilf Smarties' fabled custom-built mixing desk, a huge, unique slab of 1980 vintage recording technology. After months of revamping and tarting the Tardis up, Kev and Dave now record their own stuff. There are no amps or mics to worry about: after all, this 24-track music is hiding in those myriad electro-cables snaking twixt the S3000 sampler, four FX machines, drum machine, compressor, sound module and five keyboards.

All of which are bloody difficult to play at gigs, bearing in mind that, in the live performance environment, Kev controls everything: sound levels, mixing, the whole shooting match. Demanding stuff. As far as sampling is concerned, Skintrade don't lift other people's material - sounds created by the syndrum syndrome duo themselves are re-structured and layered, to produce their own original music. An interesting development was their joint performance with The Loveless: unrehearsed computers meet prime, live Aberdeen funk. Kev, Dave and Titch were messing on with a new Aberdeen label to complement Hook and Bellboy. . . good on yer, Skintraders and the vertically challenged DJ.

The John Pearson Group and Spoil The Dog reside on the power soul side of Aberdeen's pleasuredome. The John Pearson guys were sitting in the Bell's Hotel soon after forming the combo in 1991. A pin was stuck randomly and repeatedly into the Aberdeen phone book, from whence various names were scribbled and put into envelopes. Mr John Pearson was the one selected by a band whose lineage is traceable to Katch 22, Refugee, Young Doctors, Klunk Brothers, Benny's Dream, Fear of Flying, The Mark Inside, Joe Public and Previous Convictions.

Dave McIntosh was in that first posse with vocalist Gary Sutherland, keyboardist Steve Craig, drummer Colin Fraser and guitarist Ewan McKay. Gary had developed a taste for soul stew in London and Cardiff. He brought the recipe back to Aberdeen, necessitating the recruitment of a horny brass section. But why go the bother of finding your own Muscle Schoals tooters when The Jive Bombers already have them? So the double-dipping Hyland, Gerry Dawson and Willie Munroe were for a period simultaneously JBs and JPs until Stroud's crowd got brassed off. The errant trio were therefore poached by John Pearson who added Colin Fraser Snr; don't be taken in by his welcome grin, he hatched from Eddie Watson's Alligators 30 years previously. Colin's trombone had lain up in the loft unused for a decade. "When I joined the Pearsons it took a wee while to blow all the spiders and dust out of it.'

Within six months Ewen left, being replaced by Doug Bruce, as the message was broadcast at Kit Carson's (oh my gawd. . . the names of these Aiberdeen pubs: whatever happened to The Filleters' Sock ?) and the Malt Mill, bastion of local music. Both Colins left as Sandy Thain arrived. During 1994 they appeared at a music festival near Stuttgart, performing a handful of gigs arranged by a friend resident in the area. Only when they arrived did they discover they were the event's headliners, and that other bands performed original material. Hence The Pearsons were the sole (soul) covers group. In front of a 6,000 crowd they set the venue alight with their composite James Brown/Stax/Atlantic show. The Pearsons settled down as Dave McIntosh (bass), Graham Chapman (keyboards), Sandy Thain (drums), Willie Munro (trombone) and 67 % of The Famous Marijuana Brass (Al and Gerry.) Vocals were shared between Leanne Harrison, Robbie the Roarer and Dilys Cooper (ex of Busco and dance-hall bands, now a Northsound regular). For replacement windows and doors AC Yule. Sorry Dilys, the world had to be told. As a diversion from the soul discipline a couple of the guys play in the occasional Hole In The Wall Gang. Their partners in crime on this Santana/Journey influenced quintet are veteran My Dear Watsons Iain Lyon and Ziggy Slater.

According to Dave McIntosh The Pearsons began "leaning more on the R 'n' B side of the fence'. This fence surely then carries the notice 'Beware of Spoil The Dog.' STD are a nine-piece pack, well entrenched in the North East's tradition of trans-Atlantic soul: Motown, irresistable R 'n' B, and (with half of their number coming from Dundee), The Average White Band. In Mike Ferrie, Patrick 'raptures of the deep' Sorley and Susie McDonald they have three vocalists and a back line of drummer Andy Davie, bassist Robert 'Fez' Ferrier and rhythm/lead guitarist Niall Scott. The Discovery Horns have provided "the proverbial icing on the cake over the band's seven- year history' according to the drummer. The DHs are Euan Ferguson, Gregor Irvine, Alistair Derrick, Frank 'Reggie Perrin' Rossiter, and Al McGlone. Their current armoury boasts 60 numbers and a 'liberal sprinkling of original material' which they put to dynamic effect: if Roddy Doyle reckoned that his Commitments were the "negroes of Europe' then Spoil The Dog are the Irish of Aberdeen. Work that one out. (And this one. . . Cadem MMM. Emnae MMM. Iso MMM. Oi MMM). Andy Davie is barking up the right tree when he proclaims "Wherever we go we take with us the bold claim: if you can't dance to Spoil The Dog, you can't dance!'

NEW LEAF
4th Left Jeremy Thoms

KORPSE

ONE GOD UNIVERSE

THE DAWN TREADERS

Chapter 20

Coda and acknowledgements

As we approach the end of our musical expedition that began with the youth club skiffle groups in the Fifties, this is the appropriate time to reflect on what happened on the Granite rock scene over the last few years. . . February 15, 1980 has UB 40 playing the opening date of their inaugural nation-wide tour supporting The Pretenders. This is their very first major league gig at which they promote their new single King/Food For Thought at Aberdeen University Union. UB 40's Ali and Robin Campbell are the sons of pre-historic Aberdeen-Birmingham folkie, Ian Campbell. The Argument release a seven-inch flexi Corner Of My Eye: no they don't, yes they do. The bickering band feature Stewart Smith, Neil Edleston, Stuart Robertson and Ron Pirie. "I've never been so bored in all my life' yawns one-time Alligator Jimmy Gray, as he finds himself playing old-time sequence music at the Beach Ballroom on Thursday nights. Superior heavy metal band Blaze release Cry Of The Wolfen. They appear several times on BBC Scotland television, and have a strong vocalist in David McLeod, son of TV presenter Donnie. Stereo Exit's single Burning Fire is released.

May 11, 1983: Ray-al, bang bang bang! Ray-al, bang bang bang! That Spanish drummer doesn't realise just how close he is to requiring expensive Swedish surgery to have his instrument removed from his ole. In Gothenburg we are Singing In The Rain and in the fountain, but it's wetter inside than out even at four pounds-odd for a half-litre of fizzy, weak Pripps lager (thank you, thank you, Aberdeen airport duty-free shop and God bless Pierre Smirnoff and his sublime blue label). Entering the NME indie chart at number 14 in June are Aberdeen Football Club with that classic European Song (We're Gonna Do It For You.) The unpredictable choice for the white-labelled flipside is The Northern Lights Of Old Aberdeen. At the recording session a decision goes the wrong way and Willie Miller, wedding ring taped-up, races into the control box to tell the producer what he is doing wrong. For reasons of an obvious limbly nature, Jim Leighton has no problems playing the cello. Boozy Dons fans become the Legion Of The Damned and are kicked out of Union Street pubs to stumble erratically down Windmill Brae. Three hours later they emerge even more unsteadily from a night club, which in recognition of happenings therein, earns the name Happy Valley, Crappy Valley, Clappy Valley and Death Valley. The Little Angels are waking up the sleepy East Yorkshire holiday resort of Scarborough with their big-hair, ear-ringed, check-yourself-in-the-mirror pose rock. Two of the Angels are former pupils of Dyce Academy Bruce John Dickinson (guitar) and brother Jimmy (keyboards). They go on to play sell-out British, European and Japanese tours. Their roster of albums includes Too Posh To Mosh, Don't Prey For Me, Young Gods and Jam. Closer to home, Gavin McDonald releases his single Rufus Snake on the Sunlight label.

The Flintstones are on the jazzier end of Aberdeen rock. Thousands of miles away on stage at the Philadelphia end of Live Aid in July 1985 is old folkie/old fogie Joan Baez. She is included on the bill on the strength of her pioneering civil rights campaigning during the Sixties. Her maternal grandfather originated in the Edinburgh area and held the ministry at Forgue Episcopal Church. The Shamen play support to Love And Money at The Venue in May of 1986 and in July an Oil Aid event at The Capitol raises money for African famine relief. Compered by Rose McDowall and Jill Bryson of Strawberry Switchblade, local acts include Grey By The Gun, Inspector Blake's Toxik Ephex and sensible Sid Ozalid.

1988 sees Rod Stewart playing to a massive crowd (remember them?) at Pittodrie where he gets the opportunity to show off his Hot Legs as tonight he wears a white Richard Irvine sponsored football strip instead of leopard-skin tights, because the occasion is a testimonial match for Alex McLeish. No pint wi' the boys afterwards though, and he is wheeked back up to the Craigendarroch in Ballater. . . It would be seven years before he graced the Pittodrie turf again for his June 1995 gig with Run Rig. . . Still on fitba', June of 1990 finds Rod amidst the fading, yacht-saturated beauty of Portofino on the Italian Ligura. This is a ten minute, 7000 lira boat trip away from Rapallo, temporary home for the Italia 90 Tartan Army. A posse (including your author and Mrs Author, Ian Selbie from Blackie, and the Cumnock tribe of Davie 'The Fish' McPherson, Tequila Tam and Wild Willie Johnston) are drowning their sorrows in the sunshine outside Giorgio's pub. The latter returns from the brewery with his fourth van-load of birra in two days (he sold more in that week than is normally shifted in five months.) Having done the touristy things and now fed up of lying on Rapallo's small beach the consensus seems to be "let's get wrecked, there's nothin' else to do.'

The opening game against Costa Rica had been a disaster and the face-saving Swedish match was up and coming. Out for a sea-front stroll, enter ex-Lads' Club hero Denis Law who sits down for a swift half with the troops. "Hey Denis bet you wish you could play against Sweden on Setterday?' was one of the less daft questions thrown at him. In that strange accent Denis replies "Waul of coars ah would lowave to play but the oaald legs are noaat up to it.' The Fish (overweight, hung-over, 30-a-day, unshaven, beer-stained AFC shirted) jumps in immediately with "Hey nae bother there big man. Just jump on my shooders, tell me whit t'dae and a'll run aboot.'

Aberdeen Sixties rocker Eric Duncan, one-time regular performer at the Hop Inn, is now resident in Florida. His country music act, for which he wears the kilt, wins him steady work at the Disney facility in Orlando. He is billed as 'the Scottish cowboy' and you may sneer away dear reader but does $800 a show put a different spin on the subject?. . . Albert Bonici dies in 1990. Union Street fearties The Pretty Things have released a handful of gems over the last few years so if raw, gutsy R 'n' B rock still does the trick for you then investigate Out Of The Island, The Chicago Blues Tapes 1991, A Whiter Shade Of Dirty Water, and Wine Women Whiskey. Their tempestuous years are encapsulated on the double CD set Unrepentant: Bloody But Unbowed. Steve Gibbons recovered from that Union Street doing-over and continues on the UK and European club circuit. He is still Eddie Vortex, playing a terrific set that your author recommends unreservedly. . . check out his latest collection Stained Glass. Gibbons recently bumped into Billy Bremner in Sweden, sitting in for a few numbers. Steve's terrific guitarist PJ Wright is out of that same chunky, picking-across-the chords rockabilly school as Bremner himself. Says Gibbons of Billy "He's a great guy and he's got that group playing really well. I had a ball.' Rosie Flores' debut album has been reissued in the USA on the Rounder label complete with bonus tracks, under the title A Honky Tonk Reprise: wonder yet again Billy's startling talent.

Former APB drummer George Cheyne surfaced with a band called Shift. Former resident of The Twighlight Zone Ronnie Sinclair plays the city's lounge bar circuit. Sadly his old china John Whyte died prematurely in 1996. Ex-Tsars drummer Stephen Wiseman was sighted in Grantown-On-Spey in school jannie mode. Ally Begg, a former pupil of Ellon Academy, leaves the teen-idol boy band Bad Boys Inc and announces that he has landed a film role with a British TV station. . . The Les McKeown version of The Bay City Rollers has Aberdonian Dave Innes on drums. . .

New year 1995 marks the third successive and final reunion gig for Seventies Banff rockers Benny's Dream. They had originally split in 1977 but this time it seems to be permanent, as vocalist Eric Paterson is off to work and live in the USA. Similar nostalgic performances in the previous two years were sell-outs. The other dream-teamers are George Sandison, John Sutherland, David Duncan and John Baird.

Rod The Mod plays at Pittodrie for the second time in his career. He doesn't have perfect pitch but the turf is in great condition due to all the shite they put on it during the nearly-down season. During the furore about potential noise problems for local residents, one wifie tells a TV reporter "Fin it's fitba the oanly time ye hear a noise is fan the Dons score a goal, an' thats nae very oaften.' Waterboys' leader Mike Scott was trapped in New York in 1993, unhappy in his task of auditioning musicians for the new version of his band. Within three months he had willingly thrown his life to the winds, sacrificing recording career, home, marriage, and anything else that was left. He checked into the Findhorn Foundation and hung up his star status with his jacket. He pitched-in, chopped carrots and mashed his ego along with the tatties. Two years on, he ventured back out into the big world to unveil his Findhorn-created persona on his Bring 'Em All In album. Now encalmed by his Moray Firth experiences, his 1995 return to touring may have been in-part inspired by his impromptu guest spot with Charlie Love's Tinderbox in Elgin.

The cat's whiskers up Buckie way are Johnny Stewart, Rob Lawson, Iain Lyon and bassist John Cumming. Not one to mince his words, John says "The group is called King Harvest (after The Band's album) and we are not into rehearsing much. But we just canna stop playing, it's in the blood.' Iain and Ziggy Slater also occasionally form part of The Hole In The Wall Gang with The John Pearson Group's Sandy Thain, Dave McIntosh and Doug Bruce.

After his days as the UK's top touring act Geno Washington disbanded the Ram Jam Band in the early Seventies at the peak of their success, returning only sporadically for one-night-stands and abortive tours. Despite clamouring demands he was unable to resolve or justify the disparity between his person-al needs and those of the manipulative concerns of the music industry. The Nineties however, have seen Geno achieve his personal ambitions and once again return to the spotlight, this time on his own terms. Amid a triumphal return to the British club scene, his appearance at Aberdeen's Lemon Tree in April of 1995 was described as "absolutely superb, a happy night on which he had the crowd eating out of his hand.' He arrived at the venue early, in time to be unexpectedly invited to play live for Radio Scotland: his invited couple of numbers developed into five and he had to be dragged away from the mic. General Geno also featured in Aberdeen Alternative Festival roster and ITV's Papparazzo (starring Nick Berry), had Geno playing a nightclub blues singer.

With a repertoire encompassing Herbie Hancock, Frank Zappa and Miles Davis, Manray are back in action in 1995, with Al Hyland, Stuart Cordiner on guitar, Willie Milne, and Martin Wood on keyboards. The Lemon Soul will return on a sporadic basis. . . Could Big Jim Paterson be enticed back North to impart his invaluable savvy to some of our current hopefuls. . . ?

Frantik Zimmer's drummer Chiz worked with ex-Ephexers Gary and Mikey in Diatribe, performing some of the old material mixed with reggae and ska. Inverness rockers Joe feature Malcolm Dent on gui-tar who is inspired by his Godfather Jimmy Page, and is apparently no mean 12-string player himself. Malcolm's father was Page's factor at Boleskine House during the Led Zepper's tenure there. Let's hope Crowley's curse doesn't visit the band who hoped to record an album at Uncle Jimmy's private studio.

From the frozen outposts of Reyjavik and Hill Of Ardo Methlick came Björk and Evelyn. Past dif-ferences are patched up: Miss Gudmundsdottir puts the 1967 ECWC score to the back of her mind, and Mrs Malcangi doesn't mention those Icelandic gunboats raking the Millwood's decks with bullets during the Seventies cod war. Björk's bands included Tappi Takarrass (the English translation is well worth inves-tigating), KUKL, and The Sugarcubes. Her solo album Debut attracted even more plaudits than the mil-lions of copies it sold. Undoubtedly the quirkiest, off-the-wallest event in jazz-pop, Debut was an unex-pected, left-field gem. For all its avant-garde un-pigeonhole-ability, the album sold internationally by the trawlerful. And as certain certain reporters have discovered, the diminutive Björk aint really up for taking shit from nobody. Evelyn has also fought her corner admirably. Despite being diagnosed profoundly deaf at the age of 14, against all odds she is now the world's premier percussionist. From early idyllic Aberdeenshire farm days she has displayed strength and a determination which puts the rest of us to shame. She has grown up in the public eye, since her first adolescent Cowdray Hall performances through to centre-stage position on every major classical concert hall in the world. Her OBE in 1993 was simply another milestone in a career already littered with awards and doctorates. Despite the international accolades heaped on her 5' 2" frame, she proudly lapses back to broad Doric when talking to friends and family. Even more commendable is the insistence that focus be placed upon her music, rather than on her disability. The nearest her work strayed into pop territory had been Hollywood movie music treatments until the innovative Icelander Björk sought Evelyn's talents on a collaborative basis early in 1994. Initially the duo worked together on an MTV Unplugged video. Venus As A Boy was selected for frequent, repet-itive MT loop-format broadcasting. Their association continued into Björk's Telegraph remix album and their co-composed song My Spine which appeared as a track on the Its Oh So Quiet single. The 1997 BMG label CD Evelyn Glennie, Her Greatest Hits reprised both My Spine and another Björk-assisted composition, Oxygen. And the girls worked together again on the Icelandic elfette's Homogenic album.

A fire destroys Runrig's office at Wellington Street in Aberdeen. Marlene says 'We are heart-broken but the show must go on.' The fire didn't stop the release of Run Rig's 'best of' CD. The Tear Gas LP Piggy Go Getter with Ricky Munro on drums, re-surfaced on the Italian label Limited as a bootleg CD.

Originally named Sunfish, Aberdeen band Geneva grew up listening to The Jesus and Mary Chain, but guitarist Steven Dora recalls "I've been into pop music since I was a toddler. My father had a juke box in his chip shop and I used to play stuff in there. He didn't change the records very often, so I ended up listening to Manfred Mann rather a lot.' So the chances are that Steve's lugs had been exposed to fellow North Eastern rockers Davie Flett and Speedy King without him realising it. Their first gig takes place at Cafe Drummond and a couple of years on, Geneva's debut on the Nude label No One Speaks is selected by NME as their Single Of The Week and immediately crashes into the chart. Andrew Montgomery (the lad has vocal chords mid-way between Tim Booth and the Vienna Boys' Choir) and the guys spent the summer of 1996, in between the odd British festival commitment, in a recording studio amid the serenity of Normandy. Kind of like Newburgh with garlic. Gentleman Jim Gellatly describes No

One Speaks as "a groover until the end of time', and he's spot on as usual. The follow-up Into The Blue also hits the top-30 as Geneva prepare to headline the NME Brat Bus Tour 1997. The singles all feature on the superb debut album Further. Mesmeric, beguiling music.

There's a bewildering array of clubs out there in the Granite City, a bit of something for everyone with names like Joy, Pussy Galores, Reds, Stork, Pegasus, Exodus, Bishops, Glider and The Works. Maybe not Stringfellows or Ibiza but a long way away from The Bilermakkers. If you prefer mainstream live acts, you could Box Clever by jumping on your Tandem with a Gaucho or Mr Pitiful, making sure that you're wearing The Shoes on your Big Foot as you head for the Soul Station for a Diet Coke or a glass of Poteen to see Cathy Brown or Terry McBain, and Salem's Lot or Lieutenant Pigeon might fly in as well. And there would be No Justice if The Billy Shears Band met up with Smokin' Bert Cooper without taking care of their Dicky Hart and the Pacemakers. On a rockier tip are Second Motion, The Laments, Fitzbee, The Needles Dusk and, with their demo Breathe, Phone Freak. With bright sparks Billy Sangster and Stephen Rafferty, Mighty Human Generator are throbbing spasmodically but Inertia aren't doing that much. At the early Stone Roses end of the BS 3704 cucumber are Ellon's The Unflavoured. By contrast The River Women, related to other Aberdeen GGG (Germaine Greer's Grandaughters) bands Amoeba Red and Midnight Blue, "perform songs written especially for the Nineties woman.' Debbie Boyd, Lynn Sangster and Liz Mowat confusingly take inspiration from native American history; fem-lib, war-painted, feathered-hair, shrill girlie BB Queens. Wonderboy are new kids on the block starring DT Tony's younger brother. Venue-wise, Exodus is at the Triple Kirks upstairs from the classrooms where yours truly did his RE and music, with the Manny Riddell and Doc 'Mad Dog' McCloy respectively. The Playhouse was sticking to reliable bets, an each-way punt on the noses of The Pearsons and The Jive Bombers.

Annie Lennox returns yet again to the pop charts as an instantly idenfiable backing vocalist on Whitney Houston's Step By Step. Annie also wrote the song. If you happened to be hiking across the wild and windy North Yorkshire moors between Guisborough and Whitby at the back-end of 1996, you might have heard a strangely familiar sarcastic voice emanating from the Jolly Sailors pub. Just who could this follically-challenged guitar and moothie chappie be, extracting the urine willy-nilly? He used to raise hell at the Alley. . . Frank Robb, that's who. Which takes us more or less up to date.

. . . .

I extend my thanks and the promise of a couple of pints to the persons indicated below, who assisted in my efforts in putting this book together. I am especially indebted to Bob Spence, Jim Allardice, Bill Mowat (Chapter 6 is a Tim Hunt special) and Mike Stobbie. For these afore-mentioned heroes I will also buy the crisps.

James Addison at Bankhead Academy, Billy Allardyce, Mark Ashton at Now and Then Records, Trevor Atkinson, Ross Baird, Danny Barbour, Mark Beavan, Beefy Keith, Robbie Elvis Benzies, Greg Brechin, Billy Bremner, Daniele Brockie, Patrick Campbell - Lyons, CD Services Dundee, Chiz, Dilys Cooper, Fred Craig, Brian Crombie, Sandy Davidson, Andy Davie, Fred Dellar at Vox, Tommy Dene, Julian de Takats, Jim Diamond, Ellie Doherty at Nude Records, Mrs. Daisy Donald, Marc Ellington, Tommy Findlay, Dave Firth, Roy Foreman, Colin Fraser Snr and his loon, Paul Fyfe, Jim Gellatly, Keith Gerrard, Steve Gibbons, Sam Gill, Deborah at Evelyn Glennie's office, Byron Grant, Jimmy Gray, Johnny Gray, Kev Gunn, Gordon Hardie, Trevor Hart, Heather Hawkins at AAM New York, Kevin Henderson, Duncan Hendry, Paul Hitchman at Sugar Records, John Hunter at Grampian Records Wick, Al Hyland, Kris Ife, Alex and Julie Joobs, Gerry Jablonski, Stewart Kemp, Brian Kennedy, Pat King, Marek Kluczynski, Mick Kluczynski, Stefan Kocemba, Andy Lawson, Gordon Lemon, Harry Lord, Charlie Love, Alistair Mabbott at The List, Robbie Manson, Paul Massie, Chris McClure, Dave McIntosh, Kenny McKay, Jim 'Get Back In Your Store' McLean, Gerry McRobb, Ian Middleton, Frank Milne, Denis 'Mad Mitch' Mitchell, Marj Mitchell, Bill Mowat, Graham Nairn, Roger Niven, Allan Park, Big Jimmy Paterson, Mark Paytress at Record Collector, Sonny Pearce, Eoan Elvis Pritchard, Alan Proctor at the Evening Telegraph and Post, Tommy Reid, Mike Reoch, Alan Rennie at City of Aberdeen Arts and Recreation Dept, John Rennie, Frank Robb, Alan Robinson at Demon Records, Gordon Rossi Ross, Norman Shearer, Ronnie Sinclair, Ian Semple, Iain Slater, Graham Spry, Jim Stephen at Osprey Promotions, Johnny Stewart, Mike Stobbie, Dave 'Goldfinger' Stroud, Gary Sutherland, Iain Sutherland, Johnny Sutherland, Rob Swan, Taff, Dick Taylor, Jeremy Thoms, Titch, Tom Waller, Stanley West, Peter Whimster, Ricky Whitelaw, Fred Wilkinson, Barry Winton, Billy Wright.

The lyrics used in the foreword come from Rip Off Train, a track on The Pretty Things' Freeway Madness album. They were written by Phil May about his (then) new guitarist Pete Tolson, but I felt that they express perfectly one of the central themes of this book - the loneliness of the long distance rocker. © Lupus Music Co. Ltd, and used with kind permission of the copyright holders and the composer. Thanks awfully, Philip my boy. The Johnny Gentle quotes in Chapter Two and Eurythmics financial data in Chapter 17 come from Rock Gold - The Music Millionaires by George Tremlett. Published by Unwin Hyman in 1990 and used with kind permission from Mr. Tremlett's agents. The Dave Wendels quote in Chapter Two comes from the gov'nor US freak-beat publication Ugly Things. Buy, buy, buy from: Mike Stax, 3707 Fifth Avenue # 145, San Diego, CA 92103, USA. An $8 post-paid thing from heaven. I didn't ask Mike for his permission, but he's a cool dude. Merci bien Michel. The Bill Wyman quotes in Chapter Two come from Stone Alone: The Story Of A Rock 'n' Roll Band by Bill Wyman and Ray Coleman. Published by Viking, © Ripple Productions Limited, 1990. Reproduced by kind permission of Penguin Books Limited. The Cliff Bennett quote in Chapter Seven comes from The Complete Rock Family Trees by Pete Frame published by Omnibus Press. Used with their kind permission. Some of the Davie Flett jive in Chapter 12 came via the fanzine Black Rose, which Thin Lizzy freaks just gotta have. Zap your dough (£1.50) to: Adam Winstanley, 1 Parson Court, Maynooth, County Kildare, Northern Ireland. Mange tak Adam. The Bob Last quote in Chapter 14 comes from Johnny Rogan's Starmakers And Svengalis: The History Of British Pop Management. Published by MacDonald Queen Anne Press, © Johnny Rogan. Danke to John for his permission to use the words and the kind offer of further help.

My uncle George Innes came back to Aberdeen from Australia in 1997 for a family funeral. I mailed him a draft version of this book and some weeks after he arrived home in Oz, he wrote me a letter. When he read about how the Strollers emigrated in 1966, he realised how small the world really is. Up in the North West on holiday, he and Mary had been introduced to an expat Aberdonian brother and sister act performing at a Darwin casino club. Guess who. . . George and Julie Barker. Kinda related to this is the sad fact that fellow veterans of the Strollers, Frankie Milne and Bill Spiers, had a serious fall-out a few years back. In retrospect it was all about something quite trivial as these things often are. A pre-publication article about this book in the Evening Express brought the guys to contacting each other and to talking again: the hatchet is well and truly buried and they have resumed their friendship that stretches back some 40 years. For your author that's a lovely feel-good story and an appropriate way to end Fit Like, New York? with the very guys who launched us on our musical journey. I'm now putting this thing to bed, which doesn't sound like a bad idea. It's been a helluva catalogue of late nights so I hope you think it was worth the effort. Didn't mean to take up all your sweet time. . .

GENEVA

CAST

Chapter 21
Discography

Your author has attempted to cover all releases relevant to the subject matter of this book. In view of Eurythmics and Shamen multi-format vinyl and CD, I identify the basic release of their work only. I apologise now for any which I have missed. I gave it my best shot, but drop me a line via the publisher if you have any additions or corrections. . . particularly label and catalogue numbers for Dekka Dance, Academy Street, Nervous Quoir, Iain McDonald, Mea Culpa, MHG, Sound Control and The Last Divide.

SINGLES

Artist	Title	Year	Label	Release #	Format	Notes
Lord Rockingham's XI	*Hoots Mon*	1958	Decca	F 11059	7"	Let's start at the top : chart # 1
Lord Rockingham's XI	*Wee Tom*	1959	Decca	F 11104	7"	Chart # 16
Johnny & The Copycats	*I'm A Hog For You Baby / I Can Never See You*	1964	Norco	AB 102	7"	Moray marauders get the R 'n' B bacillus
The Sorrows	*Take A Heart*	1965	Piccadilly	7N35260	7"	Chart # 21
The Sorrows	*You've Got What I Want*	1965	Piccadilly	7N35277	7"	
The Copycats	*Angela / I'll never Regret You*	1966	Cornet	3005	7"	Coming out of their Buckie on this first German release
The Copycats	*Start Thinking About Me / Pain Of Love*	1966	Cornet	5008	7"	German release
The Facells	*If You Really Love Me (I Won't care) / So Fine*	1966	Norco	AB 116	7"	Taped at the Two Red Shoes
The Misfits	*You Won't See Me / Hanging Around*	1966	ASCC		7"	Shaka Can
My Dear Watson	*Elusive Face / The Shame that Drained*	1968	Parlophone	R5687	7"	Phil Spector sick as a pig
My Dear Watson	*Stop Stop, I'll be There / Make This Day Last*	1968	Parlophone	RF737	7"	100 mph stonker
The Tremors	*Sing La La / Little Liza Jane*	1969	Metronom	M25121	7"	Grosse Freiheit pop

Artist	Title	Year	Label	Release #	Format	Notes
Mr Dear Watson	Have You Seeen Your Saviour / White Line Road	1970	DJM	JJS 224	7"	The year's best, or I'll go and eat hay wi' the donkeys
The Tremors	Ring A Ding Dong / It's So Good	1970	Fontana	269413 TF	7"	Trems Spielen Eurovision
Rebellion	When I'm Singing Rock 'n' Roll	1971	CBS	3050	7"	Spiggy Topes with Cliff Bennett, 1 track on CBS EP
Rebellion	Amos Moses / Movin' And Travellin' On	1971	CBS	7321	7"	B side actually Skid Row
Royal Scots Dragoon Guards	Amazing Grace	1972	RCA	2191	7"	John Thompson on drums; chart topper
Pilot	Magic	1974	EMI	2217	7"	Stuart Tosh on drums, chart # 11
Pilot	January	1975	EMI	2255	7"	Chart # 1
Pilot	Call Me Round	1975	EMI	2287	7"	Chart # 34
Pilot	Just A Smile	1975	EMI	2338	7"	Chart # 31
Rod Stewart	Sailing	1975 1976 1987	Warner Brothers	K16600	7"	Rod the Mod with The Sutherlands' classic; chart positions 1, 3 & 41 respectively
Sutherland Brothers & Quiver	Arms of Mary / Secrets	1976 1987	CBS Old Gold	4001 OG9402	7" 7"	Chart # 5
10 CC	Things We Do For Love	1976	Mercury	6008 019	7"	Stuart Tosh on drums, chart # 6
Sutherland Brothers & Quiver	Secrets	1976	CBS	4668	7"	Chart # 35
Atlas	Easy Money / Losing You	1976	Action	7603	7"	
10 CC	Good Morning Judge	1977	Mercury	6008 025	7"	Chart # 5
Billy Murray	Downtown Hoedown / Rhyme And Reason	1977	Polydor		7"	

Artist	Title	Year	Label	Release #	Format	Notes
The Catch	Borderline / Black Blood	1977	Logo	GO 103	7"	Annie and Dave
10 CC	Dreadlock Holiday	1978	Mercury	6008 035	7"	Chart # 1
Nick Lowe	I Love the Sound of Breaking Glass	1978	Radar	ADA 1	7"	Smashing time for Billy B, # 7
Billy Murray	The Heart And The Stone / I Don't Want To Be A Hero	1978	State		7"	
Dave Edmunds	Deborah / What Looks Good On You	1978	Swansong	SSK 19413	7"	Rockpile
Dave Edmunds	Television / Never Been In Love	1978	Swansong	SSK 19414	7"	Rockpile
The Squibs	On the Line / Satisfy Me	1978	Oily	Slick 1	7"	Oily and The Squibs ignite
Dave Edmunds	A-1 On the Juke Box / It's My Own Business	1979	Swansong	SSK19417	7"	Rockpile
Dave Edmunds	Girl's Talk / Bad is Bad	1979	Swansong	SSK19418	7"	Rockpile
The Tourists	Blind Among the Flowers / He Who Laughs Last	1979	Logo	GO350	7	Chart # 52
Sutherland Brothers & Quiver	Easy Come Easy Go	1979	CBS	7121	7"	Chart # 50
Nick Lowe	Crackin' Up	1979	Radar	ADA 34	7"	Rockpile, chart # 34
The Tools	Gotta Make Some Money Somehow / TV Eyes	1979	Oily	Slick 2	7"	
Dave Edmunds	Queen of Hearts / Creature From The Black Lagoon	1979	Swansong	SSK19419	7"	Rockpile, chart # 11
Dave Edmunds	Crawling From The Wreckage / As Lovers Do	1979	Swansong	SSK19420	7"	Rockpile, chart # 59
Pallas	Reds Under The Bed / Thought Police / CUUK / Willmot Dovehouse MP	1978	Sue-i-cide	PAL 101	7"	"The Pallas EP"
Tucker Donald	What Did I Do Wrong / Deborah / Just In Case	1978	Clubland	SJP 792	7"	Torry rock

Artist	Title	Year	Label	Release #	Format	Notes
Bunion	Boys on the Rig / Dreamer	1978	Malt Mill	CPS 012	7"	Double B side from the corny duo
The Tourists	The Loneliest Man In the World / Don't Get Left Behind	1979	Logo	GO360 GOP 360	7" 7" pic	Chart # 32
The Tourists	I Only Want To Be With You / Summer Night	1979	Logo	GO 370	7"	Chart # 4
The Shapiros	Waitress In a Hotel / Isolde	1979	North of Watford	N702	7"	
The Kids	C'mon Kids / Travelling Man	1979	Agenda	GM479/ 480	7"	The Bash Street Kids
Nick Lowe	Cruel to be Kind	1979	Radar	ADA43	7"	Billy Bremner, chart # 43
The Tourists	So Good to be Back Home / Circular Saw	1980	Logo	Tour 1	7"	Chart # 8
Dave Edmunds	Singing The Blues / Boys Talk	1980	Swansong	SSK19422	7"	Rockpile : Chart # 28
Nick Lowe & Dave Edmunds	Sing The Everly Brothers	1980	F Beat		7" EP	Rockpile, freebie with LP Seconds Of Pleasure
The Squibs	Parades / Out on the Town	1980	Oily	Slick 3	7"	Why don't ya?
Dexy's Midnight Runners	Dance Stance / I'm Just Looking	1980	Oddball Productions	R6028	7"	Chart # 40
Dexy's Midnight Runners	Geno / Breakin' Down The Walls of Heartache	1980	Late Night Feelings	R6033	7"	It's number one, it's Top Of The Pops
Dexy's Midnight Runners	There There My Dear / The Horse	1980	Late Night Feelings	R6038	7"	Chart # 7
Hustler	Jukebox Queen / Street Fighter / Lifestyle	1980	Refined	Refined 1	7"	
The Naturals	Strange Days / Maybe Someday / My Only Friend	1980	Refined	Refined 2	7"	

Artist	Title	Year	Label	Release #	Format	Notes
Rockpile	Wrong Way / Now and Always	1980	FBeat	XX9 XX9C	7" 7"	Billy's boys rock it up
The Tourists	Don't Say I Told You So / Strange Sky	1980	RCS	Tour 2	7"	Chart # 40
The Presidents Men	Out In The Open / State Of Mind / When Someone Says No	1980	Oily	Slick 4	7"	
Rockpile	Teacher Teacher / Fool Too Long	1980	FBeat	XX11	7"	
Dexy's Midnight Runners	Keep it Part 2 / One Way Love	1980	Parlophone	R6042	7"	
Manray	The Duke's Den / Baked Alaska	1980	Hardy High	HH 01	7"	Celebrating Aberdeen pub grub
The Presidents Men	Reasons For Leaving / Cry / I've Got My Best Suit On Today	1981	Oily	Slick 5	7"	
Kirsty McColl	There's A Guy Works Down The Chipshop Swears He's Elvis.	1981	Polydor	POSP 250	7"	Billy Bremner, # 14
APB	Chain Reaction / Power Crisis	1981	Oily	Slick 6	7"	'I know it's only a lust affair'
Dexy's Midnight Runners	Plan B / Soul Finger	1981	Parlophone	R6046	7"	Chart # 58
Eurythmics	I'm Never Gonna Cry Again / Le Sinistre	1981	RCA	RCA 68 RCAT 68	7" 12"	Chart # 63
Eurythmics	Belinda / Heartbeat	1981	RCA	RCA 115	7"	
Thin Lizzy	Trouble Boys	1981	Vertigo	Lizzy 9	7"	Lynott sings Bremner
APB	Shoot You Down / Talk To Me	1981	Oily	Slick 7	7"	Granite city funk takes off
Private ID	A Little Fun / Stay Back	1981	Dodo's	Dodo 1	7"	
Billy Bremner	Loud Music in Cars / Price Is Right	1981	Stiff	BUY 125	7"	"It wisna' that great"
Rue de Remarx	One Way Trip / Full circle	1981	Underground Music	UMA003	7"	Superklute adrift in London

Artist	Title	Year	Label	Release #	Format	Notes
Dexy's Midnight Runners	Liars A To E / And Yes We Must Remain The Wildhearted Outsiders	1981	Mercury	Dexys 7	7"	
Sutherland Brothers	When Will I Be Loved / Love Sick	1981	RCA	RCA 110	7"	Suthbruths sing Evbruths
Billy Bremner	Laughter Turns To Tears / Tired And Emotional	1982	Stiff	BUY 143	7"	
Dexy's Midnight Runners	The Celtic Soul Brothers / Love Part 2	1982 1983	Mercury	Dexys 8 Dexys 12	7" 7"	Chart # 45 Chart # 20
Dexy's Midnight Runners	Come On Eileen / Dubious	1982	Mercury	Dexys 9 Dexys 912	7" 12"	Chart # 1
Pallas	Arrive Alive / Stranger At The End Of Time	1982	Granite Wax	GWS1	7"	
Dexy's Midnight Runners	Jackie Wilson Said / Let's Make This Precious	1982	Mercury	Dexys 10	7"	Chart # 5
Eurythmics	This Is The House / Home Is Where The Heart Is	1982	RCA	RCA 199 RCAT 199	7" 12"	Live material
PhD	I Won't Let You Down	1982	WEA	K79209	7"	Mesmeric, Euro-tinged chart-buster from Tony Hymas and adopted loon Jim D. Chart # 3
APB	Palace Filled With Love / All Your Life With Me	1982	Oily	Slick 8	7"	
Eurythmics	The Walk / Step On The Beast / The Walk - Part 2	1982	RCA	RCA 230 RCA 230T	7" 12"	Live material
The Grip	Keeping The Peace / Musicland	1982	Gripping Youth	GRIP 1	7"	
Billy Bremner	Meek Power	1982	Demon	D1014	7"	"I could do something with the singer"
APB	Rainy Day / From You and Back to You	1982	Oily	Slick 9	7"	
Eurythmics	Love is a Stranger / Monkey Monkey	1982	RCA	DA1 DAP1/ DAT1	7" 7" &12"	UK Chart # 54 7" pic disc

Artist	Title	Year	Label	Release #	Format	Notes
The Pretenders	Back on the Chain Gang	1982	Real	ARE 19	7"	Chart # 17 - Billy with Big Country's rhythm section
No Human Eye	Wet Your Lips / The Owners Lose a Package	1982	Rhodium	SRS 801 TT 826	7"	
Dexy's Midnight Runners	Let's Get This Straight From The Start / Old	1982	Mercury	Dexys 11 Dexys 1112	7" 12"	
Eurythmics	Sweet Dreams / I Could Give You a Mirror	1983	RCA	DA2 DAP2/DAT2	7" 7" & 12"	Chart # 2, Who Am I To Disagree ?
Segue	Christine / Three On The Trot	1983	Tart 'n' Records	Storm 1	7"	
Jimmy The Hoover	Tantalise (Wo Wo Ee Yeh Yeh)	1983	Innervision	A 3406	7"	Derek Dunbar cleans up at # 18
Pallas	Paris is Burning / The Hammer Falls	1983	Cool King	CK010 12CK010	7" 12"	
Never Amber	Who the Hell / I've got Feelings Too	1983	Bait	Bait 1	7"	
APB	One Day / Help Yourself	1983	Oily	Slick 10	7" & 12"	UK Indie Chart # 6 Rockpool club chart # 2
Eurythmics	Who's That Girl / You Take Some Lentils	1983	RCA	DA 3	7"	UK Chart # 3
Iain Sutherland	It Coulda Been Buddy Holly	1983	RCA	AVAT 5	7"	A Blue Toon belter
Eurythmics	Right By Your Side / Party Mix	1983	RCA	DA 4	7"	UK Chart # 10
Segue	Working in a Factory	1983	Storm	Storm 1	Flexi	
Eurythmics	Here Comes The Rain Again / Paint A Rumour	1984	RCA	DA 5	7"	Aberdeen's weather forecast at # 8
Pallas	Eyes in the Night / East West (as above plus Crown of Thorns)	1984	Harvest	PLS1 12PLS1	7" 12"	

Artist	Title	Year	Label	Release #	Format	Notes
APB	Danceability Parts 1 and 2 / Crazy Grey / Rainy Day / Palace Filled With Love	1984	Albion	12 ION 160	12"	Rockpool Club Chart # 1 Billboard Club Chart # 9
Jasmine Minks	Think	1984	Creation	CRE 004	7"	
Billy Bremner	Shatterproof / Look at that Car / Musclebound	1984	Arista	Arist 557 Arist 12557	7" 12"	
Jasmine Minks	Where The Traffic Goes	1984	Creation	CRE 008	7"	
Iain Sutherland	The Wheel (Fait Vos Jeux)	1984	Avatar	AVAT 9	7"	
Billy Bremner	Love Goes to Sleep / Fire In My Pocket	1984	Arista	Arist 566 Arist 12556	7" 12"	
The Bluebells	Young At Heart	1984	London	LON 49	7"	Chart # 8, Billy on acoustic
APB	What Kind of Girl (3 versions)	1984	Albion	ION 170 12ION 170	7" 12"	
Jim Diamond	I Should Have Known Better	1984	A & M	AM 220	7"	Aftershave-less chart # 1
Alone Again Or	Drum the Beat (In My Soul) / Smartie Edit	1984	All One	ALG 1	7"	Pre-Shamen indie pop-rock
Private I.D.	Cold Cold Sweat / Dreams of You Cold Cold Sweat / Perfect Lady	1984 1984	Gabriels Metropolis War. Bros	GAB1 WAR 3 12WAR 3	7" 7" 12"	
Pallas	Shock Treatment / March on Atlantis As above plus Heart Attack	1984	EMI	PLS 2 12PLS 2	7" 12"	
Billy Connolly	Super Gran	1985	Stiff	BUY 218	7"	The Twa' Billys, chart # 32
Jasmine Minks	What's Happening	1985	Creation	CRE 018	7"	
APB	Summer Love / Is the Music Loud Enough	1985	Red River	Ythan 1 Ythan T1	7" 12"	

Artist	Title	Year	Label	Release #	Format	Notes
APB	Something to Believe In / So Many Broken Hearts / Versions	1985	Red River	Ythan 2 Ythan T2	7" 12"	
Pallas	The Knightmoves : Strangers / Nightmare (as above plus Sanctuary)	1985	EMI	PLS3 12PLS3	7" 12"	
Alan Reed	A Stitch in Time / Mad Man Machine	1985	EMI		7"	Promo free with 12PLS3
Billy Bremner	Endless Sleep	1985	Rock City	RCR 6	7"	
Alone Again Or	Dream Come True / Smarter Than The Average Bear	1985	Polydor	ALG 2 ALGX 2	7" 12"	
Pallas	Thowing Stones At The Wind (as above plus live tracks Cut and Run & Crown of Thorns)	1985	EMI	PLS4 12PLS4	7" 12"	
Kevin Henderson	Skinny Minny / Pick Up	1985	zyx	zyx 1149 zyx 5304	7" 12"	German cut by Lemon Soul's bassman
Kevin Henderson	Pattaya	1985	zyx	zyx 1118 zyx 5217	7" 12"	Ich bin ein Frankfurter
Jim Diamond	Hi Ho Silver	1986	A & M	AM 296	7"	A Boon to the pop charts
Toxik Ephex	Punk as Fuck EP : Fallout Shelter / Always Skint / Nothing's Permissive	1986	Green Vomit Records	Puke 11/2	7"	
The Shamen	They May Be Right EP Happy Days / Velvet Box / I Don't Like the way the World Is	1986	One Big Guitar	OBG 003T	12"EP	
The Shamen	Wayward Wednesday in May Affair.... Four Letter Girl / Stay in Bed	1986	Skipping Kitten		7"	One sided flexi with Skipping Kitten fanzine
The Shamen	Young Till Yesterday / World Theatre / Golden Hair	1986	Moksha	Soma 1 Soma 1T	7" 12"	

Artist	Title	Year	Label	Release #	Format	Notes
Jasmine Minks	Cold Heart	1986	Creation	CRE 025 CRET 025	7" 12"	
5 Star	Rain or Shine / Summer Groove	1986	RCA	PB40901 12PB40901	7" 12"	Mike Stobbie
Northern Lights	Numero Uno / The Big Black Cloak	1986	Mysterious Publishing Co.	MPC 4	7"	Bankhead bop
A Girl Called Johnny	Hello It Isn't Me / Shallow	1986	10 Records	10-144	7"	The Presidents Man returns
APB	Open Your Eyes / Sunset Song	1986	Red River	Ythan 3 Ythan T3	7" 12"	
Nirvana	Black Flower / Save My Soul	1987	Demon	OPRA 078	7"	Billy Bremner
APB	Missing You Already / Best of Our Love / Boy, You're Not so Great	1987	Red River	Ythan 6 Ythan T6	7" 12"	
The Shamen	Something About You / Do What You Will	1987	Moksha	Soma 2 Soma 2T	7" 12"	
Loveless	Fields of Yellow / Low Down Sneak / Big Fat Cow/ Hypocrite	1987	Embryo	EMB 01	12"	APB as was
The Shamen	Christopher Mayhew Says / Shitting on Britain	1987	Moksha	Soma 3 Soma 3T	7" 12"	Mescaline a go-go
1, 2, 3	Where Do We Go From Here ? / Let Go	1987	Virgin	109379	7"	Mike Stobbie
1, 2, 3	Love Me / I Know You So Well	1987	Virgin	109586	7"	Mike Stobbie
The Shamen	Knature of a Girl / Happy Days	1988	Moksha	Soma 4 Soma 4T	7" 12"	
Toxik Ephex	Does Someone Have to Die / Life's For Living	1988	Words of Warning	WOW 6	7"	Split EP with Welsh spikeys Shrapnel

Artist	Title	Year	Label	Release #	Format	Notes
The Shamen	Jesus Loves Amerika / Darkness In Zion	1988	Ediesta	Calc 069 Calc T/CD 069	7" 12"/CD	Guitar funkateering mode
Jive Bombers	Sock It To 'Em JBs EP : Run Run Rudolph / Drift Away / Hard to Handle / Devil In The Blue Dress	1988		Bouncing Bomb 1	CD	Loud, proud and Stroud
The Shamen	Transcendental / House Version	1988	Desire	WANTX 10	12"	
The Shamen	You, Me and Everything / Reraptyouare	1989	Moksha	Soma 6 Soma 6T/CD	7" 12"/CD	
The Shamen	Omega Amigo / Pre-mix	1989	One Little Indian	30 TP 12 30 TP7 CD	12" CD	
1, 2, 3	Love Reigns	1989	Strada	12STRAD2	12"	Co-produced by Mike Stobbie
Another Wild Rose		1989		acp2	Cass	
The Shamen	Pro > Gen	1990	One Little Indian	36 TP 7 36 TP 12	7" 12"	Chart # 55: Many, many mixes moving mountains
The Shamen	Make It Mine	1990	One Little Indian	46 TP 7 46 TP 12	7" 12"	Chart # 42 Various Mixes
The Other Side	Got This Feeling / Don't Take Me Down / Got to Find a Better Way / Mad World	1991	City Arts	ACLMC 9	Cassette	Melodic pop at its best
The Shamen	Hyperreal	1991	One Little Indian	48 TP 7 48 TP 12	7" 12"	Chart # 29 Various mixes
Coast	Headlight / Sound Hole / Blue Green	1991	Fluxus	FL 001	7"	
The Shamen	Move Any Mountain (Progen 91)	1991	One Little Indian	52 TP 7 52 TP 12	7" 12"	Chart # 4 Dance Icons R Us
The Shamen	LSI	1992	One Little Indian	68TP 7 68TP 12	7" 12"	Chart # 6

Artist	Title	Year	Label	Release #	Format	Notes
The Shamen	*Ebeneezer Goode*	1992	One Little Indian	78TP 7 78 TP 12	7" 12"	Chart # 1
The Shamen	*Boss Drum*	1992	One Little Indian	88TP 7 88TP 12	7" 12"	Chart # 4
The Shamen	*Phorever People*	1992	One Little Indian	98TP 7 98TP 12	7" 12"	Chart # 5
The Dreaming	*I Want Out / For The Children / The Haunting / Fake*	1992	Feaked Records	MC 001	Cass EP	
Korpse	*X / Rusted*	1992	F	F001	7"	Rag, Tag and Bobtail
The Dawntreaders	*Today / Time*	1993		DTV 001	7"	
The Shamen	*Re-evolution*	1993	One Little Indian	118TP 7 118TP 12	7" 12"	Chart # 19
Loveless	*Low Down Sneak*	1993	M8		Cass	Freebie with *M8* Magazine
The Dreaming	*Rain on the Level*	1993	M8		Cass	*M8*
Greenblade	*Are We A Warrior*	1993	M8		Cass	*M8*
Nothing Like Monday		1993			Cass	Broch & Roll
Party On Plastic	*Give Myself To You*	1993	Hook	HK 001	12"	
Bubble Up	*Barimba*	1993	Hook	HK 002	12"	
The Shamen	*SOS*	1993	One Little Indian	108TP	12"	EP, Chart # 14
Skintrade	*Subuman / Uman*	1993	Bellboy	Bellboy 001	12"	
The Foundation	*Everybody Looks The Same*	1993	Pop Art	ART x 1	7"	
Skintrade	*Shape Shifter / Slither / Psalm*	1994	Soma	Soma 17	12"	

Artist	Title	Year	Label	Release #	Format	Notes
Brother Sledge	*Keep On Pumping It Up*	1994	Hook	HK 003	12"	
The Turnbull ACS	*Bring It On Down*	1994	Hook	HK 004	12"	
Canyon	*Tumbleweed*	1994	Bellboy	Bellboy 002	12"	
Wavelength	*Morpheus*	1994	Bellboy	Bellboy 003	12" EP	
Inertia	*Inertia*	1994	Bellboy	Bellboy 004	12" EP	
Brother Sledge	*The Trade Marks*	1994	Hook	HK 005	12" EP	
The Dawntreaders	*Talk EP : Close Your Eyes / Save / John Says*	1994	Cannonball	DTCD 002	CD EP	
Skintrade	*Andomraxess*	1995	Soma	Soma 027	12"	
Annie Lennox	*No More 'I Love You's'*	1995	RCA-BMG	74321255512 74321157164	CD Cass	Live acoustic tracks on CD and *Ladies Of The Canyon* on cassette
Coast	*Polly's Domain / Sleepy / You Can Look*	1995	Sugar	Sugarcd	CD EP	
The Shamen	*Destination Eschaton*	1995	One Little Indian		You name it	Two riders of the Apocalypse
Canyon	*Planet Source*	1995	Hook	HK 006	12"	
Scan Carriers	*Ezascumby*	1995	Bellboy	Bellboy 006	12"	
Excabs	*Neuro / Outcast*	1995	Bellboy	Bellboy 007	12"	

Artist	Title	Year	Label	Release #	Format	Notes
Annie Lennox	Whiter Shade Of Pale	1995	RCA/BMG	Aquarium 2	CD	Promo
Ian Elvis Pritchard	Zed's Dead Baby	1995	Bellboy	Bellboy 008	12"	
Coast	Slugs / Shag Wild / Pretend	1995	Sugar	SUGA5CD SUGA5V	CD 7"	
Coast	Now That You Know Me / Tender Cage / She Wears A Frown	1996	Sugar	SUGA 8CD SUGA8V	CD 7"	
Amoeba Red	Amoeba Red	1996		ar 100	Cassette	3-tracks "for the modern woman'
Coast	Britannia	1996	Melody Maker	MMMC KER 96	CD	Cassette freebie with Melody Maker
Geneva	No One Speaks / Closer To The Stars	1996	Nude	NUD 22CD	CD	Recorded in Newburgh with garlic
Geneva	Into The Blue / Riverwatching / Land's End	1997	Nude	NUD 25CD	CD	Top 30 again (cassette & 7-inch versions backed by At The Core
Coast	Do It Now	1997	Sugar		CD	
Geneva	Tranquiliser / Dead Giveaway / Strung Out On You Tranquiliser / Michaelmas / Compulsive Love Disorder	1997	Nude		CD	7-inch backed by Driftwood

ALBUMS

Artist	Title	Year	Label	Release #	Format	Notes
Mike Reoch and The Tremors	*Beaten An International Evergreens*	1964	Elite Special	SOLPF 236	LP	Rockin' the Reeperbahn
The Sorrows	*Take a Heart*	1965	Picadilly	NPL38023	LP	Stompin' drums from Huntly's Neil Finlay
Various Artists	*16 Beat Groups On The Hamburg Scene*	1965	Polydor	237639	LP	2 tracks aus Tremors
Various Artists	*Beat City*	1965	Polydor	237660	LP	More Hamburg heat
The Steele Combo	*Good Times*	1968	Grampian	MOR 4007	LP	Garioch groovers taped in Wick
The Crofters	*The Crofters*	1969	Beltona-Decca	ARL 8842P	LP	Frankie's folk roots are showing
Light Of Darkness	*Light Of Darkness*	1970 1992	Philips Second Battle	SB 019	LP CD	The Tremors let it all hang out
Tear Gas	*Piggy Go Getter*	1970 1993 1993	Famous Limited Renaissance	LMTRCD 06 RCD 1005	LP CD CD	Ricky Munro on drums Italian pic disc bootleg US reissue
Trifle	*First Meeting*	1971	Dawn	DNLS 3017	LP	Pat King at Marble Arch
Pilot	*Second Flight*	1975	EMI	EMC 3075	LP	Chart # 48
Sutherland Brothers and Quiver	*Reach For The Sky*	1976 1995	CBS Columbia	CBS 69191 480526-2	LP CD	Gavin and Iain arrive… and return in 1995.
Neil Innes & Eric Idle	*The Rutland Weekend Songbook*	1976	BBC Records	REB 233	LP	Billy B plays Rutley guitar

Artist	Title	Year	Label	Release #	Format	Notes
Manfred Mann's Earth Band	*The Roaring Silence*	1976	Bronze	ILPS 9357	LP	Davie Flett on the road again to #
		1977	Bronze	BRON357	LP	10 in the album Chart
		1981	Bronze	BRON 357	LP	
		1987	Legacy	LLP 122	LP	
Sutherland Brothers & Quiver	*Slipstream*	1976	CBS	CBS 81593	LP	
Various Artists	*The New Bronze Age*	1977	Bronze	-	LP	Promo including MMEB
10 CC	*Deceptive Bends*	1977	Mercury	9102 502	LP	Chart # 3
10 CC	*Live And Let Live*	1977	Mercury	6641 698	LP	Chart # 14
				838 861-2	CD	
The Beatles	*Live at the Star Club, Hamburg*	1977	Lingasong	LNL 1	LP	6 days before the Beach Ballroom
10 CC	*Bloody Tourists*	1978	Mercury	9102 503	LP	Chart # 3
		1983		826 921-2	CD	
Mickey Jupp	*Juppanese*	1978	Stiff	Seez 10	LP	Rockpile line-up
Dave Edmunds	*Trax On Wax 4*	1978	Swangsong	SSK59407	LP	Rockpile line-up, with the massed guitars of Dave E and Billy B
Manfred Mann's Earthband	*Watch*	1978	Bronze	Bronze 507	LP	Chart # 33, Speedy and Flettie
		1981	Bronze	Bronze 507	LP	
		1987	Legacy	LLP 123	LP	
Nick Lowe	*Jesus of Cool*	1978	Radar	Radar 1	LP	Rockpile
Rebellion	*Rebellion*	1979	CBS	64487	LP	Cliff Bennett & Spiggy Topes
Jimmy Hibbert	*Heavy Duty*	1979	Logo	Logo 1021	LP	Speedy King on bass

Artist	Title	Year	Label	Release #	Format	Notes
Manfred Mann's Earthband	*Angel Station*	1979 1981 1987	Bronze Bronze Legacy	BRON516 BRON 516 LLP 124	LP LP LP	Speedy King again, chart # 30
Dave Edmunds	*Repeat When Necessary*	1979	Swangsong	SSK 59409	LP	Rockpile : Chart # 39
The Tourists	*The Tourists*	1979 1981	Logo RCA	1018 INTS5096	LP LP	La Lennox Post-Catch, pre-Eurythmics. Chart # 72
Nick Lowe	*Labour of Lust*	1979 1985	Radar	Radar 21 Pile 1	LP CD	Rockpile, chart # 43
The Tourists	*Reality Effect*	1979	Logo	1019	LP	Chart # 23
Dexy's Midnight Runners	*Searching For The Young Soul Rebels*	1980 1982	Parlophone Fame	PCS7213 FA 3032	LP LP	Chart # 6 for Big Jim
The Tourists	*Luminous Basement*	1980	RCA	RCALP 5001	LP	End of the Tourists...
Manfred Mann's Earthband	*Chance*	1980 1981	Bronze Bronze	BRON529 BRON529	LP LP	Extremorist plays bass.
Carlene Carter	*Musical Shapes*	1980	F Beat	XXLP3	LP	Former Tremor Billy B on guitar
Rockpile	*Seconds of Pleasure*	1980	F Beat Demon	XXLP 7 XXC7 Fiend CD28	LP Cassette CD	and again
Dave Edmunds	*Twangin'*	1981	Swangsong	SSK59411	LP	and again, chart # 37
Pallas	*Arrive Alive*	1981 1983	Granite Wax Cool King	GCW001 CKLP002	Cass. LP	Smoke bombs R Us....
Eurythmics	*In the Garden*	1981	RCA	RCALP5061	LP	*Who's That Girl?*
Dave Edmunds	*The Best Of...*	1981	Swangsong	SSK59413	LP	Rockpiling it on...
Kirsty McColl	*Desperate Character*	1981	Polydor	POLS 1035	LP	RockaBilly strikes again

Artist	Title	Year	Label	Release #	Format	Notes
Deke Leonard	*Before Your Very Eyes*	1981			LP	and yet again
Frank Robb	*Life Lines*	1982	Frank Robb Productions		Cass.	Gie us some Jimi Hendrix
Various Artists	*Bullshit Detector 2*	1982	Crass		Double LP	*Police Brutality* from Toxik Ephex
Dave Edmunds	*DE 7th*	1982	Arista Fame	SPART1184 FA4130901	LP LP	Chart # 60 for Billy
PhD	*PhD*	1982	WEA	K 99150	LP	Gully Foyle no more: chart # 33
Various Artists	*Scottish Kulchur* (Barclay Towers compilation)	1982	Supermusic	SUP-LP-2004	LP	Premium Aberdeen crude from APB & The Squibs
Nick Lowe	*Nick The Knife*	1982	F Beat	XX LP14	LP	Billy Bremner
Various Artists	*Pleasantly Surprised*	1982	Klark	Klark 002	LP	Oil city slickers
Patrick Campbell - Lyons	*The Hero I Might Have Been*	1982	Shonackie	82001	LP	US Release with Billy on guitar
Dexy's Midnight Runners	*Too - Rye - Ay*	1982	Mercury	MERS 5	LP	Chart # 2
Dexy's Midnight Runners	*Geno*	1983	EMI	EMS 1007	LP	Chart # 79
Dave Edmunds	*Information*	1983	Arista	205-348	LP	Chart # 92 for the Twang Brothers
Eurythmics	*Sweet Dreams (Are Made Of This)*	1983	RCA	RCALP 6063	LP	Chart # 1 for the odd couple
Pallas	*The Sentinel*	1984 1992	EMI Centaur	SHSP 2400121 CENCD001	LP & Cassette CD	Pallas sign with EMI
Eurythmics	*Touchdance*	1984	RCA	PG70354	LP	Chart # 31

Artist	Title	Year	Label	Release #	Format	Notes
Eurythmics	*1984 (For The Love of Big Brother)*	1984 1988 1989	Virgin	V1984 OVED 207 CDV 1984	LP LP CD	Orwell's that ends well : chart # 23
Eurythmics	*Be Yourself Tonight*	1985	RCA	PL 70711 PD 70711	LP CD	Chart # 3 : Where's that fish house now?
Frank Robb	*Silver City*	1985	Frank Robb Productions		Cassette	"I get my heckles in first".
APB	*Something To Believe In*	1985 1988	Link	Link 002 Link 002	LP CD	Noo Yoiyk discovers Caledonian funk *par excellence*
Dexy's Midnight Runners	*Don't Stand Me Down*	1985 1997	Mercury Creation	MERH 56 CRECD 154	LP CD	Chart # 22
Pallas	*The Wedge* Knightmoves to Wedge	1986 1992	EMI Centaur	SHVL 850 CENCD002	LP &Cas CD	Pallas come of age
Pallas	*Live in Southampton 8/3/86*	1986			Cassette	Fan club only release
APB	*Cure For The Blues*	1986	Red River Link	Ythan LP 4 Link 004	LP LP & cass	Buchan bass. . . . In the USA
Jasmine Minks	*1234567, All Good Preachers Go To Heaven*	1986	Creation	CRELP 003	LP	
Jasmine Minks	*Sunset*	1986	Creation	CRELP 013	LP	
Eurythmics	*Revenge*	1986	RCA	PL 71050 PD 71050	LP CD	Chart # 3
The Shamen	*What's Going Down*		Communion	COMM 4CD	CD	They're gonna keep coming on. . .
Toxik Ephex	*Mad as Fuck*	1987	Green Vomit Records	Puke 2 •	LP	Split album with Edinburgh punk thrashers Oi Polloi

Artist	Title	Year	Label	Release #	Format	Notes
The Shamen	*Drop*	1987	Moksha	Soma LP 1 Soma CD 1 Soma C 1 Mau 613	LP CD Cassette CD	Told ya. . .
			Demon			
Phil Everly	*Louise*	1987	Magnum Force	MFLP 053	LP	Session King Billy returns
Eurythmics	*Savage*	1987	RCA	PL 71555 PD 71555	LP CD	Chart # 7
Pallas	*Voices In The Dark*	1987			Cassette	Demo for unreleased album
APB	*Something To Believe In*	1988	Red River	Ythan LP5	LP	
Jasmine Minks	*Another Age*	1988	Creation	CRELP 025	LP	
Mabel Meldrum's Band	*"Limited Edition"*	1988	Red Rock Records	MM 001	Cassette	
Mojo Pep	*Little Pleasures*	1988		Mojostoo 1	LP	A doozie from Dobies
The Shamen	*In Gorbachev We Trust*	1989	Demon	Fiend 666 Fiend CD 666 Fiend Cass 666	LP CD Cassette	Eee, they're good
Mabel Meldrum's Band	*Brownie Snaps*	1989	Red Rock Records	MM 002	Cassette	
The Shamen	*Phorward*	1989	Moksha	Soma LP 3 Soma C 3 Soma CD 3	LP Cassette CD	
Toxik Ephex	*The Adventures of Nobby Porthole, The Cock of the North*	1989	1 Up	Puke 4 1/2	LP	

Artist	Title	Year	Label	Release #	Format	Notes
Jasmine Minks	*Scratch The Surface*	1989	Creation	CRELP 044 CRECD 044	LP CD	
Desperate Danz Band	*Send 3/4d*	1989	Happas	Happas 1	LP	Electric ceilidh from Carnie & Francis
The Shamen	*Strange Days Dream*	1989	Materiali Sonori	MASO 33041	LP	Italian release
Pallas	*Sketches*	1989			Cassette	Fan club only release
Eurythmics	*We Too Are One*	1989	RCA	PL 74251 PD 74251	LP CD	We two are back at # 1
The Pretenders	*Packed*	1990	WEA	WX 346	LP	Chrissie and Billy
The Shamen	*En-Tact*	1990	One Little Indian	TPLP 22 TPLP 22 SP TPLP 22 C TPLP 22 CD TPLP22CDUS TPLP 22 CUS TPLP 22 US COCY 7060 EK 48722 ET 48722	LP LP Cassette CD CD Cassette LP CD CD Cassette	US issue US issue US issue Japanese issue
			Nippon Columbia			
			EPIC			
Old Blind Dogs	*Old Blind Dogs* (First)	1990			Cassette	
Wozani	*Dancing in the Moonlight*	1990	RPM	RPM 7135	LP	Mike Stobbie on keyboards
Jasmine Minks	*Jasmine Minks*	1990	Creation	CRELP 007 CRECD 007	LP CD	An Iain Slater bedroom production
Snakebite	*The Angel and The Devil*	1990			Cassette	Heads-down-no-nonsense-boogie

Artist	Title	Year	Label	Release #	Format	Notes
Mojo Pep	*Pep Talk*	1990			CD	
Eurythmics	*Greatest Hits*	1991	RCA	PL 74856 PD 74856	LP CD	Out with a bang at # 1
Blah !	*Or What ?*	1991	City Arts	ACL MC5	Cassette	
Jasmine Minks	*Soul Station*	1991	Creation	CRELP 112 CRECD 112	LP CD	Compilation from a right bunch of minkers
The Shamen	*Progeny*	1991	One Little Indian	TPLP 32	LP & CD	
Various Artists	*Aberdeen Rock Volume 1*	1991	City Arts	ACL MC 7	Cassette	Battle of the Bands spin-off
Dexy's Midnight Runners	*The Very Best Of.....*	1991	Mercury	846 460 - 2	CD	
Various Artists	*Wild Summer, Wow!*	1991	Creation	CRECD 002	CD	Jasmine Minks summer-ised
Various Artists	*Purveyors Of Taste*	1991	Creation	CRECD 010	CD	The Minks in bitter balladesque mode on *Cold Heart*
Various Artists	*Doing God's Work*	1991	Creation	CRECD 024	CD	Creation revisits The Minks
The Rutles	*The Rutles*	1991	Rhino		CD	Legendary sessions from Shabby Road
Old Blind Dogs	*Old Blind Dogs 2*	1991			Cassette	
Korpse	*Mauler*	1991			Cassette	6 track debut
Various Artists	*SI magazine compilation*	1992	SI	Simply 7	CD	1 from Pallas : *War of Words*
Geoff Mann and Clive Nolan	*Casino*	1992	SI Music	Simply 15	CD	Mike Stobbie on keyboards
Annie Lennox	*Diva*	1992	BMG	PL 75326 PD 75326	LP	Chart # 1
One God Universe	*One God Universe*	1992	Fluxus	SL 002	LP	

Artist	Title	Year	Label	Release #	Format	Notes
Old Blind Dogs	*New Tricks*	1992	Lochshore/ KRL	LOC 1068	CD & Cass.	
The Beatles	*Rockin' At the Star Club*	1992	Columbia	468950-2	CD	Hogmanay in Hamburg, hangover in Aiberdeen. . .
The Shamen	*Boss Drum*	1992	One Little Indian	TPLP 42 TPLP 42 C TPLP 42 CD	LP Cassette CD	Chart # 3
Manfred Mann's Earthband	*Spotlight : 1971 - 1991*	1992	Cohesion	COMME 13	CD	Compilation
Big Blue		1993			CD	
The Dreaming	*Let the Feast of Fools Begin*	1993	Freaked Records	MC 002	Cassette	
Frantik Zimmer	*Liars, Leaders and The Law*	1993	City Arts	ACL MC 14	Cassette	A Wilkinson wonder
Various Artists	*New Stars in Country*	1993	Modi	931001	CD	2 tracks from Lemon Soul bassist Kevin Henderson
Kevin Henderson	*Kentucky Bound*	1993	Gnoth	120 004-2	CD	Germany calling
Various Artists	*SI Magazine compiliation*	1993	SI	Simply 22	CD	1 track from Pallas : *Never Too Late*
Jim Diamond	*Jim Diamond*	1993	Polydor	843 847-2 843 847-4	CD Cassette	All Jim's hits and some new stuff
Various Artists	*Bucket Full of Rubbish*	1993	Grants	GR-D 1974 (1011-038)	LP	Spiggy Topes bootlegged in America

Artist	Title	Year	Label	Release #	Format	Notes
Old Blind Dogs	*Close to the Bone*	1993	Lochshore/ KRL	CD LDL1209 ZC LDL1209	LP CD	
The Dawntreaders	*The Dawntreaders*	1993		DTMC 002	Cassette	
Dexy's Midnight Runners	*Because of You*	1993	Karussell	5500032	CD	Compilation
Various Artists	*British Progressive Rock Directory - Part 1*	1994			CD	1 track from Pallas : *Refugee*
Manfred Mann's Earthband	*The Very Best Of*	1994	Arcade	ARC 3100162 ARC 3100174	CD Cassette	Compilation
Various Artists	*British Progressive Rock Directory - Part 3*	1994			CD	Mike Stobbie 1 track : *Exordium*
Old Blind Dogs	*Tall Tails*	1994	Lochshore / KRL	CD LDL 1220 ZC LDL 1220	CD Cassette	
New Leaf	*On Safari*	1994	Foundation	Found CD 001	CD	Sublime pop from Jeremy
Korpse	*Hold The Flood*	1994	Candlelight	CANDLE 005CD	CD	
Lemon Soul	*Lemon Soul - LIVE !*	1994	Rockin' Horse		Cassette	Reunion gig, Lemon Tree 3/4/94
Elvis Costello	*Almost Blue*	1994	Demon	DPAM 7	CD	5 tracks live in Aberdeen
Various Artists	*Feast of the Mau Mau*	1994	Mau Mau	MMM 1	CD	Shamen 1 track : *Strange Day's Dream*

Artist	Title	Year	Label	Release #	Format	Notes
The Lorelei	*Headstrong*	1994	Lochshore / KRL	ZCLDL 1213 CDLDL 1213	Cassette CD	
Nirvana	*Black Flower*	1994	Edsel	ED 278	CD	Billy's guitar on 2 tracks
Foreigner	*Mister Moonlight*	1994	Arista	74321232852	CD	Nashville noise from Billy
Rosie Flores	*Once More With Feeling*	1994	Hightone	HCD 8047	CD	and yet more . . . .
One God Universe	*Schiffer*	1994	Background Radiation	OGU CD 003	CD	Rico booked again
Nirvana	*Secret Theatre*	1995	Edsel	ED 407	CD	Billy on 4 tracks
Kevin Henderson	*Lights of Heaven*	1995	Gnoth	110.003	CD	Kevin on a Cajun kick in Germany
Annie Lennox	*Medusa*	1995	RCA-BMG	7432125712	CD	Under the covers with Greselda
Tinderbox	*The Haunting*	1995	Freaked Records	MCT 001 CDT 001	Cassette CD	
The Fabians	*Locomotive*	1995		FAFA 1 CD	CD	
Frank Robb	*Watching Time*	1995	Frank Robb Productions	CD FRP003	CD	
Ian F. Benzie	*So Far*	1995	Lochshore / KRL	CDLDL 1228 ZCLDL 1228	CD Cassette	
The Promise	*The Promise*	1995	Now and Then	NTHEN 14	CD	
Various Artists	*Celtic Connections*	1995	Living Tradition	LTCD 001	CD	1 track from Old Blind Dogs
The Lorelei	*Progression*	1995	Lochshore / KRL		CD	

Artist	Title	Year	Label	Release #	Format	Notes
The Shamen	*Axis Mutatis*	1995	One Little Indian	TP 52	CD	The Shamen : *Destination Eschaton / Escadid*
Various Artists	*Future Music magazine freebie CD*	1995	Future Music	October	CD	
Björk	*Telegraph*	1995	One Little Indian		CD	Evelyn Glennie guest appearance
Dexys Midnight Runners	*1980 - 1982 The Radio One Sessions*	1995	Strange Fruit	NT 009	CD	*NME*: "Masterpieces of soul catharsis'
Dexys Midnight Runners	*It Was Like This*	1996	EMI Premier		CD	The stage is set for Alan McGee's arrival. . .
The Lorelei	*Progression*	1996	Lochshore / KRL	CDLDL 1236	CD	
Various Artists	*Folk 'n' Hell*	1996	Hemisphere	85334429	CD	*Willie's Aul' Trews & The Auld Reels* from Old Blind Dogs
Rosie Flores	*A Honkytonk Reprise*	1996	Rounder	CD 3136	CD	Old new country with Billy Bremner
Barrelhouse Blues Band	*In Town*	1996	BB Music	CD 0001	CD	Where's Prince Moulay?
Various Artists	*Rough Guide To Scottish Music*	1996	World Music Network	RGNET1004	CD	*Malcolm Ferguson, Finbar Saunders*, double entendres & Old Blind Dogs
Dawntreaders	*Puppy*	1996		DTCD 003 DTMC 003	CD Cassette	Don't listen to me. Listen to this instead.
Coast	*Big Jet Rising*	1997	Sugar	SUGACD 13 SUGALP 13	CD Vinyl	We have lift off. . .?
Geneva	*Further*	1997	Nude	Nude 7	CD	*Q*: "Rapturous stuff'
Various Artists	*Come On You Reds*	1997	Cherry Red	Gaffer 15	CD	Chipper time!